THE MOST TRUSTED NAME IN TRAVEL: **FROMMER'S**

FROMMER'S EasyGuide to
WASHINGTON, D.C.
2020

7th Edition

D0030254

By Meredith Pratt

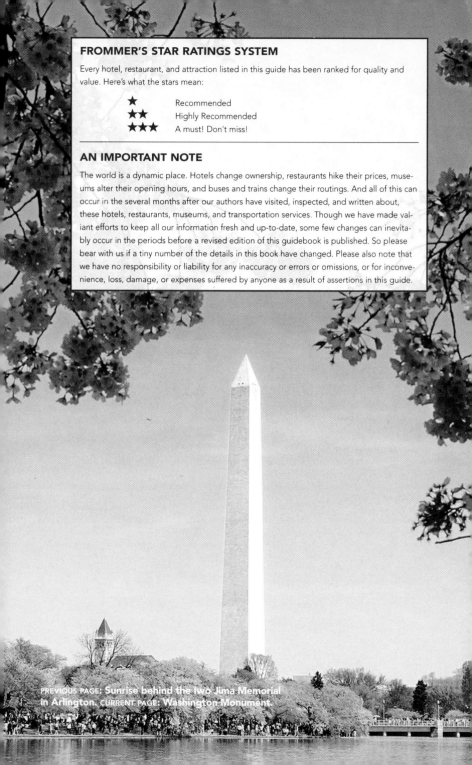

FROMMER'S STAR RATINGS SYSTEM

Every hotel, restaurant, and attraction listed in this guide has been ranked for quality and value. Here's what the stars mean:

★ Recommended
★★ Highly Recommended
★★★ A must! Don't miss!

AN IMPORTANT NOTE

The world is a dynamic place. Hotels change ownership, restaurants hike their prices, museums alter their opening hours, and buses and trains change their routings. And all of this can occur in the several months after our authors have visited, inspected, and written about, these hotels, restaurants, museums, and transportation services. Though we have made valiant efforts to keep all our information fresh and up-to-date, some few changes can inevitably occur in the periods before a revised edition of this guidebook is published. So please bear with us if a tiny number of the details in this book have changed. Please also note that we have no responsibility or liability for any inaccuracy or errors or omissions, or for inconvenience, loss, damage, or expenses suffered by anyone as a result of assertions in this guide.

PREVIOUS PAGE: Sunrise behind the Iwo Jima Memorial in Arlington. CURRENT PAGE: Washington Monument.

CONTENTS

1 THE BEST OF WASHINGTON, D.C. 1

2 WASHINGTON, D.C., IN CONTEXT 11

3 SUGGESTED ITINER-ARIES & NEIGHBOR-HOODS 28
Iconic Washington, D.C., in 1 Day 28
Iconic Washington, D.C., in 2 Days 33
Iconic Washington, D.C., in 3 Days 35
Washington, D.C., for Families 36
A Women's History Tour of Washington, D.C. 39
An African-American History Tour of Washington, D.C. 42
The Neighborhoods in Brief 47

4 WHERE TO STAY 53
Getting the Best Deal 53
Capitol Hill 56
Capitol Riverfront 60
National Mall 62
Southwest Waterfront 63
Penn Quarter 64
Midtown 67
Adams Morgan 70
Dupont Circle 73
Foggy Bottom/ West End 75

Georgetown 78
Shaw 80
U & 14th Street Corridors 81
Woodley Park 82

5 WHERE TO EAT 84
Atlas District 84
Capitol Hill & Barracks Row 85
Capitol Riverfront ("Navy Yard") 91
Southwest Waterfront 92
Downtown & Penn Quarter 94
Midtown 100
U & 14th Street Corridors 102
Adams Morgan 106
Dupont Circle 107
Foggy Bottom/West End 110
Georgetown 111
Woodley Park & Cleveland Park 114

6 EXPLORING WASH-INGTON, D.C. 117
Capitol Hill 117
The National Mall & Memorial Parks 133
Southwest of the Mall 163
Midtown 168
Penn Quarter 176
Dupont Circle 184
Foggy Bottom 187
U & 14th Street Corridors 188

Upper Northwest D.C.: Glover Park, Woodley Park & Cleveland Park 189
Georgetown 193
Northern Virginia 195
Parks 199
Especially for Kids 203
Outdoor Activities 205

7 SHOPPING 209
The Shopping Scene 209
Great Shopping Areas 209
Shopping A to Z 211

8 ENTERTAINMENT & NIGHTLIFE 222
The Performing Arts 223
The Bar Scene 228
The Club & Music Scene 231
The LGBTQ Scene 235
Spectator Sports 236

9 DAY TRIPS FROM D.C. 238
Mount Vernon 238
Old Town Alexandria 243

10 SELF-GUIDED WALKING TOURS 257

11 PLANNING YOUR TRIP 285

INDEX 307

MAP LIST 316

ABOUT THE AUTHOR 318

The United States Capitol, seen from the Capitol reflecting pool.

A LOOK AT WASHINGTON, D.C.

For many visitors, a trip to Washington, D.C., isn't just a vacation. It's a pilgrimage of sorts. Schoolchildren are bused in by the thousands and swarm the Mall in organized platoons, determined teachers feeding them facts about its importance. Veterans pay homage at memorials to fallen comrades. And ordinary citizens arrive in droves to be part of the most powerful city in the world, at least for a short time. Where else, after all, are decisions made that affect not only the lives of every American citizen, but also the lives of people across the planet? The city was designed, from its very inception, to be a worthy place for pilgrimage, with its monuments, broad avenues, and traffic circles (symbolic of the rays of the sun). But over the years, Washington has become even more multifaceted than the original planners could have envisioned. It's a highly cosmopolitan, multiracial, and wonderfully diverse city, thanks to its embassies (and their resident staff), large immigrant populations, and proud African American community. What follows is just a sampling of the impressive sights you'll see and adventures you'll have in this engrossing capital.

The treasures inside the National Archives include the country's most important documents—the Declaration of Independence, the Constitution, and the Bill of Rights—and the original 1297 Magna Carta.

The National Mall stretches from the Lincoln Memorial, seen here, in the west, to the U.S. Capitol in the east. See p. 149.

Lincoln Memorial (see p. 141).

Giacometti's bronze *Walking Man II* sculpture, on display in the East Building of the National Gallery of Art (see p. 147).

The ornate interior of the U.S. Capitol Dome (see p. 118).

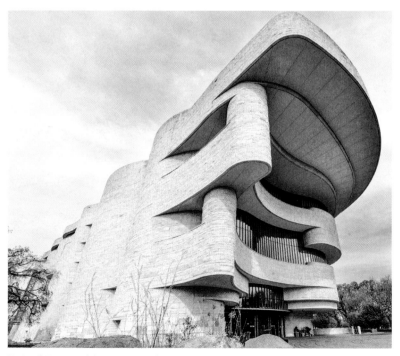

National Museum of the American Indian (see p. 154).

A National Parks ranger leads a guided tour of the Vietnam Veterans Memorial (see p. 160).

The Boeing Milestones of Flight Hall in the National Air and Space Museum (see p. 143).

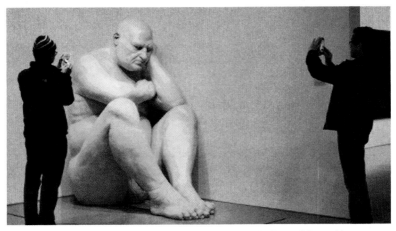

Contemporary art, like this untitled sculpture by Ron Mueck, is the focus of the Hirshhorn Museum and Sculpture Garden (see p. 138).

The Apollo 11 command module at the National Air and Space Museum.

District of Columbia War Memorial.

Great Historical Clock at the National Museum of American History (see p. 153).

Le Diplomate on 14th Street in Logan Circle (see p. 102).

Lively nightlife in Adams Morgan.

Robert Emmet statue in the Dupont Circle neighborhood (see p. 280).

Panda at the National Zoo (see p. 190).

The Municipal Fish Market.

The Dupont Circle Fountain is one of 18 Civil War memorials in the city.

Homes along the C&O Canal in Georgetown (see p. 202).

Penn Quarter Farmers Market.

Rose's Luxury restaurant (see p. 89).

An evening stroll along Georgetown's waterfront.

Beautiful tree-lined streets in Georgetown's historical district.

Healy Hall on the main campus of Georgetown University (see p. 266).

OTHER D.C.

Celebrants in Washington's annual Capital Pride Parade.

Spring in D.C. brings the beautiful cherry blossoms along the Tidal Basin (see p. 199).

The White House (see p. 171).

The Eisenhower Executive Office Building.

On April 15, 1865, President Abraham Lincoln died from an assassin's bullet in this room in the Petersen House, opposite Ford's Theatre.

A performance at the 10-day DC Jazz Festival.

The African American Civil War Memorial (see p. 188).

NORTHERN VIRGINIA

Over 1 million people visit George Washington's home, Mount Vernon, yearly (see p. 238).

Outdoor dining in Old Town Alexandria, Virginia.

Alexandria's waterfront draws crowds with its al fresco restaurants, street performers, and Potomac River views (see p. 255).

Historic brick row houses in Old Town Alexandria, Virginia.

The Tomb of the Unknown Soldier at Arlington National Cemetery (see p. 196).

A fully functioning distillery and gristmill (pictured here) are among the working exhibits at Mount Vernon.

THE BEST OF WASHINGTON, D.C.

The Georgetown University rowing team glides gracefully along the Potomac River as the sun paints the surface of the water. Museums open their doors and docents take their places. Jets take off from nearby Reagan National Airport and roar overhead. The Metro hums along its maze of tunnels and over the Potomac River. Commuters of all sorts, from diplomats to nonprofit wonks to shopkeepers, spill from cars and buses and Metro stations onto downtown streets armed with briefcases, coffee cups, smartphones, and newspapers. Chefs plot the day's menu in preparation for the throngs of D.C. restaurant-goers. Reporters gather at the White House to cover stories that will ripple across the country. All rub elbows from sunup to sundown in downtown coffee shops, in the halls of Congress, in waterfront restaurants, in Georgetown shops, in Penn Quarter theaters, in bars along 14th Street. Washington, D.C., is waking up.

But D.C.'s awakening is bigger than any one day. The city is coming into its own, becoming more than a haven of staunch politicos and white-marbled monuments. (Although it's still that, too.) Those who have power, those who want power, and those who are trying to change how power works are constantly shaping the here and now of Washington. A young generation is framing new neighborhoods, like the Wharf in Southwest, a formerly sleepy area abuzz with new restaurants, hotels, music halls, and nightlife; or Union Market, an epicenter for good food and artful retail. Avant-garde and "protest" art is making a statement on our streets and in our museums, giving volume to the city's often unheard voices. And D.C.'s sports teams are finally on the national map again, following the Washington Capitals' big Stanley Cup win in 2018.

Politics are here and will always be here in this "city of magnificent intentions," as Charles Dickens called it, but Washington is so much more. Each day is different. Things happen here that can happen nowhere else on earth. You're in the heartbeat of a nation, in a city that belongs to you. Make the most of it!

1 most unforgettable WASHINGTON, D.C., EXPERIENCES

o **Viewing Washington Landmarks by Moonlight:** There is nothing as spectacular as the Lincoln Memorial illuminated at night, unless it's the sight of the White House, the Capitol, or the Washington Monument lit up after dark. Go via the Old Town Trolley, by bike on a Bike and Roll excursion, or by boat aboard a Potomac Riverboat Company cruise; all three operations offer narrated day and nighttime tours. See p. 298.

o **Watching the Supreme Court in Action:** Behind the stately marble facade of the Supreme Court building, the nation's nine black-gowned justices reveal their intellectual brilliance and individual personalities as they listen to and question both sides of an argument. Will the famously silent Justice Thomas talk today? Will Justice Sotomayor tell one of her charming personal anecdotes to illustrate a point? Will Chief Justice Roberts reveal a willingness to assume the "swing vote" role long held by the now-retired Justice Kennedy? Who will volley the wittiest remark into the discourse? Only one way to find out: Wait in line for entry and a coveted seat inside the courtroom. See p. 130.

o **Taking in a Show at the Historic Ford's Theatre:** It's memorable if not a bit eerie to see the Presidential Box where John Wilkes Booth shot President Abraham Lincoln on April 14, 1865, while the president watched the comedy "Our American Cousin." The renovated theater is still staging compelling productions today, and an attached museum holds surprisingly affecting exhibits on Lincoln's presidency and assassination, including the actual Derringer Booth used in the shooting. See p. 176.

o **Perusing the Constitution:** Nowhere else in the U.S. can you see the original documents that grounded this nation in life, liberty, and the pursuit of

The Lincoln Memorial and the Reflecting Pool.

A reported 1 million people marched in Washington, D.C., during the 3rd Annual Women's March.

happiness. The National Archives in Washington displays the Declaration of Independence, the Constitution of the United States, and the Bill of Rights behind glass. Sealed in scientifically advanced housing inside a low-lit marble rotunda designed to preserve the "Charters of Freedom," the documents are faded but still readable—and no less impressive when you consider their enormous impact on the beginnings of the United States. See p. 145.

○ **Visiting the U.S. Capitol:** Washington is the capital of the United States, one of the world's greatest democracies, and it can be thrilling, inspiring, and just plain fun to tour the historic U.S. Capitol Building. Tours begin inside the Emancipation Hall, with its grandiose sandstone columns and Statue of Freedom. Pick up passes to a session inside the Capitol's original Senate and House chambers and observe your elected politicians at work. Reserve Capitol Tour passes online. See p. 118.

THE best FAMILY EXPERIENCES

○ **Hanging Out at the National Zoo:** Make faces at the cute giant pandas, hear the mighty lion's roar, laugh at the playful monkeys, watch an elephant exercise, ride the solar-powered carousel. The National Zoo is essentially one big (163 acres!), family-friendly park, offering the chance to observe some 1,500 animals at play (or snoozing or eating). See p. 190.

○ **Ice Skating at the National Gallery:** The pond in the National Gallery of Art Sculpture Garden is transformed into an ice-skating rink in winter. Rent some skates and twirl around on the ice, admiring the sculptures as you go. Warm up with a hot chocolate at the garden's Pavilion Café. See p. 208.

○ **Getting the Wiggles Out at Rock Creek Park:** If you have little ones with lots of energy, then Rock Creek Park is for you. The Woodland Trail begins behind the Nature Center, while a quarter-mile, stroller-accessible Edge of the Woods trail leads from the Nature Center's front door. Inside the Nature Center itself are live turtles, fish, snakes, an active beehive, and a bird observation deck. The Planetarium offers scheduled daily shows, some for those under 5. See p. 200.

○ **Riding a Roller Coaster, Piloting a Jet, and Other Adventuring:** Relax, parents. The Smithsonian's 17 museums and zoo have you covered. Kids will marvel at the suspended airplanes and astronaut and cosmonaut space suits, among 9,000 other artifacts, at the National Air and Space Museum. Or they can brave the simulated rides—inside a jet aircraft, a vintage airplane, or a spacecraft exploring the Milky Way. The National Museum of American History has cars, trains, and the interactive "Wegman's Wonderplace," designed exclusively for kids, where they can cook in a kid-sized Julia Childs' model kitchen, shop in a scaled-down market, and climb to their heart's content. Simulated adventures feel real in futuristic, high-speed race car and roller-coaster machines. *Note:* Height requirements and fees apply. See p. 143 and 155.

THE best FOOD

○ **Best for a Splurge:** Dining at Dupont Circle's **Komi** (p. 108) is as close to having a personal chef as many of us may come. Chef Johnny Monis gracefully cooks nightly and presents a dozen or so Mediterranean-inflected tasting dishes followed by family-style finales. Each is wondrously delicious, from branzino drizzled with olive oil to the house-aged beef rib. The dining room is very intimate, but thankfully reservations are accepted as early as a month in advance.

○ **Best for Romance:** Romance is everywhere at **Iron Gate** (p. 108), in the cozy wood-beamed main dining room with its crackling fire and red banquettes; in the twinkly lit, wisteria-canopied, brick-paved courtyard; even in the high-walled and narrow bar/lounge. The menu of inventive Mediterranean fare, such as oak-roasted manicotti or grilled oysters with goat butter, seals the deal. If Iron Gate is rustic romance, **Plume** (p. 73) in the historic Jefferson Hotel oozes classic charm. Elegant table-clothed tables are set in cozy nooks by the fire, while waiters serve an American menu of Alaskan halibut, bison with heirloom eggplant, or a Moulard duck breast with brussels sprouts. *Tip:* Begin or end your evening at Quill, also in the Jefferson, for live piano music and delicious aperitifs.

○ **Best for Families:** It can be hard to get kids to sit still through dinner. At **Pinstripes** (p. 103) in Georgetown, the enormous Italian-American menu comes with plenty of bowling lanes and bocce courts to keep little ones entertained. Thin-crust, wood-fired pizzas fill you up at **Pizzeria Paradiso** (p. 109; with locations in Dupont Circle and M St. NW). More safe bets: chicken tenders and milkshakes at **Ted's Bulletin** (www.tedsbulletin.com; with locations on Capitol Hill and 14th St.); burgers and fries at **Good Stuff Eatery** (p. 90; with locations on Capitol Hill and Georgetown); or the lively, convenient **Hill Country Barbecue** (p. 95) in Penn Quarter for good ol' American barbecued chicken and mac and cheese.

○ **Best for Regional Cuisine:** While Washington doesn't have its own cuisine per se, its central location in the Mid-Atlantic/Chesapeake Bay region gives it license to lay claim to the area's culinary specialties. And locals say

Ben's Chili Bowl is a D.C. institution.

nobody does Eastern Shore seafood better than Wharf newcomer **Rappahannock Oyster Bar** (p. 94), the place to go for superb oysters, fresh from the waters off Virginia or Maryland. Try the briny Olde Salts from Chincoteague, Virginia, a personal favorite. The U-shaped seafood bar also serves up seafood classics like peel-and-eat shrimp steamed with Old Bay seasoning, clam chowder, and crab cakes.

o **Best All-Around for Fun and Food:** Oh, gosh, all sorts of D.C. restaurants satisfy this category, but Jose Andres' **Zaytinya** (Mediterranean tastes; p. 98) and **Jaleo** (Spanish tapas; p. 96) both offer imaginative and playful tasting menus. **Taco Bamba** (p. 99) is another favorite option for inventive Mexican, while **Tiger Fork** (p. 115) in Shaw transports diners to a Hong Kong food market for crispy pork belly, soya chicken, and steamed rice noodles.

o **Best for a "Taste of Washington" Experience:** Real locals claim chicken and mumbo sauce, a bright orange sauce made by combining ketchup with a dash of BBQ and some sweet-and-sour sauce, as the hometown specialty. Find it at **Wingo's** in Glover Park, **Yums II Carryout** on 14th Street NW, and the **Hamilton** (p. 232) downtown. For some down-home fare, sit at the counter at **Ben's Chili Bowl** (p. 104) and chat with the owners and your neighbor over a chili dog or a plate of blueberry pancakes. The place is an institution, and you can stop by anytime—it's open for breakfast, lunch, and dinner.

o **Best for Vegetarians:** Fans flock to fast-casual **Shouk** for its polenta fries and eggplant burgers, plus cauliflower, either in a bowl or pita. **Beefsteak** (p. 110) is Chef Jose Andres' healthy and delicious salute to made-to-order vegetarian fast food. **Bombay Club** (p. 100) and **Rasika** (p. 97) are excellent choices for vegetarian-friendly Indian cuisine served in sophisticated surroundings.

THE best THINGS TO DO FOR FREE IN WASHINGTON, D.C.

o **Visit the White House:** Yes, believe it or not, touring the country's most famous house is entirely free. You'll just need to contact your member of Congress and submit a request up to 3 months in advance and no less than 21 days prior to your visit. Several rooms in the East Wing are made public during the tour, as well as a view of the White House Rose Garden. See p. 171.

o **People-Watch at Dupont Circle:** This traffic circle is also a park—an all-weather hangout for mondo-bizarre bike couriers, chess players, street musicians, and lovers. Sit and watch scenes of Washington life unfold around you—or join in the fun: The Circle is also the setting for outdoor yoga classes, sports screenings, and an annual snowball fight. See p. 184.

o **Attend a Millennium Stage Performance at the Kennedy Center:** Every evening at 6pm in its Grand Foyer, the Kennedy Center presents a free 1-hour concert performed by local up-and-coming, national, or international musicians. And though the Kennedy Center doesn't advertise it, you might be interested to know that the Grand Foyer's bars near Millennium Stage host food-and-drink happy hours between 5 and 6pm nightly. Purchase a cocktail and head through the glass doors to the terrace, where you can enjoy your drink and views of the Potomac River. See p. 224.

o **Groove to the Sounds of Live Jazz in the Sculpture Garden:** On summery Friday evenings at the National Gallery of Art Sculpture Garden, you can dip your toes in the fountain pool and chill out to live jazz from 5 to 8pm. The jazz is free; the sandwiches, wine, and beer served in the Pavilion Café are not. See p. 147.

o **Pick a Museum, (Just About) Any Museum:** Because this is the U.S. capital, many of the museums are federal institutions, meaning admission is free. The National Gallery of Art, the U.S. Botanic Garden, and the Smithsonian's 17 Washington museums, from the National Air and Space Museum to its newest, the National Museum of African American History & Culture, are among many excellent choices. See chapter 6.

o **Watch Planes Take Off and Land at Gravelly Point:** Take the short drive to this waterfront park bordering Reagan National Airport, just minutes outside of D.C. Bring picnic eats and watch jet after jet descend and fly directly overhead. Not for the fainthearted! You can also see the planes from Hains Point, located on the other side of the Potomac River at the tip of East Potomac Park.

o **Attend an Event on the Mall:** Think of the National Mall as the nation's public square, where something is always going on—more than 3,500 events annually, according to the National Park Service. There's the Kite Festival during cherry blossom season in the spring; the splendid Independence Day celebration every Fourth of July; special events reserved by individuals and random organizations that have obtained a permit, from weddings to speeches to yearly jamborees of, for instance, the National Astronomy Festival; and walking tours, biking, Frisbee throwing, and assorted impromptu sports happenings year-round. See p. 23 for a calendar of annual events.

THE best NEIGHBORHOODS FOR GETTING LOST

- **Georgetown:** The truth is, you *want* to get lost in Georgetown, because it's the neighborhood's side streets that hold the history and centuries-old houses of this one-time Colonial tobacco port. Don't worry—Georgetown is so compact that you're never far from its main thoroughfares, M Street, and Wisconsin Avenue. For a backstreets tour of Georgetown, see p. 264.
- **Capitol Hill:** Take the Capitol Hill walking tour (p. 120) if you like, then continue east down Pennsylvania Ave. SE into the heart of one of the most storied neighborhoods in D.C. East of 2nd Street, blocks of large-scale government buildings fade into rows of beautifully restored 19th-century town houses. Coffee shops, restaurants, and stores frequented by resident Hill staffers abound. The historic Eastern Market (p. 125) lies just north of Pennsylvania Avenue; and fun and lively Barracks Row (p. 85) follows just south to the Washington Navy Yard, the oldest shore establishment of the U.S. Navy.
- **Old Town Alexandria:** Just a short distance from the District (by Metro, car, boat, or bike) is George Washington's Virginia hometown. On and off the beaten track are quaint cobblestone streets, boutiques and antiques stores, 18th-century architecture, and fine restaurants, many laying claim to the best crab cakes in town. See p. 243.
- **Dupont Circle:** Explore Dupont Circle's lovely side streets extending off Connecticut and Massachusetts avenues. You'll discover picturesque 19th-century town houses, small art galleries, historic museums, and actual residences (this is the Obama family's old neighborhood). Stroll Embassy Row (northward on Massachusetts Ave.) to view Beaux Arts mansions, many built by wealthy magnates during the Gilded Age. See p. 184.

THE best WAYS TO SEE WASHINGTON, D.C., LIKE A LOCAL

- **Shop at Eastern Market:** Capitol Hill is home to more than government buildings; it's a community of old town houses, antiques shops, and the venerable Eastern Market. Here, locals shop and barter every Saturday and Sunday for fresh produce, baked goods, and flea-market bargains, just as they've done for well over a century. *A must:* the blueberry pancakes at the Market Lunch counter. See p. 125.

The Best Ways to See Washington, D.C., Like a Local

Attending a hometown game at Nationals Park.

o **Pub and Club It in D.C.'s Hot Spots:** Join Washington's footloose and fancy-free any night of the week (but especially Thurs–Sat) along 14th Street, in Shaw, Adams Morgan, the Capitol Riverfront, the Wharf in southwest waterfront, Georgetown's waterfront, and the Penn Quarter.

o **Go for a Jog on the National Mall:** Lace up your running shoes and race down the Mall at your own pace, admiring famous sights as you go. Your fellow runners will be buff military staff from the Pentagon, speed-walking members of Congress, and downtown workers doing their best to stave off the telltale pencil-pusher's paunch. It's about 2 miles from the foot of the Capitol to the Lincoln Memorial. See p. 149.

o **Attend a Hometown Game:** Take yourself out to a Washington Nationals baseball game at Nationals Park, drive to FedEx Field to root for Washington's NFL team along with its rabid fans, catch a Washington Wizards or Mystics basketball game at the downtown Capital One Arena, or hop the Metro to the new soccer stadium at Buzzard Point for a D.C. United match. To experience the true soul of the city, attend a Washington Capitals ice hockey match. Wear red. See p. 236.

o **Take in Some Live Music:** One of the best ways to feel at one with locals is by enjoying the live music scene together, not so much in large concert halls, but in smaller, seated venues such as **Blues Alley** (jazz and blues; p. 232) in Georgetown; the **Hamilton** (blues, rock, or country; p. 232) in the Penn Quarter; **The Anthem** (rock, country, pop; 901 Wharf St., SW; www.theanthemdc.com; © **202/888-0020**) in the Southwest Wharf district; and **Gypsy Sally's** (bluegrass; p. 232) also in Georgetown. See p. 231.

o **Sit at an Outdoor Cafe and Watch the Washington World Go By:** Locals watching locals. What better way to keep tabs on one another? The capital is full of seats offering front-row views of D.C. on parade. Here's a bunch:

Fiola Mare (not a cafe, but its terrace tables can't be beat for watching Georgetown's waterfront scene; p. 112), **Belga Café** (p. 89), **Café du Parc** (p. 100), **Central** (p. 94), **Zaytinya** (p. 98), **Le Diplomate** (p. 102), and **Martin's Tavern** (p. 113).

THE best PLACES TO STAY

- **Best Historic Hotel:** The **Willard InterContinental** celebrates its 114th anniversary in 2020, and recently reopened after another renovation. The original, smaller "City Hotel" existed here as early as 1816 before its name changed in 1906. The hotel has hosted nearly every U.S. president since Franklin Pierce was here in 1853. President Ulysses S. Grant liked to unwind with a cigar and brandy in the Willard lobby after a hard day in the Oval Office, and is even said to have popularized the term "lobbyist" after so many locals would approach him there. Literary luminaries such as Mark Twain and Charles Dickens used to hang out in the Round Robin bar. See p. 68.

- **Best for Romance:** Its discreet service, intimate size, and exquisitely decorated guest rooms, and the fact that you need never leave the hotel for pampering or dining, makes the **Jefferson** (p. 73) perfect for a romantic rendezvous. A pianist plays classic melodies Tuesday through Saturday in the cozy-comfortable bar, Quill; and the hotel's small spa offers massages.

- **Best When You Have Business on Capitol Hill:** **The George** (p. 57) lies a short walk from the Capitol and offers a rooftop pool, a 24/7 fitness center, and an excellent in-house power-dining spot, Art and Soul.

- **Best Bang for Your Buck:** Its great location near Georgetown, the White House, and the Metro and less than a mile from the National Mall, plus spacious studio and one-bedroom suites with kitchens, free Wi-Fi, and reasonable rates, make Foggy Bottom's **River Inn** (p. 77) one of the best values in town.

- **Best Views:** The **Hay-Adams** (p. 67) has such a great, unobstructed view of the White House that the Secret Service comes over regularly to do security sweeps of the place. Ask for a room on the H Street side of the hotel, on floors six through eight. Many of the guest rooms at the **Watergate** (p. 75) survey the Potomac River and the Georgetown waterfront, but the best view of all is from the hotel's Top of the Gate rooftop bar and lounge. Nearly half of the guest rooms in the **InterContinental Washington D.C. – The Wharf** (p. 63), in the Southwest Waterfront neighborhood, capture a stunning view of the Washington Channel and East Potomac Park.

- **Best for Families:** The **Marriott Residence Inn DC/Capitol** (p. 63) is within walking distance of the National Mall, the Smithsonian museums, and the Metro. Breakfast is free every day along with a free "social hour" in the evenings. Kids will love the indoor heated pool and parents will love the large, suite-style rooms with fully equipped kitchenettes. It's also pet-friendly if your family includes the four-legged variety.

THE best OFFBEAT EXPERIENCES

o **Join the Drum Circle at Meridian Hill Park:** Sunday afternoons, when the weather is right, Meridian Hill Park (p. 201) is the setting for an all-comers-welcome African drum circle. The tradition is 50 years old and dates from the tumultuous days of the 1960s, when activists sought a way to celebrate black liberation but also mourn the death of African-American leader Malcolm X. One drummer started, others gradually joined in, and over time the sonorous Sunday drum circle turned into a steady gig. The park is stunning, designed to resemble an Italian garden, complete with statuary, a cascading fountain, and landscaped grounds.

o **Dine at a Drag Brunch:** Sassy drag queens dressed to the hilt sashay around the room, lip-syncing to the DJ's tunes and entertaining all who've turned up for the $29.95 all-you-can-eat buffet at **Perry's Drag Brunch,** 1811 Columbia Rd. NW (www.perrysam.com; ✆ **202/234-6218**), held every Sunday from 10am to noon and 1pm to 3pm. The brunch is a Washington institution, so expect to see partiers burning the candle at both ends and suited types heading to the office after the show.

o **Explore Washington from an Unconventional Angle:** Yes, it's a graveyard, but Georgetown's **Oak Hill Cemetery** is also a handsome wooded and landscaped garden with a grand view of the city from its hillside perch. Here lie monuments for some of Washington's most illustrious residents, from the city's early days as well as recent years. See p. 271.

o **Play Street Hockey in Front of the White House:** Pennsylvania Avenue in front of the White House is closed to traffic, which makes it a perfect place for street hockey fanatics to show up Saturdays and Sundays at 10am. All you need are Rollerblades and a stick, although gloves and shin pads are also recommended. Go to www.whitehousehockey.com for info.

o **Participate in an Eccentric Yoga Class:** We Washingtonians love our yoga, so any way you can imagine it, D.C. likely offers it. Try "Outdoor Yoga Mortis" at the historic **Congressional Cemetery** (www.congressional cemetery.org), where notables such as J. Edgar Hoover and John Philip Sousa are buried. Head underground for yoga in a **salt cave** in Bethesda, Maryland (www.bethesdasaltcave.com). Do your downward dog with adoptable kittens and cats at **Crumbs and Whiskers** (www.crumbsand whiskers.com) every Sunday morning. The **Yoga Factory** (www.wharfdc. com/upcoming-events) also hosts free beginner-friendly yoga classes seasonally on Saturday mornings at the Wharf in the Southwest Waterfront. Or take your yoga love indoors for an all-levels vinyasa class in the **Kennedy Center's Grand Foyer** almost every Saturday at 10:15am (www.kennedy-center.org/festivals/soundhealth).

WASHINGTON, D.C., IN CONTEXT

2

T he Federal City. The Nation's Capital. Hollywood for Ugly People. Chocolate City. A swamp. The DMV. Over the years, Washington, D.C., has garnered quite a few identities. Some pleasant; others not so much. Even Washingtonians have argued over what Washington, D.C., should really be called if it's ever granted its statehood. The New Columbia? The D.C.?

Whatever nickname best describes D.C., you are bound to formulate your own after visiting. The city is that multi-hued and diverse. Sure, most visitors are here to see some of the country's most celebrated landmarks: the Washington Monument standing tall next to the Lincoln Memorial, the stately U.S. Capitol Building staring down Pennsylvania Ave. toward the porticoed White House, the National Mall in all its shimmering green glory. But Washington is not just a city of iconic sites. It's a dynamic metropolis full of life: marble-clad monuments providing a stately backdrop to a morning excursion on the Potomac River, a delicious meal at a Michelin-starred restaurant, a bike ride through Rock Creek Park on a beautiful fall day, a stroll past handsome embassies along Embassy Row, a tour of the Smithsonian's compelling National Museum of African American History & Culture, or a live jazz performance on a summer night in the Sculpture Garden of the National Gallery of Art.

This chapter, specifically, aims to put the story of Washington, D.C. into context beyond all of those monikers. It's also where we offer practical information on the best times to visit, the weather by season, and the city's most celebrated events.

WASHINGTON, D.C., TODAY

What Washington, D.C., was, is, and wants to be is constantly shifting. D.C., is both the capital of the United States and a city unto itself; therein lie its charms, but also a host of complications. Control of the city is the main issue. The District is a free-standing jurisdiction, but because it is a city with a federal rather than a state overseer, it has never been entitled to the same governmental powers as the states. Congress supervises the District's budget and legislation. Originally, Congress granted the city the authority to elect its own governance, but it rescinded that right when the District overspent its budget in attempts to improve its services and appearance after the Civil War. The White House then appointed three commissioners to oversee D.C.'s affairs.

It wasn't until a century later, in 1973, that the city regained the right to elect its own mayor and city council—although Congress still retains some control of the budget and can veto municipal legislation. The U.S. president appoints all D.C. judges and the Senate confirms them. District residents can vote in presidential primaries and elections and can elect a delegate to Congress, who introduces legislation and votes in committees but cannot vote on the House floor. This unique situation, in which residents of the District pay federal income taxes but don't have a vote in Congress, is a matter of great local concern. D.C. residents publicly protest the situation by displaying license plates bearing the inscription TAXATION WITHOUT REPRESENTATION.

Another wrinkle in this uncommon relationship is the fact that Washington's economy relies heavily on the presence of the federal government, which accounts for about 24% of all D.C. jobs (according to an October 2018 report by D.C.'s Office of the Chief Financial Officer), making it the city's second-largest employer. The city struggles toward political independence, although it recognizes the economic benefits of its position as the seat of the capital.

As you tour the city in 2020, you will see that Washington, D.C., is a remarkably vibrant place. The economic hard times that afflicted other parts of the country in recent years have been muted here. For the time being, income remains higher than the national average, unemployment is down, and residents are better educated than elsewhere. Around 52.6% of the population is female, more than one-third are between the ages of 18 and 34, and the people are remarkably diverse: 47.1% African American, 45.1% white, 11% Hispanic, 4.3% Asian, 14% foreign-born, and 17.5% speaking a language other than English at home. The presence of embassies and the diplomatic community intensifies the international flavor.

The city's thriving culture includes a restaurant scene showcasing an immense variety of international cuisines, from Ethiopian to Peruvian, as well as soul food and such regional specialties as oysters and crab (served softshell, hard-shell, soup, cake, you name it). The city's dining creds mount as critics from *Bon Appétit* magazine to the *New York Times* give high marks to the capital's restaurants. Eating out is a way of life here, whether simply for the pleasure of it or for business—the city's movers and shakers break bread at breakfast, lunch, and dinner.

Theaters, music venues, assorted historic and cultural attractions, hotels, brand-name stores, and homegrown boutiques abound, and Washingtonians make the most of their bounty. But whatever it is—exhibit, play, concert, or restaurant meal—it had better be good. As well-traveled, well-educated, and, let's face it, pretty demanding types, capital dwellers have high standards.

It wasn't always this way. About 20 years ago, Washington wasn't as attractive. Tourists came to visit federal buildings and the city's memorials but stayed away from the dingy downtown and other off-the-Mall neighborhoods. The city had the potential for being so much more, and certain people—heroes, in my book—helped inspire action and brought about change themselves: Delegate Eleanor Holmes Norton, who fought (and continues to fight) steadfastly for D.C. statehood and economic revival and equality; former Mayor Anthony Williams, who rescued the District's budget when his predecessor, the notoriously mismanaging Mayor Marion Barry, brought the city to the brink of financial ruin; and the community-minded developers Abe and Irene Pollin, who used their own funds to finance the $200 million MCI sports center in the heart of town, spurring development all around it. Today, the wildly successful arena (renamed the Verizon Center in 2006 and now known as Capital One Arena) anchors the utterly transformed Penn Quarter neighborhood.

The city's resident population has grown for the 13th straight year and now stands at approximately 702,000, a size not seen since 1975. (At its peak, during and immediately following World War II, more than 900,000 people called D.C. home.) The growth spurt is especially significant given that the District's population reached a relative low point in 1998, when the U.S. Census counted 565,000 D.C. residents.

"Revitalization" is too mild a word to describe the changes taking place in neighborhoods throughout the District. The city is literally reinventing itself. Look to the Capitol Riverfront neighborhood in southeast D.C., where a grand baseball stadium, Nationals Park, opened in March 2008, followed ever since by new restaurants and bars and hotels and housing; to the Columbia Heights enclave in upper northwest D.C., now a mélange of Latino culture, loft condominiums, and ethnic eateries; to historic Shaw, which has turned overnight from a quiet residential area into a hot new foodie destination; and to the Southwest Waterfront, whose new Wharf complex of watersports and recreational activities, lodging, nightlife venues, shops, and eateries gives people plenty of reasons to come here, when they had few before. Add one more reason: Audi Field at Buzzard Point, the gorgeous stadium that debuted in 2018 as home base for D.C. United, the city's soccer team. And more development is underway, including Capital Crossing, a mixed-use, 7-acre development between Union Station and Capital One Arena that actually adds three new city blocks, by way of its placement atop the I-395 Freeway! Meanwhile, the city's evergreens—the memorials and monuments, the historic neighborhoods, and the Smithsonian museums—remain unflaggingly popular.

But D.C. continues to have its share of problems, including crime, poverty, and lingering inequality. Some issues relate to the city's gentrification efforts, such as the displacement of residents from homes they can no longer afford in increasingly expensive neighborhoods. Mayor Muriel Bowser, who overwhelmingly won the 2018 election, continues to work hard to connect the city to its residents, as different as they may be, and to the politicians who reside here. Despite D.C.'s remarkable growth, many residents still struggle with access to all of those economic benefits, including healthcare, good schools, safe neighborhoods, adequate housing, and basic social services.

Diverse in demographics, residents are alike in loving their city, despite the issues it faces. Visitors seem to share this love, as statistics bear out: D.C. welcomes 22 million visitors a year, including more than 2 million from abroad.

THE MAKING OF THE CITY

As with many cities, Washington, D.C.'s past is written in its landscape. Behold the lustrous Potomac River, whose discovery by Captain John Smith in 1608 led to European settlement of this area. Take note of the city's layout: the 160-foot-wide avenues radiating from squares and circles, the sweeping vistas, the abundant parkland, all very much as Pierre Charles L'Enfant intended when he and Congress envisioned the "Federal District" in 1791. Look around and you will see the Washington Monument, the U.S. Capitol, the Lincoln Memorial, the White House, and other landmarks, their very prominence in the flat, central cityscape attesting to their significance in the formation of the nation's capital.

But Washington's history is very much a tale of two cities. Beyond the National Mall, the memorials, and the federal government buildings lies "D.C.," the municipality. Righteous politicians and others speak critically of "Washington"—shorthand, we understand, for all that is wrong with government. They should be more precise. With that snide repudiation, critics dismiss as well the particular locale in which the capital resides. It is a place of lively neighborhoods and vivid personalities, a vaunted arts-and-culture scene, international diversity, rich African-American heritage, uniquely Washingtonian attractions and people—the very citizens who built the capital in the first place and have kept it running ever since.

Early Days

The European settlers who arrived in 1608 weren't the region's first inhabitants, of course. Captain John Smith may have been the first European to discover this waterfront property of lush greenery and woodlands, but the Nacotchtank, Powhatan, and Piscataway tribes were way ahead of him. As Smith and company settled the area, they disrupted the American Indians' way of life and introduced European diseases. The Native Americans gradually were driven away or sold into slavery.

By 1751, immigrants had founded "George Town," named for the king of England and soon established as an important tobacco-shipping port. African Americans lived and worked here as well. Several houses from its early days still exist in modern-day Georgetown: The Old Stone House (on M St. NW), a cabinetmaker's home built in 1765, is now operated by the National Park Service and open to the public, and a few magnificent ship merchants' mansions still stand on N and Prospect streets, though these are privately owned and not open to the public. The Vigilant Firehouse at 1066 Wisconsin Ave., NW., is the oldest surviving in the District. For a walking tour of Georgetown, see p. 264.

The Old Stone House, a woodworker's house built in the 1760s in Georgetown.

Birth of the Capital

After colonists in George Town and elsewhere in America rebelled against British rule, defeating the British in the American Revolution (1775–83), Congress, in quick succession, unanimously elected General George Washington as the first president of the United States, ratified a U.S. Constitution, and proposed that a city be designed and built to house the seat of government for the new nation and to function fully in commercial and cultural capacities. Much squabbling ensued. The North wanted the capital; the South wanted the capital. Alexander Hamilton, Thomas Jefferson, and James Madison hashed out a compromise, which resulted in the Residence Act of 1790, giving President George Washington the authority to choose his spot: The nation's capital would be "a site not exceeding 10 miles square" located on the Potomac. The South was happy, for this area was nominally in their region; Northern states were appeased by the stipulation that the South pay off the North's Revolutionary War debt, and by the city's location on the North–South border. Washington, District of Columbia, made its debut.

The only problem was that the city was not exactly presentable. The brave new country's capital was a tract of undeveloped wilderness, where pigs, goats, and cows roamed free, and habitable houses were few and far between. Thankfully, the city was granted the masterful 1791 plan of the gifted but temperamental French-born engineer, Pierre Charles L'Enfant. Slaves, free blacks, and immigrants from Ireland, Scotland, and other countries worked to fulfill L'Enfant's remarkable vision, starting construction first on the White House in 1792 (making it the city's oldest federal structure) and months later the Capitol, the Treasury, and other buildings. (Read *The Great Decision: Jefferson, Adams, Marshall and the Battle for the Supreme Court*, by Cliff Sloan and David McKean, and *Empire of Mud: The Secret History of Washington, D.C.*, by J. D. Dickey, for excellent descriptions of the early days of the city.)

Gradually, the nation's capital began to take shape, though too slowly perhaps for some. British novelist Anthony Trollope, visiting during the Civil War, declared Washington "the empire of King Mud."

The Early 1800s

Living in early "Washington City" was not for the faint-hearted. Functional roads went only to Maryland and the South, essentially stranding the city on its own. The roads that were in place, mainly Pennsylvania Avenue, were so full of potholes and tree stumps that carriages frequently overturned. Politicians "slipped into the gutter or stumbled against a bank of earth" walking home from the Capitol. L'Enfant's plans for the National Mall as a "grand and majestic avenue" were also derailed. The cofounder of the National Institute (the predecessor to the Smithsonian) described the Mall as "a magnificent Sahara of solitude and waste—appropriated as a cow pasture and frog pond...." To make matters worse, British forces stormed the city in August 1814 during the War of 1812 and torched the Capitol, the Library of Congress, and the White House before heading north to Baltimore. The city lay in tatters.

The Civil War & Reconstruction

During the Civil War, the capital became an armed camp and headquarters for the Union Army, overflowing with thousands of followers. Parks became campgrounds; churches, schools, and federal buildings—including the Capitol and the Patent Office (now the National Portrait Gallery)—became hospitals; and forts ringed the town. The population grew from 60,000 to 200,000, as soldiers, former slaves, merchants, and laborers converged on the scene. The streets were filled with the wounded, nursed by the likes of Louisa May

The inauguration of Abraham Lincoln in 1861 while construction of the U.S. Capitol continued.

Alcott and Walt Whitman, two of many making the rounds to aid ailing soldiers. In spite of everything, President Lincoln insisted that work on the Capitol continue. "If people see the Capitol going on, it is a sign we intend the Union shall go on," he said.

Lincoln himself kept on, sustained perhaps by his visits to St. John's Church, across from the White House. Lincoln attended evening services when he could, arriving alone after other churchgoers had entered and slipping out before the service was over. Then on the night of April 14, 1865, just as the war was dwindling down and Lincoln's vision for unity was being realized, the president was fatally shot at Ford's Theatre (p. 176) while attending a play.

In the wake of the Civil War and President Lincoln's assassination, Congress took stock of the capital and saw a town worn out by years of war—awash with people but still lacking the most fundamental facilities. Indeed, the city was a mess. There was talk of moving the capital city elsewhere, perhaps to St. Louis or some other more centrally located city. A rescue of sorts arrived in the person of public works leader Alexander "Boss" Shepherd, who initiated a "comprehensive plan of improvement" that at last incorporated the infrastructure so necessary to a functioning metropolis, including a streetcar system that allowed the District's overflowing population to move beyond city limits. Shepherd also established parks, constructed streets and bridges, and installed water and sewer systems and gas lighting, gradually nudging the nation's capital closer to showplace design. Notable accomplishments included the completion of the Washington Monument in 1884 (after 36 years) and the opening of the first Smithsonian museum in 1881.

Washington Blossoms

With the streets paved and illuminated, the water running, streetcars and rail transportation operating, and other practical matters in place, Washington, D.C., was ready to address its appearance. In 1901, as if on cue, a senator from Michigan, James McMillan, persuaded his colleagues to appoint an advisory committee to develop designs for a more graceful city. With his own money, McMillan, a retired railroad mogul, sent a committee that included landscapist Frederick Law Olmsted (designer of New York's Central Park), sculptor Augustus Saint-Gaudens, and noted architects Daniel Burnham and Charles McKim to Europe for 7 weeks to study the landscaping and architecture of that continent's great capitals.

"Make no little plans," Burnham counseled fellow members. "They have no magic to stir men's blood, and probably themselves will not be realized. Make big plans, aim high in hope and work, remembering that a noble and logical diagram once recorded will never die, but long after we are gone will be a living thing, asserting itself with ever growing insistency."

The committee implemented a beautification program that continued well into the 20th century. Other projects added further enhancements: A presidential Commission of Fine Arts, established in 1910, positioned monuments and fountains throughout the city; FDR's Works Progress Administration (WPA) erected public buildings embellished by artists. The legacy of these programs is on view today, in the Federal Triangle, the cherry trees along the Tidal Basin, the Lincoln Memorial, the Library of Congress, Union Station, East Potomac Park, Lafayette Square, and many other sights, each situated in its perfect spot in the city.

The American capital was coming into its own on the world stage, as well, emerging from the Great Depression, two world wars, and technological advancements in air and automobile travel as a strong, respected global power. More and more countries established embassies here, and the city's international population increased exponentially.

Black Broadway Sets the Stage

As the capital city blossomed, so did African-American culture. The many blacks who had arrived in the city as slaves to help build the Capitol, the White House, and other fundamental structures of America's capital stayed on, later joined by those who came to fight during the Civil War, or to begin new lives after the war. From 1900 to 1960, Washington, D.C., became known as a hub of black culture, education, and identity, centered on a stretch of U Street NW called "Black Broadway," where Cab Calloway, Duke Ellington, and Pearl Bailey often performed in speakeasies and theaters. Many of these stars performed at the Howard Theatre, the first full-size theater devoted to black audiences and entertainers when it opened in 1910. Nearby Howard University, created in 1867, distinguished itself as the nation's most comprehensive center for higher education for blacks. (The reincarnated "U & 14th Street Corridors," or "New U," is now a diverse neighborhood of blacks, whites, Asians, and Latinos, and a top dining and nightlife destination.) The fact remained, however, that the city was a divided society, in which segregation and discrimination prevented blacks from achieving parity with whites.

The Civil Rights Era Ushers in a New Age

By the late 1950s, African Americans made up more than half of Washington's total population of 805,000, and their numbers continued to grow, reaching a peak of 70% in 1970, before beginning a steady decline that continues to this day. One hundred years or so after the passage of the 13th Amendment to the Constitution (abolishing slavery) and the 15th Amendment to the Constitution (outlawing the denial of voting rights based on race or color), African Americans generally remained unequal members of society. Despite the best efforts and contributions of individuals—from abolitionist Frederick Douglass (p. 195), a major force in the human rights movement in the 19th century, to educator and civil rights leader Mary McLeod Bethune (p. 189), who served as an advisor to President Franklin Delano Roosevelt in the 1930s—the country, and this city, had a long way to go in terms of equal rights. (Read Edward P. Jones, the Pulitzer Prize–winning author whose short-story collections, *Lost in the City* and *All Aunt Hagar's Children,* will take you into D.C.'s black neighborhoods during the mid–20th century.)

The tipping point may have come in 1954, when Thurgood Marshall (appointed the country's first black Supreme Court justice in 1967) argued and

Martin Luther King, Jr., speaking at the March on Washington for Jobs and Freedom.

won the Supreme Court case Brown v. Board of Education of Topeka, which denied the legality of segregation in America. This decision, amid a groundswell of frustration and anger over racial discrimination, helped spark the civil rights movement of the 1960s. On August 28, 1963, black and white Washingtonians were among the 250,000 who marched on Washington for jobs and freedom and listened to an impassioned Rev. Dr. Martin Luther King, Jr., deliver his stirring "I Have a Dream" speech on the steps of the Lincoln Memorial, where 41 years earlier, during the memorial's dedication ceremony, black officials were required to sit separately from the white attendees.

The assassination of John F. Kennedy on November 22, 1963, added to a general sense of despair and tumult. On the day before his funeral, hundreds of thousands of mourners stood in line outside the Capitol all day and night to pay their respects to the president, who lay in state inside its Rotunda.

Then Martin Luther King, Jr., was assassinated on April 4, 1968, and all hell broke loose. For 3 days, angry, frustrated, and heartsick blacks rioted, setting fire to and looting businesses and homes. Three neighborhoods in particular were decimated: Shaw's Seventh Street NW, the H Street Corridor in northeast D.C. (now known as the Atlas District), and the U & 14th Street

President Kennedy lying in state in the Capitol Rotunda.

Corridors. The corner of 14th and U streets served as the flashpoint. Ben's Chili Bowl (p. 104) was ground zero and remained open throughout the riots to provide food and shelter to activists, firefighters, and public servants. Rehabilitation of these neighborhoods has been decades in the making.

As the 20th century progressed, civil rights demonstrations continued and led to Vietnam War protests, which in turn led to revelations about scandals, from President Nixon's Watergate debacle to the late D.C. Mayor Marion Barry's drug and corruption problems to President Bill Clinton's sexual shenanigans.

Beyond the sordid headlines, the city itself was flourishing. A world-class subway system opened, the Capital One Arena (originally the MCI Center, then the Verizon Center) sports and concert venue transformed its aged downtown neighborhood into the immensely popular Penn Quarter, and arts-and-culture venues like the Kennedy Center and Shakespeare theaters came to worldwide attention, receiving much acclaim.

Twenty-First-Century Times

Having begun the 20th century as a backwater, Washington finished the century a sophisticated city, profoundly shaken but not paralyzed by the September 11, 2001, terrorist attacks. Barack Obama's landmark win as the first African-American president in 2008 lifted the country at a critical time, conveying an "all things are possible" perspective.

But nearly 2 full decades into the 21st century, the sense of American unity and fellowship that prevailed after the tragedy of 9/11, and the hopefulness that attended the election of President Obama, has faded, done in by pervasive differences of political opinion coupled with an unwillingness to compromise. The divisive 2016 presidential campaign drove most of these deep differences—and the subsequent long government shutdown in 2018 only provoked them.

What this means for Washington, D.C., in its dual role as the nation's capital and as a culturally, historically, and socially integral city in its own right, is that the District has become even more of a focal point for the worries and dreams of the nation. Always a place for protests, the city continues to serve in that regard, but now the demonstrations are often huge, starting with the Women's March on January 21, 2017, continuing in spring 2018 with the inaugural March for Our Lives demonstration to end gun violence, and the Climate Change Rally in March 2019—with more to come certainly in 2020.

As the seat of the federal government, the city is a natural venue for demonstrations and celebrations of American values. But it helps that in this very Democratic District (where only 4.1% of voters turned out for Trump), the city's own leaders embrace the idea that this is what democracy looks like. Women rule: Congresswoman Eleanor Holmes Norton, now in her 15th term in office, represents residents of the District of Columbia; and Mayor Muriel Bowser, likewise, is a strong champion for the city, tackling education, housing, transportation, and crime issues.

History informs one's outlook, but so does the present. Look again at the Potomac River and think of Captain John Smith, but observe the Georgetown

LITTLE-KNOWN facts

o **What's in a name?** Many people—including Washington, District of Columbia, residents themselves—wonder how the city wound up with such an unwieldy name. Here's how: President Washington referred to the newly created capital as "the Federal City." City commissioners then chose the names "Washington" to honor the president and "Territory of Columbia" to designate the federal nature of the area. Columbia is the feminine form of Columbus, synonymous in those days with "America" and all it stood for—namely, liberty. In 1871, the capital was incorporated and officially became known as Washington, District of Columbia.

o **Green city:** More than 27% of Washington, D.C., is national parkland, which makes the capital one of the "greenest" cities in the country. The biggest chunk is the 2,100-acre Rock Creek Park, the National Park Service's oldest natural urban park, founded in 1890.

o **Taking the measure of landmarks:** The distance between the base of the Capitol, at one end of the National Mall, and the Lincoln Memorial, at the other, is nearly 2 miles. The circumference of the White House property, from Pennsylvania Avenue to Constitution Avenue and 15th Street to 17th Street, is about 1½ miles.

o **A global perspective:** Every country that maintains diplomatic relations with the United States has an embassy in the nation's capital. There are more than 170 foreign embassies in D.C., mostly located along Massachusetts Avenue, known as Embassy Row, and other streets in the Dupont Circle neighborhood. Each May, the embassies open their doors to visitors during Passport DC in addition to holding events throughout the year.

University crew teams rowing in unison across the surface of the water and tour boats traveling between Georgetown and Old Town Alexandria. As you traverse the city, admire L'Enfant's inspired design, but also enjoy the sight of office workers, artists and students, and people of every possible ethnic and national background making their way around town. Tour the impressive landmarks and remember their namesakes, but make time for D.C.'s home-grown attractions, whether a meal at a sidewalk cafe in Dupont Circle, jazz along U Street, a walking tour past Capitol Hill's old town houses, or a visit to a church where slaves or those original immigrants once worshiped.

WHEN TO GO

The city's peak seasons generally coincide with two activities: the sessions of Congress, and springtime—beginning with the appearance of cherry blossoms.

Specifically, from about the second week in September until Thanksgiving, and again from about mid-January to June (when Congress is "in"), hotels are full of guests whose business takes them to Capitol Hill or to conferences.

Mid-March through June is traditionally the most frenzied season, when families and school groups descend upon the city to see the cherry blossoms and bask in Washington's sensational spring. Hotel rooms are at a premium, and airfares tend to be higher. This is also the most popular season for protest marches, although in these tempestuous days, protests take place year-round.

If crowds turn you off, consider visiting Washington at the end of August or in early September, when Congress is still "out" and families have returned home to get their children back to school, or between Thanksgiving and mid-January, when Congress leaves again and many people are busy with their own at-home holiday celebrations. Hotel rates are cheapest at this time, too, so check hotel websites for attractive packages.

If you're thinking of visiting in July or August, be forewarned: The weather is very hot and humid. Despite the heat, Independence Day (July 4th) in the capital is a spectacular celebration. Summer is also the season for outdoor concerts, festivals, parades, and other events (see chapter 8 for performing-arts schedules). If you can deal with the heat, it's a good time to visit: Locals are on vacation elsewhere, so streets, subway trains, and attractions are somewhat less crowded. In addition, hotels tend to offer their best rates in July and August.

Weather

Season by season, here's what you can expect of the weather in Washington:

FALL: This is our favorite season. The weather is often warm during the day—in fact, if you're here in early fall, it may seem entirely *too* warm. But it cools off, and even gets a bit crisp, at night. By late October, Washington has traded its famous greenery for the brilliant colors of fall foliage.

WINTER: People like to say that Washington winters are mild—and sure, if you're from Minnesota, you'll find Washington warmer, no doubt. But D.C. winters can be unpredictable: bitter cold and windy one day, an ice storm the next, followed by a couple of days of sun and higher temperatures. In 2017–2018, snow was minimal but Arctic temperatures arrived in November and pretty much stayed through April; the winter of 2018-2019 included a little bit of everything: big snowstorm, lots of heavy rain, fierce winds, and periods of mild temps. Who knows what to expect in 2020? *Best advice:* Check before you go and pack with all possibilities in mind.

SPRING: Early spring tends to be colder than most people expect. Cherry blossom season, late March to early April, can be iffy—and very often rainy and windy. As April slips into May, the weather usually mellows, and people's moods with it. Late spring is especially lovely, with mild temperatures and intermittent days of sunshine, flowers, and trees colorfully erupting in gardens and parks all over town. Washingtonians sweep outdoors to stroll the National Mall, relax on park benches, or laze away the afternoon at outdoor cafes.

SUMMER: Anyone who has ever spent July and August in D.C. will tell you how hot and steamy it can be. Though buildings are air-conditioned, many attractions, like the memorials and organized tours, are outdoors and unshaded, and the heat can quickly get to you. Make sure you stop frequently for drinks (vendors are plentiful), and wear a hat, sunglasses, and sunscreen.

Average Temperatures & Rainfall in Washington, D.C.

	JAN	FEB	MAR	APR	MAY	JUNE	JULY	AUG	SEPT	OCT	NOV	DEC
TEMP (°F)	44/29	47/31	57/39	68/48	76/58	85/67	89/72	87/71	80/64	69/52	59/42	48/34
TEMP (°C)	7/–2	8/–.6	13/3.9	20/9	24/14	29/19	32/22	30/22	27/18	21/11	15/6	9/–1
RAINFALL (in.)	2.46	2.41	3.02	3.41	4.14	5.04	4.41	3.12	3.66	3.89	2.58	3.50

Holidays

Banks, government offices, post offices, and many stores, restaurants, and museums are closed on the following legal national holidays: January 1 (New Year's Day), the third Monday in January (Martin Luther King, Jr., Day), the third Monday in February (Presidents' Day), the last Monday in May (Memorial Day), July 4 (Independence Day), the first Monday in September (Labor Day), the second Monday in October (Columbus Day), November 11 (Veterans Day/Armistice Day), the fourth Thursday in November (Thanksgiving Day), and December 25 (Christmas). In addition to these national holidays, the District of Columbia celebrates Emancipation Day on April 16; D.C. public schools and government offices and courts are closed but most everything else, including federal offices, are open. See below for details.

Washington, D.C., Calendar of Events

The capital's signature special event takes place every 4 years, when the winner of the presidential election is sworn in on Inauguration Day, January 20. Otherwise, the city's most popular annual events are the National Cherry Blossom Festival in spring, the Fourth of July celebration in summer, and the lighting of the National Christmas Tree in winter. But some sort of special activity occurs almost daily. For the latest schedules, check **www.washington. org**, **www.culturaltourismdc.org**, **www.dc.gov**, **www.washingtonpost.com**, and **washingtoncitypaper.com**. When you're in town, grab a copy of the *Washington Post* (or read it online), especially the Friday "Weekend" section, and/or a free copy of the weekly *Washington CityPaper* (or read it online).

The phone numbers below were accurate at press time, but these numbers change often. If the number you try doesn't get you the details you need, call **Destination D.C.** at ℂ **202/789-7000.**

JANUARY

Martin Luther King, Jr.'s Birthday. Events include a Martin Luther King Jr. Memorial peace walk, parade, and festival in Anacostia (www.mlkholidaydc.org); ongoing park-ranger talks about the civil rights hero at the **Martin Luther King Jr. National Memorial** (www.nps.gov/mlkm); and other commemorations of the slain leader's life at the **National Museum of African American History & Culture** (www.nmaahc.si.edu), the **Kennedy Center** (www.kennedy-center.org), and elsewhere around town. The national holiday is marked on the third Monday in January; King's actual birthday is January 15. For more info, check the websites listed above, or call the National Park Service at ℂ **202/426-6841.**

Restaurant Week. Dining out at some of D.C.'s most popular restaurants becomes much more affordable during the city's biannual Restaurant Week, held in January and again in August. More than 100 restaurants citywide offer three-course, prix-fixe meals for brunch, lunch, and dinner, with brunch and lunch priced at $22 and dinner at $35. Visit www.ramw.org/restaurantweek for a list of participating restaurants. Call the restaurant directly to make a reservation, but call early—reservations fill up fast.

FEBRUARY

Black History Month. Every month is Black History Month at the **National Museum of African American History & Culture** (www. nmaahc.si.edu), but the NMAAHC and its fellow Smithsonian museums further highlight the contributions of African Americans to American life with special concerts, talks, films, discussions, and exhibits. Park rangers give black-history-related talks at the **Frederick Douglass House** (p. 195; www.nps.gov/frdo), the **MLK** and **Lincoln memorials,** and other National Park sites. For details, check the websites listed in the intro to this section and the Smithsonian Institution calendar at www.si.edu/Events.

Chinese New Year Celebration. A Friendship Archway, topped by 300 painted dragons and lighted at night, marks the entrance to Chinatown at 7th and H streets NW. The Chinese New Year celebration begins on the day of the first new moon of the new year, which might fall anywhere from late January to mid-February, and continues for 14 or so days. Festivities center on the Friendship Archway and include a big parade throughout downtown, with firecrackers, dragon dancers, and live musical performances. The Smithsonian's Asian art museum, the **Freer Gallery** (www.freersackler.si.edu), often hosts Chinese cooking and art demonstrations and performances on a day close to the official start of the new year. Get details at www.washington.org. Late January to early February.

Abraham Lincoln's Birthday. Expect quiet recognition of Lincoln's birthday at **Ford's Theatre** and its **Center for Education and Leadership,** an exploration of Lincoln's legacy in the time since his assassination (p. 176). The commemoration at the **Lincoln Memorial** usually includes a wreath-laying and a reading of the Gettysburg Address. For more details, check the websites listed in the intro to this section. February 12.

George Washington's Birthday/Presidents' Day. The city celebrates Washington's birthday in two ways: on the actual day, February 22, with a ceremony that takes place at the **Washington Monument;** and on the federal holiday, the third Monday in February, when schools and federal offices have the day off. The occasion also brings with it great sales at stores citywide. For information on the bigger celebrations held at **Mount Vernon** and in **Old Town Alexandria** on the third Monday in February, see chapter 9.

D.C. Fashion Week. This biannual event features designers from around the world. The weeklong extravaganza stages parties, runway shows, and trunk shows at citywide venues, sometimes including an international couture fashion show at an embassy. Most events are open to the public but may require a ticket. Call ☏ **202/600-9274** or visit www.dcfashionweek.org. Mid-February and mid-September.

MARCH

Women's History Month. Count on the Smithsonian to cover the subject to a fare-thee-well. For a schedule of Smithsonian events, visit www.si.edu/events. Be sure to check out the **Belmont-Paul Women's Equality National Monument**'s schedule of women's history events; visit www.nps.gov/bepa. The historic house is headquarters for the National Woman's Party and is a stop on "A Women's History Tour of Washington, D.C." (p. 39). For other events, check sites listed above in the section intro.

St. Patrick's Day Parade. Celebrating its 50th year, this big parade on Constitution Avenue NW, from 7th to 17th streets, is complete with floats, bagpipes, marching bands, and the wearin' o' the green. For parade details, visit www.dcstpatsparade.com. The Sunday before March 17.

APRIL

National Cherry Blossom Festival. Strike up the band! 2020 marks the 108th anniversary of the city of Tokyo's gift of cherry trees to the city of Washington. This event is celebrated annually; if all goes well, the festival coincides with the blossoming of the nearly 3,800 Japanese cherry trees by the Tidal Basin, on Hains Point, and on the grounds of the Washington Monument. Events take place all over town and include the Blossom Kite Festival on the grounds of the Washington Monument; a Japanese Street Fair on Pennsylvania Avenue; "Petalpalooza," an outdoor celebration with fireworks, art activities, and live music at the Wharf on the Southwest Waterfront; special art exhibits; park-ranger-guided tours past the trees; and sports events. A grand parade winds down the festival, with floats, marching bands, celebrity guests, and more. Most events are free; exceptions include the Japanese Street Fair ($10 per ticket), and grandstand seating at the parade (from $20 per person). For details, go to www.nationalcherryblossomfestival.org. March 20 to April 12, 2020.

White House Easter Egg Roll. A biggie for kids 13 and under, the annual White House Easter Egg Roll continues a practice begun in 1878. Entertainment on the White House South Lawn and the Ellipse traditionally includes appearances by cartoon characters, clowns, musicians (Idina Menzel and Ariana Grande are among those who have performed in the past), egg-decorating exhibitions, puppet and magic shows, an Easter egg hunt, and an egg-rolling contest. To get tickets, you must use the online lottery system, www.recreation.gov, up and running about 7 weeks before Easter Monday. For details, visit www.nps.gov/whho/planyourvisit/easter-egg-roll.htm. Easter Monday 8am to 5pm.

Emancipation Day. On April 16, 1862, Pres. Abraham Lincoln signed the D.C. Compensated Emancipation Act, ending slavery in Washington, D.C., and freeing more than 3,000 slaves, reimbursing those who had legally owned them, and offering money to the newly freed women and men to help them emigrate. Lincoln issued this decree 8 months before the Emancipation Proclamation liberated slaves in the South. To mark the occasion, the D.C. government closes its public schools and government offices on the day itself, and throws a parade, concert, and fireworks show downtown either on the day or the weekend preceding the holiday. (Federal offices and all else stay open.) For details, visit https://emancipation.dc.gov. April 16.

Smithsonian Craft Show. Held in the National Building Museum (401 F St. NW), this juried show features one-of-a-kind, limited-edition crafts by more than 120 noted artists from all over the country. There's an entrance fee of $20 (or $17 in advance) per adult each day; it's free for children 12 and under. No strollers. For details, visit www.smithsoniancraftshow.org. Four days in mid- to late April.

MAY

Embassy Open Houses. If you're in D.C. in May, you may have the opportunity to tour embassies that participate in either or both the **Around the World Embassy Tour,** held on the first Saturday in May, and the **EU Open House,** held on the second Saturday in May. Go to www.culturaltourismdc.org and click on "Passport DC" for more information.

Washington National Cathedral Annual Flower Mart. Now in its 81st year, the flower mart takes place on cathedral grounds, featuring displays of flowering plants and herbs, decorating demonstrations, ethnic food booths, children's rides and activities (including an antique carousel), costumed characters, puppet shows, tower climbs, and other entertainment. Free admission. For details, visit www.allhallowsguild.org. First Friday and Saturday in May, rain or shine.

Memorial Day. Ceremonies take place at **Arlington National Cemetery's Memorial Amphitheater** (p. 196) and the **Tomb of the Unknowns,** at the **National World War II** (p. 157) and **Vietnam Veterans memorials** (p. 160), at the **Women in Military Service for America Memorial,** and at the **U.S. Navy Memorial.** A National Memorial Day

Soldier places flags in Arlington National Cemetery for Memorial Day ceremonies.

Parade marches down **Constitution Avenue** from the Capitol to the White House. On the Sunday before Memorial Day, the National Symphony Orchestra performs a free concert at 8pm on the West Lawn of the **Capitol** to honor the sacrifices of American servicemen and servicewomen. Last Monday in May.

JUNE

DC Jazz Festival. The 10-day festival, now in its 16th year, presents more than 125 performances in dozens of venues all over the city. Performers include both stars and up-and-comers, and some performances are free. www.dcjazzfest.org. Early to late June.

Smithsonian Folklife Festival. A major event celebrating both national and international traditions in music, crafts, food, games, concerts, and exhibits, staged between 4th and 7th streets on the National Mall. Each Folklife Festival showcases two or three cultures or themes. All events are free; most take place outdoors. To learn more, visit www.festival.si.edu, or check the listings in the *Washington Post*. Ten days in late June and early July, always including July 4.

JULY

Independence Day. There's no better place to be on the Fourth of July than in Washington, D.C. The all-day festivities include a massive National Independence Day Parade down **Constitution Avenue,** complete with lavish floats, marching groups, and military bands. A morning program in front of the National Archives includes military demonstrations, period music, and a reading of the Declaration of Independence. In the evening, the National Symphony Orchestra plays on the west steps of the **Capitol** with guest artists. And big-name entertainment precedes the fabulous fireworks display behind the **Washington Monument.** For details, go to www.july4thparade.com or www.nps.gov/subjects/nationalmall4th/fireworks.htm. July 4.

Citi Open. This week-long tennis tournament brings some of the top players from the WTA and ATP tours to D.C. for a series of nail-biting matches at the Rock Creek Park Tennis Center. www.citiopentennis.com. Late July to early August.

Capital Fringe Festival. Celebrating experimental theater in the tradition of the original Fringe Festival in Edinburgh, Scotland. Nearly 100 separate productions take place at multiple venues daily for 3 weeks or more, sometimes throughout the city and sometimes in one locale, as in 2019 when the festival took over the Southwest Waterfront. Local and visiting artists perform in theater, dance, music, and other disciplines. All single tickets are $17, plus a one-time fee of $7 for an admission button; purchase at www.capitalfringe.org. The Capital Fringe organization produces performances and events year-round, including a music festival, all worth checking out; same website as above. Three weeks in mid- to late July.

AUGUST

Shakespeare Theatre Free for All. This free theater festival presents a different Shakespeare play every year for a 2-week run at the Sidney Harman Hall, across from the Verizon Center, in the Penn Quarter. Tickets are required, but they're free. Go to www.shakespearetheatre.org/events/free-for-all. Evenings and some matinees in late August through early September.

SEPTEMBER

Labor Day Concert. The National Symphony Orchestra closes its summer season with a free performance at 8pm on the West Lawn of the Capitol. Sunday before Labor Day (rain date: same day and time at Constitution Hall or the Kennedy Center).

Library of Congress National Book Festival. The Library of Congress sponsors this festival, now in its 20th year, welcoming more than 100 established authors and their many fans. It was previously held on the National Mall, but the festival's popularity and the toll the turnout took on Mall grounds necessitated its relocation in 2014 to the Walter E. Washington Convention Center in downtown D.C. (btw. 7th and 9th sts. NW, and N St. and Mt. Vernon Place). The festival takes place over the course of one long day, from 10am to 10pm in late August or early September and includes readings, author signings (2019 authors included Ruth Bader Ginsberg, Barbara Kingsolver, and Chef José Andrés), panel discussions, and general hoopla surrounding the love of books. For details, visit www.loc.gov/bookfest. A Saturday in late August/early to mid-September.

H Street Festival. What started as a neighborhood block party has grown into a 150,000-participant festival along the H Street Corridor between 4th and 14th streets, NE. Expect to hear live music of different genres, catch youth performances, participate in interactive children's programs, and enjoy fashion, poetry, and arts programs throughout the 1-day festival. For details, visit www.hstreetfestival.org. Late September.

OCTOBER

Marine Corps Marathon. A maximum of 30,000 may compete in this 26.2-mile race (the third-largest marathon in the United States). The 2020 race marks its 45th year. The start line is at a spot located between the Pentagon and Arlington Memorial Cemetery, and the course takes racers through Georgetown, through Rock Creek Park almost to the National Zoo, along the Potomac River, past memorials and museums on the National Mall, and so on, before reaching the finish line at the Marine Corps Memorial (the Iwo Jima statue). Participants must be 14 or older. Register online for the lottery system that determines entry in the marathon. A 1-mile kids' run is held the day before and is open to anyone ages 5 to 12. Registration is $10. For details, go to www.marinemarathon.com. Third or fourth Sunday in October.

NOVEMBER

Veterans Day. The nation's tribute to those who fought in wars to defend the United States, and to those who died doing so, takes place with a wreath-laying ceremony at 11am at the **Tomb of the Unknowns** in **Arlington National Cemetery,** followed by a memorial service in the **Amphitheater.** The president of the United States or a stand-in officiates, as a military band performs. Wreath-laying ceremonies also take place at other war memorials in the city. November 11.

DECEMBER

National Christmas Tree Lighting. At the northern end of the **Ellipse,** the president lights the National Christmas Tree to the accompaniment of orchestral and choral music, and big-name performers take the stage. The lighting ceremony inaugurates several weeks of holiday concerts performed mostly by local school and church choruses, afternoons and evenings on the Ellipse. (Brrrr!) The 17,000 tickets (3,000 seated, 14,000 standing) are free but required for the tree-lighting ceremony. (No tickets are required to attend the other holiday concerts.) To enter the lottery to try to score tickets, visit the website www.recreation.gov—the lottery opens in mid-October. For further details, visit www.thenationaltree.org. The tree-lighting ceremony takes place at 5pm in late November to early December. Following the ceremony, the tree stays lit until January 1.

SUGGESTED ITINERARIES & NEIGHBORHOODS

3

"Washington is a city of Southern charm and northern efficiency," John F. Kennedy famously declared. You'll certainly feel that way if you're caught up in the throng on the National Mall on a sunny day or waiting for a table at one of the city's hottest restaurants. The crowd is intense and the wait can be long. There's so much to see here, and everyone has his or her own way of seeing it. This chapter lays out suggested itineraries to help make your Washington, D.C., trip as fun-filled and stress-free as possible. It includes a 3-day tour of the capital's iconic sites, plus three themed itineraries: one for families, another to explore women's history, and the third an African-American history tour. Follow them to the letter or adapt them for your own purposes—it's entirely up to you.

Prepare to be calm and flexible: Lines to enter public buildings can be lengthy; depending on the season and security clearance procedures, you'll need to enter many of the federal buildings. Reserve spots on tours whenever possible to avoid some of those waits. Most important, don't be afraid to ask questions. The U.S. Capitol tour guides, the National Park Service rangers, and the staff at all the museums know an awful lot; take advantage of their expertise.

Following the itineraries is an overview of D.C.'s neighborhoods. Among the most enjoyable activities in D.C. is exploring its neighborhoods on foot, so if you tire of crowded museums, choose a neighborhood and simply stroll. See chapter 10 for walking tours of a few standout neighborhoods.

ICONIC WASHINGTON, D.C., IN 1 DAY

If you have limited time in Washington, D.C., and would like to do a deep dive into several specific landmark attractions (rather than the rushed experience of many), then this is the itinerary for you.

An ideal Washington, D.C., itinerary would include a visit to the **National Museum of African American History & Culture** (p. 150), a trip to the top of the **Washington Monument** (p. 161), and a tour of the **White House** (p. 171). However, the popularity and/or admission procedures of these sites can make visits difficult to incorporate into a set schedule. For instance, the only way to visit the interior of the White House is by making a reservation through the office of your congressional representative or senator, as much as 3 months in advance. Best advice? Absolutely try in advance to 1) book a White House tour, 2) order advance tickets to visit the Washington Monument, and 3) obtain an African American Museum entry pass. Then, if you're successful, tweak the following itineraries accordingly.

3

SUGGESTED ITINERARIES

Iconic Washington, D.C., in 1 Day

Start: *Metro on the Blue, Orange, or Silver Line to the Capitol South stop on Capitol Hill or on the Red Line to Union Station.*

---

1 The U.S. Capitol Building ★★★

This is Congress's "House," its cornerstone laid in 1793 by President George Washington. The Capitol was officially completed in 1826, but by 1850, Congress had grown and there was already need for expansion. In 1868, the larger building was finally finished and the impressive Statue of Freedom placed atop the dome. Head inside the Capitol Visitor Center to take the hour-long guided Capitol tour (highly recommended), armed with the timed passes you've ordered in advance online. If you've neglected to order these, you may well be in luck: Go to the "Visitors Without Reservations" walk-up line to see if any same-day passes are available—they usually are (I've put this to the test even at the busiest times of year). The Visitor Center is itself worth checking out. See. p. 123.

Exit the Capitol and head south on First St. SE to return to the Capitol South Metro station, where you take a Blue, Orange, or Silver Line train to the L'Enfant Plaza stop. Exit at Maryland Ave. and 7th St. SW, walk down 7th St. SW to cross Independence Ave., and continue along 7th St., stopping midway to take in the:

2 National Mall ★★★

Stroll the long green promenade, buttressed end-to-end by the Capitol, where you started, and the Lincoln Memorial, westward in the distance, where you'll end up later today. Once you've had a chance to catch your breath, it's time to resume touring.

Continue across the Mall and cross Madison Dr. to enter the West Building of the:

3 National Gallery of Art ★★★

If you have time to visit only one of the city's free art museums, make it this one. The freshly renovated East Building showcases modern and contemporary art, while the West Building's galleries display European paintings and sculptures spanning the 13th to 19th centuries and American art.

Iconic Washington, D.C.

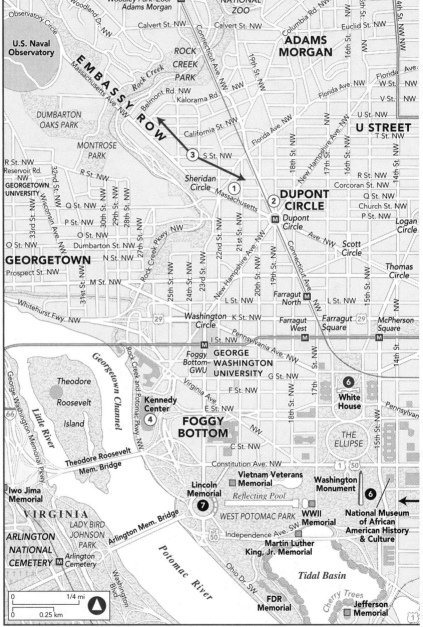

Woodley Park–Zoo/
Adams Morgan

NATIONAL
ZOO

Observatory Circle

Woodland Dr. NW

Calvert St. NW

Calvert St. NW

Columbia Rd. NW

Euclid St. NW

15th St. NW

14th St. NW

U.S. Naval
Observatory

ROCK
CREEK
PARK

ADAMS
MORGAN

16th St. NW

EMBASSY ROW

Massachusetts Ave. NW

Rock Creek

Belmont Rd. NW

Kalorama Rd.

19th St. NW

Florida Ave.
NW

Florida Ave.
W St. NW

V St. NW

DUMBARTON
OAKS PARK

California St. NW

Florida Ave. NW

U St. NW

U STREET
T St. NW

MONTROSE
PARK

3 S St. NW

18th St. NW

17th St. NW

16th St. NW

14th St. NW

R St. NW
Reservoir Rd.
NW

R St. NW

Sheridan
Circle

Massachusetts

1

R St. NW

Corcoran St. NW

Logan
Circle

GEORGETOWN
UNIVERSITY

32nd St. NW

Q St. NW

DUPONT
CIRCLE

2

Q St. NW

Wisconsin Ave. NW

Q St. NW

P St. NW

Church St. NW

M Dupont
Circle

P St. NW

33rd St. NW

31st St. NW

30th St. NW

29th St. NW

28th St. NW

27th St. NW

P St. NW

O St. NW

Scott
Circle

O St. NW

Dumbarton St. NW

22nd St. NW

21st St. NW

20th St. NW

19th St. NW

15th St. NW

GEORGETOWN

N St. NW

Ave. NW

Thomas
Circle

Prospect St. NW

Rock Creek Pkwy. NW

25th St. NW

24th St. NW

23rd St. NW

New Hampshire Ave. NW

Connecticut Ave. NW

M St. NW

31st St. NW

L St. NW

Farragut
North

L St. NW

Whitehurst Fwy. NW

Washington
Circle

K St. NW

M

Pennsylvania Ave. NW

Farragut
West

Farragut
Square

29

McPherson
Square

29

M

I St. NW

Foggy
Bottom–
GWU

GEORGE
WASHINGTON
UNIVERSITY

17th St.

M

14th St.

Georgetown Channel

Rock Creek and Potomac Pkwy. NW

Virginia Ave.

G St. NW

6

White
House

Pennsylvan

Theodore

Roosevelt

Island

66

Little River

George Washington Memorial Pkwy.

Kennedy
Center

4

F St. NW

E St. NW

18th St. NW

17th

THE
ELLIPSE

15th St. NW

FOGGY
BOTTOM

NW

C St. NW

Theodore Roosevelt
Mem. Bridge

Constitution Ave. NW

Vietnam Veterans
Memorial

Washington
Monument

1 50

6

Iwo Jima
Memorial

Lincoln
Memorial

7

Reflecting Pool

National Museum
of African
American History
& Culture

VIRGINIA

LADY BIRD
JOHNSON
PARK

Arlington Mem. Bridge

WEST POTOMAC PARK

WWII
Memorial

ARLINGTON
NATIONAL
CEMETERY M

50

Independence Ave. SW

Martin Luther
King, Jr. Memorial

Arlington
Cemetery

Washington Blvd.

Potomac River

Ohio Dr. SW

Tidal Basin

Cherry Trees

0   1/4 mi

0   0.25 km

FDR
Memorial

Jefferson
Memorial

1

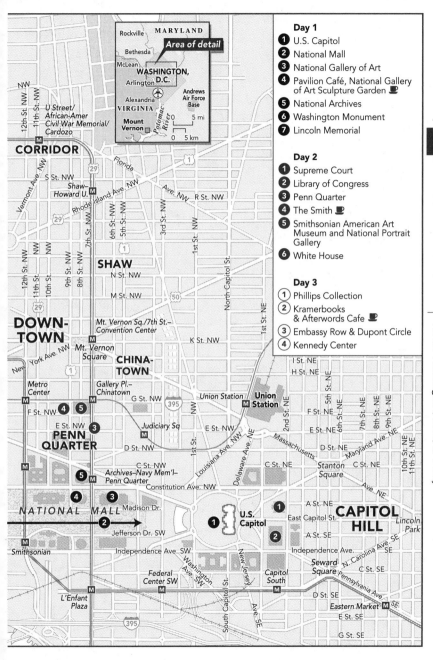

Day 1
1. U.S. Capitol
2. National Mall
3. National Gallery of Art
4. Pavilion Café, National Gallery of Art Sculpture Garden ☕
5. National Archives
6. Washington Monument
7. Lincoln Memorial

Day 2
1. Supreme Court
2. Library of Congress
3. Penn Quarter
4. The Smith ☕
5. Smithsonian American Art Museum and National Portrait Gallery
6. White House

Day 3
1. Phillips Collection
2. Kramerbooks & Afterwords Cafe ☕
3. Embassy Row & Dupont Circle
4. Kennedy Center

Don't leave without checking out the gallery's special exhibits, which are always superb. See p. 147.

Exit the Gallery's West Building and cross 7th St. NW to the:

Hall of the National Gallery of Art.

4 Pavilion Café at the National Gallery Sculpture Garden ☕
Order a grilled vegetable wrap or an Asian chicken salad and maybe a glass of rosé, and if the weather's pleasant, try to snag a seat at one of the outside tables. Be sure to wander through the entire garden to admire all 20 sculptures and a delightful mosaic by Chagall, one of the garden's newer pieces. See p. 148.

Exit the Sculpture Garden and proceed westward down the Mall, or hop a DC Circulator bus at Madison Dr. and 7th St. to reach the:

5 The National Archives ★★★

No trip to Washington is complete without a visit to this museum located just behind the Gallery of Art's Sculpture Garden. Here, the three "Charters of Freedom" reside: the Declaration of Independence, the Constitution, and the U.S. Bill of Rights, among other important historical documents, photos, and audio recordings. Housed behind glass in a low-lit rotunda, it can be a hushed, almost reverent, experience to read the documents in the Founding Fathers' own script. The gallery almost always has a special exhibit on view, too.

Exit the museum to Madison Dr. and cross 15th street to reach the grounds of the:

6 Washington Monument ★★★

People often ask: Which is taller, the Washington Monument or the Capitol? The answer is the Washington Monument. The monument reopened in 2019 after an extensive renovation of its interior, including an elevator that delivers you to the observation tower and its panoramic views stretching for miles (20 miles on a clear day!). A ticket to enter the monument can be elusive in peak season. If tickets are gone for the day or the monument isn't open, you can still stand back and consider the fact that this 555-foot, 5⅛-inch-high obelisk, D.C.'s version of a skyscraper, is one of the world's tallest freestanding works of masonry. See p. 161.

Walk the rest of the way or hop the DC Circulator bus at the 15th St. and Madison Dr. stop to arrive at the:

7 Lincoln Memorial ★★★

Visit this temple-like memorial to contemplate the inspiring life and spirit of the nation's 16th president. Citizens of the world surround you, reading aloud the words inscribed on its walls: "FOUR SCORE AND SEVEN YEARS AGO OUR FATHERS BROUGHT FORTH ON THIS CONTINENT A NEW NATION, CONCEIVED IN LIBERTY, AND DEDICATED TO THE PROPOSITION THAT ALL MEN ARE CREATED EQUAL…" Stand at the top of the memorial's steps to take in the sweeping view across the Reflecting Pool and green expanse of the National Mall. See p. 141.

ICONIC WASHINGTON, D.C., IN 2 DAYS

With a second day added on, you can return to Capitol Hill for more capital attractions, tour the Penn Quarter neighborhood, and cap off the day with a presidential flourish. ***Start:*** *Metro on the Blue, Orange, or Silver Line to the Capitol Hill South stop.*

1 Supreme Court ★★★

You may be shocked to know that the U.S. Constitution does not specify an age, an education level, or even a citizenship requirement for a person to become a Supreme Court justice. No, all that is required is that the president nominates the person and that the Senate confirms the nomination, a simple process often complicated by politicking. One of the "newer" federal buildings, the Supreme Court first sat here in its own building in 1935. If the Court is in session (Mon–Wed mornings, starting the first Mon in Oct and continuing through late Apr), I highly recommend that you attend an argument, which is only possible if you arrive 90 minutes in advance of the scheduled 10am-to-noon time slots. If the Court is not in session, you can at least attend a docent lecture. See p. 130.

Boats on the Tidal Basin and the Jefferson Memorial.

Exit and head right next door to tour the:

2 Library of Congress ★★

The world's largest library is not only a keeper of books; ongoing exhibits show off early maps of the U.S., Jefferson's own library collection, and a preliminary draft of the Emancipation Proclamation in Abraham Lincoln's own hand. See p. 127.

Exit and proceed north on First St. NW (closed to car traffic but not pedestrians), crossing Constitution Ave. and walking a couple of blocks to reach Union Station, where you catch Metro's Red Line train to the Gallery Place stop, putting you right in the thick of the:

3 Penn Quarter

This lively neighborhood just north of the National Mall is full of restaurants, bars, and assorted sightseeing attractions, all within a short walk of one another. Wander down to Pennsylvania Avenue and up 7th Street, the main arteries, and explore side streets. Then head to lunch at:

4 The Smith 🍺

Expect great tastes and a fun vibe at this lively restaurant and raw bar serving a bite of everything: a breakfast of omelets and French toast, lunch featuring burgers and salads, and a delicious dinner of oysters or a pot of mussels. See p. 98.

Exit The Smith, walk 1 block east on G St., and then turn right onto 7th St:

5 Smithsonian American Art Museum & National Portrait Gallery ★★★

Nothing reveals the essence of the American spirit and character better than its art. Pop in here and look into the portraiture faces of America's presidents (and First Ladies—don't miss Michelle Obama's portrait on the third floor), its poets, its heroes, its historic figures, its celebrities. Study Georgia O'Keeffe's southwestern landscapes, and admire the creations from self-taught folk artists, from exquisite quilts to outlandish sculptures made of metallic foil and found objects. The enclosed Kogod Courtyard with its wavy, glass and steel roof is a work of art itself.

Make your way eastward on G St. until you hit 15th St. Cross 15th St. and walk briefly north to reach Pennsylvania Ave. and:

6 The White House ★★★

A tour of the White House is a highlight of a trip to the nation's capital, but one that can be hard to procure. If you have not managed to book an advance reservation, I encourage you to admire its exterior view and consider the facts: Its cornerstone was laid in 1792, making the White House the capital's oldest federal building. It's been the residence of every president but George Washington (although the nation's second president, John Adams, lived here for only 4 months). The British torched the mansion in 1814, so what you see is the house rebuilt in 1817, using the original sandstone walls and interior brickwork. Consider following the "Strolling Around the White House" tour in chapter 10. See p. 257.

The Capitol.

ICONIC WASHINGTON, D.C., IN 3 DAYS

Time for some off-the-Mall attractions. Take in a beloved museum, explore a neighborhood, and get a taste of the city's international identity. *Start: Metro on the Red Line to reach Dupont Circle, exiting at Q St.*

1 Phillips Collection ★★

Tour this charming museum to view French, American, post-Impressionist, and modernist art, all housed in an 1897 mansion and its modern wings. Always keep an eye out for favorites, such as Renoir's *Luncheon of the Boating Party,* numerous Bonnards, the gallery devoted to Mark Rothko's bold artworks, and, on display from time to time, *Night Baseball,* a painting by founder Duncan Phillips's wife, Marjorie Phillips. See p. 186.

Turn right outside the museum, turn left onto Q St., NW, then right on Connecticut Ave.:

2 Kramerbooks and Afterwords Cafe 📖

Open early in the morning and late at night, this neighborhood institution (with bookstore attached) serves a generous American menu (1517 Connecticut Ave., NW; www.kramers.com; ✆ **202/387-1400**).

Return to Q St., follow it to Massachusetts Ave. heading north to start your tour of:

3 Embassy Row & Dupont Circle

Stop in shops along Connecticut Avenue, and then follow side streets to discover boutiques, little art galleries, and quaint, century-old town houses. If you look carefully, you'll notice that some of these buildings are actually embassies or historic homes. The most evocative embassies lie on Massachusetts Avenue, west of Dupont Circle. Turn onto S Street NW and look for no. 2340 to see where President Woodrow Wilson lived after he left the White House. The **Woodrow Wilson House** (p. 187) is worth touring if you have time. A bit farther along Massachusetts Avenue, turn onto Belmont Road NW to find Barack and Michelle Obama's post-presidency digs, at no. 2446. Few embassies are open to the public; those that are limit their hours. For an in-depth tour of Dupont Circle and Embassy Row, take the self-guided walking tour outlined in chapter 10. See p. 273.

Walk, if you feel up to it, or take a taxi to the:

4 Kennedy Center ★★★

Head to the Kennedy Center for the 6pm nightly free concert in the Grand Foyer (part of the center's Millennium Stage program). See p. 224. At concert's end, proceed through the glass doors to the terrace overlooking Rock Creek Parkway and the Potomac River, and enjoy the view. You're a short walk around the bend of the river from Georgetown; why not head there next for dinner? See p. 111.

WASHINGTON, D.C., FOR FAMILIES

Here's a bold statement: Few if any other U.S. cities are truly as perfect for kids as D.C. From the countless museums that keep them entertained (and educated, too) to the vast expanse of the National Mall (perfect for letting off steam), Washington is made for families. *Start: The National Building Museum.*

1 National Building Museum ★

Aside from the impressive Great Hall, perfect for letting kids roam safely, the museum hosts PLAY, WORK, BUILD, a year-round hands-on play area with supersized foam blocks and small-scale structures. The Building Zone, specially designed for kids 2 to 6, features toy trucks, LEGOs, and a life-size "green" playhouse. Tickets to the Building Zone are first come, first served. See p. 181.

Exit to 6th St and walk south to the National Mall; head diagonally across the Mall from the National Gallery of Art Sculpture Garden to the:

2 Carousel

For little and not-so-little children, the carousel is a treat, operating year-round, weather permitting. See p. 203. (Good to know: Another carousel awaits at your final destination, the National Zoo, where a solar-powered, custom-designed carousel with 58 animal figures operates daily.)

Now cross the Mall on the diagonal, heading west to reach the:

3 National Museum of American History ★★★

Like all the Smithsonians, this one has tons of kid-friendly activities and exhibits. If your children are younger than 6, visit Wegmans Wonderplace, full of fun activities and toys related to the museum's collections. Kids 6 and older will appreciate the 23-room dollhouse; Spark!Lab, a hands-on "invention activity" space for tinkering; interactive carts of objects, such as a stereoscope, that children can pick up and experiment with; carriages, cars, and trains that children can sit in; artifacts on

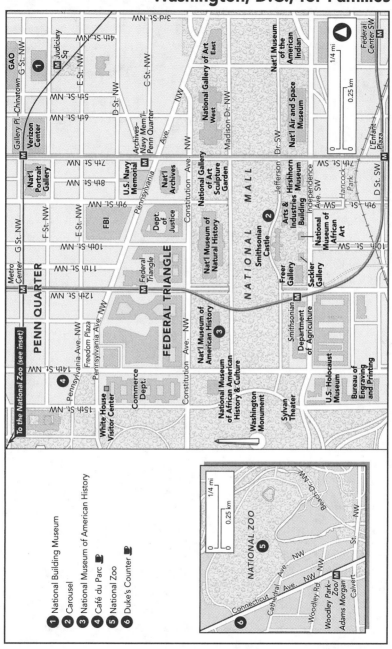

Washington, D.C., for Families

NATIONAL MALL

PENN QUARTER

FEDERAL TRIANGLE

GAO

Verizon Center

Gallery Pl.-Chinatown

National Museum of the American Indian

National Gallery of Art East

National Gallery of Art West

Nat'l Air and Space Museum

Federal Center SW

L'Enfant Plaza

Archives-Navy Mem'l-Penn Quarter

Nat'l Portrait Gallery

U.S. Navy Memorial

Nat'l Archives

National Gallery of Art Sculpture Garden

Arts & Industries Building

Hirshhorn Museum

Smithsonian Castle

National Museum of African Art

FBI

Dept. of Justice

Nat'l Museum of Natural History

Freer Gallery

Sackler Gallery

Metro Center

Federal Triangle

Smithsonian

Department of Agriculture

Nat'l Museum of American History

National Museum of African American History & Culture

Commerce Dept.

White House Visitor Center

Washington Monument

Sylvan Theater

U.S. Holocaust Museum

Bureau of Engraving and Printing

To the National Zoo (see inset)

Judiciary Sq

3rd St. NW

4th St. NW

5th St. NW

5th St. NW

4th St. NW

D St. NW

G St. NW

E St. NW

Pennsylvania Ave. NW

Constitution Ave. NW

Madison Dr. NW

Jefferson Dr. SW

Independence Ave. SW

D St. SW

4th St. SW

6th St. SW

7th St. SW

Hancock Park

7th St. NW

8th St. NW

9th St. NW

10th St. NW

11th St. NW

12th St. NW

14th St. NW

15th St. NW

Pennsylvania Ave. NW

Freedom Plaza

F St. NW

G St. NW

E St. NW

1/4 mi

0.25 km

National Building Museum ❶
Carousel ❷
National Museum of American History ❸
Café du Parc ❹
National Zoo ❺
Duke's Counter ❻

NATIONAL ZOO

Woodley Park-Zoo-Adams Morgan

Connecticut Ave. NW

Cathedral Ave. NW

Woodley Rd. NW

Calvert St.

Beach Dr. NW

1/4 mi

0.25 km

Children riding the National Mall carousel.

display including Kermit the Frog; and simulator rides that make you feel like you're riding a roller coaster or driving a race car. See p. 153.

You must be starving! You can dine here in the Smithsonian's **museum cafes** or from the **food trucks** parked outside, but if your family has the energy, it's worth the short walk to get to your next stop. Exit to Constitution Ave. and cross it to reach 14th St., then follow 14th St. to Pennsylvania Ave. Cross Pennsylvania Ave. and walk past the main entrance to the Willard Hotel to find a seat inside or outside at the lovely Parisian brasserie:

4 Café du Parc 🍽

It's open daily 7am to 10pm, has a children's menu of delicious items ($5–$16), and is a satisfying mashup of French tastes and D.C. ambience. The White House is across 15th St., just beyond all those barriers and trees (Willard InterContinental Hotel; www.cafeduparc.com; ℂ **202/942-7000**).

Now head north on 14th St. to G St., turn right, and follow G St. to 13th St. to find the entrance to the Metro Center subway station. Board a Red Line train going in the direction of either Shady Grove or Grosvenor. Debark at the Woodley Park–Zoo station and walk up Connecticut Ave. to reach the:

5 National Zoo ★★

Certain children's exhibits (the Kids' Farm, the seasonal Zoo-Tubing down Lion/Tiger Hill) lie at the very bottom of this large zoo, situated on a hill. Keep that part in mind as you explore the zoo, since it'll be all uphill—and quite a long hill it is—back to Connecticut Avenue. (*Tip:* A

Storytelling in a tipi in the imaginNATIONS Activity Center at the National Museum of the American Indian.

free shuttle does loop continuously between the upper and lower zoo.) But you need not go all the way to the bottom of the hill, as pandas, a solar-powered carousel, a fab elephant exhibit, and nearly 1,500 other animals are on view elsewhere in the zoo. See p. 190.

Head across Connecticut Ave. to:

6 Duke's Counter 🍵
Located directly across the street from the National Zoo, this British gastropub has a little something for everyone, including a kids' menu with fish n' chips and a "Proper Cheeseburger." Open early to late. See p. 103.

A WOMEN'S HISTORY TOUR OF WASHINGTON, D.C.

"Remember the ladies," Abigail Adams famously advised her husband, John Adams, in 1776, when he was attending the Continental Congress and busy formulating his ideas about the new government. John Adams, who went on to become the second president of the United States in 1797, did his best. But that was a long time ago, and women have long acted as their own advocates. One day, perhaps, Americans might marvel that there was ever a time when a woman couldn't vote, own property, succeed in sports, run a large company, or become the president. In the meantime, let us now celebrate the achievements of women in many realms. *Start: The Belmont-Paul Women's Equality National Monument on Capitol Hill.*

---

1 Belmont-Paul Women's Equality National Monument ★
On April 12, 2016, President Obama proclaimed the historic Sewall-Belmont House a national monument to women's equality, the first of its kind in the National Park Service. As the headquarters for the National Woman's Party since 1929, the house serves as both a museum honoring the many women who have struggled for women's equality and a center supporting activities to educate the public on the women's rights fight. The monument takes its name from National Woman's Party founder Alice Paul and the party's benefactor, Alva Belmont. See p. 125.

From the house, head up to 1st St. and continue on Constitution Ave. Give a nod to the Supreme Court, where three of the nine justices are women, and the U.S. Capitol, where 127 women now hold seats in Congress. Then make a left to cross the National Mall to the:

2 National Air and Space Museum ★★★
Throughout history, women pilots have played an integral part in aviation. But it wasn't until the 1970s that women gained full access to military and commercial cockpits, as well as the Space Shuttle. From Amelia Earhart's red Lockheed Vega (the one she flew solo across the Atlantic Ocean in 1932) to the clothes Sally Ride wore during her Space Shuttle

A Women's History Tour of Washington, D.C.

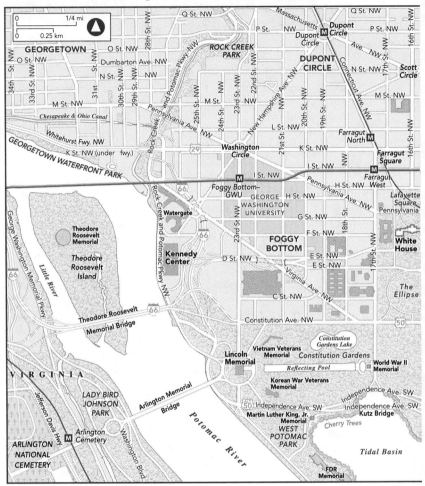

mission aboard *Challenger* in June 1983, when she became the first U.S. woman in space, this museum honors the lasting legacy women have made in flight.

Head north to Madison Dr., then turn left and walk to the:

3 National Museum of American History ★★★

The most popular exhibit in the museum is the First Ladies exhibit, which gives First Ladies their due as strong and interesting people in their own right. Also don't miss Julia Child's Kitchen (in the "Food: Transforming the American Table 1950–2000" exhibit), a tribute to a different kind of icon; "Uniformed Women in the Great War," presenting the role of women in World War I; and the individual stories of ordinary women

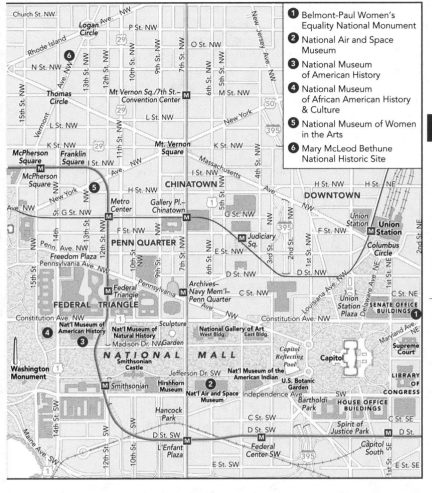

3

SUGGESTED ITINERARIES | A Women's History Tour of Washington, D.C.

Map Legend

1. Belmont-Paul Women's Equality National Monument
2. National Air and Space Museum
3. National Museum of American History
4. National Museum of African American History & Culture
5. National Museum of Women in the Arts
6. Mary McLeod Bethune National Historic Site

woven throughout the museum's exhibits, such as that of abolitionist Lucy Caldwell, who lived "Within These Walls," an occupant of the old Ipswich House on view, from 1836 to 1865. And the Star-Spangled Banner? The handiwork of a woman, or rather, several women: Mary Pickersgill and her daughter, nieces, and a maid. See p. 153.

Exit the museum and walk west along Madison Dr. toward the Washington Monument until you come to the:

4 National Museum of African American History & Culture ★

African American women and their contributions to politics, academics, arts, and athletics are reflected throughout this impressive museum. The newest museum to the National Mall, it details the entire African American experience from slavery to modern times, so much of which features the contributions of women. Exhibits include Rosa Parks' handmade dress from 1955–56 and Althea Gibson's Wightman Cup blazer when she became the first African American Grand Slam tennis champion in 1957. Stories of lesser-known African American women, including Mae Reeves, who fashioned hats in Philadelphia for more than 50 years, are also on display. *Note:* I strongly recommend that you reserve visitor passes before arriving. See p. 150.

Walk to 14th St. and head north, until you reach New York Ave., then turn right until you reach the:

5 National Museum of Women in the Arts ★

From Renaissance paintings to contemporary sculptures to silver pieces created by 18th- and 19th-century Irish and British female silversmiths, this museum is full of masterpieces by women. It's also the only major museum in the world created exclusively to highlight women in art. The graceful portraits of Mary Cassatt are here, along with the iconic self-portraits of Frida Kahlo. Check out the calendar, too: The museum frequently hosts gallery talks, films, and concerts. See p. 182.

Walk to 14th St. and head north, going around Thomas Circle at Massachusetts Ave. to pick up Vermont Ave. on the other side. Proceed about a block to the:

6 Mary McLeod Bethune National Historic Site

Mary McLeod Bethune bought this house not as a residence, but to serve as headquarters for the National Council for Negro Women. So although she did live here from 1943 to 1949, it is the sense of her professional rather than personal life that you absorb from the exhibits—which speak volumes. Look for a black-and-white photo of FDR's cabinet in the 1930s, and there you will see a panel of white men and, in their midst, a black woman—Bethune, appointed as a national advisor to the president. When you consider that Bethune was born poor, the 15th of 17 children of former slaves, you start to truly appreciate her accomplishments. See p. 189.

AN AFRICAN-AMERICAN HISTORY TOUR OF WASHINGTON, D.C.

The story of African Americans in Washington, D.C., actually predates the founding of the capital, for African Americans were here from the get-go. Records show that blacks were living and working in Alexandria, Virginia, in its early days as a tobacco port. (And worshipping: See p. 273 for information about Georgetown's **Mount Zion United Methodist Church,** which celebrates its 206th year in 2020, making its worshippers the city's oldest black congregation.) In 1800, African Americans made up 29% of the District's roughly 14,000 residents, but 80% of them were enslaved. The capital's very design was plotted by self-taught mathematician/surveyor Benjamin Banneker, who in 1791 assisted Andrew Ellicott in mapping out Pierre L'Enfant's

10-square-mile territorial vision. Slaves built many of the capital's historic buildings, the White House and the U.S. Capitol among them. The population of African Americans in the capital, always significant, now stands at about 48%. This tour aims to shed some light on the local and national history of African Americans, from pre-Revolutionary War times to the present. ***Start: Frederick Douglass National Historic Site in Anacostia.***

1 Frederick Douglass National Historic Site (Cedar Hill) ★★

Douglass is best known for being an abolitionist, but his story doesn't stop there. After the Civil War, Douglass held a number of government positions, including U.S. Marshal, appointed by President Rutherford Hayes in 1877. His office was in the U.S. Capitol. He was 60. Douglass walked the 5 miles daily to and fro. So let me ask you something: Do you think the Anacostia site is too far away to visit? You could make the same trek as Douglass, but actually, it's quite easy to get there: From Union Station, take the DC Circulator bus headed in the direction of Congress Heights and travel 7 stops farther to the corner of W Street SE and Martin Luther King, Jr. Avenue SE, hop off and walk 4 blocks east to 14th and W streets SE. Easy-peasy. See p. 195.

From the house, simply reverse the steps listed above, picking up the DC Circulator at Martin Luther King Jr. Ave. SE and W St. SE, headed toward Congress Heights, and travel 1 stop to the Anacostia Metro station, where you catch the Green Line train to the L'Enfant Plaza Metro station. From here you can either exit and walk to your next

3

SUGGESTED ITINERARIES | An African-American History Tour of Washington, D.C.

The Duke Ellington mural on U Street.

An African-American History Tour of Washington, D.C.

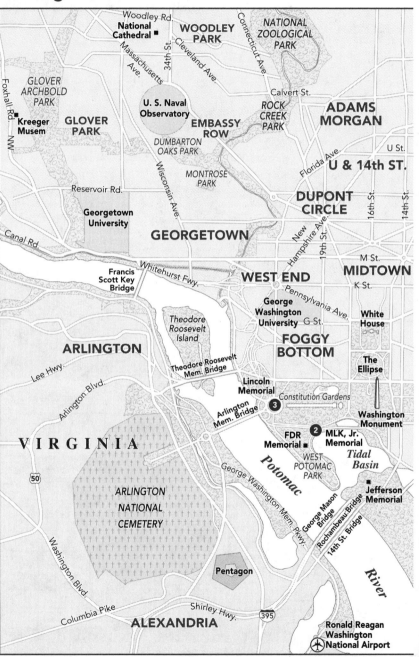

Woodley Rd.

National Cathedral ■

WOODLEY PARK

NATIONAL ZOOLOGICAL PARK

34th St.

Cleveland Ave.

Massachusetts Ave.

Connecticut Ave.

GLOVER ARCHBOLD PARK

Kreeger Musem ■

Foxhall Rd. NW

GLOVER PARK

U. S. Naval Observatory

EMBASSY ROW

DUMBARTON OAKS PARK

MONTROSE PARK

Calvert St.

ROCK CREEK PARK

ADAMS MORGAN

Florida Ave.

U St.

U & 14th ST.

Reservoir Rd.

Wisconsin Ave.

DUPONT CIRCLE

16th St.

14th St.

Georgetown University

GEORGETOWN

New Hampshire Ave.

19th St.

M St.

MIDTOWN

Canal Rd.

Whitehurst Fwy.

Francis Scott Key Bridge

WEST END

Pennsylvania Ave.

K St.

White House

Theodore Roosevelt Island

George Washington University

G St.

FOGGY BOTTOM

ARLINGTON

Lee Hwy.

Theodore Roosevelt Mem. Bridge

Lincoln Memorial ③

Constitution Gardens

The Ellipse

Arlington Blvd.

Arlington Mem. Bridge

FDR Memorial ■

② **MLK, Jr. Memorial**

WEST POTOMAC PARK

Washington Monument

Tidal Basin

V I R G I N I A

50

George Washington Mem. Pkwy.

Potomac

■ **Jefferson Memorial**

ARLINGTON NATIONAL CEMETERY

George Mason Bridge

Rochambeau Bridge

14th St. Bridge

Washington Blvd.

Pentagon

Columbia Pike

Shirley Hwy.

395

ALEXANDRIA

River

Ronald Reagan Washington ✈ National Airport

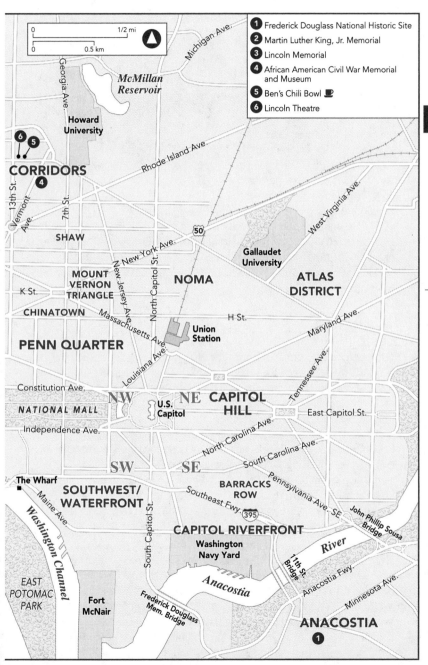

0 ----- 1/2 mi
0 ----- 0.5 km

1 Frederick Douglass National Historic Site
2 Martin Luther King, Jr. Memorial
3 Lincoln Memorial
4 African American Civil War Memorial and Museum
5 Ben's Chili Bowl
6 Lincoln Theatre

Michigan Ave.

Georgia Ave.

McMillan Reservoir

Howard University

6 5

CORRIDORS
4

13th St.
Vermont Ave.
7th St.

Rhode Island Ave.

West Virginia Ave.

SHAW

New York Ave.

50

Gallaudet University

ATLAS DISTRICT

MOUNT VERNON TRIANGLE

New Jersey Ave.
North Capitol St.

NOMA

K St.

CHINATOWN

Massachusetts Ave.

H St.

Maryland Ave.

PENN QUARTER

Louisiana Ave.

Union Station

Constitution Ave.

NW   NE CAPITOL HILL

Tennessee Ave.

NATIONAL MALL

U.S. Capitol

East Capitol St.

Independence Ave.

North Carolina Ave.

South Carolina Ave.

SW   SE

The Wharf

Maine Ave.

SOUTHWEST/ WATERFRONT

South Capitol St.

BARRACKS ROW

Southeast Fwy.

Pennsylvania Ave. SE

John Phillip Sousa Bridge

395

Washington Channel

CAPITOL RIVERFRONT

Washington Navy Yard

River

11th St. Bridge

Anacostia Fwy.

Minnesota Ave.

EAST POTOMAC PARK

Fort McNair

Frederick Douglass Mem. Bridge

Anacostia

ANACOSTIA

1

3

SUGGESTED ITINERARIES | An African-American History Tour of Washington, D.C.

stop, or switch to the Blue Line, travel to the Smithsonian station, exit to 12th St. SW, and walk along Independence Ave. until you reach the:

2 Martin Luther King, Jr. National Memorial ★★

In his 39 years, the Rev. Dr. Martin Luther King, Jr. helped found the Southern Christian Leadership Conference, wrote and delivered 2,500 speeches, organized massive protests and drives to register black voters, won the Nobel Peace Prize, and led the August 28, 1963, historic March on Washington for Jobs and

The Martin Luther King, Jr. National Memorial.

Freedom that helped convince Congress to pass the Civil Rights Act of 1964. The memorial at the northwest corner of the Tidal Basin has 15 quotes inscribed into the walls that attempt to define the man, including one that inspired the memorial's design: OUT OF THE MOUNTAIN OF DESPAIR, A STONE OF HOPE. (See p. 142.) Your next stop is the place where King delivered that line.

Cross Independence Ave. and walk westward along the avenue until you reach a lane leading to the:

3 Lincoln Memorial ★★★

Forty-one years before Martin Luther King, Jr. delivered his famous "I Have a Dream" speech from the steps of the Lincoln Memorial, another black man addressed a crowd here. Dr. Robert Russa Moton, the president of Tuskegee Institute, gave the keynote speech at the memorial's dedication on May 30, 1922. The attendees were mostly white and the seating segregated, but the occasion, nevertheless, was momentous for paying honest tribute to Lincoln's legacy. It's not certain where Dr. Moton stood that day, but Dr. King's step is clearly marked: Ascend to the top of the steps, then count down to the 18th and look for the stone inscribed with the words I HAVE A DREAM. MARTIN LUTHER KING, JR. THE MARCH ON WASHINGTON FOR JOBS AND FREEDOM. AUGUST 28, 1963. See p. 141.

Catch the DC Circulator headed toward Union Station and debark at the stop near the Hirshhorn Museum, at 7th St. and Jefferson Dr. Cross Independence Ave. and return to the L'Enfant Plaza Metro station. Board the Green Line train to the U Street/African-American Civil War Memorial/Cardozo stop and exit to 10th St., which puts you right in front of your next destination:

4 African American Civil War Memorial and Museum

When you exit the Metro station at 10th Street, you'll exit to the plaza that holds the African American Civil War Memorial: *The Spirit of Freedom* sculpture portraying uniformed soldiers and a sailor on one side of the rounded pedestal, a family on the other side. The sculpture sits within a semicircular Wall of Honor, a series of stainless steel plaques on which are engraved the names of 209,145 United States Colored Troops mustered into military service during the Civil War. Now cross Vermont Street to visit the African American Civil War Museum to view exhibits that tell the story of the slaves and freed blacks who fought in the Civil War.

When you leave the museum, walk 3 blocks westward on U St. until you reach 1213 U St.:

5 Ben's Chili Bowl 🍽

In the 1950s and '60s, the capital was a violent hotbed of civil rights activism. Ben's, around since 1958, was one establishment that somehow remained open during the tumultuous days of race riots and heartbreak following Dr. King's assassination in 1968. And it's still going strong. Famous for its half-smokes and chili fries, Ben's also serves decent vegetarian fare. See p. 104.

From here you need go no farther than right next door to view the historic:

6 Lincoln Theatre

The greater U Street neighborhood is a place for dining out, hanging out, and nightlife. But for decades, this area was predominantly a cultural and residential stronghold for African Americans, who had started to settle here after the Civil War. In the 1920s, '30s, and '40s, the popularity of jazz venues and their stars, like D.C.'s own Duke Ellington, led fans to dub the area "Black Broadway." The Lincoln Theatre, open since 1922, was at the center of it all, welcoming Duke Ellington, Pearl Bailey, Ella Fitzgerald, Billie Holliday, Cab Calloway, Louis Armstrong, and others to its stage. See a show if you're here at night.

The Neighborhoods in Brief

Adams Morgan This bohemian-trendy, multi-ethnic neighborhood is crammed with shops, bars, clubs, and restaurants. Most everything is located on either 18th Street NW or Columbia Road NW. Parking is manageable during the day but difficult at night, especially on weekends (a parking garage on Champlain St., just off 18th St., helps a little). Luckily, you can easily walk to Adams Morgan from the Dupont Circle or Woodley Park Metro stop, or take the bus or a taxi there. (Be alert in Adams Morgan at night and try to stick to the main streets: 18th St. and Columbia Rd.).

Anacostia When people talk about the Washington, D.C., that tourists never see, they're talking about neighborhoods like this; in fact, they're usually talking about Anacostia, specifically. Named for the river that separates it from "mainland" D.C., it's an

old part of town, with little commercial development and mostly modest, often low-income housing. Anacostia does have three attractions: the Smithsonian's **Anacostia Community Museum** and the **Frederick Douglass National Historic Site** (see the African-American History Tour, above, and "Museums in Anacostia" box, p. 195); and the **Anacostia Riverwalk Trail** (p. 205), a popular walking and bicycling path that connects southwest and southeast neighborhoods fronting the Anacostia River. Also be alert if here, especially at night.

Atlas District The Atlas District, also known as the H Street Corridor, stretches along H St. NE between 4th and 14th streets, but centers on the 12th to 14th streets segment. Primarily known as a nightlife and restaurant destination, the neighborhood has lately sprouted a cafe and coffeehouse

Washington, D.C., at a Glance

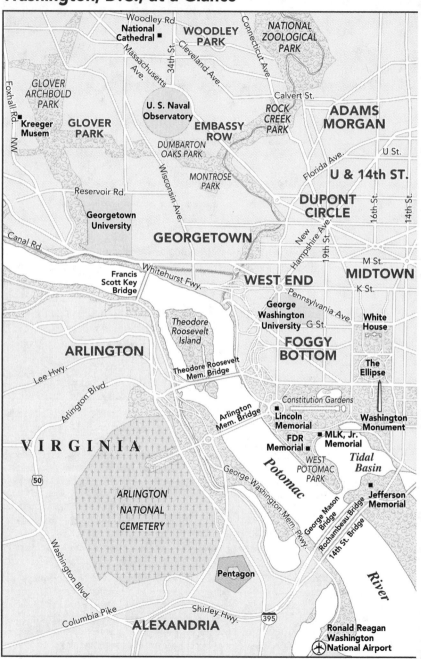

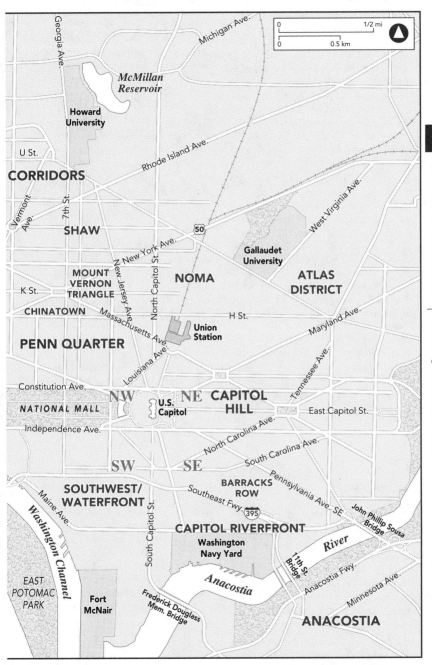

culture that attracts young entrepreneurs and locals during the day.

Barracks Row Barracks Row refers mainly to a single stretch of 8th Street SE, south of Pennsylvania Avenue SE, but also to side streets occupied by Marine Corps barracks since 1801. This southeastern subsection of Capitol Hill is known for its lineup of shops, casual bistros, and pubs. Its attractions continue to grow as a result of the 2008 opening of the Nationals baseball team's stadium, Nationals Park, half a mile away. In fact, the ballpark has spawned its own neighborhood, dubbed Capitol Riverfront (see below).

Capitol Hill Everyone's heard of "the Hill," the area crowned by the Capitol building. The term, in fact, refers to a large section of town, extending from the western side of the Capitol to the D.C. Armory going east, bounded by H Street to the north and the Southwest Freeway to the south. It contains not only this chief symbol of the nation's capital, but also the **Supreme Court Building,** the **Library of Congress,** the **Folger Shakespeare Library, Union Station,** and **Eastern Market.** Much of it is a quiet residential neighborhood of tree-lined streets, rows of Federal and Victorian town houses, and old churches. Restaurants keep increasing their numbers, with most located along Pennsylvania Avenue SE on the south side of the Capitol and near North Capitol Street NW on the north side of the Capitol—the north side, near Union Station, is where most of the hotels are, too. Keep to the well-lit, well-traveled streets at night, and don't walk alone—crime occurs more frequently in this neighborhood than in some other areas.

Capitol Riverfront The opening of **Nationals Park** in 2008 spurred the development of this once-overlooked part of town. Known also as "Navy Yard" (that's the name of the subway stop here), the revitalized 500-acre neighborhood abuts 1½ miles of the Anacostia River. Besides the ballpark, the area has five hotels, tons of restaurants and bars, a brewery or two, the city's first winery, numerous shops, and public parks, trails, and docks. Much, much more to come.

Cleveland Park Cleveland Park, just north of Woodley Park, is a picturesque enclave of winding, tree-shaded streets dotted with charming old houses with wraparound porches. The streets extend off the main artery, Connecticut Avenue. With its own stop on the Red Line Metro system and a respectable number of good restaurants, Cleveland Park is worth visiting when you're near the zoo (just up the street) or seeking a good meal after a bike ride or stroll through nearby Rock Creek Park.

Columbia Heights Hispanic immigrants have long settled here but now are joined by millennials and others seeking more affordable housing. Here you'll find historic mansions, colorful town houses, Hispanic cultural attractions, the gorgeous **Meridian Hill Park** (p. 201), and loads of good ethnic restaurants. The neighborhood lies north of U Street to Quincy Street NW, and east of 16th Street to Georgia Avenue NW.

Downtown The area bounded roughly by 6th and 21st streets NW to the east and west, and M Street and Pennsylvania Avenue to the north and south, is a mix of the Federal Triangle's government office buildings; K Street, ground zero for the city's countless law and lobbying firms; Connecticut Avenue restaurants and shopping; historic hotels; the city's poshest small hotels; **Chinatown;** the huge Walter E. Washington Convention Center; and the White House. You'll also find the historic **Penn Quarter,** one of D.C.'s hottest locales, which has continued to flourish since the 1997 opening of the MCI Center, now renamed the **Capital One Arena** (sports and concerts, see p. 227). A number of off-the-Mall museums, such as the massive **National Building Museum** and the **Smithsonian's National Portrait Gallery** and **American Art Museum,** are here. Besides hip restaurants, boutique hotels, and nightclubs, the Penn Quarter claims ultra-trendy **CityCenterDC,** a mini-Manhattan of chic shops and restaurants. The total downtown area encompasses so many blocks and sites that I've divided discussions of attractions, restaurants, and hotels in this area into two sections: **"Midtown,"** referring to the area from 15th Street west to 21st Street, and from Pennsylvania Avenue north to M Street; and **"Penn Quarter,"** from 15th Street east to 6th Street, and

Pennsylvania Avenue north to New York Avenue.

Dupont Circle One of my favorite parts of town, Dupont Circle provides easy fun, day or night. It takes its name from the traffic circle minipark, where Massachusetts, New Hampshire, and Connecticut avenues converge. Washington's famous **Embassy Row** centers on Dupont Circle and refers to the parade of grand embassy mansions lining Massachusetts Avenue and its side streets (see walking tour, p. 273). The streets extending out from the circle are lively, with all-night bookstores, good restaurants, wonderful art galleries and art museums, hip nightspots, and Washingtonians at their loosest. Once the hub of D.C.'s LGBTQ community, the neighborhood continues to host the annual High Heel Drag Queen Race the Tuesday preceding Halloween and the Capital Pride Parade every June, despite the fact that LGBTQ residents live throughout the city now. The neighborhood has plenty of hotel choices, most of them moderately priced.

Foggy Bottom/West End The area west of the White House, south of Dupont Circle, and east of Georgetown encompasses both Foggy Bottom and the West End. Foggy Bottom, located below, or south, of Pennsylvania Avenue, was Washington's early industrial center. Its name comes from the foul fumes emitted in those days by a coal depot and gasworks, but its original name, Funkstown (for owner Jacob Funk), is perhaps even worse. There's nothing foul or funky about the area today. The West End edges north of Pennsylvania Avenue, booming with the latest big-name restaurants and new office buildings. Together, the overlapping Foggy Bottom and West End neighborhoods present a mix: the **Kennedy Center,** town house residences, George Washington University campus buildings, offices for the World Bank and the International Monetary Fund, State Department headquarters, small- and medium-size hotels, student bars, and several fine eateries, lining either side of Pennsylvania Avenue and its side streets.

Georgetown This historic community dates from Colonial times. It was a thriving tobacco port long before the District of Columbia was formed, and one of its attractions, the **Old Stone House,** dates from pre-Revolutionary days. Georgetown action centers on M Street and Wisconsin Avenue NW, where you'll find hundreds of boutiques, chic restaurants, and popular pubs. Expect lots of nightlife here. Detour from the main drags to relish the quiet, tree-lined streets of restored Colonial row houses, stroll the beautiful gardens of **Dumbarton Oaks,** and check out the **C&O Canal.** Georgetown is also home to **Georgetown University.** (See chapter 10 for a walking tour of Georgetown.) The neighborhood gets pretty raucous on weekends.

Glover Park Mostly a residential neighborhood, this section of town just above Georgetown and just south of the **Washington National Cathedral** is worth mentioning because of several good restaurants and bars located along its main stretch, Wisconsin Avenue NW. Located between the campuses of Georgetown and American universities, Glover Park has a large student presence.

Midtown This refers roughly to the part of downtown from 15th Street west to 21st Street, and from Pennsylvania Avenue north to M Street. See "Downtown," above.

Mount Vernon Triangle Yet another old neighborhood experiencing renewal, Mount Vernon lies east of the convention center, its boundary streets of New Jersey, Massachusetts, and New York avenues defining a perfectly shaped triangle. Within that triangle, trendy restaurants are starting to multiply.

The National Mall This lovely, tree-lined stretch of open space between Constitution and Independence avenues, extending for nearly 2 miles from the foot of the Capitol to the steps of the Lincoln Memorial, is the hub of tourist attractions. It includes most of the Smithsonian Institution museums and several other notable sites. Tourists as well as natives—joggers, food vendors, kite flyers, and picnickers among them—traipse the 700-acre Mall. Hotels and restaurants are located beyond the Mall to the north, and, increasingly, south of the Mall across Independence Avenue all the way to the waterfront, thanks to intense development. The proper name for the entire parkland area is actually **National Mall and Memorial Parks,** which is how I refer to it in chapter 6.

NoMa NoMa, as in "North of Massachusetts," is a curious mix of a neighborhood. Located east of downtown D.C. and directly north of Union Station, NoMa's got old residential streets of real character, but also major thoroughfares slicing through, which makes it not the most walkable of areas. Wide swaths of commuter and Amtrak train tracks form the neighborhood's eastern boundary. Except for the smattering of pleasant side streets, the place has an industrial look about it. And yet, NoMa won't be ignored, and here's why you shouldn't: You're close to Capitol Hill and Union Station; you have access to two Metro stations, bike stations, and a bike path; and the neighborhood has caught the eye of developers, who have built three hotels here in the last few years and more and more restaurants. If you're here on Capitol Hill business, this might be a good pick.

Northern Virginia Across the Potomac River from the capital lies Northern Virginia and its close-in city/towns of Arlington and Old Town Alexandria. The Arlington Memorial Bridge leads directly from the Lincoln Memorial to Arlington National Cemetery, and beyond to Arlington and Alexandria (see chapter 9). Commuters travel back and forth daily between the District and Virginia.

Penn Quarter This refers roughly to the part of downtown from 15th Street east to 6th Street, and Pennsylvania Avenue north to New York Avenue. See "Downtown," above.

Shaw Located due north of the Penn Quarter, this historic district encompasses the area between 11th and 6th streets NW going west to east, and Massachusetts Avenue to U Street NW going south to north. Shaw remains largely a neighborhood of longstanding houses and old churches, even as it undergoes a renewal that started with the

opening of the Walter E. Washington Convention Center in 2003. Shaw has been garnering a lot of attention lately for its hot new restaurants and bars, a city market, and interesting shops. Suddenly, Shaw is the place to go for the best dining in D.C.

Southwest/Waterfront With the fall 2017 opening of the **Wharf,** the waterfront complex of eateries, shops, live music venues, bars, and outdoor recreation activities, this neighborhood has been transformed quite suddenly into an attractive, vital area of the city. As development goes on and new buildings go up, this stretch of waterfront continues as a working marina, with vendors selling fresh crabs and fish straight off their docked fishing barges. This is where locals and restaurateurs come to buy fresh seafood. The neighborhood is also home to the acclaimed **Arena Stage** (p. 223) and **Anthem** music hall (p. 227). Traffic congestion can be a problem, especially at night and in pleasant weather when people descend on the Wharf; even though it does have a large parking garage, take advantage of the many transportation alternatives to driving (see p. 293).

U & 14th Street Corridors The diverse U Street NW and 14th Street NW neighborhood is rooted in black history and culture, but is better known these days as a dining and nightlife destination. During its "Black Broadway" heyday in the first half of the 20th century, jazz and blues legends Duke Ellington, Louis Armstrong, and Cab Calloway performed at the **Lincoln Theatre** (p. 228) and other venues. Jazz lovers in 2020 might still be satisfied at the tiny **Twins Jazz,** but most folks flocking here at night are the young and the restless in search of a hot new eatery or bar hangout.

Woodley Park Home to two large hotels, including the Omni Shoreham (p. 82), Woodley Park is mainly a pretty residential neighborhood. Its biggest attractions are the **National Zoo, Rock Creek Park**, good restaurants, and some antiques stores.

WHERE TO STAY

Tourism continues to break all records in Washington, D.C., and new hotels of all kinds are popping up fast. At least 18 hotels are currently in the pipeline, bringing the total number of hotels in the capital to 158 in 2020.

That number represents an increasingly diverse selection, among them bed-and-breakfasts, "pod" hotels (with tiny but stylish guest rooms and low rates), convention hotels, historic gems, properties catering to business visitors, those beckoning to families, and those appealing to millennials. D.C. even lays claim to a hotel targeted to "changemakers and creatives." Check it out: The **Eaton Hotel DC** (www.eatonworkshop.com) includes a radio/podcasting studio, a co-working space for 370 members, a newsstand, a library, and a wellness center offering alternative treatments like reiki and sound baths. Rooms contain a "curated selection" of vinyl, artwork, books, Himalayan salt lamps, and organic bedding, while the bathrooms all feature chemical-free products. D.C.'s location is the first of three such hotels opening in the United States.

This chapter describes properties in different neighborhoods and the features that make them uniquely recommendable. They include the posh **Hay-Adams** (p. 67) with its view of the White House; the **Capitol Hill Hotel** (p. 57), the only hotel truly located on "The Hill"; the **Fairfax at Embassy Row** (p. 73), situated among embassies and elegant residential town houses; and the **Hampton Inn & Suites Washington DC-Navy Yard** (p. 61), for baseball fans—you can watch the action at Nationals Park from its rooftop lounge!

GETTING THE BEST DEAL

Want the secret for getting the best hotel deal ever in Washington? Easy: Come to Washington when Congress is out, when cherry blossom season is over, or during the blazing-hot days of July or August or the icy-cold days of a non-inauguration-year January or February. Not possible? Okay, let's put it this way: Don't try to negotiate a good deal for late March or early April (cherry blossom season); hotel reservationists will laugh at you. I've heard them.

But do consider these money-saving tips:

o Check out hotels that are **located away from big events taking place** while you are visiting the capital. For example, during cherry blossom season, look at properties in Georgetown, upper Dupont Circle, Woodley Park, or otherwise a few miles from downtown and the National Mall. When the Washington

WHAT YOU'LL really PAY

The prices given in this chapter are based on web searches of both discounter sites and the hotels' own websites; they're the lowest average rates and the highest ones, for both double rooms and suites. At most hotels, you probably won't pay the top rate unless you visit in the spring—especially during cherry blossom season from late March through mid-April. These categories are intended as a general guideline only, because rates rise and fall dramatically.

It's important to note that when the timing's right, it's possible to obtain a room at an expensive property for the same rate as a more moderate one. And if you're persistent, or book at the last minute, you might get a steal. Or you could end up paying through the nose, especially if you're visiting during a special event. It's all the luck of the draw, though I do have some tips for savings below.

Three things to keep in mind: 1) Quoted discount rates almost never include the hefty **14.95% hotel sales tax.** 2) Some hotels tack on a **"guest amenity fee"** to your daily room rate when you book your reservation. Not all hotels charge this fee, but for those that do—for example, the Capitol Hill Hotel (p. 57) and the Kimpton hotels George (p. 57), Monaco (p. 65), and Mason & Rook (p. 81)—the fee is not optional. Also known as a "resort fee," it can be substantial (Kimpton's fee is $25 plus tax) and covers services that you may not even be interested in. 3) Finally, the word **"double"** refers to the number of people in the room, not to the size of the bed. Most hotels charge one rate, regardless of whether one or two people occupy the room.

Nationals are playing home games at Nationals Park, consider hotels on the other side of town.

o **Visit on a weekend.** Hotels looking to fill rooms vacated by weekday business travelers lower their rates and might even be willing to negotiate further for weekend arrivals. Sundays usually have the lowest nightly rates. Also ask whether a room less expensive than the first one quoted is available.

o **Ask about special rates or other discounts.** You may qualify for substantial corporate, government, student, military, senior, trade union, or other discounts. Members of the **National Trust for Historic Preservation** (https://savingplaces.org) get up to 30% off stays at the Trust's affiliated Historic Hotels of America. Washington has 14 National Trust properties, including the Willard and the Morrison-Clark Inn.

o **Book online.** Because booking online is often the best way to get a discount, I've devoted a box to a discussion of how to get the best deals. See p. 56.

o **Look into group or long-stay discounts.** If you come as part of a large group, you should be able to negotiate a bargain rate because the hotel can then guarantee occupancy in a number of rooms. Likewise, if you're planning a long stay (at least 5 days), you might qualify for a discount. As a general rule, expect 1 night free after a 7-night stay.

o **Consider enrolling in hotel loyalty programs.** In 2016, all of the major chains announced they'd be reserving special discounts for travelers who booked directly through the hotel websites (usually in the portion of the site reserved for loyalty members). They weren't lying: These are always the lowest rates at the hotels in question, though discounts can range widely, from as little as $1 to as much as $50. *Our advice:* Search for a hotel that's in your price range and ideal location (see the online booking box on p. 56) and then, if it is a chain property, book directly through the online loyalty portal.

○ **Check out deals listed in the "Places to Stay" tab on the homepage of D.C.'s tourism bureau, Destination DC** (www.washington.org; ☏ **202/ 789-7000**). For example, in 2019, the Eaton Hotel offered a "book in advance" deal that offered 15% off for guests who booked more than 7 days in advance.

○ **Subscribe to e-mail alerts.** Alerts from your favorite hotels or booking sites can keep you informed of special deals.

○ **Even if you haven't gotten the best deal possible on your room rate, you can still save money on incidental costs.** D.C. hotels charge unbelievable rates for overnight parking—more than $50 a night at some hotels, plus 18% tax!—so if you can avoid driving, you can save yourself quite a bit of money. Also resist the pricey minibar offerings.

Note: D.C.'s hotel sales tax is a whopping 14.95%, merchandise sales tax is 6%, and food and beverage tax is 10%, all of which can rapidly increase the cost of a room.

Consider Alternative Accommodations

These alternatives to traditional hotels are another smart way to save:

○ **Hostelling International Washington, DC** (1009 11th St. NW, at K St.; www.hiwashingtondc.org; ☏ **888/464-4872** or 202/737-2333) is well-located in the Penn Quarter and nicely equipped, with free Wi-Fi, bike racks, and air-conditioning. Breakfast is complimentary, and the hostel often hosts complimentary dinners. Guests are welcome to use the full kitchen. Self-serve washers and dryers are available ($1 to wash, $1 to dry, $1.25 for soap if needed). The hostel hosts free daily walking tours and other activities. Almost all of the 238 beds are dorm rooms with shared bathrooms ($32–$62 a night per person). Of the 10 private bedrooms, two have their own bathrooms ($129–$144 a night per person). A staffperson is on-site 24/7.

○ **Go the Airbnb route: Airbnb, VRBO, HomeAway.com,** and **FlipKey. com,** among others, match people looking for a place to stay with locals interested in renting out space in their home, or sometimes entire apartments or homes, often for far less than you might pay at a hotel. According to the website **Inside Airbnb** (www.insideairbnb.com), D.C. has roughly 9,000 active listings, two-thirds of which are for entire houses or apartments.

○ **Consider house swapping.** Try such organizations as **HomeExchange** (www.homeexchange.com) or **HomeLink International** (www.homelink. org), which offer tens of thousands of would-be swaps worldwide (take into account membership fees when looking at costs).

○ **Call Washington's tourism bureau, Destination DC** (www.washington. org; ☏ **202/789-7000**) and ask for the names and numbers of any **new** or

TURNING TO THE internet or apps FOR A HOTEL DISCOUNT

It's not impossible to get a good deal by calling a hotel, but you're more likely to snag a discount online and with an app. Here are some strategies:

1. **Browse extreme discounts on sites where you reserve or bid for lodgings without knowing which hotel you'll get.** You'll find these on Priceline.com and Hotwire.com, and they can be money-savers, particularly if you're booking within a week of travel (that's when the hotels get nervous and resort to deep discounts). Both feature major chains, so it's unlikely you'll book a dump.

2. **Review discounts on the hotel's website.** As we said above, the hotels generally give the lowest rates to those who book through their sites rather than through a third party. But you'll only find these truly deep discounts in the loyalty section of these sites—so join the club.

3. **Use the right hotel search engine.** They're not all equal, as we at Frommers.com learned in the spring of 2017 after putting the top 20 sites to the test in 20 cities (including Washington, D.C.) around the globe. We discovered that **Booking.com** listed the lowest rates for hotels in the city center, and in the under $200 range, 16 out of 20 times—the best record, by far, of all the sites we tested. And Booking.com includes all taxes and fees in its initial results (not all do, which can make for a frustrating shopping experience). For top-end properties, again in the city center, both Priceline.com and HotelsCombined.com came up with the best rates, tying at 14 wins each.

about-to-open hotels. If the rep isn't sure, ask her to check with the marketing director. Up-and-coming hotels may have affordable rooms, for the simple reason that few people know about them.

o **Consider staying outside the city.** You'll find lower lodging prices in Arlington, Virginia, and its location, directly across the Potomac River from D.C., offers easy access to the city: Each of Arlington's close-in "urban villages"—Rosslyn, Crystal City, Pentagon City, Ballston, Clarendon, and Courthouse—has a Metro stop. Rosslyn, located just the other side of Key Bridge from Georgetown, is the most convenient, and some of its hotels even proffer spectacular views of the river and capital.

CAPITOL HILL

For proximity to the U.S. Capitol, the Supreme Court, the Library of Congress, and other Capitol Hill attractions, the hotels in this section can't be beat. I've included the one hotel that's truly located on the Hill and two others that lie due north of the Capitol, a quick walk away. Union Station (both the Amtrak station and Metro stop) is here, right across the street from two of the hotels and not far from the other.

Best for: Travelers who have business at the Capitol and tourists whose priority is visiting the Capitol, its sister sites, and the Capitol Hill neighborhood, while staying within easy reach of other attractions throughout the city.

Drawbacks: These streets are in the thick of things during the day; not so much at night.

Expensive

Kimpton George ★★   The Kimpton George is the best hotel closest to the Capitol. Celebrities often stay here, and not just those visiting Congress to plead the case for their pet cause. Big-name musicians (ladies and gentlemen, the Rolling Stones!) like the Kimpton George, and this is interesting, because the hotel is not the most obvious choice. Its location is not the hot spot of, say, a Penn Quarter or Georgetown property. Nor is the George associated with the kind of over-the-top luxury of a Ritz-Carlton or a Four Seasons. Rather, the George offers playful personality, sumptuously comfortable guest rooms, and total discretion. The 270-square-foot guest rooms have a touch of whimsy, with their parchment and ink-stylized graphics of George Washington's inaugural address on the wallpaper, and accent pillows based on GW's notable uniform. The Capitol is a pleasant 8-minute walk from the hotel. The only other hotel closer is the Capitol Hill Hotel (see below), an entirely different kind of place. The hotel's restaurant, **Bistro Bis,** is a favorite among locals and visitors alike.

15 E St. NW (at N. Capitol St.). www.hotelgeorge.com. ℂ **800/546-8331** or 202/347-4200. 139 units. $159–$459 double; $459–$859 suite. Children 17 and under stay free in parent's room. Rates include hosted evening wine hour. Parking $49 plus tax. Metro: Union Station (Massachusetts Ave. exit). Pets accepted (free). **Amenities:** Restaurant; bar; children's amenity program; concierge; small exercise room w/steam rooms; room service; Wi-Fi (free when you sign up for the no-cost loyalty program).

Moderate

Capitol Hill Hotel ★   This hotel's foremost distinction is its unbeatable location: It is the only hotel in the city actually *on* Capitol Hill (on the House side of the Capitol). The property occupies two buildings on a residential street lined with old town houses. Neighbors include the Library of Congress, the Capitol, and the Supreme Court; just a block away is Pennsylvania Avenue SE's stretch of fun bars and restaurants. Guest rooms are comfortably furnished, with pleasing touches here and there, such as L'Occitane products in the bathroom and accent pillows embossed with the D.C. skyline on beds and sofas. Rooms in the west wing have kitchenettes (coffeemaker, microwave, refrigerator, utensils); rooms in the east wing have full kitchens. Some suites have pullout sofas. Whatever the configuration, rooms are generally spacious, ranging in size from 320 to 510 square feet. Best room? The northwest corner suite on the fifth floor of the west wing, where you have a partial view of the Capitol and the Library of Congress. Each morning in the east wing breakfast

PRICE CATEGORIES

Expensive	$300 and up	Inexpensive	Under $200
Moderate	$200–$300		

Washington, D.C., Hotels

Garfield St. NW

1

Fulton St. NW

Woodley Rd. NW

2

Woodley Park–Zoo/
Adams Morgan

**NATIONAL
ZOO**

Harvard St. NW

Ontario Rd. NW

Lanier Pl. NW

Columbia Rd. NW

4

Euclid St. NW

Calvert St. NW

3

Calvert St. NW

5

Woodland Dr. NW

Observatory Circle

**U.S. Naval
Observatory**

EMBASSY ROW

Massachusetts Ave. NW

Rock Creek

**ROCK
CREEK
PARK**

**ADAMS
MORGAN**

Florida Ave

Belmont Rd. NW

Kalorama Rd.

Wyoming Ave.

6

Florida Ave. NW

W St. NW

V St. NW

**DUMBARTON
OAKS PARK**

California St. NW

S St. NW

U St. NW

T St. NW

U STREET

**MONTROSE
PARK**

Sheridan
Circle

Massachusetts

7

**DUPONT
CIRCLE**

Corcoran St. NW

Q St. NW

Church St. NW

P St. NW

R St. NW

Reservoir Rd.
NW

**GEORGETOWN
UNIVERSITY**

R St. NW

R St. NW

Q St. NW

P St. NW

O St. NW

Dumbarton St. NW

N St. NW

8

Dupont
Circle

17

Scott
Circle

18

Thomas
Circle

23

GEORGETOWN

Prospect St. NW

M St. NW

9

10

11

12

13

L St. NW

16

Washington
Circle

K St. NW

Farragut
North

Farragut
West

Farragut
Square

McPherson
Square

20

**DOWN-
TOWN**

**Francis Scott
Key Bridge**

Whitehurst Fwy. NW

Rock Creek Pkwy. NW

Pennsylvania Ave. NW

I St. NW

**Foggy
Bottom–
GWU**

**GEORGE
WASHINGTON
UNIVERSITY**

19

21

22

Georgetown Channel

14

Virginia Ave.

G St. NW

**White
House**

Pennsylvania

**Theodore
Roosevelt
Island**

**Kennedy
Center**

15

F St. NW

E St. NW

**FOGGY
BOTTOM**

**THE
ELLIPSE**

Little River

George Washington Memorial Pkwy.

C St. NW

**Theodore Roosevelt
Mem. Bridge**

Constitution Ave. NW

**Iwo Jima
Memorial**

VIRGINIA

**LADY BIRD
JOHNSON
PARK**

**Vietnam Veterans
Memorial**

**Lincoln
Memorial**

Reflecting Pool

**WWII
Memorial**

**Washington
Monument**

**ARLINGTON
NATIONAL
CEMETERY**

Arlington Mem. Bridge

Arlington
Cemetery

Washington Blvd.

WEST POTOMAC PARK

Independence Ave. SW

Potomac River

Ohio Dr. SW

Cherry Trees

Tidal Basin

**FDR
Memorial**

**Jefferson
Memorial**

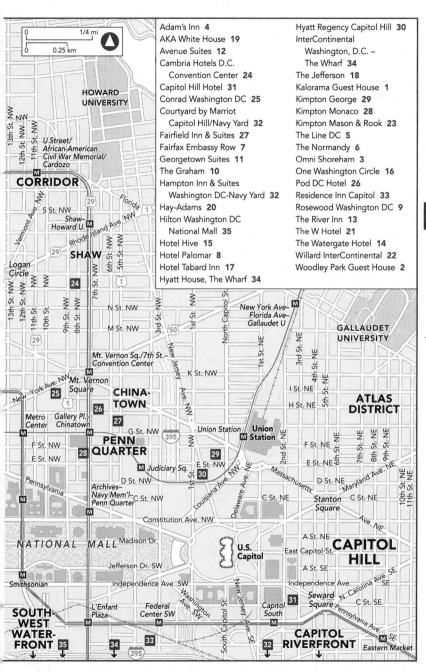

Adam's Inn **4**
AKA White House **19**
Avenue Suites **12**
Cambria Hotels D.C.
 Convention Center **24**
Capitol Hill Hotel **31**
Conrad Washington DC **25**
Courtyard by Marriot
 Capitol Hill/Navy Yard **32**
Fairfield Inn & Suites **27**
Fairfax Embassy Row **7**
Georgetown Suites **11**
The Graham **10**
Hampton Inn & Suites
 Washington DC-Navy Yard **32**
Hay-Adams **20**
Hilton Washington DC
 National Mall **35**
Hotel Hive **15**
Hotel Palomar **8**
Hotel Tabard Inn **17**
Hyatt House, The Wharf **34**

Hyatt Regency Capitol Hill **30**
InterContinental
 Washington, D.C. –
 The Wharf **34**
The Jefferson **18**
Kalorama Guest House **1**
Kimpton George **29**
Kimpton Monaco **28**
Kimpton Mason & Rook **23**
The Line DC **5**
The Normandy **6**
Omni Shoreham **3**
One Washington Circle **16**
Pod DC Hotel **26**
Residence Inn Capitol **33**
Rosewood Washington DC **9**
The River Inn **13**
The W Hotel **21**
The Watergate Hotel **14**
Willard InterContinental **22**
Woodley Park Guest House **2**

room, an ample continental breakfast of baked goods, yogurt, scrambled eggs, oatmeal, sausage, cheeses, meat, and fruit is laid out. A grab-and-go breakfast is available in the west wing library for guests who don't have time to linger. The library is also the spot for the hotel's nightly wine reception (5–6pm). Other pluses include a well-equipped gym and a tiny gift shop that includes perfect presents for those at home, like chocolates decorated with cherry blossoms, the Capitol, and other iconic images of the capital. A daily, per-room amenities fee of $20 plus tax covers the costs for the wine reception, Wi-Fi, bike use, and all-day coffee and tea; the fee is non-optional.

200 C St. SE (at 2nd St.). www.capitolhillhotel-dc.com. © **202/543-6000.** 153 units. $159–$400 double, plus daily $20 amenities fee (see "What You'll Really Pay," p. 54). Extra person $25 for rollaway only. Children 12 and under stay free. Parking $50 including tax. Metro: Union Station (Massachusetts Ave. NW exit). Pets accepted ($150 fee per pet per stay). **Amenities:** Business center; fitness center; coin-op washer/dryers; Wi-Fi (included in amenities fee).

Hyatt Regency Washington on Capitol Hill ★ Travelers can't go wrong with this venerable hotel set within sight of the U.S. Capitol building and National Mall, and just 3 blocks to Union Station. Business travelers will love the sleek, soaring atrium lobby with communal tables and 24/7 business center, while families will love the skylit indoor pool and complimentary amenity for kids upon check-in. The standard guest rooms range from 276 to 328 square feet, with contemporary finishes like sleek silver lamps, mod carpeting, and spacious work tables. Bathrooms are exceptionally spacious for a D.C. hotel. The renovated **Article One** restaurant offers an extensive continental breakfast, free for guests, with an omelet bar, flaky pastries, and fresh fruit, as well as a decent dinner. The adjoining Article One lounge is best for a quick bite, cocktails, and craft beer. Sports fans can catch the big game on a massive jumbotron above the bar in the lounge. For best views and spaciousness, ask for a king corner room facing south. For the quietest rooms, request a room on the upper floors facing 1st Street NW, a decidedly less busy street than New Jersey Avenue. The Old Town Trolley stops right at the front door, making getting around town a snap.

400 New Jersey Ave., NW (btw. D and E sts.). www.hyatt.com. © **202/737-1234.** 838 units. $136–$189 double; $336–$654 suite. Parking $62 plus tax. No pets allowed. Metro: Union Station (Massachusetts Ave. NW exit). **Amenities:** Lounge; exercise room; pool; room service; Wi-Fi (free).

CAPITOL RIVERFRONT

About 1 mile south of the U.S. Capitol is this southeast riverside enclave where development has been going full throttle ever since the 2008 opening of the Washington Nationals' baseball stadium, Nationals Park. (The Southwest Waterfront lies due west of the Capitol Riverfront, a single Metro stop away on the Green Line.) The Courtyard by Marriott Capitol Hill/Navy Yard, the sole hotel here for a decade, now has several rivals, including the Hampton Inn & Suites Washington DC-Navy Yard, described below, and the brand-new

Thompson D.C., expected to open in 2020 after this book goes to print. The only hotel to be located in The Yards, a 500-acre riverfront development of restaurants, apartments, a winery, and shops next to Nats Stadium, Thompson D.C. will be a boutique hotel offering 225 rooms with 38 suites, a massive meeting space, a restaurant, and a rooftop bar.

Best for: Those with business on Capitol Hill or visitors who want to experience a young and vibrant waterfront neighborhood located just south, but within easy reach, of the city's core. And during baseball season, baseball fans!

Drawbacks: Sights and sounds of construction will continue on these streets for many years to come.

Moderate

Courtyard by Marriott Capitol Hill/Navy Yard ★

When this hotel opened in 2006, its guests probably felt like outliers in nowheresville. No longer. The beckoning features of the Capitol Riverfront neighborhood now includes Nationals Park, a waterfront walkway, pubs and breweries, scores of restaurants, an award-winning public park that stages Friday-night concerts in summer and sundry festivals year-round, and a trapeze school, to boot. Glance northward on New Jersey Avenue and you'll spot the Capitol preening for you, just a mile away.

Most rooms at the Courtyard have king beds and a sofa bed, and about 50 rooms have two queen beds. There are 12 spacious suites. For a lovely view of the river, ask for a room at the L Street and New Jersey corner of the hotel. (*Note:* These rooms have a king bed but no pullout sofa.) *Other pluses:* The Metro stop is just across the street; the fitness center is available 24 hours, the pool from 7am to 10pm; a market is open 24/7; and the lobby is a sea of media pods, rounded banquettes with individual TVs, and power outlets.

140 L St. SE (at New Jersey Ave.). www.marriott.com/wasny. ✆ **202/479-0027.** 204 units. $109–$359 double (rates usually less than $250 a night). Limited parking $40 plus tax. Pets (1 per room) under 60 lb. allowed ($150 nonrefundable fee). Metro: Navy Yard/Ballpark (M St. and New Jersey Ave. exit). **Amenities:** Restaurant; bar/lounge; pool and hot tub; fitness center; Wi-Fi (free).

Hampton Inn & Suites Washington DC-Navy Yard ★

Baseball fans, this is your hotel. Situated directly across the street from Nationals Park, this new lodging has guest rooms facing the stadium from floors 9 through 14 (just ask for a "park view" room) that provide an unobstructed view of the infield, most of right field, and a bit of center field. Best rooms are nos. 1402, 1404, 1406, and 1408. Otherwise, guests (and locals) can enjoy an even better view, as well as cocktails and bar fare, from the rooftop **Top of the Yard** lounge. Here, the panoramic vistas takes in not just the ballpark, but the Anacostia River, the neighborhood, and the Washington Monument and U.S. Capitol in the distance.

Year-round reasons to stay at the Hampton Inn are its location in the increasingly popular Capitol Riverfront neighborhood, and its smart amenities and furnishings, from ergonomic desk chairs to a contemporary decor of dark woods and leather and metal accents. Meanwhile, Hampton Inn's signature features are on hand: the complimentary hot breakfast that includes eggs, sausage or bacon, and waffles; "on-the-run" breakfast bags for those in a hurry; and a 24-hour **Pavilion Pantry** market.

1265 First St. SE (at N St.). www.hamptoninnwashingtondcnavyyard.com. 🕿 **800/ HAMPTON** (426-7866) or 202/800-1000. 168 units. $155–$357 double; $195–$387 suite. (Rates are at the low end during Aug away games and in Nov and Dec, and at the high end during home games in baseball season.) Parking $43 plus tax. Pets under 50 lb. allowed (free). Metro: Navy Yard/Ballpark (Half and M sts. exit). **Amenities:** Concierge; fitness center; coin-op laundry room; Wi-Fi (free).

NATIONAL MALL

Several neighborhoods bordering the National Mall are less than a mile away, an easy walk from the Mall, including the Penn Quarter to the north and Capitol Hill to the east. Closest of all is the neighborhood immediately to the south, across Independence Avenue from the National Mall. The streets in this southwest quadrant of the city have long been home to government buildings and old residences, joined gradually over the last 15 years or so by a smattering of hotels and other developments. In addition to the phalanx of Smithsonian museums and other Mall sites, area attractions include the International Spy Museum, newly relocated here in 2019; the Museum of the Bible; and the U.S. National Holocaust Memorial Museum. Affordable family-oriented properties predominate.

Best for: Travelers who want to be as close as possible to the National Mall, as well as within easy access to Capitol Hill.

Drawbacks: You're in the thick of things during the day, but these streets shut down at night. You will need to travel elsewhere in the city for restaurants, nightlife, and urban liveliness. You should also be aware that passenger and freight trains run on tracks that lie close to all of the hotels in this neighborhood, so ask for a room away from the train-track side of the hotel for maximum quiet.

Expensive

Hilton Washington DC National Mall ★★   Luxury and practicality abound in this hotel, which reopened in 2019 after a redesign. Its location can't be beat: within walking distance to the White House and the Wharf, facing the International Spy Museum, and on top of the L'Enfant Metro station (with an elevator that takes you directly to the Metro platform). All rooms are spacious, bright, and modern, with one (or two!) king platform beds, floor-to-ceiling windows, plank flooring, and a 65-inch HDTV. Families will love the large suites, which come with a dining room table, sofa bed, and guest powder room. The heated outdoor hotel pool on the 12th floor has views of the monuments and also features cabanas, fire pits, and cozy lounge seating. *Other pluses:* an expansive fitness center, 24-hour dining options including a **Market Express,** and a large business center.

480 L'Enfant Plaza. SW (at 9th St.). www3.hilton.com. 🕿 **800/445-8667** or 202/484-1000. 367 units. $225–$399 one-king room; $325–$489 two-king room; $889–$1,325 2-bedroom suite. Parking $59 plus tax. Pets under 75 lb. accepted ($50 nonrefundable fee). Metro: L'Enfant Plaza. **Amenities:** Restaurant; bar; Starbucks Café; concierge; fitness center; pool; room service; solarium; Wi-Fi (free).

Residence Inn Capitol ★   It's no accident that this Residence Inn is located within walking distance of the National Museum of the American Indian. Three Native American tribes are 49% owners of the hotel, which made it the first multi-tribal partnership with non-tribal partners on land off the reservation when the hotel opened in 2005. Although certain features, such as the sandstone walls in the lobby and artwork throughout, hint at its Native-American heritage, the hotel is otherwise similar to standard Residence Inns. All rooms are spacious suites (studio, one-bedroom, or two-bedroom) equipped with full kitchens. A major renovation, completed in 2018, endowed guest rooms and the lobby with a more modern look, furnishings (think chaise lounges and stainless-steel accessories), and amenities, such as 52-inch flatscreen TVs that offer access to Netflix, Hulu, and other subscription services, for guests who are subscribers. The hotel lies close to a train track, so ask for a room on the other side.

333 E St. SW (at 4th St.). www.marriott.com/wascp. ℂ **800/331-3131** or 202/484-8280. 233 units. $179–$419 studio suite; $209–$449 1-bedroom suite; $249–$589 2-bedroom suite. Rates include hot breakfast, light fare Mon–Wed evenings, and grocery delivery service. Parking $42 plus tax. Metro: Federal Center SW or L'Enfant Plaza. Pets accepted ($200 nonrefundable cleanup fee and an additional $10 added to room rate). **Amenities:** Concierge; fitness center; indoor pool; sundeck; Wi-Fi (free).

SOUTHWEST WATERFRONT

Arena Stage, boating activities, and fish markets have long been the main reasons anyone, out-of-towner or local, might visit this neighborhood located on the Washington Channel, south of downtown. The debut of the **Wharf** complex in October 2017 reinvented the quarter overnight, adding many more reasons to visit: live music venues, restaurants and bars, tons of watersports and other outdoor recreational activities, shops, and hotels, all strewn along the picturesque waterfront. In spring, summer, and fall, day and night, the place is lively—crazy lively on the loveliest days. In winter, however, the neighborhood can seem quiet and out of the way. But you're less than a mile south of the National Mall, and a free shuttle travels continuously daily, connecting the Wharf, Metro stations, and the Mall. Water jitneys and water taxis travel the waterfront, taking you to and from Georgetown, Old Town Alexandria, or National Harbor in Maryland.

Best for: Those who prefer water views and activities over city views and vibes, and for anyone wanting to experience D.C.'s newest trendy neighborhood.

Drawbacks: The Wharf's location, between Maine Avenue and the waterfront, limits its access, which can create traffic nightmares when there's a lot going on in the city and at the Wharf itself. Insufficient and/or poorly placed signage can make travel confusing; be sure to get precise directions from your hotel. Ongoing construction also interferes with traffic and scenery as the Wharf works on Phase 2 of the development, scheduled for completion in 2022.

Expensive

InterContinental Washington, D.C. – The Wharf ★★   All three of the Wharf hotels overlook the lovely Washington Channel, boats docked or cruising along, and the **East Potomac Park** island (p. 199), which, for 2 weeks in spring, is gorgeously aflower in blossoming cherry trees. And each property has its particular advantages. **Hyatt House Washington DC/The Wharf** (https://washingtondcthewharf.house.hyatt.com/en/hotel/our-hotel/map-and-directions.html) is recommended for extended stays, with some suites equipped with full kitchens. **Canopy by Hilton Washington DC/The Wharf** (http://canopy3.hilton.com/en/hotels/district-of-columbia/canopy-by-hilton-washington-dc-the-wharf-DCACUPY/index.html), the Hilton brand's "lifestyle" lodging, offers complimentary artisanal breakfast and bikes and a lively mix of pop-up shops, nightly tastings, and filtered spring water stations on each floor.

The Intercontinental is the largest of the hotels at the Wharf. All guest rooms are spacious, measuring at least 340 square feet, and on-site amenities are a cut above, including its Afro-Caribbean restaurant, **Kith and Kin;** the fully equipped and waterfront-facing fitness center; and **L'Occitane Spa** (the Inter-Conti is the sole Wharf hotel with a spa). The hotel's lively, light-filled living-room-like lobby opens directly onto the Wharf's wide strand of a walkway and the waterfront, blending pleasantly into the scene; the hotel also operates a seasonal open-air "watering hole" across this strand, so you can enjoy a drink as you people-watch. One very helpful practical feature off the lobby is a real-time monitor displaying arrivals and departures of shuttles, Metro trains, jitneys, and other modes of neighborhood transportation. Not all guest rooms overlook the water; rooms on the sides and at the rear of the hotel view Maine Avenue, buildings, and passageways. Waterfront rooms with balconies are the best.

801 Wharf St. SW (at 7th St.). https://wharfintercontinentaldc.com. ✆ **202/800-0844.** 278 units, including 33 suites. $259–$500 double; $400–$607 suite. Children 17 and under stay free. Parking $50 including tax. Pets accepted up to 40 lb. ($75 fee). Metro: Waterfront (M and 4th sts.) or L'Enfant Plaza (7th and D sts.). **Amenities:** Restaurant; bar; 12th-floor lounge; rooftop bar and seasonal pool; children's amenity program; concierge; expansive fitness center; room service; full-service spa; Wi-Fi (free).

PENN QUARTER

At the center of the city is this hot locale, jammed with restaurants, bars, museums, theaters, the Capital One Arena, and the posh CityCenterDC shopping arcade. Hotels include modern venues catering to convention crowds, historic properties switched up for luxury-loving fun-seekers, and one of D.C.'s new pod hotels.

Best for: Those who love being in the thick of it all. Business travelers are within easy reach of downtown offices, the convention center, and Capitol Hill. Likewise, the Penn Quarter is a prime home base for tourists, with attractions within its boundaries and the National Mall just across Pennsylvania Avenue.

Drawbacks: Crowded sidewalks and noisy traffic can be annoying—and sometimes even overwhelming.

Expensive

Conrad Washington DC ★★   Just north of the busiest blocks of Penn Quarter but set within CityCenterDC, the city's sparkling new (and growing) hub of shops, restaurants, and condos, you'll find this all-glass hotel, which opened in 2019. Rooms are spacious—from 416 to 465 square feet—with either two queens or one king. All rooms have floor-to-ceiling windows, marble bathrooms, and calming white and cream interiors. If you can, book a premium corner king room with views stretching down New York Avenue. Guests who book rooms on the 10th floor have access to the **Sakura Club,** a lounge that offers meals made to order by a private chef, a club concierge, an evening cocktail program, and afternoon tea. *Top Chef* alums (and brothers) Bryan and Michael Voltaggio anchor the hotel's seafood-centric restaurant **Estuary,** focused on the flavors of the Chesapeake Bay. **Summit,** its rooftop bar and terrace, offers unobstructed views of the U.S. Capitol and Washington Monument, and filtered views all the way to the Potomac River. The hotel's ground level features 30,000 square feet of luxury retail space, which now includes a Tiffany & Co.

950 New York Ave. NW (at 10 St. NW). www.conradwashingtondc.com. ✆ **202/844-5900.** 360 units. $400–$500 double. Parking $60 plus tax (more for oversized vehicles). Pets accepted ($75 one-time fee). Metro: Gallery Place–Chinatown (9th and G sts. exit). **Amenities:** Restaurant; bar; 24-hr. fitness center; room service; Wi-Fi (free).

Kimpton Hotel Monaco Washington DC ★★ For deluxe accommodations in a terrific location, you can't beat the Monaco. When it was completed in 1866, this historic, four-story marble building served as a general post office and tariff building for an area that was a developing mishmash of big government and small-town buildings. Hard to imagine now. It's one of the city's top hotels, surrounded by wondrous museums, like the Smithsonian American Art/National Portrait Gallery, and trendy restaurants such as **Zaytinya** (p. 98). The hotel has an "elegance-meets-bold" design. Note the playful architectural details in each guest room, like a 5-foot lion's head medallion above the bed, and the night table resembling the top of a Corinthian column, as well as the eye-catching features in the lobby/living room, with its brilliant green walls, contemporary Murano glass chandeliers, and modern art. Guest rooms are spacious, averaging about 400 square feet, and feature vaulted ceilings, long windows, and vibrant hues of bronze, plum, champagne, and royal blue. Ask for an F Street or 7th Street–facing Monte Carlo room (525 sq. ft.) for best views, or a first-floor guest room if quiet is preferred (some guests call this "the basement," because it is nearly subterranean). The hotel restaurant, **Dirty Habit DC,** gets good reviews for its take on global cuisine, and for its bars in the atrium and courtyard.

700 F St. NW (at 7th St.). www.monaco-dc.com. ✆ **800/649-1202** or 202/628-7177. 184 units. $179–$479 double; $459–$899 suite. Children 17 and under stay free. Rates include complimentary coffee in the morning and a hosted evening wine hour. Parking $52 including tax. Pets welcome (free). Metro: Gallery Place (7th & F sts. exit). **Amenities:** Restaurant; bar; children's amenity program; concierge; spacious fitness center; room service; Wi-Fi (free when you sign up for the no-cost loyalty program).

Moderate

Fairfield Inn & Suites ★ You're really in the thick of things at this hotel, situated on a busy Chinatown street in the bustling Penn Quarter, a block north

family-friendly HOTELS

Hyatt House D.C., The Wharf ★★ (p. 64)

Located in the bustling Wharf district, the Hyatt House always offers plenty for kids to see and do, which includes not just restaurants and shops, but also tour boats, an ice-skating rink or mini-golf at the waterfront, a fountain to splash in nearby, and the National Mall with its museums within walking distance (or take the free shuttle). Spacious suites offer kitchenettes so you can feed the hungry mob at any hour. A nice complimentary breakfast is offered every morning and a heated rooftop pool (seasonal) is perfect for kiddos. Another plus: Ben & Jerry's ice cream is located right outside the lobby.

Omni Shoreham Hotel ★★★

(p. 82) With two pools (including a kiddie pool), loads of lawn out back to run around on (and Rock Creek Park beyond that), the National Zoo up the street, as well as the Metro nearby, the Omni is one of the best hotels in town for families. The hotel sweetens the deal with a backpack filled with games that your child can wear when you set off sightseeing, and cookies and milk left in the room at turndown the first night. The hotel sometimes partners with the zoo for special packages that include a furry stuffed animal and zoo backpack.

Willard InterContinental ★★★

(p. 68) You're in the heart of the city, with the White House across 15th St. to your right, the National Theatre next door, the National Mall essentially down the street, and many other attractions nearby. Add to its great location the Willard's stellar Kids Concierge program: Tailored to children 11 years and younger, highlights include a complimentary in-room dessert, a children's library of books that kids can check out using their specially issued Willard Library card, a borrowable treasure chest of board games and toys, and family-friendly history tours of the Willard led by a member of the hotel's concierge team on Saturdays. In addition, the Willard's Café du Parc has a substantial children's menu featuring much more than just standard hot dogs and mac and cheese.

of the Capital One Arena, and surrounded by hip eateries. But this is an old neighborhood, too: The bells of St. Mary Mother of God, the 1890 Catholic church across 5th Street from the Fairfield, peal from 7am to—don't worry—9pm. And if you walk down H Street to no. 604, you'll notice a plaque on the facade of what is now the Wok and Roll restaurant, identifying the structure as Mary Surratt's Boarding House. (Surratt conspired here with John Wilkes Booth to assassinate President Lincoln.) The property plays up the Chinatown connection, with the color red and Chinese symbols predominating in furnishings. Most spacious are 10th-floor rooms (which also have high ceilings) and corner suites ending in "24." Fifth Street–facing rooms offer nice city views. Executive king rooms have pullout sofas. Suites and double-queen rooms have mini-fridges, which are available upon request in king and executive king rooms. Guests also like the key-only access to elevators, the availability of a coin-operated washer/dryer, as well as same-day dry-cleaning service (for a fee), and the complimentary hot breakfast buffet, which includes eggs, sausage, and waffles.

500 H St. NW (at 5th St.). www.marriott.com/wasfc. ☏ **202/289-5959.** 198 units. $99–$599 double. Add $10 for an executive king room, $20 for a suite. Children 17 and

under stay free. Parking $49 plus tax (more for oversized vehicles). Metro: Gallery Place–Chinatown (7th and H sts. exit). **Amenities:** Restaurant; bar; 24-hr. fitness center; room service; Wi-Fi (free).

Inexpensive

Pod DC Hotel ★ It's inexpensive and centrally located, but also small and so efficient it borders on uncomfortable. Even still, the Pod is a worthy contender for business or young travelers who want to be in the heart of the action without having to pay a lot of money to do so. As befits its Penn Quarter locale, the Pod DC is lively from the jump, welcoming you into an open space that serves as both lobby and the hotel's **Crimson Diner.** Of-the-moment music plays, as guests check in at the little reception counter or chill on one of the teal-colored barstools in Crimson. Downstairs is the **Crimson Whiskey Bar,** and on the rooftop is the **Crimson View bar,** with views of the city and the Washington Monument, and—a rarity for D.C. hotels—the capability to stay open year-round, thanks to enclosable glass doors. Guest rooms are all the same tiny size, 150 square feet, but you can choose from full bed, queen bed, or bunk beds options. Everything fits just so, the frosted bathroom door sliding to close (yes, each guest room has its own bathroom) and space left beneath the bed for luggage storage. Despite the allure of bunk beds, I wouldn't recommend the hotel to families unless your children are old enough to stay alone in a room (there are no connecting rooms). But millennials? Solo travelers? Thrifty types? Fun lovers? Go for it. The hotel has its own fitness center, but guests also have free access to a nearby sports club and yoga studio.

627 H St. NW (7th St.). www.thepodhotel.com/pod-dc. ✆ **202/847-4444.** 245 units. Off-peak $94–$170; peak $170–$284. No on-site parking, but hotel partners with nearby public garages. No pets. Metro: Gallery Place–Chinatown (7th and H sts. exit). **Amenities:** Restaurant; bar; year-round rooftop bar; fitness center; Wi-Fi (free).

MIDTOWN

Think of the White House as center stage, with an array of hotels, law and lobbyist office buildings, and restaurants at its feet. Several historic hotels, as well as contemporary, more affordable properties, are among the options.

Best for: Travelers interested in a central location that's less raucous than the Penn Quarter at night. Also those doing business with the executive branch or at one of the law, lobbying, or association offices that line K Street.

Drawbacks: Urban sounds (traffic, construction, garbage collection) may be part of the experience.

Expensive

The Hay-Adams ★★★ This 92-year-old hotel's tagline, "Where nothing is overlooked but the White House," would be corny if it were not true. The Hay-Adams is known not only for its sublime service but for being the hotel that lies closest to the White House, and the only one with such straight-on views, best seen from guest rooms on the top floors, six through eight. (You can also see Lafayette Square, the Washington Monument, and the Jefferson

Memorial.) Views in other rooms are of historic **St. John's Episcopal Church** and downtown buildings. So it makes sense that views determine guest-room rates. Guest rooms are similarly sized, about 385 square feet, and furnished with creamy white and tan toile fabrics, European linens, and marble bathrooms. The interior designs that were here when Amelia Earhart stayed at the Hay in 1928—intricate plaster moldings, walnut wainscoting, and high ceilings—are still in place. One thing that was not here then was the **Off the Record**

View of the White House from the Federal Suite of the Hay-Adams.

bar, a regular hangout for the press and politicos. The hotel's restaurant, the **Lafayette,** is one of the most elegant in the capital, chandeliers and white-linen-topped tables pointing up the decor, contemporary American cuisine taken to new heights by French chef Nicolas Legret. *Conde Nast Traveler*'s Readers' Choice Awards recognized the Hay-Adams as the best hotel in the capital in 2018.

800 16th St. (at H St.). www.hayadams.com. ℂ **800/853-6807** or 202/638-6600. 145 units. $339–$439 double; from $839 junior suite; from $1,299 1-bedroom suite. Two-bedroom suites available. Third person $30. Children 17 and under stay free. Valet parking $62. Dogs up to 25 lb. allowed (free); however, you'll be charged for dog-sitting services if you leave your dog alone in the room and for repair to any damage done to the room. Metro: Farragut West (17th St. exit). **Amenities:** Restaurant; bar; bikes (available for adults only); concierge; state-of-the-art fitness facility; room service; Wi-Fi (free).

Willard InterContinental ★★★ The guest list at this historic hotel has always included illustrious figures. President Abraham Lincoln actually lived here for 10 days in 1861 before moving into the White House, 1 block away. Dr. Martin Luther King, Jr. sat in the lobby here in August 1963, finishing the writing of his historic "I Have a Dream" speech before delivering it on August 28 from the steps of the Lincoln Memorial. And from its very start, the Willard has hosted foreign dignitaries, from Japan's first delegation to the U.S. (three Samurai ambassadors and their entourage of 74 in 1860) to…well, take a look at which head of state is scheduled to visit the White House, and there's a good chance that dignitary is booked at the Willard.

The spacious guest rooms, completely refurbished in 2018, are elegantly decorated with dark wood furnishings; shades of blue, cream, and gold; and comfortable extras like a velvet armchair and ottoman. Ask for courtyard-facing rooms for quiet, or Pennsylvania Avenue–facing rooms for views of the Washington Monument, the Lincoln Memorial, and even the Jefferson Memorial (the higher your floor, the better the sights). The expansive oval suites offer the best views, from floor-to-ceiling windows that sweep down Pennsylvania Avenue almost to the Capitol.

The Willard InterContinental Hotel.

But you're here as much for the history and ambience as for a place to sleep. You must enjoy a cocktail at the **Round Robin Bar,** expertly mixed by barman Jim Hewes as he tells tales about Willard guests, from Charles Dickens to Bill Clinton (Hewes also hosts a popular monthly History Happy Hour in the Willard Room, where he and a guest historian or author serve up potent libations and entertaining stories from Washington's past); stroll through the lobby and admire its mosaic floor, marble columns, and ornate ceiling; and tour the history gallery filled with memorabilia, such as a copy of Lincoln's hotel bill. Check out the Willard's calendar. In addition to the History Happy Hour mentioned above, varied events—afternoon tea, Kentucky Derby Day soiree, Christmas tree viewing and caroling throughout December—attract as many locals as hotel guests. Finally, stop by **Café du Parc** (p. 100) and sit on the terrace if possible, to savor the views and the lovely French brasserie flavors of boeuf bourguignon and *croque monsieur.*

1401 Pennsylvania Ave. NW (at 14th St.). www.washington.intercontinental.com. ⓒ **866/ 487-2537** or 202/628-9100. 335 units. $259–$599 double; $459–$899 basic suite. Parking $55 plus tax. Small pets (up to 40 lb.) accepted ($200 nonrefundable cleaning fee). Metro: Metro Center (13th and F sts. exit). **Amenities:** Brasserie w/seasonal terrace; 2 bars; seasonal afternoon tea in Peacock Alley; concierge; kids' concierge program (details, p. 66); complimentary chauffeur service Mon–Fri 7–9am; health club with sauna; room service; luxurious Red Door Spa; Wi-Fi (free).

Moderate

The W Hotel ★   As with so many hotels in the capital, the history of this hotel built in 1917 is extensive: from Harrison Ford buying a round of drinks for everyone at the bar, President Reagan and Clinton attending balls here, and

Travelers to Washington, D.C., who plan to visit for a week or longer should know about the centrally located **AKA White House ★★★** apartments/hotel, 1710 H St. NW (www.stayaka.com; ℂ **202/ 904-2500**). The D.C. location is one of 11 AKA properties (others are in NYC, Beverly Hills, Philadelphia, and London), all of which offer luxuriously furnished one- and two-bedroom apartments. AKA can offer tremendous value, especially if your timing is right. Check out the website to see for yourself some of the property's fine appointments and amenities, including fully equipped kitchens, stylish decor, free Wi-Fi, an on-site fitness center, and laundry services. K Street law offices, the White House, the Renwick Gallery, and excellent restaurants, such as **Founding Farmers** (p. 110), are just some of the property's notable neighbors. *FYI:* While AKA serves mainly as an extended-stay property, it also accommodates visitors for nightly stays as availability allows.

parts of *The Godfather Part II* being filmed on the rooftop. But this stylish hotel, formerly the Hotel Washington, unveiled a full renovation of its rooms, restaurants, and lobby in 2019. One of its new restaurants, **Cherry,** is centered around a 15-foot hearth, where chef Will Morris cooks everything on the grill from vegetables to seafood. **Corner Office,** its second restaurant, serves wood-fired pizzas and nearly 40 beers on tap. Rooms can be tight but are comfortable and modern. For peace and quiet, ask for a room with a courtyard view. For rooms with views of the Washington Monument and National Mall, you'll want one facing south on the 8th to 10th floors. Views of the White House from the hotel's rooftop **POV** lounge are so close you can see federal officers patrolling the roof of the president's mansion. *A plus for pet lovers:* The hotel offers canine guests a welcome treat bag, food and water bowls, a custom bed, and dog-sitting services.

515 15th St. NW (at F St.). www.marriott.com/hotels/travel/waswh-w-washington-dc. ℂ **844-631-0595** or 202/661-2400. 324 units. $299–$429 double. Parking $59 daily plus tax. Rates include free continental breakfast. Maximum two pets per room (up to 40 lb. each) accepted ($25 supplemental room charge and nonrefundable $100 cleaning fee). Metro: Metro Center. **Amenities:** 2 restaurants; lounge; babysitting; concierge; valet dry cleaning; fitness center; 24/7 room service; Wi-Fi (free).

ADAMS MORGAN

Inns and bed-and-breakfasts are far more common than hotels in Adams Morgan. In fact, only one hotel lies truly inside Adams Morgan boundaries, the **Line,** which is included below. I've also listed the Normandy, which technically is situated in the Kalorama neighborhood (where the Obamas now live), but is geographically close to Adams Morgan (a 5-minute walk eastward, crossing Connecticut Ave.).

Best for: Travelers who want to stay in a 24-hour neighborhood with a more quirky/gritty vibe than downtown.

Drawbacks: The closest Metro stops (Dupont Circle and Woodley Park) are each about half a mile away.

Entrance to the Line DC Hotel.

Expensive

The Line DC ★★★   If you want to be charmed and intrigued and wowed, book a room here. Opened in late 2017, the Line Hotel occupies a former First Church of Christ, Scientist, which was built in 1912 at the crest of the hill that defines the Adams Morgan neighborhood. The building sits right at the crossroads of 18th Street NW and Columbia Road. Its architecture is Neoclassical Revival style, temple-like in other words, with colossal columns framing the grand entrance.

A renovation transformed the church interior into a spectacular gallery of a lobby. The hotel employed local artists and designers to create an imaginative decor throughout, incorporating found objects and original features of the church as much as possible. In the lobby, for example, the enormous chandelier was sculpted by a local artist from brass pieces of the church's pipe organ. The talent behind the restaurants and bars are locals, too, but with national acclaim: Spike Gjerde (A Rake's Progress) and Erik Bruner-Yang (Brothers and Sisters). Continuing the community vibe is the hotel's radio station, Full Service Radio, broadcasting live news about the city from the lobby.

Guest rooms are located in the U-shaped, eight-floor annex at the rear of the structure. Rooms are 300 square feet or larger, and each is outfitted with hand-hewn oak floors, brass beds, copper accessories, and whimsical original artworks. About one-third of the rooms capture a glimpse of the Washington Monument; all have long windows that bring in lots of light.

1770 Euclid St. NW (at Columbia Rd.). www.thelinehoteldc.com. ✆ **202/588-0525.** 220 units. Mid-$200s off-peak to mid-$300s peak for a double; add $150–$200 for suite. Extra person $25. Children 12 and under stay free. Parking $54 including tax. Pets allowed (free). Metro: Woodley Park (Adams Morgan exit) or Dupont Circle (North/Q St. exit). **Amenities:** 3 restaurants; 2 bars; coffee shop; fitness center; room service; Wi-Fi (free).

Moderate

The Normandy Hotel ★★   This six-floor boutique hotel has a pretty, Parisian charm. The Normandy lies on a tree-shaded street lined with embassies; not surprisingly, the clientele is an international mix. You're a peaceful detour only minutes away, by foot, from the heart of the Dupont Circle, Adams Morgan, and Woodley Park neighborhoods. The Normandy's 75 rooms range in size, measuring between 210 and 352 square feet, and each makes good use of the space with cleverly designed and positioned furnishings: long, skinny desks; nifty little reading lamps with stems you can twist out of the walls just so; and compact Nespresso coffee machines and glass-fronted fridges placed out of the way. Front-facing rooms overlook tranquil Wyoming Avenue, while those at the back survey the courtyard. Three first-floor rooms open to a private garden terrace. Also on the first level is the parquet-floored lounge, with little sofas, armchairs, and a fireplace.

The Normandy is perfect for couples and solo travelers, but a larger hotel might be a better choice for groups, large families, and those who crave lots of space.

2118 Wyoming Ave. NW (at Connecticut Ave.). www.thenormandydc.com. © **202/483-1350.** 75 units. $129–$299 double. Rates include evening wine-and-cheese hour and coffee and tea throughout the day. Extra person $20. Children 12 and under stay free. Limited parking $40 plus tax. Pets $25 per pet per night. Metro: Dupont Circle (North/Q St. exit). **Amenities:** Free fitness passes to nearby Mint Fitness Center; Wi-Fi (free).

Inexpensive

Adam's Inn Bed & Breakfast ★   Adam's Inn is nice but lacks any frills; it's a place to lay your head, pure and simple. Located on a lovely residential street, just a stone's throw from (but not within earshot of, fortunately) the rowdy Adams Morgan nightlife strip, the inn's three 100+-year-old brick row houses hold 27 rooms that satisfy sundry needs. School groups sometimes reserve an entire house, while families with two or three children are happy to find that the inn's English basement suite, with full kitchen and washer/dryer, can accommodate them all. The more typical single and couple travelers have plenty of standard rooms from which to choose, with the option of a shared or private bathroom. Guest rooms are individually decorated with comfortable furnishings. Sixteen rooms have private bathrooms; 10 of these rooms also have 55-inch TVs with full cable access. All guests are welcome to socialize and watch TV in the communal living rooms. Two guest kitchens are equipped with a refrigerator, microwave, and toaster. The inn is plumly situated close to the National Zoo, Rock Creek Park, and good restaurants and bars, and within easy access to the rest of the city. Best are its good-for-D.C. prices, especially if you take advantage of one of the online sales. The inn is not wheelchair-accessible.

1746 Lanier Place NW (btw. Calvert St. and Adams Mill Rd.). www.adamsinn.com. © **202/745-3600.** 27 units, 16 with private bathroom, 11 with shared bathroom. $79–$209 room with shared bathroom; $89–$254 room with private bathroom. Rates include extensive continental breakfast. Children 8 and under stay free. Extra person $20. Parking $40 plus tax (only 4 spaces available), very limited street parking, plus nearby public parking garages. Pets allowed ($50 nonrefundable fee). Metro: Columbia Heights or Woodley Park/Adams Morgan, also DC Circulator and Metrobus. **Amenities:** Free access to computer with printer; guest kitchens; coin-operated laundry; Wi-Fi (free).

DUPONT CIRCLE

This neighborhood of quaint town houses and beautiful embassies, bistro restaurants, art galleries, and bars is home to more hotels than any other neighborhood in the city. Boutique hotels reign supreme, though several chains have outposts here, too.

Best for: Travelers who love a city scene minus the office buildings. Also for gay and lesbian visitors, since Dupont Circle is LGBTQ central.

Drawbacks: If you have business on Capitol Hill or in the Penn Quarter, this might not be your first choice, since there are plenty of closer options.

Expensive

The Jefferson ★★★ If you can afford to, stay at the Jefferson, which I consider to be D.C.'s best hotel. (I'm hardly alone: *Conde Nast Traveler*'s Readers' Choice Awards voted it one of the top 5 best hotels in D.C. in 2018 and *U.S. News & World Report* named the Jefferson the 3rd best hotel in the entire U.S. in 2017.) And if you can't afford to, at least stop in at **Quill ★★★** (p. 231), the hotel's delightful bar, where a pianist plays jazz standards Tuesday through Saturday evenings starting at 9pm. Located slightly off the beaten track, about a half-mile north of the White House, the Jefferson exudes the ambience of a country-house hotel. Decor throughout pays homage to Thomas Jefferson in all his passions, from Quill's display of 18th-century maps tracing the oenophile's journeys through the wine regions of France, to guest-room fabrics imprinted with architectural and agricultural scenes of Monticello. A handful of rooms catch glimpses of the Washington Monument a mile away, and another few look to the White House, at the end of 16th Street; none, alas, capture the sight of the Jefferson Memorial a bit beyond. In addition to Quill and the lovely, skylit **Greenhouse** restaurant, the hotel's dining options include the sublime and intimate, Michelin-starred **Plume** restaurant, which serves seasonal menus inspired by the harvest from Thomas Jefferson's kitchen gardens at Monticello.

1200 16th St. NW (at M St.). www.jeffersondc.com. ✆ **202/448-2300.** 99 units. $320–$725 double; $800–$8,000 suite. Extra person $30. Children 18 and under stay free. Valet parking $55. Dogs welcome ($50 fee). Metro: Farragut North (L St. and Connecticut Ave. exit). **Amenities:** 3 restaurants; bar/lounge; children's amenities; concierge; 24-hr. fitness center; petite spa w/massages and facials; 24-hr. room service; Wi-Fi (free).

Moderate

The Fairfax at Embassy Row ★★ When this historic hotel opened in 1927, guests paid an extravagant sum of $4 for a double occupancy suite. The hotel has since been home to congressmen, senators, and ambassadors, most notably, a young Al Gore and George H. Bush. Now, after a sleek renovation in 2019, the hotel is refreshed, combining the artistic vibe of Dupont Circle with warm woods and pops of emerald green while still reflecting its diplomatic and historic past. Guest rooms further blend old world with new, with ornate wooden headboards hand-painted in black, original crown moldings, crisp white linens, an iPod docking station, and laptop safes. Grand deluxe rooms offer sweeping views of Embassy Row, while other rooms offer glimpses of the National Cathedral. Guests enjoy complimentary wine during the nightly reception 3pm to 5pm, and coffee from 6am to 10pm in **The Market cafe**. Its new restaurant, The **Sally,** serves American fare with locally sourced produce and beef from the DuPont Circle Farmer's Market.

2100 Massachusetts Ave. NW (at 21st St.). www.fairfaxwashingtondc.com. © **855/559-8899** or 202/293-2100. 259 units. High season $207–$333 double; low season $180–$280 double. $23 daily amenity fee. Parking $49 plus tax. Metro: Dupont Circle (Q St. exit). **Amenities:** Restaurant/lounge; market cafe/pantry; 24/7 fitness center; Wi-Fi (free with guest amenity fee).

Hotel Palomar ★★   The Hotel Palomar is another property by Kimpton, which operates 12 hotels in the capital. In that sense it's a chain, but guests will feel pampered here. (It was voted one of the best hotels in Washington, D.C., in 2019 by *U.S. News and World Report* if you need any extra sway.) Studio rooms are 500 square feet, decorated with bright colors, mod lamps, and bold geometric prints. If you're visiting in the summer, don't miss the chance to sit around the outdoor courtyard pool, which whisks guests away from the sounds of the city. **Urbana** is the hotel's acclaimed Italian restaurant, serving handcrafted pastas with fresh ingredients. The hotel is just 2 blocks from Dupont Circle, which is the name not only for the neighborhood but also for the urban park around which the traffic swirls. The park is a performance space in its own right, perfect for sitting and watching the goings-on.

2121 P St. NW (across from Dupont Circle). www.hotelpalomar-dc.com. © **877/866-3070** or 202/448-1800. 327 units. $200–$299 double; from $479 suite. Extra person $20. Children 17 and under stay free. Daily amenity fee of $25 plus tax. Rates include evening wine hour (5–6pm) and morning coffee and tea (6:30–10:30am). Parking $49 plus tax. Pets allowed (free). Metro: Dupont Circle (either exit). **Amenities:** Restaurant; bar; business center; concierge; state-of-the-art fitness center; pool; room service; Wi-Fi (free).

Inexpensive

Hotel Tabard Inn ★   Fans of quaintness and quirks—and I am one of them—will continue to find them throughout the three joined 19th-century town houses that make up the inn. Nooks, bay windows, exposed brick, vibrantly hued walls (shades of purple, or chartreuse, or periwinkle, for instance), flea-market finds, and antiques are some of the characteristics of individual guest rooms (plus no TVs). Quaintness also means a certain creakiness throughout. There is no elevator, which may pose a challenge to those trudging upstairs with (or without) luggage to lodging on the third or fourth floor. That, and narrow hallways, may make a stay here challenging for travelers with disabilities.

The Tabard is a beloved institution to locals, who flock to the inn's charming **restaurant** (p. 109) and the adjoining paneled lounge for drinks and, on Sunday through Tuesday nights, jazz.

1739 N St. NW (btw. 17th and 18th sts.). www.tabardinn.com. ℂ **202/785-1277.** 35 units, 27 with private bathroom (6 with shower only). $125–$210 single with shared bathroom; $165–$385 single with private bathroom. No charge for second person. Rates include $15 meal voucher per person. Limited street parking, plus nearby public parking garages. Valet parking $39/day. Small and confined dogs allowed ($100 fee). Metro: Dupont Circle (South/19th St. exit). **Amenities:** Restaurant w/lounge (free live jazz Sun–Tues eves.); free access to nearby Washington Sports Club; Wi-Fi (free).

FOGGY BOTTOM/WEST END

This section of town is halfway between the White House and Georgetown; Foggy Bottom lies south of Pennsylvania Avenue, and the West End north. Together, the neighborhoods are home to town house–lined streets, George Washington University, International Monetary Fund offices, World Bank headquarters, and lodging that includes all-suites, upscale, quaint, and budget-friendly options.

Best for: Parents visiting their kids at GW, international business travelers, and those who desire proximity to the Kennedy Center, also located here.

Drawbacks: Around 12,000 undergraduate students attend GW and some-times make their presence known throughout the Foggy Bottom neighborhood in ways you'd rather they wouldn't. On the flip side, the West End might seem too quiet if you like being where the action is.

Expensive

The Watergate Hotel ★★★   This latest iteration of the Watergate Hotel opened in June 2016, 9 years after its former self closed. New owners spent $200 million to transform the iconic structure into an "unapologetically luxurious" property, complete with a wellness floor (spa, fitness center, pool), a highly styl-ized modern decor (heavy on the metalwork, minimalist and streamlined furnish-ings, and lots of curvy artwork and other features suggesting the wavy shape of the Watergate building), and the absolute-best rooftop bar and lounge in the city. Come winter, the rooftop features a synthetic skating rink, a bar serving boozy cocoa, and comfy seating around fire pits. The hotel lies within the six-building Watergate complex of condos, shops, and offices, one of which made the name Watergate famous, when five men working for the Nixon presidential cam-paign were arrested on June 17, 1972, while breaking into and attempting to bug Democratic National Committee headquarters. Next door to the complex is the Kennedy Center. Cross Rock Creek Parkway to stroll the lovely waterfront, reaching the Lincoln Memorial if you walk south, and Georgetown harbor 5

A "Diplomat" room at the sleek Watergate Hotel.

minutes away in the other direction. Thompson Boat Center, almost directly across from the hotel, rents bikes and boats. Guest rooms have minibar/fridges and spa-like marble bathrooms; suites feature deep soaking tubs. Some 117 rooms have balconies, many with views of the Potomac River and George-town. ***Bottom line:*** The hotel is cleverly posh but also comfortable, the service impeccable, and its Potomac River front perch unique in the city.

2650 Virginia Ave. NW (at Rock Creek Pkwy.). www.thewatergatehotel.com. (C) **855/256-3966** or 202/827-1600. 336 units, including 34 suites. Rates start in the mid-$200s for rooms and in the mid-$500s for suites. Extra person $30. Children under 16 stay free. A daily "urban resort fee" is $25 plus tax. Parking $52 including tax. Pets up to 50 lb. allowed (free). Metro: Foggy Bottom. **Amenities:** Restaurant; 3 bars, including rooftop bar/lounge/wintertime skating; weekend afternoon tea; concierge; fitness center; indoor pool; room service; spa; Wi-Fi (free).

Moderate

Avenue Suites ★★   Each of the 124 suites in this all-suite hotel is one-bedroom, measures a remarkably spacious 600 to 650 square feet, and includes a sleeper sofa in the separate living room, a fully equipped kitchen (Whole Foods and Trader Joe's stores are nearby), and trendy but comfortable decor, all at an affordable rate, though that varies by peak/off-peak times. Another plus: a stock-the-fridge program that allows you to order groceries ahead of your stay. I also like Avenue's prime location (on the cusp of George-town and within walking distance of the White House, a Metro stop, and other attractions) and that guests get pool privileges at nearby sister hotel, **One Washington Circle** (see below). The hotel's restaurant/bar and terrace lounge, with its comfy furniture, fire pit, and green garden wall, is a charming place to enjoy the nightly happy hour, as the city's 20-somethings often do. ***Note:*** Inte-rior rooms at the back of the house overlook the lounge, so during the warm season you might want to try for a top-floor room on the 25th Street side.

2500 Pennsylvania Ave. NW (at 25th St.). www.avenuesuites.com. (C) **888/874-0100** or 202/333-8060. 124 units. Peak $276–$349; off-peak $129–$239. Extra person $20. Children 12 and under stay free. Parking $42 including tax. Pets welcome (free). Metro: Foggy Bottom. **Amenities:** Restaurant; bar; concierge; fitness center; room service; Wi-Fi (free).

The River Inn ★★ Nestled among quaint town houses on a quiet side street a short walk from the Kennedy Center, Georgetown, the White House, and the Foggy Bottom Metro station, the River Inn is a comfortable refuge for all sorts except rabble-rousers. Most of the units in the all-suite property are studios, in which the bedroom and living room are combined; 33 units are one-bedrooms, which are roomier and include either a king-size bed or two double beds, as well as a second TV in the separate bedroom. All guest rooms provide a full kitchen, bed with pillowtop mattress, cushy armchair, a sleeper sofa, and a sophisticated decor. Upper-floor suites offer views of the Potomac River and two, nos. 702 and 802, catch sight of the Washington Monument. (These are always in demand, so seldom available.) Complimentary bikes (based on availability in spring/summer months), on-site coin-operated laundry machines, a "stock-the-fridge" program that allows guests to have groceries waiting for them, and an especially gracious staff are among the pluses that keep the inn steeped in bookings from happy repeat customers.

924 25th St. NW (btw. K and I sts.). www.theriverinn.com. © **888/874-0100** or 202/337-7600. 125 units. Peak weekdays $239–$399 double, weekends $179–$350 double; off-peak weekdays $179–$269 double, weekends $169–$259 double. Add $30 for upgrade from studio to 1-bedroom suite. Extra person $20. Children 17 and under stay free in parent's room. Rates include complimentary seasonal cocktails during nightly social hour 5–6pm. Parking $42 plus tax. Pets welcome (free). Metro: Foggy Bottom. **Amenities:** Restaurant; bar; bikes; small fitness center; concierge; room service; Wi-Fi (free).

Inexpensive

Hotel Hive ★★ The District now has two micro-hotels (with more opening in 2021), but the Hotel Hive was the first (the Penn Quarter's Pod Hotel is the other), and it is adorable, from its tagline—"Buzz More. Spend Less."—to the individual decorative elements that cleverly maximize the use of space. Let's start with the guest rooms, which average 150 square feet in size, with some a little smaller, some a little larger. Most rooms have queen beds, some have bunk beds, and all come with a private bathroom. Pocket doors, cubbies beneath platform beds, and built-in nightstands and plasma-screen TVs help create an uncluttered feel. Hexagonal outlines suggesting hives crop up in carpet designs, headboard fabrics, and in bathroom amenities bearing the special Hotel Hive logo. The Hive concept derived in part from the early-20th-century building's unique architectural feature, a hexagonal pocket punctuating the western end of each floor in the six-level structure. On the first floor, the hotel's cool bar occupies the space and beyond, joining up with **&Pizza,** a local favorite restaurant; on the rooftop terrace, the hive area is incorporated into a seasonal cocktail lounge with views of the Lincoln Memorial. On all other levels, the turret holds the best rooms in the house, with six windowed walls letting in lots of light, and connecting, if desired, to the bunk-bed room next door: Voilà! Instant suite. Although the budget rates and small rooms may speak most to millennials, families should consider the hotel, too. The Hive's location is pretty sweet: at the edge of George Washington University's campus, close to the Foggy Bottom Metro station, up the street from the Kennedy Center, and within walking distance of the National Mall. *Note:* The Hive has no parking, but its website directs you to nearby garages that allow reserve-ahead parking.

2224 F St. NW (at Virginia Ave.). www.hotelhive.com. (C) **202/849-8499.** 83 units. $125–$249 year-round, with higher prices expected during peak occasions, such as cherry blossom season. Children 16 and under stay free. Pets 20 lb. and under allowed (free). Metro: Foggy Bottom. **Amenities:** Restaurant; bar; seasonal lounge; Wi-Fi (free).

One Washington Circle Hotel ★ Even this hotel's smallest room (measuring 390 sq. ft.) is more spacious than the largest room at some other D.C. hotels. The biggest suites here encompass more than 700 feet. All of the rooms are suites, with separate full kitchens in 90% of the units and kitchenettes in the remainder. Families especially love the outdoor pool, the on-site restaurant, and the location near the Foggy Bottom Metro stations, Georgetown, and the White House. Most rooms have walkout balconies. One Washington Circle is situated, as it sounds, right on Washington Circle, and across from the George Washington University Hospital. Double-paned windows help screen some of the siren sounds, but for quietest sleep, ask for a room on the eighth or ninth floor facing L Street or New Hampshire Avenue. George Washington University–affiliated guests may be eligible for discounts.

1 Washington Circle NW (btw. 22nd and 23rd sts. NW). www.thecirclehotel.com. (C) **800/424-9671** or 202/872-1680. 151 units. Weekdays $159–$299 smallest suites, $199–$339 largest suites; weekends $109–$199 smallest suites, $159–$239 largest suites. Call hotel or check the website for the best rates, including special offers. Extra person $20. Children 12 and under stay free. Rates include complimentary wine 5–6pm nightly in the lobby. Parking $42 plus tax. Pets accepted (free). Metro: Foggy Bottom. **Amenities:** Restaurant; bar; fitness center; outdoor pool; room service; Wi-Fi (free).

GEORGETOWN

Bustling day and night with shoppers and tourists, Georgetown's handful of hotels ranges from the city's most sublime accommodations to one that offers good value, especially for families.

Best for: Shopaholics; tourists; and parents, students, and academics visiting Georgetown University.

Drawbacks: Crowds throng sidewalks; cars snarl traffic daily. College kids and 20-somethings party hearty here nightly, but especially on weekends.

Expensive

The Graham ★★ The Graham Georgetown is named for the inventor of the telephone, Alexander Graham Bell, who once lived and worked nearby (who knew?). The seven-story hotel holds 57 rooms, nearly half of them deluxe guest rooms with a king bed; the rest are suites, either junior or full, each with a king bed. Largest are king suites, which have an extra-large pullout sofa in the adjacent living room. Each unit is similarly and stylishly decorated in shades of grays, whites, and pale blue, with white, tufted-leather headboards on beds made up in Irish linens. The pretty bathrooms feature white marbled floors and walls, Mexican accent tiles, and L'Occitane amenities. On the lower level lies the restaurant, the **Alex Craft Cocktail Cellar & Speakeasy** (after you-know-who). The seasonal rooftop lounge offers one of the best views in town; it wraps around the building, so you're able to take in Georgetown and the cityscape, including the Washington Monument. The bar attracts a sea of scene-seeking Washingtonians, which means 1) you must reserve a spot, and 2) you might want to consider wearing something slightly trendy: There is a dress code!

1075 Thomas Jefferson St. NW (just below M St.). www.thegrahamgeorgetown.com. ✆ **202/337-0900.** 57 units. $289–$429 king room; $379–$529 king suite. Extra person $25. Children 7 and under stay free. Parking $48 plus tax. Metro: Foggy Bottom. Small pets accepted ($100 cleaning fee). **Amenities:** Restaurant; rooftop bar; concierge; exercise room; room service; Wi-Fi (free).

Rosewood Washington D.C. ★★   The Rosewood is unabashedly luxurious and, after a refresh and reopening in 2019, even more fit for the discerning traveler. Want to tour a museum after hours? Done. Craving a personal shopping experience in Georgetown after the shops have closed? Also done. Staff is on hand 24 hours a day to take care of your every need and whim. The Rosewood sits along the C&O Canal, and some of its 49 rooms overlook the canal, as do the bar and the seasonal outside terrace. The hotel just added six town houses to the property in 2019, each approximately 1,000 square feet of living space, including a well-appointed kitchen and bathroom. The town houses are furnished with curated works of art created by local artists and photographers. A **rooftop lounge** includes a fitness center, indoor/outdoor relaxation pool, and views of Georgetown, the Kennedy Center, a bit of the Potomac River, and the Washington Monument. **CUT by Wolfgang Puck** is the Rosewood's new restaurant, a steakhouse with regional influences and design from surrounding Georgetown.

1050 31st St. NW (at Waters Alley NW). www.rosewoodhotels.com/washington-dc. ✆ **888/767-3966** or 202/617-2400. 49 units. Peak from $626 double, from $2,295 suite; off-peak from $595 double, from $1,545 suite. Parking $52 plus tax. Pets 50 lb. and under allowed (with $100 nonrefundable cleaning fee). Metro: Foggy Bottom. **Amenities:** Restaurant; 2 bars; babysitting; children's programs; concierge; rooftop fitness center and pool; room service; in-spa services; Wi-Fi (free).

Inexpensive

Georgetown Suites ★★   You won't find better value in Georgetown, and even in the city, especially in the summer, when weekend specials can go as low as $115 a night. Note that this is a two-location hotel, with one building on 30th Street, and the second building one street over and down the block, on 29th Street. Here is a breakdown of the two locations:

30th Street   *The pros:* The 30th Street address is unbeatable, just off busy M Street in Georgetown, seconds away from the picturesque C&O Canal and its towpath, but also near posh shops and fun restaurants and bars. Staff is cheery. Suites are quite spacious (studios measure 500 sq. ft., one-bedrooms 800 sq. ft.). All have full kitchens equipped with granite countertops and modern appliances. The one-bedroom suites all have sleeper sofas. The expanded and updated lobby lounge is the location for a complimentary continental breakfast. Ask for a room on an upper floor, or if budget allows, consider one of the two-level, two-bedroom town houses or one of the penthouse suites, with terraces that overlook Georgetown rooftops.

The cons: The 30th Street building has a whiff of college campus about it, thanks to its architecture and layout, and a clientele often made up of college-visiting students. The noise of traffic and revelers can be an annoying factor for rooms on the lower floors.

29th Street *The pros:* The hotel's Harbour Building on 29th Street lies just across from the Washington Harbour complex (attractions there include waterfront restaurants, tour boats that cruise the Potomac River, and the largest ice-skating rink in the city). Ask for a courtyard-side suite or the stunning two-level penthouse suite, with a wall of windows that captures sweeping views of the Potomac, the Kennedy Center, and the bustling waterfront.

The cons: The Harbour Building lies right next to the Whitehurst Freeway, so rooms facing the freeway get those unattractive views and the din of traffic, though double-paned and insulated windows somewhat muffle the sound. The hotel is a bit of a hike (⅔ mile) to the closest Metro station.

1111 30th St. NW (just below M St.) and 1000 29th St. NW (at K St.). www.georgetown suites.com. © **800/348-7203** or 202/298-7800. 221 units. Weekdays $195 studio, $225 1-bedroom suite; weekends $165 studio, $185 1-bedroom suite; penthouse suites from $375; town houses from $475. Rollaway or sleeper sofa $15 extra. Rates include continental breakfast. Limited parking $35 including tax. Pets allowed ($75 per pet one-time fee). Metro: Foggy Bottom or take the DC Circulator Bus, which stops right at the corner of 30th and M sts. **Amenities:** Small exercise room; Wi-Fi (free).

SHAW

Shaw is now home to several hotels, including the city's largest, with 1,175 rooms and 49 suites: the Marriott Marquis Washington, D.C., adjacent to the Walter E. Washington Convention Center. Only one hotel, the Cambria Hotel & Suites, is located in the very heart of the historic neighborhood.

Best for: Travelers who are attending a conference or event at the convention center or are visiting nearby Howard University. Also: those who enjoy an urban residential feel and prefer to be within walking distance of nighttime attractions over sightseeing venues.

Drawbacks: The city's major attractions, from Capitol Hill to the National Mall, are at least a mile away. In addition, there's a lot of construction going on, so be prepared for building sights and sounds and road obstructions.

Moderate

Cambria Hotels DC Convention Center ★★   In this old neighborhood of historic churches, modest houses, colorful town homes, and corner shops, the modern, glass-fronted 10-story Cambria Hotel stands out. Or it did when it opened in 2014. Construction is going on all around the hotel these days, as new apartments and condos rise. Two blocks away is the convention center, on surrounding streets are scores of new and well-reviewed restaurants (p. 114), and a few blocks north are U Street clubs and bars and Howard University beyond. From the rooftop patio, you'll have grand views of the neighborhood, as well as of D.C. sites awaiting you in the distance: the Capitol, the Washington Monument. Ask for an O Street–side room, or best of all, a corner king overlooking both 9th and O streets, the higher up the better, for these same views. Of the 182 suites, 168 are studio suites, spacious certainly, with an abbreviated partition and work table separating the bedroom from the living room, which has a sleeper sofa and its own TV. The remaining 14 suites are one-bedrooms. The hotel has its own restaurant, open for breakfast and dinner, but really, you need to check out the many excellent restaurants in the 'hood.

899 O St. NW (btw. 8th and 9th sts.). www.CambriaDC.com. ℂ **202/299-1188.** 182 units. Weekends year-round: $129–$199; Mon–Thurs: Dec–Feb and July–Aug $129–$242, Mar–June $242–$329, Sept–Nov $189–$242. Add $50 for 1-bedroom suite. Extra person (beyond 4) $30. Children 18 and under stay free. Parking $45 including tax. No pets. Metro: Mt. Vernon Sq./7th St./Convention Center. **Amenities:** Restaurant; bar; business center; 24-hr. fitness center; self-serve laundry room; in-room microwave and mini-fridge; indoor rooftop pool; rooftop patio and fire pit; Wi-Fi (free).

U & 14TH STREET CORRIDORS

Hotels abound in nearby Dupont Circle and downtown, but in the U & 14th Street Corridors proper, only one hotel truly can claim to be in the neighborhood.

Best for: Travelers who prefer to stay close to the buzziest restaurants, bars, and clubs than to cultural attractions.

Drawbacks: Sometimes the party never ends! (Especially in pleasant weather when the hotel's rooftop lounge itself is a nightlife destination.)

Moderate

Kimpton Mason & Rook ★★   The conversation at check-in is all about the really good restaurants nearby, such as Le Diplomate (p. 102) and Doi Moi (better book restaurant reservations when you book your hotel stay). But there are plenty of other reasons to stay here: complimentary bikes, spacious guest rooms (double rooms run 300 to 425 sq. ft.; suites measure 645 sq. ft.), a rooftop pool, and the spanking-fresh newness of the property. You're meant to hang out in the living room–like lobby, with its set-up chessboard and clusters of armchairs and rounded-armed sofas; this is the site of a complimentary wine hour each evening and coffee/tea every morning. Guest rooms are equally inviting, featuring nubby gray fabrics, pumpkin-hued accents, expansive desks, enormous 65-inch TVs, large marble bathrooms with walk-in glass showers (plenty of room for two), and a truly stacked bed.

1430 Rhode Island Ave. NW (btw. 14th and 15th sts.). www.masonandrookhotel.com. ℂ **800/706-1202** or 202/742-3100. 178 units, including 18 suites. $159–$429 double; $279–$599 suite. Room rates do not include daily "facilities fee" of $25 plus tax. Rates include evening wine hour 5–6pm and morning coffee and tea 6–9am weekdays, 7–10am weekends. Parking $49 plus tax. Pets allowed (free). Metro: McPherson Sq. (14th St. exit) or U St./Cardozo (13th St. exit). **Amenities:** Restaurant; bar; rooftop pool and lounge; bikes; concierge; 24-hour fitness center; room service; Wi-Fi (free when you sign up for the no-cost loyalty program).

WOODLEY PARK

This Connecticut Avenue–centered upper northwest enclave is a residential neighborhood of little stores and restaurants, Rock Creek Park, the National Zoo, and one of Washington's biggest hotels.

Best for: Families who prefer a tamer experience than found downtown, plus proximity to Rock Creek Park and the zoo. Travelers interested in lodging that lies close to nightlife hotspots but not actually in their neighborhood (Adams Morgan is a quick stroll east of the hotel, over the Duke Ellington Bridge). Groups requiring a big hotel without a convention ambience.

Drawbacks: This area may be a little too quiet for some, especially at night.

Moderate

Omni Shoreham Hotel ★★★ Step from the lively streets of the city into the Omni Shoreham's lovely and enormous lobby, and it really does feel like you've arrived at a resort. It's the towering ceiling, the chandeliers, and the sheer expanse of lobby leading back down through the dining room and out the French doors to the terrace and the acres of landscaped lawns, all backing up to Rock Creek Park. Truly, one of the pleasures of staying here is exploring the premises. Poke your head in the Palladian Ballroom to inspect its muraled scenes of Monticello, or check out the Diplomat Ballroom, modeled after the East Room of the White House. The Omni Shoreham was built in 1930 as a hotel and apartment building, so its guest rooms are of varying sizes and shapes. For best views and quiet, ask for a park-view room at the back, preferably with a balcony (15% of the rooms have them). You should also opt for the Omni Select Guest Loyalty program (it's free), which gets you free Wi-Fi upon signing up, plus a bundle of other privileges, such as morning-beverage room service, pressing service, and shoeshine, on subsequent stays at Omni hotels. The Omni attracts groups, thanks to its size (11 acres, 834 rooms, 24 meeting rooms, several ballrooms), but families love it, too, for its large seasonal pool, children's amenities (backpack of games given at check-in, cookies and milk delivered on the first evening), its on-site restaurants, and its proximity to Rock Creek Park and the National Zoo. The **buffet breakfast** is a veritable groaning board of deliciousness, from smoked salmon to teddy-bear waffles to omelettes made to order; look for stay/dine packages that include it.

2500 Calvert St. NW (near Connecticut Ave.). www.omnihotels.com/dc. © **800/843-6664** or 202/234-0700. 834 units. $159–$359 double; from $359 suite. Extra person $20. Children 12 and under stay free. Parking $52 plus tax. Pets under 25 lb. allowed ($50 cleaning fee). Metro: Woodley Park–Zoo. **Amenities:** 2 restaurants; bar; poolside bar (summer only); bike rentals; children's amenities program; concierge; fitness center; heated outdoor pool (open Apr–Oct); room service; spa services; Wi-Fi (free when you sign up for the loyalty program).

Inexpensive

Kalorama Guest House ★ Kalorama's rambling redbrick house blends right in among the large town houses and family dwellings in this residential neighborhood. Built in 1910, the house retains an old-timey feeling about it. That's partly due to its 119-year-old design: old wood floors, fireplaces (decorative only), paneled wainscoting along the stairwell, a tin ceiling here and there. And it's partly due to the furnishings, which come from estate sales and antiques auctions. Owner Jack Shrestha adds to the homey feel, offering cookies and coffee and pointing out the communal family room, kitchen, and laundry-room facilities, even as he's pulling out photos of his 6-year-old daughter. (Speaking of children, Shrestha notes that the inn is best for well-behaved children ages 6 and older.) The least expensive rooms are two in the basement that share a bathroom; these two rooms, plus a large room on this floor with its own television, have their own entrance from the street. Basement rooms, by the way, do have windows, and are as pleasantly furnished as any upstairs. Nicest, in my opinion, is the sole room on the first floor; built-in bookcases and a sleigh bed are part of its charm. You're in a great area, with the zoo, good restaurants, Rock Creek Park, and the Woodley Park Metro stop all within a short walk.

2700 Cathedral Ave. NW (off Connecticut Ave.). www.kaloramaguesthouse.com. ℂ **202/588-8188.** 10 units, 8 w/private bathroom. $99–$249 single or double. Rates include hot breakfast buffet and afternoon refreshment of lemonade and cookies. Extra person (including children) $25. Street parking permit $20 plus tax. Metro: Woodley Park–Zoo. **Amenities:** Wi-Fi (free).

Woodley Park Guest House ★   This charming 14-room B&B offers clean, comfortable, and cozy lodging, inexpensive rates, a super location, and a personable staff. The innkeepers own the Embassy Circle Guest House as well, and the same graciously welcoming ambience prevails. Special features of this 1906 guest house include a wicker-furnished, tree-shaded front porch; exposed, century-old brick walls; and beautiful antiques and original art. (The innkeepers buy works only from artists who have stayed at the house.) Rooms are of every possible configuration: three are singles; three have full beds; five have queen beds; two have kings; and two rooms come with two beds, one of which can accommodate three people (it's $50 extra for a third person). The guesthouse benefits from its across-the-street proximity to the Washington Marriott Wardman Park Hotel, where airport shuttles and taxis are on hand. The Woodley Park-Zoo Metro stop, good restaurants, Rock Creek Park, and the National Zoo are all within a very short walk. *Note:* The B&B has no TVs.

2647 Woodley Rd. NW (off Connecticut Ave.). www.dcinns.com. ℂ **202/667-0218.** 14 units, 11 w/private bathroom. Low season $125–$225; high season $145–$275. Rates include breakfast buffet, midday snacks, and evening wine or beer. Children 8 and older only. Limited parking $20. Metro: Woodley Park–Zoo. **Amenities:** Wi-Fi (free).

WHERE TO EAT

S hould you have any doubts about the quality—or even existence—of a worthy dining scene in the nation's capital, consider the fact that more than 100 restaurants in D.C. earned coveted Michelin stars in 2019. *Bon Appétit* magazine named Washington, D.C., its "Restaurant City of the Year" in 2016. Plus, the city's restaurants, chefs, sommeliers, and other top pros in the trade regularly show up on the vaunted James Beard Foundation Awards lists (the Oscars for excellence in championing American cuisine).

So that's settled. Now comes the two-fold tricky part: how to choose where you want to eat from a world's choice of options, and then score a table. Washingtonians dine out a lot. *A lot.* Wheeler-dealers and socializing urbanistas fill restaurants throughout the city, from the newly bustling waterfront communities to hot-hot-hot Shaw (see box, p. 114) to Barracks Row on Capitol Hill and old reliable chestnuts near the White House. Be sure to make a reservation.

The city is also notable for its casual dining, and often the food is as sensational in these places as at higher-priced restaurants, from the empanadas at **Colada Shop** (p. 105) to the oysters at **Rappahannock Oyster Bar** (p. 94). Bistros serving "small plates" are here to stay, no matter whether the cuisine is American, as at **Rose's Luxury** (p. 89), or the Middle Eastern *mezze* of **Zaytinya** (p. 98). Some restaurants, like **Hank's Oyster Bar** (p. 93), hedge their bets with menus of small plates *and* large plates. Something else you should know: A boisterous bar scene is now a dining-out fact of life. And it can get loud.

Good restaurants are in every neighborhood, and this chapter leads you to a range of possibilities, spanning diverse cuisines, budget considerations, even trendiness (some of the best restaurants have been around for a while).

ATLAS DISTRICT

Moderate

Fancy Radish ★ VEGETARIAN The greater Washington, D.C., area has become a hotbed for vegetarians, and based on the number of restaurants catering to plant-based eaters that have opened recently, it shows. But even non-vegetarians find this restaurant a treat. James Beard Award nominees Rich Landau and Kate Jacoby opened this "vegetable restaurant" in 2018, and it's been a hit since for presenting veggies in new and interesting ways, and for keeping texture in its dishes. No mushy green stuff here. A recent dinner started with stuffed avocado filled with pickled cauliflower in a crispy "rice" shell, and a rutabaga fondue served with hot pretzel bread and pickled veggies, followed by "ramen" tossed in a burnt miso sauce and topped with swiss chard. Also perfect: the chermoula tofu, plated beautifully with a smear of eggplant puree and olives. The key lime pie panna cotta was refreshing and not overly filling; while the strawberry rhubarb tart earned praise for its true-to-Midwest flavor. Try the natural wines or craft sodas, like the Happy Go Lucky with pear and chai or the raspberry truffle with chocolate orange syrup. With its rum, pear, lime, and soda mix, the Prickly Pete tastes like spring. Delicious and fresh.

600 H St. NE (at 7th St.). www.fancyradishdc.com. ℭ **202/675-8341.** Reservations accepted for dinner. Main courses $12–$19. Tues–Thurs 5pm–10pm; Sat 5pm–11pm; Sun 5pm–10pm. Metro: Union Station, then walk, take a taxi, or ride the streetcar.

Maketto ★★ CAMBODIAN/TAIWANESE   Stop by Maketto during the day and you'll find locals seated at tables and counters throughout the place— in the downstairs restaurant, the upstairs cafe, the open kitchen, the courtyard, and the roof deck—typing away on laptops, a cup of coffee and a sticky bun within reach. (All the baking is done in-house.) They look like they live here, and that's the idea. But Maketto is first and foremost a restaurant, one of several operated by Chef Erik Bruner-Yang, including Brothers and Sisters at the **Line hotel** (p. 71) in Adams Morgan. And the food is delish: steamed pork *bao* (doughy bun filled with shredded pork in hoisin sauce), crispy dumplings with braised beef, flash-fried broccoli with peanuts, and a crispy sweet and spicy version of Taiwanese fried chicken, served atop bread. Maketto grows livelier as the day progresses—this is the nightlife-happy Atlas District, remember. *Other things to note:* Maketto sells men's contemporary fashion (p. 216) and stages assorted events, from pop-up shops to yoga classes.

1351 H St. NE (btw. 12th and 13th sts.). www.maketto1351.com. ℭ **202/838-9972.** Reservations accepted for dinner. Restaurant $6–$12 lunch items, $6–$34 dinner items (most items under $16), $4–$15 dim sum. Cafe: Most items $2–$6. Mon–Thurs 7am– 10pm; Fri–Sat 7am–11pm; Sun 7am–5pm. Metro: Union Station, then walk, take a taxi, or ride the streetcar.

CAPITOL HILL & BARRACKS ROW

Along with the recommendations below, for solid diner fare and lively local color, I recommend **Pete's Diner and Carryout** at 212 2nd St. SE (btw.

Washington, D.C., Restaurants

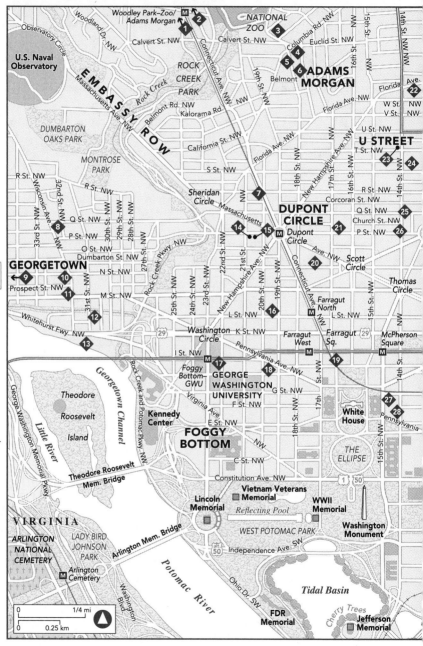

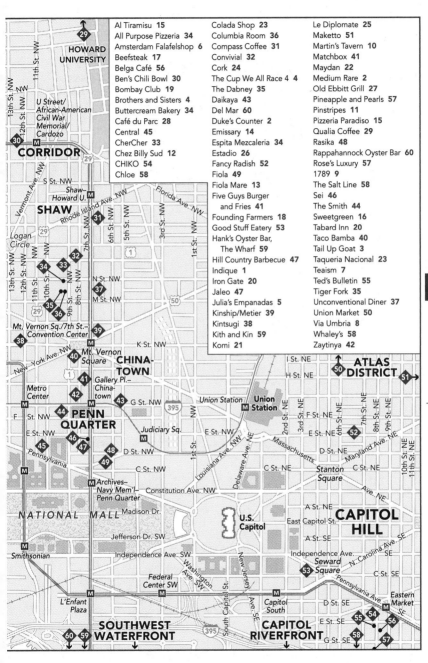

Al Tiramisu **15**
All Purpose Pizzeria **34**
Amsterdam Falafelshop **6**
Beefsteak **17**
Belga Café **56**
Ben's Chili Bowl **30**
Bombay Club **19**
Brothers and Sisters **4**
Buttercream Bakery **34**
Café du Parc **28**
Central **45**
CherCher **33**
Chez Billy Sud **12**
CHIKO **54**
Chloe **58**

Colada Shop **23**
Columbia Room **36**
Compass Coffee **31**
Convivial **32**
Cork **24**
The Cup We All Race 4 **4**
The Dabney **35**
Daikaya **43**
Del Mar **60**
Duke's Counter **2**
Emissary **14**
Espita Mezcaleria **34**
Estadio **26**
Fancy Radish **52**
Fiola **49**
Fiola Mare **13**
Five Guys Burger
  and Fries **41**
Founding Farmers **18**
Good Stuff Eatery **53**
Hank's Oyster Bar,
  The Wharf **59**
Hill Country Barbecue **47**
Indique **1**
Iron Gate **20**
Jaleo **47**
Julia's Empanadas **5**
Kinship/Metier **39**
Kintsugi **38**
Kith and Kin **59**
Komi **21**

Le Diplomate **25**
Maketto **51**
Martin's Tavern **10**
Matchbox **41**
Maydan **22**
Medium Rare **2**
Old Ebbitt Grill **27**
Pineapple and Pearls **57**
Pinstripes **11**
Pizzeria Paradiso **15**
Qualia Coffee **29**
Rasika **48**
Rappahannock Oyster Bar **60**
Rose's Luxury **57**
1789 **9**
The Salt Line **58**
Sei **46**
The Smith **44**
Sweetgreen **16**
Tabard Inn **20**
Taco Bamba **40**
Tail Up Goat **3**
Taqueria Nacional **23**
Teaism **7**
Ted's Bulletin **55**
Tiger Fork **35**
Unconventional Diner **37**
Union Market **50**
Via Umbria **8**
Whaley's **58**
Zaytinya **42**

HOWARD UNIVERSITY

U Street/
African-American
Civil War
Memorial/
Cardozo

CORRIDOR

SHAW

Shaw-
Howard U.

Logan
Circle

Mt. Vernon Sq./7th St.–
Convention Center

Mt. Vernon
Square

CHINA-
TOWN

Metro
Center

Gallery Pl.–
Chinatown

PENN
QUARTER

Union Station   Union
                Station

Judiciary Sq.

Archives–
Navy Mem'l–
Penn Quarter   Constitution Ave. NW

NATIONAL MALL   Madison Dr.

U.S.
Capitol

East Capitol St.

CAPITOL
HILL

Jefferson Dr. SW

Smithsonian   Independence Ave. SW   Independence Ave.

Seward
Square

Federal
Center SW

L'Enfant
Plaza

Capitol
South

Eastern
Market

ATLAS
DISTRICT

Stanton
Square

SOUTHWEST
WATERFRONT

CAPITOL
RIVERFRONT

UNION market

Where can you sample savory Indian crepes one minute, poke bowls the next, and finish with delicious doughnuts and homemade gelato? It's all found in **Union Market** (1309 5th St. SE; https://union marketdc.com). This vibrant, historic market is an all-in-one hotspot for eating, drinking, and shopping. Wander among the nearly 50 vendor stalls and you may feel as though you're on a foodie world tour. Sample the craft-roasted **Blue Bottle Coffee** (www.bluebottlecoffee.com) and cheese from **Trickling Springs Creamery,** then head over to **Rappahannock Oyster Company** for Chesapeake bivalves (p. 94). Italian eatery **Masseria** (1340 4th St. NE; www.masseria-dc.com; ℂ **202/608-1330**), one of the only freestanding restaurants in Union Market, stands out for its elegant Italian menu in a country-chic setting. Shops include **District Cutlery** (www.districtcutlery. com), a chef's knife shop; the lifestyle/homegoods shop **Salt & Sundry** (www.shopsaltandsundry.com); and **Sabah** (https://shop.sabah.am), selling handmade Turkish shoes. It's an eclectic mix and worthy of a stop for the tastes alone.

La Cosecha (http://lacosechadc.com), a 20,000-square-foot contemporary market celebrating Latin American culture, opened in Union Market in 2019, adding at least six new food vendors. Among them is **El Cielo** (www.elcielorestaurant. com), from Colombian chef Juan Manuel "Juanma" Barrientos; **Ali Pacha** (https://alipachadc.com), a vegan tasting room; and **Amparo Fondita** (www.amparo fondita.com), a modern Mexican restaurant from the chef of Oyamel and featuring a menu of coastal Mexican fare.

Steps from Union Market, **Coconut Club** (540 Penn St. NE; www.hello coconutclub.com; ℂ **202/544-5500**) bustles nearly every night. Built into an electric company's former loading docks, the Club is an "island vacation spot" in the city from chef Adam Greenberg, the "all-time winningest Food Network competitor" (his words). Greenberg won *Chopped* five times and took down the host of *Beat Bobby Flay* before opening this tropical-themed restaurant serving fish flown in fresh from Hawaii nightly, poke with lotus root chips, pork belly and pineapple, and even Spam, a Hawaiian favorite, presented three ways.

Union Market is open Sunday to Wednesday 8am to 8pm and Friday to Saturday 8am to 9pm (Metro: NoMa-Gallaudet/New York Ave., just a few blocks north of the Atlas District).

Independence and Pennsylvania aves. in Capitol Hill), and for an insider's experience, **Market Lunch** inside Eastern Market (p. 125).

Expensive

Pineapple and Pearls ★★★ MODERN AMERICAN   Welcome to the city's most sublime dining experience. At $325 per person, it is also one of the most expensive. The magic happens Tuesday through Saturday nights, when chef/owner Aaron Silverman and his able staff ply you with an improbably wondrous menu of 12 exquisite tastes in a warm, gracious atmosphere. You might start with a fennel and absinthe bonbon, going on to the likes of spring garlic egg drop soup (with snow peas) and mole-smoked beef rib, and finishing with a little box of doughnuts in Chartreuse, Campari, Grappa, and Nardini flavors (just examples—the menu is always changing). The congenial welcome and the overall attention to details, decor to cuisine to charming service, are likely to win you over, and you'll appreciate that service again the next morning, as you enjoy the house-made breakfast bar you were sent home with.

Your three seating options—in the main dining room, at the chef's counter, and at the bar—determine the price of your tasting menu (the prix-fixe bar menu does not include the cost of beverages); see service information below. Reservations are available exclusively on the restaurant's website for dates 5 weeks out for the dining room. You may also snag same-day reservations by checking the restaurant's Instagram page (@lastminutedinnerplans), where available last-minute seats are posted. For the same gracious ambience but a less expensive meal, try for a table at nearby sister restaurants **Rose's Luxury** (see below) and **Little Pearl,** 921 Pennsylvania Ave. SE (www.littlepearldc. com; ℂ **202/618-1868**), a darling cafe by day and wine bar at night.

715 8th St. SE (at G St.). www.pineappleandpearls.com. ℂ **202/595-7375.** Reservations required. Prix-fixe $325 all-inclusive (dinner, drinks, tax, and tip) per person in the dining room and at the chef's table; prix-fixe $150 (includes all but the drinks) per person at the bar. Dinner only Tues–Sat. Seatings at 5–6pm and 8:15–9:15pm. Metro: Eastern Market.

Moderate

Belga Cafe ★ BELGIAN Open since 2004, Belga Cafe claims to be "the original Belgian restaurant in D.C.," and helmed by a true Bruge-native as chef, it offers a vibe and menu that rivals the old country. Come for dinner and try the waffle stuffed with crabmeat, mussels, and saffron sauce. The mussel pots (seven varieties to choose from) are big enough to share, and arrive with tasty *frites* and the traditional mayonnaise side. Brunching in D.C. is a competitive sport, so don't show up to Belga's storied brunch without a reservation. You'll be glad you did, with dishes like a Belgian omelet stuffed with lobster, shrimp, crab, and calamari and topped with a tomato-bisque sauce, and waffles "like you've never seen before." A hearty menu of classic Belgian beers is also available.

514 8 St. SE (btw. E and G sts). www.belgacafe.com. ℂ **202/544-0100.** Reservations accepted. Main courses $13–$22 brunch, $13–$27 lunch, $18–$38 dinner. Mon–Thurs 11am–10pm; Fri 11am–11pm; Sat 9am–11pm; Sun 9am–9:30pm. Metro: Eastern Market.

Rose's Luxury ★★★ AMERICAN Critics declared this quirky little labor of love in Barracks Row one of D.C.'s best restaurants almost as soon as it opened in October 2013. America's "best new restaurant" (*Bon Appétit* magazine 2014), and "Best Chef in the Mid-Atlantic" (2016 James Beard Foundation Award) are among the many accolades both the restaurant and its chef/owner Aaron Silverman have received. Its success comes down to endearing service, an eclectic decor of antiques and pretty fabrics and china, and a simple menu of unexpected taste combinations. Though the menu changes frequently, it almost always includes a pork sausage, habañero, and lychee salad among its small plates, and at least one family-style dish intended for two to four diners to share. Rose's now accepts a set number of same-day reservations, available on its website beginning at 9am (Mon–Sat). If you can't get a reservation, it's still worth it to walk in and wait. Give the receptionist your cellphone number, then head upstairs to the cute bar for a drink, or wander 8th Street until the restaurant calls to say your table is ready. Rose's siblings, the luxe **Pineapple and Pearls** right next door, and the precious and affordable **Little Pearl** one street over, also accept reservations.

717 8th St. SE (btw. G and I sts.). www.rosesluxury.com. ℂ **202/580-8889.** Small plates $10–$16. Mon–Sat 5–10pm. Metro: Eastern Market.

Ted's Bulletin ★ AMERICAN   Ted's Bulletin calls itself a family restaurant, and it is, but many of the "children" who come here are in their 20s and 30s and they're drinking milkshakes laced with coconut rum or maybe vodka and Kahlúa. So it can get rowdy. What you'll enjoy, besides the retro decor, is the well-done comfort-food menu: grilled cheese, tomato soup, fried chicken, mac and cheese, barbecued chicken, chili, sloppy joes, and breakfast items (which are served all day). Ted's Tarts (a homemade Pop-Tart), available in a variety of flavors, are a favorite. Ted's Bulletin has another District location at 1818 14th St. NW (ℂ **202/265-8337**), in the U & 14th Street Corridors.

505 8th St. SE (at E St.). www.tedsbulletin.com. ℂ **202/544-8337.** Reservations accepted. Main courses $10–$16 breakfast; $11–$29 lunch/supper (most items under $20). Mon–Thurs 7am–10pm; Fri–Sat 7am–11pm; Sun 7am–10pm. Metro: Eastern Market.

Inexpensive

CHIKO ★ CHINESE/KOREAN   Almost overnight, this little restaurant transformed from a hot dog shop into one of the city's best "fast-casual" spots for Asian fare. Co-chefs Danny Lee and Scott Drewno, along with partner Drew Kim (together as the Fried Rice Collective), opened this hit eatery in 2017, and soon drew a following for dishes like orange-ish chicken with candied mandarins, crispy chicken spring rolls, and wok-blistered Chinese broccoli and kimchi stew. Grab a seat at the reservation-only chef's counter, offering a $50 tasting menu. Another CHIKO location is in Dupont Circle at 2029 P St. NW (ℂ **202/331-3040**).

423 8th St. SE (btw. D and E sts.). www.chikodc.com. ℂ **202/558-9934.** Reservations only for chef's counter. Dinner $8–$17. Tasting menu $50. Sun–Thurs 5–10pm. Fri–Sat 5pm–12am. Metro: Eastern Market.

Good Stuff Eatery ★ AMERICAN   Spike Mendelsohn shot to fame as a *Top Chef* contestant and remains renowned thanks to the scrumptiousness of his burgers, fries, and shakes. The Prez Obama Burger (with applewood bacon, onion marmalade, Roquefort cheese, and horseradish mayo sauce) is still the most popular item on the menu, according to the staff; the toasted marshmallow milkshake will always be the #1 milkshake, to my mind. ***Warning:*** Good Stuff Eatery is always jumping, with people in line on the first floor and filling upstairs and outdoor patio tables. The line moves fast and table turnover is fairly quick, but just the same, you might consider getting the burgers to go, as so many do. The pizza place next door, **We The Pizza** (www.wethepizza.com; ℂ **202/544-4008**), is also Spike's. Other Good Stuff Eatery locations are in Georgetown at 3291 M St. NW (ℂ **202/337-4663**), and at

Reagan National Airport (Terminal B); these locations, unlike Capitol Hill's, are open daily, including Sundays.

303 Pennsylvania Ave. SE (at 3rd St.). www.goodstuffeatery.com. © **202/543-8222.** Reservations not accepted. Burgers $7–$8; milkshakes $6; salads $8–$12. Mon–Sat 11am–10pm. Metro: Capitol South.

CAPITOL RIVERFRONT ("NAVY YARD")

This neighborhood bustles with Washington Nationals fervor in baseball season (the ballpark is here), waterfront fun when weather permits, and restaurant and bar crowds year-round. Among your many choices are these keepers.

Moderate

Chloe ★★ AMERICAN   This glass-enclosed bistro sits at the corner of 4th and Tingey streets right across the road from Bluejacket Brewery (p. 228). Weekdays, this part of town is a workaday world, with not much of interest for the tourist. If it weren't for the presence of the Anacostia River and Nationals Park, you might imagine yourself in a modern suburban development complex. Nighttime and weekends are really when the restaurant, like the rest of the neighborhood, comes alive. Happy hour's a crush, as is weekend brunch. Dinner's the winner, with favorite dishes including roasted cod with tastes of coconut, curry, and ginger; seafood gumbo with Andouille sausage and sassafras; and crispy brussels sprouts and burrata with roast squash and apples. The cuisine is multi-culti American, drawing from diverse cuisines, New Orleans to India, Vietnamese to Lebanese. This, you might say, is what America tastes like.

1331 4th St. SE (at Tingey St.). www.restaurantchloe.com. © **202/313-7007.** Reservations recommended. Main courses $5–$15 brunch, $14–$29 dinner. Sun 11am–9pm; Mon–Thurs 4–10pm; Fri 4–11pm; Sat 11am–2pm and 4–11pm. Metro: Navy Yard/Ballpark (M St. and New Jersey Ave. exit).

The Salt Line ★ SEAFOOD   This restaurant stands out among the growing number of good ones in the neighborhood for two reasons: its unimpeded view of the Anacostia River—especially from the outdoor bar areas, which bump up against a wideplanked boardwalk—and for the fresh seasonal seafood, with lobster rolls, crispy-skin rockfish, and oysters taking center stage. The menu also includes items like a farro and kale salad for vegetarians and surf and turf for carnivores. Delicious desserts are baked in-house (as are the breads) and include a s'mores lava cake. Wash down your meal with the restaurant's potent cocktails, some of which have delightfully New England-y names like the "Caper Codder G&T."

79 Potomac Ave. SE (at First St.). www.thesaltline.com. © **202/506-2368.** Main courses $22–$38 brunch and dinner. Sat–Sun 11am–3pm; nightly 4:30–10:30pm; weekdays raw bar and outdoor bar 3pm to closing. Hours change with the seasons, the Nationals home-game schedule, and sundry other reasons; check website for the latest information. Metro: Navy Yard/Ballpark (M and Half sts. exit).

5

WHERE TO EAT

Capitol Riverfront ("Navy Yard")

Whaley's ★★ SEAFOOD   You'll be hard-pressed to find fresher fish than Whaley's unless you head to the fish market on the Wharf. Cousins Nick and David Wiseman opened this casual raw bar and seafood joint on the waterfront in honor of Zedechiah Whaley, the first Maryland Navy casualty of the Revolutionary War. The space is small—only 44 seats—but the airy and nautical ambience makes it feel larger. The raw bar is where it's at—pristine oysters, littleneck clams, poached shrimp, and shellfish towers. (The large tower is pricey at $150 but feeds 4-6 people.) Pair your fish with one of the house cocktails, changed seasonally, including the Fresno chili–infused vodka and lime gimlet. The seasonal alfresco **Rosé Garden** overlooks the river and offers a wide selection of rosés, plus frozen drinks, highballs, and cold beer.

301 Water St. SE, Suite 115 SE (btw. 3rd and 4th sts. in the Lumbershed Building). www. whaleysdc.com. ℂ **202/484-8800.** Main courses $14–$25 dinner, $14–$19 brunch. Mon–Thurs 5–9:30pm; Fri 5–11pm; Sat 11am–11pm; Sun 11am–9pm. Metro: Navy Yard/Ballpark (M and Half sts. exit).

SOUTHWEST WATERFRONT

The Wharf complex's waterfront location is its main attraction, but one that poses logistical challenges for anyone driving here. Traffic jams up on Maine Avenue, the primary route leading to the Wharf and its parking garages. If you can, use one of the many alternative transportation options, which include the Metro, the DC Circulator bus, water taxis, and a shuttle that loops continuously between the Wharf and the L'Enfant Plaza Metro station. If you must drive, take care to read the section "Getting Here" posted on the Wharf's website, www.wharfdc.com, as well as specific instructions provided by the restaurant to which you're headed.

Expensive

Del Mar ★★★ SPANISH/SEAFOOD   This latest from the dynamic duo, chef Fabio Trabocchi and partner/wife, Maria (see **Fiola** [p. 95] and **Fiola Mare** [p. 112]), shimmers with waterfront light and a welcoming sparkle. The two-level restaurant is huge, but it doesn't seem so: Intimate spaces are carved out within, each with its own style, but sharing an overall attention to beauty and comfort and Spanish accents that Mallorca native Maria Trabocchi undoubtedly had a hand in. High ceilings, jade-green banquettes, a green-shuttered window-front room overlooking the waterfront, a large, circular bar punctuated with sea-blue cushioned barstools, and hand-painted ceramic tiles underfoot are just some of the charming touches. Del Mar focuses on the tastes of coastal Spain, so expect excellent grilled fish, paellas, marinated mussels, grilled wild squid, and such. Selections of tapas, Spanish cheeses, charcuterie, and raw fish are available at every meal. A short list of "principal plates" might include grilled lamb in a manchego sauce and Mallorcan-style rice (served with clams, prawns, and mussels). The *croquetas* (creamy fritters filled with *jamon Iberico;* i.e., Spanish ham, black truffles, and green garlic aioli) are a must. As comfortable as Del Mar is, it still feels special, so it's worth dressing up a little to come here, even during the day. In fact, it's required: The restaurant permits no flip-flops, athletic wear, or torn clothing and requests that "gentlemen refrain from wearing shorts, sandals, sleeveless shirts, or hats."

791 Wharf St. SW (at Maine Ave. SW). www.delmardc.com. ℭ **202/525-1402.** Reservations recommended. Tapas $10–$24 each, available at every meal; main courses $20–$28 brunch, $20–$36 lunch, $40–$38 dinner. Light "Maria" 3-course prix-fixe lunch $28. Sun 11am–2pm and 2:30–10pm; Mon 4–10pm; Tues–Thurs 11:30am–10pm; Fri 11:30am–10:30pm; Sat 11:30am–2pm and 2:30–10pm. Metro: Waterfront.

Kith and Kin ★★★ AFRO-CARIBBEAN   When a hotel, especially an enormous global chain hotel, opens a restaurant, it's hard not to be a tad skeptical. You might expect overly reheated food and a conference-room vibe. What you don't expect is Kith and Kin. Open since 2017, Kith and Kin is flourishing, thanks to the delicate hand in the kitchen of creator and executive chef Kwame Onwuachi. The former *Top Chef* star combines the flavors of his heritage—ranging from Nigeria and Jamaica to West Africa and the Caribbean, and even New Orleans and New York. Breakfast brunch might include a curried crab benedict or smoked salmon with whipped cream cheese. Mom Dukes Shrimp over buttered rice is perfection. Dinner diners can expect *sambusas* (Somali stuffed pastry pockets) with spiced lamp and *shiro* sauce or king crab curry with plantains. A large banquette snakes through the dining room, punctuated by large industrial-style lamps, a wine wall with more than 400 bottles, and a line of bi-fold doors that open directly onto the Wharf's waterfront. Also visit Onwuachi's fast-casual spot in Union Market, **Philly Wing Fry** (www.phillywingfry.com), for cheesesteaks and chicken wings.

801 Wharf St. SW (at Sutton Sq. SW, in the InterContinental Washington D.C. – The Wharf). www.kithandkindc.com. ℭ **202/878-8566.** Reservations recommended. Main courses $14–$24 breakfast, $30 breakfast buffet, $14–$32 lunch, $14-$60 dinner. Mon–Fri 6:30–10:30am; Sat–Sun 6:30–11am; daily noon–2:30pm; Sun–Thurs 5–10:30pm; Fri–Sat 5–11pm. Metro: Waterfront.

Moderate

Hank's Oyster Bar ★★ SEAFOOD   Around since 2005, Hank's just keeps getting better and better. Chef/owner Jamie Leeds now has four Oyster Bars, with the original at Dupont Circle (1624 Q St. NW; ℭ **202/462-4265**) and this one at the Wharf the newest…*and* the largest: The restaurant can seat nearly 200 people. Like every other Wharf venue, Hank's capitalizes on its waterfront location, with windows opening to covered patios on two sides, giving patrons, inside and out, great views of wharf activity and the parade of people passing by. The place always feels festive, and the food is always great; I'm particularly fond of the crab cake, the po'boys, and just about anything with oyster in the name. Leeds caters to meat lovers, as well, with a daily "Meat&2" entree. If it's Sunday, say, fried chicken is the daily special, and comes with two sides from a list of eight. Hank's other Oyster Bars are on Capitol Hill, at 633 Pennsylvania Ave. SE (ℭ **202/733-1971**), and in Old Town Alexandria, at 1026 King St. (ℭ **703/739-4265**). Leeds also has a

A seafood tower of lobster and oysters at the Old Ebbitt Grill.

Hank's Pasta Bar in Old Town, at 600 Montgomery St. (© 571/312-4117), and in 2019, opened an outpost at Nats Park, near Section 108, serving up oyster and shrimp po'boys and more to the ballpark crowd.

701 Wharf St. SW (at 7th St.). www.hanksoysterbar.com. © **202/817-3055.** Reservations accepted. Small plates $8–$23; large plates $14–$28. Sun 11am–10pm; Mon–Thurs 11:30am–10pm; Fri 11:30am–11pm; Sat 11am–11pm. Bar open later. Metro: Waterfront.

Rappahannock Oyster Bar ★★ SEAFOOD As you may have noticed by now, seafood, particularly oysters, are kind of a big deal here in D.C. Cousins Travis and Ryan Croxton opened this branch of their popular bivalve bar in 2018 in a historic oyster-shucking shed across from the bustling Maine Avenue Fish Market, the oldest fish market in the U.S. The inside is tight, with only 27 bar seats surrounded by accordion-style folding doors. The 90-seat dining patio is much airier but only open in seasonal weather. But you're really there for the oysters, right? Try the sweet and buttery Rappahannock River oysters or the briny Rochambeau from Virginia. Oyster chowder, crab cakes, and crispy whole fish round out the menu. Rappahannock's other location is in Union Market (1309 5th St. NE; © 202-544-4702).

1150 Maine Ave. SW (at the Fish Market). www.rroysters.com. © **202/484-0572.** Reservations not accepted. Small plates $10–$30; oysters $1.75–$2.50 each. Sun–Thurs 11am–12am; Fri–Sat 11am–1am. Metro: Waterfront.

DOWNTOWN & PENN QUARTER

Expensive

Central Michel Richard ★★ FRENCH BISTRO The ebullient spirit of chef Michel Richard lives on at Central, though the brilliant Richard died in August 2016. His namesake restaurant continues to win high marks for both food and ambience. A great downtown location on Pennsylvania Avenue, a generous bar, a menu that speaks to both French and American cultures (deviled eggs, croque monsieur, fried chicken, mussels in white wine with garlic, hot dogs, trout almandine), and voilà! Central is It. And the place is always full. The dining room can be loud, but the commotion signifies the happy time that most are enjoying. *A couple of tips:* For best value, order from the $25.50 three-course lunch special menu, or dine at the bar or on the patio for weekday happy hour 5 to 7pm, and enjoy some delicious deals from the bar menu, such as French fries for $5 and a plate of three sliders for $12.

1001 Pennsylvania Ave. NW (at 11th St.). www.centralmichelrichard.com. © **202/626-0015.** Main courses $16–$32 lunch; $28 prix-fixe brunch; $17–$34 dinner. Mon–Fri 11:30am–2:30pm; Mon–Thurs 5–10pm; Fri–Sat 5–10:30pm; Sun 11am–2:30pm. Metro: Metro Center (12th and F sts. exit).

Fiola ★★★ ITALIAN   For a splash-out D.C. dining experience, book a table at this local favorite and enjoy inventive Italian cuisine and a lively atmosphere. With its wide swath of bar at the front, white banquettes, and modern art, the dining room has a glamorous, head-turning, New York feel, maybe informed by chef Fabio Trabocchi's stint there not so long ago. The main event is the seasonal Italian fare, which might include lobster ravioli in cream sauce, a fisherman's stew, veal tenderloin with morel mushrooms, or arugula salad with figs. The menus change daily—and the variety of menus is always changing, too. There's a real sense that Fabio and wife/partner Maria are having fun as they create the Fabio Grand Tasting Menu, or a Celebration of Venice menu, or—you get the idea: festive dining. Also consider the Trabocchis' swank Italian seafood eatery, **Fiola Mare** (p. 112), at Georgetown's waterfront; and the stunning two-level, waterfront **Del Mar** (p. 92), serving up tastes of coastal Spain at the Wharf, in the Southwest Waterfront.

601 Pennsylvania Ave. NW (entrance on Indiana Ave., btw. 6th and 7th sts.). www.fiola dc.com. © **202/525-1402.** Reservations recommended. Lunch a la carte main courses $16–$36; prix-fixe menus $20/$28; dinner prix-fixe menus $115/$135; tasting menu $145/$220. Mon–Fri 11:30am–2:30pm; Mon–Thurs 5–9pm; Fri–Sat 5–9:30pm. Metro: Archives–Navy Memorial or Gallery Place/Chinatown (7th and F sts. exit).

Moderate

Hill Country Barbecue Market ★★ BARBECUE   Enter Hill Country Barbecue and you leave official Washington at the door. It's just not possible to cleave to lofty attitudes and politicking when the Red Dirt Rangers or some such band are playing up a storm, as you make your way through a mess of dry-rubbed Texas barbecued ribs ("smoked low and slow over Texas oak"), skillet corn bread, and sweet potato bourbon mash. Meats are priced by weight, from $5.50 per half-pound of barbeque chicken to $28 per pound of short ribs; sides range in price from $4.95 for a standard serving of coleslaw to $10.75 for a large serving of mac and cheese. You place your order upstairs in the cafeteria/kitchen, and then carry it to your seat, either in the large dining room adjoining the cafeteria or to your table downstairs. I recommend the downstairs. That's where the bands play and where the lively **Boots Bar** is. Families, however, will want to stay upstairs, and should also know about the Kids 10 & Under Combo deal: $10 gets you one pork rib, a quarter-pound of brisket, or one-eighth chicken; a small side dish or bag of Fritos; and a choco-late chunk cookie.

410 7th St. NW (at D St.). www.hillcountry/dc.com. ℰ **202/556-2050.** Reservations recommended for downstairs. Main courses $5–$28. Mon-Thurs 11am–10pm; Fri 11am–11pm; Sat 11:30am–11pm; Sun 11:30am–9:pm. Metro: Archives–Navy Memorial or Gallery Place–Chinatown (7th and F sts. exit).

Jaleo ★★★ SPANISH   Jaleo, at age 27, is now ancient in terms of restau-rant years, but sure doesn't act it…or look it. A creative redesign added art-work by contemporary Spanish artists, foosball tables with chairs made from Vespa scooter seats, "love tables" closed off by metal curtains, and other whimsical touches, even in the restrooms, where photographed faces smile up at you from the floor. Chef extraordinaire José Andrés is 27 years older as well, and in that time has grown into a culinary and personal phenomenon, with restaurants here (**Zaytinya,** p. 98; **Oyamel, Beefsteak,** p. 110), **America Eats, Minibar by José Andrés,** and elsewhere, a cooking show, courses at Harvard, and a number of cookbooks. Not to mention his humanitarian work in fighting world hunger, for which the James Beard Foundation named him its 2018 Humanitarian of the Year. But it all started here at Jaleo, when Andrés introduced his version of Spanish tapas to the capital. Andrés and his staff may fiddle with the menu of some 60 individual small plates, but you always know you're enjoying the best tapas in the city (some say in the country). Look for fried dates wrapped in bacon and served with an apple-mustard sauce; mini-burgers made from acorn-fed, black-footed Iberico pigs; and roasted sweet onions, pine nuts, and Valdeón blue cheese. Be adventurous.

480 7th St. NW (at E St.). www.jaleo.com. ℰ **202/628-7949.** Reservations recom-mended. Lunch: Sandwiches and salads $9–$10; 4–course "quick lunch" $20. Dinner: Tapas $4–$25 (most $10–$16), "big plates" and paellas $40–$55; tasting menus $55 (classic), $70 (the Jaleo Experience), $95 (José's Way); pre-theater menu (Sun–Thurs 5–6:30pm) $30. Sun 10am–10pm; Mon 11am–10pm; Tues–Thurs 11am–11pm; Fri 11am–midnight; Sat 10am–midnight. Metro: Archives–Navy Memorial or Gallery Place–Chinatown (7th and F sts. exit).

Matchbox ★ PIZZA/AMERICAN   Named for the narrow, three-story-tall matchbox-resembling space the eatery first inhabited, Matchbox was immedi-ately so popular that it soon expanded to this Chinatown location and added many other Matchboxes throughout the area, including one on Barracks Row (521 8th St. SE) and in the U and 14th Street Corridors (1901 14th St. NW). Locals love the thin-crust pizzas cooked in 900°F wood-fired brick ovens (try the spicy meatball with crispy bacon and crushed red pepper), the appetizer of mini burgers on toasted brioche topped with onion "straws" (skinny fried onion strands), the fried chicken Cobb salad, and entrees like the pan-roasted salmon. Saturday and Sunday brunch are big, too.

713 H St. NW (btw. 7th and 8th sts.). www.matchboxrestaurants.com. ℰ **202/289-4441.** Reservations accepted. Main courses $18–$32; pizzas and sandwiches $11–$23; brunch $9–$16. Mon–Thurs 11am–10:30pm; Fri 11am–11:30pm; Sat 10am–11:30pm; Sun 10am–10:30pm. Metro: Gallery Place–Chinatown (H and 7th sts. exit).

Sliders and onion rings at Matchbox on Barracks Row.

Rasika ★★★ INDIAN   Rasika serves exquisite modern Indian food in an intimate, softly lit, shimmering champagne-hued setting, frequented by a who's who in the capital and the world beyond. Little wonder that Chef Vikram Sunderam took home the prestigious James Beard Foundation award for Best Chef, Mid-Atlantic region, in 2014. Rasika's specialties are griddle, open barbecue, tandoori, and regional dishes. The *palak chaat* (crisped spinach in a yogurt sauce), black cod with honey, duck vindaloo, and tandoori salmon are among the most popular items. Intrigued? Better get out your calendar. You can dine in the bar/lounge without advance reservations, but that, too, is usually pretty full—and the seating is too low for comfortable eating. Rasika has a sister eatery in the West End, at 1190 New Hampshire Ave. NW (www.rasikarestaurant.com/westend; ☎ 202/466-2500), a larger location with a similar menu and just as popular as the Penn Quarter Rasika.

633 D St. NW (btw. 6th and 7th sts.). www.rasikarestaurant.com. ☎ 202/637-1222. Reservations recommended. Main courses $17–$28; pre-theater menu $35. Mon–Fri 11:30am–2:30pm; Mon–Thurs 5:30–10:30pm; Fri–Sat 5–11pm. Lounge stays open throughout the day serving light meals. Metro: Archives–Navy Memorial or Gallery Place/Verizon Center (7th and F sts. exit).

Sei ★★ SUSHI   During his time in office (and even after), President Barack Obama and Michelle were regulars at this sushi restaurant in the heart of Penn Quarter. In 2018, Zagat voted it the city's best sushi restaurant, and in 2016 it was listed as one of the capital's best-looking restaurants (for its sleek all-white faux-leather interior). Need more sway to visit Sei (pronounced "say")? Just take it from me and go—you won't regret it. Try the tuna poke with pickled radish and wonton chips or the pan-seared scallops with black fried rice. You can't go wrong with any sushi on the menu, but the "Snow White" roll with eel, avocado, and roasted apple puree is perfection, as is a "Fish and Chips" combo of flounder, malt vinegar, potato crisps, and wasabi tartar. Wine, beer, and cocktails are all offered, but sake is the focus, with pages and pages of the fermented rice wine to choose from. Sei overlooks the Penn

Quarter's busiest artery, 7th Street; sit at a window-side table and you're in the best spot for people-watching, inside and out.

444 7th St. NW (at E St.). www.seirestaurant.com. ℰ **202/783-7007.** Reservations accepted. Main courses (lunch and dinner) $6–$20; sushi $9–$17; brunch $12–$18. Mon–Thurs 11:30am–10pm; Fri 11:30am–11pm; Sat 11am–11pm; Sun 11am–9pm. Metro: Gallery Place/Chinatown (7th and F sts. exit) or Archives/Navy Memorial.

The Smith ★ AMERICAN It can get loud here—very loud—but this casual American brasserie is a fun and delicious experience, and a solid for good service. Specialties at this New York City offshoot include crab-cake tots, wild mushroom flatbread, ricotta gnocchi with truffle cream, and the signature Smith burger on a brioche bun with bacon shallot marmalade. You can dine in the bar/restaurant without reservations, but expect a wait—it's always packed, especially weekend nights. Locals also come here for the brunch, often jammed with millenials and downtown regulars. Try the breakfast pot pie or vanilla bean French toast. The Smith opened a second D.C. location in the U Street Corridor (1314 U St. NW; ℰ **202/250-3900**) in 2018.

901 F St. NW (at 9th St.). www.thesmithrestaurant.com. ℰ **202/868-4900.** Reservations recommended. Main courses $11–$19 breakfast, $12–$39 lunch/dinner. Mon–Wed 8am–11pm; Thurs–Fri 8am–midnight; Sat 10am–midnight; Sun 10am–11pm. Metro: Gallery Place–Chinatown (9th St. exit) or Metro Center.

Zaytinya ★★ GREEK/TURKISH/MIDDLE EASTERN When it opened in 2002, Zaytinya, with its full-on, authentic, and wide-ranging tastes of the Middle East, Greece, and Turkey, was quite the culinary adventure for Washingtonians. (Crispy brussels sprouts with coriander seed, barberries, and garlic, oh my! Olive-oil ice cream. How interesting!) But Washington was a different place then. Eighteen years, national acclaim, and a boom of restaurant openings later, Zaytinya is an old friend. Those brussels sprouts are a favorite among the dishes that appear on the four-page menu, which, in truth, has barely changed over the years. It consists primarily of *mezze,* Mediterranean small dishes, although some entrees appear as well. Other signature dishes

Dining under the trees at Zaytinya.

include scallops in yogurt and dill sauce; roasted cauliflower with sultans, caper berries, and pine-nut puree; spanakopita with house-made filo; and *kibbeh nayeh* (Lebanese-style veal tartare with bulgur wheat, radishes, mint, and pita chips). Zaytinya is enormous, seating 230 in the attractive dining rooms, another 52 on stools at the bar, and 65 outside on the patio. Best way to enjoy Zaytinya? Bring a crowd and order an array of tapas. Instant party!

701 9th St. NW (at G St.). www.zaytinya.com. ✆ **202/638-0800.** Reservations recommended. Mezze items $6–$20 (most are under $15); lunch sandwiches $11–$15; brunch items $8.50–$15. Sun–Mon 11am–10pm; Tues–Thurs 11am–11pm; Fri-Sat 11am–midnight. Metro: Gallery Place–Chinatown (9th St. exit).

Inexpensive

Daikaya ★ JAPANESE   This restaurant is an upstairs/downstairs affair—two different places with two separate entrances—but both offer authentic Japanese specialties. Downstairs is the tiny ramen noodle house, serving the city's best ramen in a 40-seat, sparsely decorated joint that lets you concentrate on slurping up one of five broths, meat-based or vegetable, filled with aged wheat noodles and topped with a bouquet of briefly stir-fried garnishes. On the second floor, which you reach via an outside staircase, is the larger *izakaya,* or Japanese tavern. The decorative woodwork and Japanese fabrics in this dimly lit bar and grill lend an exotic feel, which tastes from the menu only amplify. You might try grilled avocado with fresh wasabi, tuna poke tartar, miso salmon with carrot puree, or the pork belly and brussels sprouts skewer. Both upstairs and downstairs are always crowded and noisy.

705 6th St. NW (at G St.). www.daikaya.com. ✆ **202/589-1600.** Reservations accepted for the upstairs *izakaya.* Ramen $14; Japanese lunch, brunch, and small-plate items $4–$14. Ramen noodle house Sun–Tues 11am–10pm, Wed–Thurs 11am–10:30pm, Fri-Sat 11am–midnight. Upstairs *izakaya* lunch Mon–Fri 11:30am–2pm; dinner Sun–Tues 5–10pm, Wed–Thurs 5–10:30pm, Fri-Sat 5pm–midnight. Metro: Gallery Place (H St./Chinatown exit).

Five Guys Burgers and Fries ★ AMERICAN   Five Guys is taking over the world! Yeah, I know it's a chain, but it's our chain, a family operation that got started in Arlington 34 years ago. You've got various iterations of hamburgers, all of which come in two sizes; assorted hot dogs; a BLT; a veggie sandwich; a grilled cheese; and your choice of regular or Cajun-style fries. One immediate difference between Five Guys and most other popular burgeries, like D.C.'s Good Stuff Eatery (p. 90), is the absence of a "magic sauce." You do get to add as many as 15 toppings, grilled onions to tomatoes, for free. D.C. currently has eight Five Guys, including this Penn Quarter/Chinatown location.

808 H St. NW (at 9th St.). www.fiveguys.com. ✆ **202/393-2900.** Burgers $6–$10; fries $4–$7. Daily 10am–10pm. Metro: Gallery Place (H St./Chinatown exit).

Taco Bamba ★ MEXICAN   It's cheap, it's loud, it's authentic, and it's delicious. Veteran restaurateur Victor Albisu has opened a round of Taco Bambas in the suburbs, but this is his first in the District, and it draws a steady flow of customers throughout the day. People come here for breakfast tacos and *huevos rancheros* in the morning, and margaritas, guacamole, and carnitas tacos at dinnertime. Sit to the left of the entrance to place your order at the counter and carry it to your table; or sit in the bar to the right of the entrance for table service. Either way, your menu options are the same. Choose from the list of about 20 different tacos, all freshly made and flavorful, half "traditional" (braised pork, goat, beef, and chicken fillings) and half *nuestras* (creative versions such as the "Sid Vicious," sort of a spicy fish and chips taco, or the "T 'N T," with crispy beef tongue and tripe). Be sure to order guacamole, which is blended from roasted avocados, and one of the specialty drinks. Choose from alcoholic, such as the strawberry cilantro margarita, or non-, like the house-made grapefruit "soda."

777 I St. NW (at 8th St.). www.tacobamba.com. ℭ **202/289-7377.** Nachos $7-$8; tostadas $7–$10; tacos $3.50 (traditional)–$4.50 (nontraditional); tortas $10–$13. Mon–Thurs 8:30am–10pm; Fri 8:30am–11pm; Sat 10am–11pm; Sun 10am–10pm. Metro: Gallery Place (H St./Chinatown exit).

MIDTOWN

In addition to the restaurants below, I highly recommend **Plume** in the Jefferson Hotel (see p. 73) for info on the restaurant and lodging) for a special-occasion meal.

Expensive

Café du Parc ★★ FRENCH   Weather permitting, you should enjoy your croissant in the morning or steak au poivre at night at an umbrella'd bistro table on the sidewalk cafe. The experience comes with the sights and sounds of Washington, some compelling, like the view of the Capitol at the other end of Pennsylvania Avenue (admittedly, you'll have to crane your neck to see it), others not so much—Big Bus tour buses and Old Town Trolleys lumbering by. But the tastes on your plate will whisk you away to France, whether Provence by way of the salade niçoise or Burgundy via the boeuf bourguignon. For something more contemporary, try the chef's specialty: Marseille-style bouillabaise. When the weather is poor, you'll find the many-windowed, blue-banquette-lined dining room upstairs a comfortable place to enjoy your repast. A much smaller casual **cafe** is on the first level.

1401 Pennsylvania Ave. NW (btw. 14th and 15th sts.). www.cafeduparc.com. ℭ **202/942-7000.** Reservations recommended. Main courses $11–$29 breakfast, $15–$37 brunch, $21–$46 lunch, $19–$35 afternoon menu, $24–$52 dinner. Daily 7am–10pm. Metro: Metro Center (13th and G St. exit).

Moderate

Bombay Club ★★ INDIAN   Located across Lafayette Square from the White House, Bombay Club has been a favorite of one administration after the other (and the reporters who cover them) since it opened in 1988. This was Ashok Bajaj's first restaurant in D.C., and though he has added a slew of well-reviewed dining rooms since, most notably **Rasika** (see p. 97), Bombay Club is special, a gracious veteran appealing to everyone. A pianist plays nightly in the dining room, which is decorated in hues of pale pink and yellow. You don't have to be from India to appreciate the cuisine (although the Indians I know say it is the real thing). Among the popular dishes are the mushroom corn samosa, a savory snack served with date tamarind chutney; the chicken *tikka,* prepared with coriander, cumin, garlic, black pepper, and yogurt; mango fish curry; and tandoor oven–roasted eggplant with sautéed onions, ginger, and yogurt. If you like spicy, try the chili- and ginger-infused duck kebab appetizer. To sample an assortment of tastes, order a house *thali.*

815 Connecticut Ave. NW (H St.). www.bombayclubdc.com. © **202/659-3727.** Reservations recommended. Main courses $17–$28; Sun brunch $24. Mon–Fri and Sun brunch 11:30am–2:30pm; Mon–Thurs 5:30–10:30pm; Fri–Sat 5–11pm; Sun 5–9pm. Metro: Farragut West (17th St. exit).

Old Ebbitt Grill ★ AMERICAN   It's midnight and you're starving. Where you gonna go? Or maybe it's 8am and you want to get a good jump on the day ahead. Who serves a full breakfast at this hour not too far from the National Mall? Or maybe you want a taste of the capital's regional dishes and a dash of insider culture. Who brings that to the table? It's the Ebbitt.

It's comforting to have a conveniently located place that's nearly always open, with four capacious bars and a menu that's known for its untrendy dishes, like burgers, trout Parmesan, and the hearty house pasta, which is stuffed with spinach, mortadella ham, and three cheeses and baked in a cream sauce. Oysters are the standout, among the best and freshest in town. (All raw-bar items are half off daily 3–6pm and after 11pm.)

Old Ebbitt has been around since 1856, first in another nearby location, and here since 1983. Some furnishings date from the early days, giving the place an old-fashioned air. Popular as the restaurant is among tourists, Ebbitt also draws attorneys from neighboring law firms, politicos visiting the White House a block away, and other downtown regulars, especially in the morning for power breakfasts, at lunchtime, and late in the evening. If you're looking for more of an inside-D.C. experience, stop by.

675 15th St. NW (btw. F and G sts.). www.ebbitt.com. © **202/347-4800.** Reservations recommended. Main courses breakfast and brunch $11–$22; lunch, dinner, and late night $14–$27. Mon–Fri 7:30am–1am; Sat–Sun 8:30am–1am. Bar until 2am Sun–Thurs, until 3am Fri–Sat. Metro: Metro Center (13th and F sts. exit).

Inexpensive

Sweetgreen ★ LIGHT FARE   Another locally launched chain, Sweetgreen was the brainchild of three eco-conscious Georgetown University students who wanted to provide homegrown, healthy options for diners. The first Sweetgreen opened in 2007; today, these popular eateries number more than 80, popping up all over D.C. and in cities throughout the country. Choose one of the 15 or so signature salads (my fave, the guacamole greens: organic mesclun, avocado, roasted chicken, red onion, tomatoes, tortilla chips, fresh lime squeeze, lime cilantro jalapeno vinaigrette), or create your own. *Note:* **Teaism** (p. 109), with a location at 800 Connecticut Ave. NW, presents another excellent option for healthy dining (weekdays only; closes at 5pm).

1901 L St. NW (at 19th St.). www.sweetgreen.com. © **202/331-3355.** Salads $10–$12. Mon–Thurs 10:30am–8pm, Fri 10:30am–6pm. Metro: Farragut North (L St. exit).

U & 14TH STREET CORRIDORS

Some of the city's trendiest restaurants and bars are right here, along 14th Street and its side streets in particular. Many don't take reservations, so you'll need to be in the right mood to go with the flow (and maybe wait a bit for dinner).

Expensive

Estadio ★★ SPANISH For Spanish tapas in the city, it would be easy to go to José Andrés' Jaleo (see p. 96), but while delicious, it lacks a certain ambience that Estadio excels at—that rustic, traditional Spanish vibe you might find in a tucked-away restaurant in Madrid. Estadio is small, and features 19th-century Spanish tile, Spanish marble, and reclaimed timber tables in a terra-cotta-hued dining room. The food adheres to traditional tastes, too. Try the wide assortment of Spanish *quesos* and *embutidos* (charcuterie). The dinner menu changes seasonally but might include roasted baby chorizos or crispy cod. Estadio also overlooks busy 14th Street, making it perfect for people-watching, day or night.

1520 14th St. NW (at Church St.). http://estadio-dc.com. ✆ **202/319-1404.** Reservations recommended. Tapas $4.50–$16; cheese plates $5–$27; charcuterie plates $9–$22. Mon–Thurs 5–10pm; Fri 11:30am–2pm, 5–11pm; Sat 11am–2pm, 5–11pm; Sun 11am–2pm, 5–9pm. Metro: U St./Cardozo (13th St. exit).

Le Diplomate ★★ FRENCH Le Diplomate looks the part of a Parisian brasserie, right down to the red banquettes, large mirrors, zinc-topped bar, little lace curtains, and windows opening to the sidewalk. And it tastes the part, too, with its menu of Gallic staples, from escargots and steak frites to trout amandine and crème brûlée. And the bread! Le Dip's house-made baguettes, cranberry walnut boules, multigrain boules, and brioches are said to be the best breads in the city. Though I wouldn't call it romantic myself, others obviously do; it's frequented by couples, including May-December types, and there's lots of hand-holding going on.

1601 14th St. NW (at Q St.). www.lediplomatedc.com. ✆ **202/332-3333.** Reservations recommended. Main courses $12–$31 lunch and brunch; $14–$38 dinner (most around $27; daily specials go as high as $52). Sat–Sun 9:30am–5pm; Sun–Thurs 5–11pm; Fri–Sat 5pm–midnight. Metro: U St./Cardozo (13th St. exit).

Moderate

CherCher Ethiopian Restaurant ★★ ETHIOPIAN The greater Washington, D.C., area is said to have the largest Ethiopian immigrant community in America, so it makes sense that Ethiopian cuisine, likewise, has found a place for itself in D.C.'s expansive dining scene. If you're already a fan of Ethiopian food or are curious to try it, D.C. is the place. And CherCher, named for the mountainous region of Ethiopia known for its beef and vegetables, remains among the best. Ethiopian expats I've met routinely rave that CherCher is as close to their grandmother's home cooking as one can get in the city. Vegetarians, especially, love the veggie platter: yellow and black

family-friendly DINING SPOTS

Most restaurants welcome families, starting, most likely, with the one in your hotel. Cafes at sightseeing attractions are always a safe bet, and so are these:

Duke's Counter (3000 Connecticut Ave. NW, Suite J; http://dukescounter.com; ℂ 202/733-4808) This London-inspired pub is located directly across the street from the National Zoo. Duke's kids' menu features mac and cheese, fish and chips, a "proper hamburger," a cheese toasty (grilled cheese), and other items, each $9 to $12. Sit inside its laidback dining room or outside on picnic tables.

Pinstripes (1064 Wisconsin Ave. NW; pinstripes.com/georgetown-washington; ℂ 202/625-6500) Your kids can bowl or play bocce here while you take your time and enjoy a meal. The kids' menu includes a starter, entrée, dessert, and beverage, all for $10—and it's half off after 5pm every Sunday if you buy an adult entrée. Sunday brunch is free for kids under 5.

Old Ebbitt Grill (p. 101) Well, first of all, the hours are kid-friendly: The place opens at 7:30am weekdays, 8:30am weekends, and then just stays open, whenever you or your children need seated sustenance. Then there's the kid-friendly Ebbitt's layout: booths and nooks and lots of strategically placed plants, which all work to contain outbursts of any sort. And finally, the children's menu offers nine different items, from the usual pizza and mac and cheese to a simply prepared fish and grilled chicken breast, each priced at $6.99, which includes one choice from a list of drinks/sweets/sides.

Ted's Bulletin (p. 90) This boisterous, laidback place in the Barracks Row section of Capitol Hill (and its twin at 1818 14th St. NW) welcomes children of all ages with a retro menu of comfort food, such as grilled cheese, Pop-Tarts (called "Ted's Tarts"), mac and cheese, and tomato soup. Breakfast is served all day, so that might decide things right there. But the kids' menu offers eight choices, PB&J to buttered pasta, each priced at $5.99. Or how about this: thick and creamy milkshakes ($7.99) in awesome flavors like Oreo and Heath almond? There's always a lot going on here, so

lentils, sautéed beets, greens, salad, yogurt, and sautéed cabbage. The special *kitfo* (beef) mixed with CherCher's homemade cottage cheese, herbal butter, cardamom, and *mitmita* (chili powder), can be ordered raw, medium, or well done, and arrives with more than enough *injera* (flat Ethiopian bread). CherCher also operates a second location in the Maryland suburb of Bethesda.

1334 9th St. NW (at O St.). www.chercherrestaurant.com. ℂ **202/299-9703.** Small plates $9–$12; large plates $13–$18; main courses $9–$17. Mon–Sat 11am–11pm; Sun noon–11pm. Metro: Mount Vernon Sq./7th St.

Cork Wine Bar & Market ★ AMERICAN If I lived in this neighborhood, I would probably hang out here all the time. Upstairs is the cozy, 60-seat wine bar, with 250 bottles on offer (most from small producers) and a whopping 50 wines by the glass. The menu features about 20 small dishes nightly, half cold, half hot, all meant to be shared. Plates of cheeses and charcuterie; roasted asparagus with garlic cream sauce; duck confit with caramelized blackberry sauce; and French fries tossed with parsley, garlic, and lemon are all recommended. On the first floor is a market and a 20-seat all-day cafe. You

103

can shop for bottles of wine and gourmet food items here, and then settle in at the cafe to enjoy something from the menu of freshly prepared sandwiches and salads, quiches, spreads, and baked goods, or else take everything to go.

1805 14th St. NW (btw. S and T sts.). www.corkdc.com. ✆ **202/265-2675.** Reservations accepted. Cafe and brunch items $7–$17; dinner small plates $7–$20. Cafe/market: Daily 11am. Wine bar: Sun brunch at 11am; dinner nightly 5pm–midnight. Metro: U St./Cardozo (13th St. exit).

Maydan ★★★ MIDDLE EASTERN/NORTH AFRICAN   I opened the unmarked, dusky-blue arched door, stepping into a dimly lit antechamber leading to Maydan, and it pulled me in. That's how it felt. Past an enormous open-fire hearth sending delicious smells of roasting meats and smoky spices wafting through the two-level atrium, past the surrounding tables and prep area I went. Artful Islamic shapes flourished in wooden screens and tabletops, and lights dangled from long wooden beaded cords. At the end of the bar, I found my spot, no stool, but just enough room to stand and sip a glass of crisp sauvignon blanc, scoop up the creamy hummus and fatoosh salad with flatbread hot from the clay oven, and munch on chunks of roasted barramundi smeared with *zhough*, a spicy condiment tasting of cilantro and cumin.

Open since late 2017, Maydan shot to everyone's immediate attention, listed by both *Food & Wine* and *GQ* as one of the top new restaurants in America. Michelin also listed it in 2019 as a favorite. Its name, appropriately, means "gathering place." And that's just what Maydan does—it gathers you in and makes you feel at home. And, as I discovered that evening, the food is scrumptious. If I could recommend only one restaurant for you to go to, this is the one. But first you have to find it! Be sure to read the directions to Maydan on its website, and then look for that dusky-blue door.

1346 Florida Ave. NW (at 14th St.). www.maydandc.com. ✆ **202/370-3696.** Reservations recommended. Small plates $6–$22; large plates start at $35. Sun 5–10pm; Mon–Sat 5–11pm; bar open until midnight weekdays (until 3am Fri–Sat). Metro: U St./Cardozo (13th St. exit).

Inexpensive

Ben's Chili Bowl ★ AMERICAN   Ben's opened in 1958 and it looks like it, with its old-fashioned storefront, Formica counters, and red barstools. Its staying power is impressive enough, but Ben's history is also compelling: When riots broke out throughout the city following the assassination of Dr. Martin Luther King, Jr., in April 1968, Ben's stayed open to serve police officers, firefighters, and anyone who needed sustenance, even as surrounding establishments closed or were destroyed.

On that basis alone, a visit to Ben's is warranted. You'll find yourself among a cross-section of locals: by day, workers from nearby municipal office buildings, students, and shoppers; by night, nightclubbers, cops, and neighborhood regulars. Often, it seems that everyone knows everyone else, including the Ali family, who own Ben's. Walls are hung with photographs that cover the history of the city and of Ben's, and include snapshots of the many celebrities who've dined here, from President Obama to Mary J. Blige.

Folks go to Ben's for the homey ambience, and for the ultra-cheap and usually tasty food. Most famous is the half-smoke sandwich, a ¼-pound, half-beef, half-pork smoked sausage, served inside a warm bun and, if you so desire, smothered with mustard, chopped onions, and a spicy chili sauce. I went to Ben's recently with a friend and tried the half-smoke for the first time, sans the chili sauce and onions. And though it is near sacrilege in this city to admit it, I didn't care for it. My friend, who ordered the half-smoke plus cheese fries, says it's because I omitted the chili sauce and onions. Maybe. But I do like Ben's flavorful turkey burger sub and the vegetarian chili (vegetarians take note: Ben's has a few veggie-friendly options). Ben's has locations now at Nationals Park, in the Atlas District, and at National Airport.

1213 U St. NW (btw. 12th and 13th sts.). www.benschilibowl.com. ℭ **202/667-0058.** Reservations not accepted. Main courses $4–$10. No credit cards (there's an ATM here). Mon–Thurs 6am–2am; Fri 6am–4am; Sat 7am–4am; Sun 11am–midnight. Metro: U St./Cardozo (13th St. exit).

Colada Shop ★ CUBAN   This tiny shop has a big personality. Lively Cuban music splashes out to the patio; in fair weather, the window-front opens upward, creating an alfresco counter space for chatting. Munching diners sit on stools across from one another, inside and outside. The spirit is exuberant, the food is swell, and the prices right: *croquettas* (fritters filled with your choice of ham, chicken, or mushrooms gently blended with a bechamel sauce into a light concoction), two for $3.50; or the famous Cuban sandwich of ham, slow-roasted pork, Swiss cheese, pickles, mustard, and aioli on Cuban bread for $9.98. A dozen versions of coffee are on offer, from the Cubano (a shot of coffee sweetened with whipped sugar) to café con leche (a Cubano with hot steamed milk). And then there are the potent cocktails: daiquiris, pina coladas, mojitos, cuba libres, and the like, each $8. Colada Shop, together with Taqueria Nacional (see below), its Mexican neighbor one door down, turn this block of T Street into a party. But if you're here just to enjoy your empanadas and pastelitos, head to the back of the shop toward the kitchen and hang a right to find the quieter back room, with leather sofas, wicker chairs, and stools at high tops. Or head to the lovely rooftop garden, open daily, weather permitting, for cocktails, Caribbean tunes, and Colada's favorite bites.

1405 T St. NW (at 14th St.). www.coladashop.com. ℭ **202/332-8800.** Reservations not accepted. All items under $10. Sun 8am–10pm; Mon–Thurs 7am–9pm; Fri 7am–11pm; Sat 8am–11pm; Sun 8am–9pm. Metro: U St./Cardozo (13th St. exit) or take the DC Circulator.

Taqueria Nacional ★ MEXICAN   Just a few steps away from noisy 14th Street is this pretty little taqueria, housed inside a former post office and decorated with handsome Mexican tiles and grillwork, an old chandelier, and a vision of the Blessed Mother painted on a worn plaster wall. It seats 45 max at a jumble of brightly colored tables; throughout Saturday and Sunday brunch (breakfast quesadilla, huevos rancheros, and Mexican fritters), and from weeknight happy hour on, all tables are usually occupied. The menu is short but affordable, featuring fresh, authentic tacos and custom-made quesadillas and tostadas. Favorites, like carnitas and fish tacos, are always on the menu, but the taqueria seems always to be inventing new tastes, like the shrimp, cauliflower, and cotija cheese tacos. Yucca fries, salads, guacamole, and other sides are available. The beverage list includes full bar offerings, and features Mexican *aguas frescas* (water blended with fruit, sugar, and other ingredients) prepared in the traditional nonalcoholic form, as well as mixed with rum or tequila; locally brewed draft beer; and a $6.95 margarita.

1409 T St. NW (at 14th St.). www.taquerianacional.co. ℂ **202/299-1122.** Reservations not accepted. All items under $10. Sun 10am–9pm; Mon–Wed noon–10pm; Thurs–Fri noon–11pm; Sat 10am–11pm. Metro: U St./Cardozo (13th St. exit) or take the DC Circulator.

ADAMS MORGAN

Expensive

Tail Up Goat ★★★ MEDITERRANEAN   Fans call Tail Up Goat "Rose's Luxury with reservations." It has the same warm and whimsical vibe, as well as a menu of otherworldly combinations of tastes, similar to what you'll find at that Barracks Row restaurant (p. 89). At Tail Up Goat that means plates of crispy salt cod with smoked cauliflower, a ricotta tart with garlic chives, seared scallops with shaved green tomato and candied olives, or the *gorro de bruja* (which literally translates to "little witch's hat") pasta. If there are more than two of you, you'll want to sit at a table in the dining room, with its view of the open kitchen at the back. But if you're dining alone or with a pal, sit on a cushioned stool in the cozy bar, where you'll be coddled and amused by the charming bartenders. It's also where you can snag a seat if you haven't snagged a reservation—the bar is reserved for walk-ins.

1827 Adams Mill Rd. NW (entrance on Lanier Pl.). www.tailupgoat.com. ℂ **202/986-9600.** Reservations recommended. Small plates $10–$16; larger plates $16–$27. Mon–Thurs 5:30–10pm; Fri–Sun 5–10pm. Metro: Woodley Park–Zoo, with a walk, or take the DC Circulator.

Moderate

Brothers and Sisters ★ ASIAN AMERICAN   Upon entering the stylish Line hotel (p. 71), you'll suddenly find you've also walked right into this lobby-centered restaurant. But don't worry; the food is anything but corporate-hotel generic. Erik Bruner-Yang (also from Maketto; p. 85) is the hipster chef behind Brothers and Sisters' menu. You'll find straightforward fare here, like a Caesar salad and French fries, but also inventive dishes with an Asian flair, like oysters in a kimchi sauce, roasted brussels sprouts with an urfa ranch on top, or wide, thick noodles with fennel sausage and celery greens in a spicy red sauce. The avocado and hearts of palm salad has a light, lemony taste, perfect for spring/summer, and the salmon arrives with a soy glaze and stewed vegetables. Glimpses of the hotel as its former church self are all around, like the soaring atrium and balcony and the enormous chandelier made from organ pipes dangling above you. Another restaurant, **A Rake's Progress,** located on that balcony above, is only open for dinner. Arrive early and you'll find serious millennial types tucked into their laptops typing away while drinking espressos and cappuccinos. Come late and the Line's two bars, which flank Brothers and Sisters, are hopping, serving not-so-serious cocktails like the "Lobby Hi-Ball" and "It's You and Me and We are Back Again."

1770 Euclid St. NW (at Columbia Rd.). www.thelinehotel.com. © **202/864-4180.** Reservations accepted. Snacks $7–$12; shareable courses $15–$28. Daily 6:30am–midnight; afternoon tea 4–5:30pm; bar open until 2am Mon–Thurs, until 3am Fri–Sat. Metro: Woodley Park–Zoo, with a walk, or take the DC Circulator.

Inexpensive

Amsterdam Falafelshop ★ MIDDLE EASTERN/DUTCH Inspired by the falafel shops of Holland, the owners opened their own D.C. version in 2004, and other locations since, including a shop in the U & 14th Street Corridors at 1830 14th St. NW. The shop does a steady business all day among people who just love these toasted pita sandwiches stuffed with fried balls of mashed chickpeas, topped with as many of the 22 self-serve garnishes as you want, from crunchy onion to hummus. You can dine in or on the patio, but most customers carry out.

2425 18th St. NW (at Belmont Rd.). www.falafelshop.com. © **202/234-1969.** Reservations not accepted. Falafel sandwiches $6–$9; Dutch fries $4–$5. Sun–Mon 11am–midnight; Tues–Thurs 11am–2:30am; Fri–Sat 11am–4am. Metro: Woodley Park–Zoo, with a walk, or take the DC Circulator.

Julia's Empanadas ★ LATIN For years, I'll admit I avoided this hole-in-the-wall shop for what it looked like on the outside. But like so many things, it's what on the inside that counts. Since 1993, Julia's has baked her fresh, homemade empanadas daily, serving a steady stream of customers who keep coming back for her spiced, filled pastry. What's available changes as the day goes on, but if it's on the menu, try the Jamaican-style empanada with ground beef, potato, onions, curry, and spices, or the chorizo with black beans, white rice, onions, and spices. If you're out clubbing in the neighborhood, do what D.C.'s barhoppers do, and stop here for a snack in the wee hours. There aren't seats inside, so grab your empanada to go or walk and eat. Other locations are in Dupont Circle (1221 Connecticut Ave. NW) and Brightwood (6325 Georgia Ave. NW).

2452 18th St. NW (at Columbia Rd.). www.juliasempanadas.com. © **202/328-6232.** Reservations not accepted. $10 minimum credit card. All empanadas $5. Mon–Wed 11am–midnight; Thurs 11am–2am; Fri–Sat 11am–4am; Sun 11am–8pm. Metro: Woodley Park–Zoo, with a walk, or take the DC Circulator.

DUPONT CIRCLE

In addition to the restaurants below, consider the swank Italian eatery **Urbana** in the Hotel Palomar (p. 74).

Expensive

Al Tiramisu ★★ ITALIAN   Al Tiramisu is a find, and those who have found it include George and Amal Clooney, Hillary Clinton, and Magic Johnson. I imagine celebrities like it for the same reason everyone else does: the infectious ebullience of chef/owner Luigi Diotaiuti, who bounces out from behind a curtain to greet you as you enter; the unpretentious feeling of this snug little restaurant, which is essentially one long room in the bottom of a Dupont Circle town house (people do complain that it feels cramped, but I like it); and a menu that includes excellently prepared grilled fish, house-made spinach-ricotta ravioli with butter and sage sauce, and grilled lamb chops. This is a place to come for romance, for cheering up, for having a good time with friends, and Tiramisu has been so obliging since it opened in 1996.

2014 P St. NW (btw. 19th and 20th sts.). www.altiramisu.com. © **202/467-4466.** Reservations recommended. Main courses $23–$33. Mon–Thurs noon–2pm, 5–10pm; Fri noon–2pm, 5–10:30pm; Sat 5–10:30pm; Sun 5–10pm. Metro: Dupont Circle (19th St./ South exit).

Iron Gate ★★ MEDITERRANEAN   This romantic restaurant lies hidden away on a quiet Dupont Circle side street. But it's no secret—just try booking a reservation. Whether you sit in the long, narrow carriageway fronting the restaurant, in the wisteria-canopied brick courtyard, or in the cozy banquette-filled and paneled main dining room, you'll be smitten. (In winter, I would choose the main dining room, where the open kitchen and wood-burning hearth add a wonderfully smoky aroma and special glow.) Plates are to share or not and might include such delectable tastes as caramelized ricotta gnocchi, oak-grilled asparagus on a bed of lentil hummus, and, in season, Maryland soft-shell crab. Be sure to leave room for one of the delicious desserts, the crispy Greek yeast doughnuts with orange blossom syrup a particular favorite.

1734 N St. NW (17th St.). www.irongaterestaurantdc.com. © **202/524-5202.** Reservations recommended. Brunch/lunch a la carte dishes $6–$17; dinner a la carte $6–$75 (entrees for 2 people). Tues–Fri 11:30am–2pm; Sat–Sun 11am–2pm; Mon–Thurs 5:30–10pm; Fri–Sat 5:30–11pm; Sun 5:30–9pm. Metro: Dupont Circle (19th St. exit).

Komi ★★★ MODERN MEDITERRANEAN   There is no printed menu at this intimate, graciously serviced restaurant. Instead, chef/owner Johnny Monis sends out 12 or more tastes of what can only be described as "divine inspirations." These might include dates filled with mascarpone, or a brioche with monkfish liver, or charred octopus with tomato and fig. (Komi will accommodate those with allergies or dietary restrictions; just be sure to call ahead.) This is not a place for loud conversation, nor is it hoity-toity. I wouldn't even describe it as the domain of foodies, although foodies certainly flock here. A dinner at Komi is really about slowing down for a short while, focusing on your taste buds, and being renewed. Note that Komi serves only wine and beer, no cocktails.

Tip: If you can't book a table at Komi, try Chef Monis' **Little Serow,** a stools-only, walk-ins-only restaurant in the basement of the building next door. The Northern Thai menu is prix-fixe, $54 for seven courses served family-style, and authentic. You'll know you've found Little Serow when you see the line.

1509 17th St. NW (near P St.). www.komirestaurant.com. ⓒ **202/332-9200.** Reservations a must. Prix-fixe menu $165 per person. Tues–Sat 5:30–9:30pm. Metro: Dupont Circle (Q St. exit).

Tabard Inn ★★ AMERICAN   Locals head to the Tabard for the freshly made doughnuts and whipped cream served at weekend brunch. (Actually, the doughnuts are available daily for breakfast, too, but that will be our little secret.) Other items also prove a potent lure, such as bacon-wrapped quail, shrimp ravioli with seaweed salad, and seared diver scallops with ginger sweet potatoes. The fact that all of this is served in an absolutely charming, sky-lit room (just past the comfy old wood-paneled lounge, where live jazz performances are offered Sun–Tues eves.) and adjoining covered courtyard doesn't hurt. If you can't get in for a meal, do stop for a cocktail, just so you can experience the inn's lovely ambience (it's also a hotel; see p. 75).

1739 N St. NW (at 17th St., in the Hotel Tabard Inn). www.tabardinn.com/dining. ⓒ **202/ 331-8528.** Reservations recommended. Main courses $2–$19 breakfast, $12–$26 lunch and brunch, $21–$38 dinner. Mon–Fri 7–10am; Sat–Sun 7–9am and 10am–3:30pm (brunch); daily 11:30am–2:30pm; nightly for dinner starting at 5:30pm. Metro: Dupont Circle (19th St./South exit).

Inexpensive

Pizzeria Paradiso ★ PIZZA/ITALIAN   Pizzeria Paradiso has been around since before you were born. Okay, well, certainly before the gourmet pizza trend was born. It's 29 years old and remains a favorite among a wide field of contenders. Paradiso cooks its pizzas in a domed, wood-burning stone oven that can withstand 650-degree heat, which gives the pizza a light but doughier crust than its rivals. The pies come in 9- and 12-inch sizes, and the 44-item toppings list includes everything imaginable, from mussels to vegan mozzarella. Paninis and salads get high marks as well. Pizzeria Paradiso serves wine and also has a **Birreria,** where patrons interested in microbrews and handcrafted beers can select from 13 drafts and more than 200 bottles. Paradiso's other locations are in Georgetown, at 3282 M St. NW (ⓒ **202/337-1245**), and in Old Town Alexandria, at 124 King St. (ⓒ **703/837-1245**).

2003 P St. NW (btw. 20th and 21st sts.). www.eatyourpizza.com. ⓒ **202/223-1245.** Reservations not accepted. Pizzas $12–$21; sandwiches and salads $6–$13. Mon–Thurs 11:30am–11pm; Fri–Sat 11:30am–midnight; Sun noon–11pm. Metro: Dupont Circle (19th St./South exit).

Teaism Dupont Circle ★ ASIAN FUSION   This homegrown teahouse enterprise currently has three D.C. locations, each similar in their menus of bento boxes, aromatic teas, savory sandwiches, and sweets, though they differ in appearance. This one, in Dupont Circle, is the original, a homey, two-level restaurant and shop tucked inside a century-old building with French windows that overlook the tree-lined street. The Penn Quarter's Teaism is busier, as you might expect from the neighborhood, and its tea shop is situated separately, one storefront away from the restaurant. No matter the Teaism, you'll find these are casual eateries, where you order from a menu that changes seasonally but might include curried chicken, udon noodle soup, Korean beef brisket sandwiches, and a constantly updated inventory of about 36 teas. All three teahouses serve an afternoon tea of savories and sweets, from 2:30 to 5:30pm, for $25 per person ($30 with alcohol).

Visit **Teaism Lafayette Square,** 800 Connecticut Ave. NW (℗ **202/835-2233**), near the White House, and **Teaism Penn Quarter ★,** 400 8th St. NW (℗ **202/638-6010**); both branches serve beer and wine, and the Penn Quarter Teaism also serves cocktails.

2009 R St. NW (btw. Connecticut and 21st sts.). www.teaism.com. ℗ **202/667-3827.** Reservations not accepted. All items $3–$14. Mon–Fri 8am–10pm; Sat–Sun 9am–10pm. Metro: Dupont Circle (Q St. exit).

FOGGY BOTTOM/WEST END

Moderate

Founding Farmers ★ AMERICAN   An international clientele gathers at Founding Farmers, thanks to the fact that the restaurant is on the ground floor of the International Monetary Fund, 1 block from World Bank Headquarters, and within a short walk of the Pan American Health Organization and the State Department. But the real reason for its popularity may be that it's one of only a few real restaurants (as opposed to fast-food joints and delis) in this neck of the woods. So expect a full house, a frenetic ambience, and noise. That's especially true downstairs, which holds a big bar as well as booths and tables. Upstairs tends to be quieter, with silo-shaped booths and small clusters of intimate seating. So, what to order? Fans enthuse about the fancy cocktails, the bourbon-battered French toast at brunch, and, for lunch and dinner, the crispy shrimp; signature dishes like Yankee pot roast and chicken pot pie; and the griddled farm bread topped with brie, onion jam, and sliced apples. The options include a number of meatless entrees. Founding Farmers has several popular siblings, including **Farmers Fishers Bakers** (www.farmersfishersbakers.com), on the Georgetown waterfront at 3000 K St. NW.

1924 Pennsylvania Ave. NW (at 20th St.). www.wearefoundingfarmers.com. ℗ **202/822-8783.** Reservations recommended. Main courses $6–$15 breakfast and brunch, $12–$37 (most under $20) lunch and dinner. Mon 7am–10pm; Tues–Thurs 7am–11pm; Fri 7am–midnight; Sat 8:30am–midnight; Sun 8:30am–10pm. Metro: Foggy Bottom.

Inexpensive

Beefsteak ★ VEGETARIAN   Inside the wide, window-wrapped, street-level corner room of George Washington University's Engineering Building is another José Andrés culinary revelation, this one serving cheap, freshly made-to-order vegetable dish assemblages. If you've ever been to a Chipotle, you'll have an idea how it works. You step up to the counter and order one of four suggested favorites or else give instructions to the line cooks to create your own. First you choose your desired veggies from a wide assortment; then your grain (bulgur, quinoa, or rice); then your sauce (black bean, cilantro, garlic yogurt, or lemon honey); and finally, your crunchy toppings, everything from toasted almonds to chopped scallions. Your vegetables are flash-cooked and all ingredients assembled in a recyclable container to eat there in the sunny room or take out. (Beefsteak does offer a couple of meaty add-ons, such as chicken sausage, for those who simply can't do without.) Overwhelmed by choices, on my last visit I opted for the Eden, which combined quinoa, snap peas, edamame, green beans, asparagus, broccoli, cilantro, garlic yogurt sauce, romaine, scallions, toasted sesame seeds, and lemon honey dressing. A second Beefsteak is located at 1528 Connecticut Ave. NW (℃ **202/986-7597**), in the Dupont Circle neighborhood.

800 22nd St. NW (at I St.). www.beefsteakveggies.com. ℃ **202/296-1439.** Reservations not accepted. All items under $10. Daily 10:30am–9pm. Metro: Foggy Bottom.

GEORGETOWN

The closest Metro stop to Georgetown is the Blue Line's Foggy Bottom station; from there you can walk or catch the DC Circulator bus on Pennsylvania Avenue.

Expensive

1789 ★★ AMERICAN   One of the city's top tables, the 1789 is the standard-bearer for old-world charm. The restaurant's six dining rooms occupy a renovated Federal-period house on a back street in Georgetown. Equestrian and historical prints, tables laid with Limoges china and silver, and antique furnishings throughout add touches of elegance. Women usually dress up and, while not required anymore, men still wear jackets to dinner. Romancing couples like Nicole Kidman and Keith Urban, world leaders like President Obama and German Chancellor Angela Merkel, and locals celebrating birthdays and anniversaries are among those who dine here for the sense of momentousness the 1789 confers upon any occasion.

The kitchen has seen chefs come and go in the past few years, but the 1789, at 60 years old, is an old hand at handling change. Its cuisine has always been and always will be American, the emphasis more and more on produce grown on local farms and meats, seafood, and poultry bought "direct from their native regions." As classically formal as the 1789 is, the menu is thoroughly modern—for instance, the salmon is served with sunflower seeds and chorizo beurre blanc, and the lobster bisque comes with Parmesan brittle. One thing you can be sure of is that your meal will be luscious.

1226 36th St. NW (at Prospect St.). www.1789restaurant.com. ℃ **202/965-1789.** Reservations recommended. Main courses $32–$59. Mon–Thurs 5–10pm; Fri–Sat 5–11pm; Sun 5–10pm.

Chez Billy Sud ★★ FRENCH   With its pale green walls and gold-framed mirrors and prints, parquet floor, and wall-length banquette, Chez Billy Sud could only be French. That's how it seems to me, anyway. (The green hue of the walls reminds me of the gift boxes used by the Parisian tearoom and

Le Bar à Vin at Chez Billy Sud.

macaron shop Ladurée, which coincidentally recently opened a location in Georgetown, at 3060 M St. NW.) The cuisine showcases the dishes of southern France, satisfying the hankerings of Francophiles with escargots, steak frites, sautéed trout with fennel puree, and a flourless *torte au chocolat*. A courtyard offers additional seating in fine weather and also leads to Chez Billy's sidekick wine bar, **Le Bar à Vin,** equally charming with its exposed brick walls, dark-stained wood floor, and copper-topped bar.

1039 31st St. NW (btw. M and K sts.). www.chezbillysud.com. © **202/965-2606.** Reservations recommended. Main courses $12–$26 lunch and brunch, $21–$38 dinner. Tues–Fri 11:30am–2pm; Sun–Thurs 5–10pm; Fri–Sat 5–11pm; Sat–Sun 11am–2pm.

Fiola Mare ★★★ ITALIAN   Strictly speaking, the Potomac River is not *Il Mare,* but as the watery view for one of the trendiest and certainly one of the finest seafood restaurants in D.C., the river certainly will do. Fiola Mare's stiffest competition comes from its own siblings, **Fiola** (p. 95) in the Penn Quarter and **Del Mar** (p. 92) at the Wharf in the Southwest Waterfront. Sit at one of the many outdoor balcony tables and you'll be gazing out at Roosevelt Island, Key Bridge, and a slice of Georgetown's waterfront to your right, and the Watergate apartments and the Kennedy Center to your left. Great views are also available within. The sprawling modern interior has a front bar and a back bar, and more than one dining area in between. The quietly proficient staff serve up a slate of specialty cocktails, like the standout Bellini. Fabio Trabocchi shines in his mastery of Italian seafood (for Spanish takes on seafood, head to Del Mar). A recent dinner started with a generous portion of top-grade tuna tartare, graced with a hint of tomato essence, followed by a too-generous portion of grilled arctic char with sea salt and salsa. Also done to perfection was a bowl of lobster ravioli in a simple, herb-scented lobster broth, together with a fresh, juicy lobster claw and tail. End with the *bombolini:* half a dozen ricotta doughnuts dusted with sugar, complemented by a warm chocolate sauce and a generous portion of vanilla gelato bearing chocolate crunches.

3050 K St. NW, Suite 101 (at 31st St. NW and the Washington Harbour waterfront). www.fiolamaredc.com. © **202/525-1402.** Reservations recommended. Prix-fixe light lunch menu $26. Main courses $20–$36 lunch, $16–$34 brunch, $25–$65 dinner. Tues–Fri 11:30am–2:30pm; Sat 11:30am–2pm; Sun 11am–2pm; Sun–Thurs 5–10pm; Fri–Sat 5–10:30pm.

Moderate

Martin's Tavern ★ AMERICAN   Martin's turns 87 in 2020, and in its lifetime has served every president from Harry Truman to George W. Bush. The tavern is best known as the place where JFK, then a U.S. senator, proposed to Jacqueline Bouvier on June 24, 1953. Hard-backed wooden booths line the walls of the restaurant, and many bear plaques identifying the former president or famous person who dined within; #3 is the "Proposal Booth." Fourth-generation Billy Martin, Jr. is usually behind the bar, attending to the regulars who frequent the place. That's largely what Martin's is these days: a restaurant for folks from the neighborhood, many of them generational iterations of earlier customers. People who aren't regulars sometimes feel left out, but that's part of the experience, too. "Tavern" is exactly the word to describe Martin's food, which is okay American and, in some cases, Colonial American: Shepherd's pie and Brunswick stew are listed, and so is Martin's Delight, which is roasted turkey on toast, smothered in rarebit sauce. Martin's offers a bit of old-guard Washington and Georgetown you're not going to get anywhere else, and that's mostly why I recommend it.

1264 Wisconsin Ave. NW (at N St.). www.martinstavern.com. © **202/333-7370.** Reservations accepted. Main courses $10–$22 lunch/brunch; $16–$40 dinner. Sun 8am–1:30am; Mon–Thurs 11am–1:30am; Fri 11am–2:30am; Sat 8am–2:30am.

Inexpensive

Via Umbria ★ ITALIAN   For my family, no visit to D.C. is complete without a stop at this Italian market, cafe, Umbrian ceramics shop, popular brunch spot, Italian cooking–class venue, and, every Friday and Saturday evening, a place for "shared experiences around a table with others" at the chef's table. It's an authentic taste of both Umbria and the Georgetown neighborhood. The light-filled second floor stages the cooking classes, Saturday and Sunday brunches, and chef's table dinners in front of the open kitchen. The street-level cafe/market/shop is jammed to the gills with cool gifty things, like gorgeous hand-painted Italian ceramics (a visiting painter is sometimes on hand to sign his work), as well as Italian wines and beer and meats and cheeses. So, shop away if you desire. Head to the cafe and order delicious *sfogliatelle* (Italian pastries) at breakfast or one of the mouthwatering paninis—I've enjoyed the Verdure (broccoli, smoked burrata, salsa) and porchetta (shaved fennel, provolone, greens, pork, and aioli)—at lunch. The menu also offers pasta dishes and salads. After 5, Via Umbria sells dinners to eat in, if you like, but most take it to go, the menu changing daily. Or consider signing up for a communal dinner

Visit Shaw by day and you'll encounter conference-goers (the convention center lies within its northwest D.C. boundaries), residents, and people who work here. Few tourists, little hustle-bustle. Except for the **African American Civil War Memorial and Museum** and the **Mary McLeod Bethune Council House** (p. 188 and 189), and the smattering of retail shops on or near U Street NW, there are no notable daytime attractions worth a detour from the sites awaiting you on the Mall and elsewhere. I invite you instead to visit Shaw in the evening, to dine, perchance to drink.

Overnight, it seems, the district has turned into the place to go for some of the city's best dining and drinking experiences. At least 25 restaurants, bakeries, coffeehouses, and bars have sprouted here in the last couple of years, James Beard Award winners among them. You may be puzzled when you arrive, though—for now, at least, Shaw looks like what it was and still is: an old neighborhood of historic churches, modest housing, and corner shops, even amid the rising luxury condos and construction

sites. The restaurants are scattered over several streets, rather than primarily along a single stretch or two (as they are in the U & 14th Street Corridors or on 8th Street SE in Barracks Row). In fact, some of the hottest spots are hidden down alleyways. You have to seek them out. Among my favorites are:

1250 9th St. NW between N and M streets: Sharing the same street address, but with separate locations right next to one another on the block, are these three different and individually owned establishments: **All Purpose Pizzeria** (www.allpurposedc.com; © **202/849-6174**), creating fresh takes on pizzas and classics such as eggplant parm; **Espita Mezcaleria** (www.espitadc.com; © **202/621-9695**), with excellent southern Mexican cuisine and an awesome selection of mescals; and **Buttercream Bakery** (www.buttercreammdc.com; © **202/735-0102**), serving and selling sausage-stuffed breakfast bombs in the morning and "funfetti" cookie cream pies for take-home desserts. Now look directly across Ninth Street and what do you see? The convention center, right?

upstairs. If it's a pleasant day, I recommend taking out those paninis and Italian pastries and walking up the street to Montrose Park on R St. for a picnic.

1525 Wisconsin Ave. NW (btw. P and Q sts.). www.viaumbria.com. © **202/333-3904.** Reservations required for chef's-table dinners. Cafe: All food items under $15; chef's-table dinners: $75–$125 per person, not including wine. Sun 9am–7pm; Tues–Sat 9am–9pm.

WOODLEY PARK & CLEVELAND PARK

Moderate

Indique ★ INDIAN   Staff from the Indian Embassy and others who know authentic Indian cuisine consider Indique's regional dishes the real deal. Favorite dishes are too many to mention, but definitely order the vegetable samosa *chaat*, the chicken curry, and the lamb *vindaloo*. The two-level town house offers two different dining spaces: Upstairs is a beautiful room of

But hiding in plain sight within that glass facade is **Unconventional Diner** (1207 9th St. NW; www.unconventionaldiner. com; ☏ **202/847-0122**), open for breakfast and lunch weekdays, brunch weekends, and dinner Monday through Saturday, serving the most cunning little takes on diner food (the meatloaf has a Sriracha glaze, for example) in one large room decorated with colorful pop art and including a cafe, bar, and banquette-filled dining area.

In Blagden Alley (more like a quaint little brick-paved village with its nookish space behind buildings on 9th and 10th sts. and M and N sts.): **The Dabney** (www.thedabney.com; ☏ **202/450-1015**), whose chef, Jeremiah Langhorne, took home the 2018 James Beard Award for Best Chef: Mid-Atlantic for his inventive regional cuisine; and its adjoining **Dabney Cellar,** a basement nook with fun cocktails, raw bar fare, cheeses, and snacks; **Tiger Fork** (www.tigerforkdc; ☏ **202/733-1152**), bringing "Hong Kong's gritty, badass culinary culture" to D.C., from salt-based oysters to chili wontons; and the **Columbia Room** (www.columbiaroomdc.com; ☏ **202/316-9396**), the gift of Derek Brown—esteemed mixologist, spirits historian, and perennial James Beard Award nominee—offering a punch garden, spirits library, and a four-course tasting menu of cocktails and snacks.

On O Street NW at 8th Street: Convivial (www.convivialdc.com; ☏ **202/525-2870**) is French chef Cedric Maupillier's interpretation of "an American cafe," and it's as merry an experience as the name suggests, with a full house of happy diners enjoying the steak frites with green peppercorn and cognac sauce followed by sticky cinnamon buns or meringue.

1015 7th St. NW, between New York Avenue and L Street NW: Kinship and **Metier** (www.kinshipdc.com; ☏ **202/737-7700**) both serve creative contemporary American cuisine, in a casual dining room upstairs at Kinship and in the acclaimed and more intimate and formal, $200-a-person tasting room/ restaurant Metier downstairs; *Washingtonian* magazine named Metier the city's best restaurant in 2018.

brightly painted marigold and lime-hued walls, with the best tables overlooking the atrium; downstairs has a lively window-fronted bar area, a good spot for watching commuters bustling in and out of the Cleveland Park subway station and all else that's happening on busy Connecticut Avenue.

3512–14 Connecticut Ave. NW (btw. Porter and Ordway sts.). www.indique.com. ☏ **202/ 244-6600**. Reservations accepted. Main courses $12–$24; Sun brunch $25. Fri noon–3pm; Sat–Sun 11am–3pm; Sun 5:30–10pm; Mon–Thurs 5–10pm; Fri 5–10:30pm; Sat 5:30–10:30pm. Metro: Cleveland Park (Connecticut Ave. west exit).

Medium Rare ★ AMERICAN   If you like surprises, then this American steakhouse is not for you. But if you like what you know, and what you like is steak, then this is the best place for it. This casual restaurant has been serving the same thing for 9 years—and it's not changing anytime soon. The menu is always a prix-fixe selection of rustic bread, mixed green salad, and *culotte* steak (a sirloin strip) with "secret sauce" and hand-cut fries, and it's delicious. (A grilled portobello mushroom is available off-menu for vegetarians.) The only decision you have to make is whether to get the apple pie, key lime pie,

BUT FIRST, coffee

Starbucks isn't the only coffee game in town anymore. Independent coffee shops are pouring into D.C. and satisfying Washingtonians' love for a great cuppa joe while also supporting local businesses. Most are open early (6–7am) to late (8pm), and serve pastries or sandwiches. Seattle, eat your coffee-loving heart out.

- Owner Joel Finkelstein takes his brew seriously at **Qualia Coffee** (3917 Georgia Ave. NW; ☏ **202/248-6423**). The beans are carefully sourced from around the world and roasted frequently and in small batches on-site. The coffee is always fresh, served within 3 days of roasting. Grab a bite here, too, and sit outside on the patio.

- Two former Marines who served together in Afghanistan established the original **Compass Coffee** (1535 7th St. NW; ☏ **202/838-3139**) in 2014, and it's grown to six more locations downtown. The coffee menu regularly rotates nine varieties/flavors, and the interiors are spacious and airy, with free Wi-Fi.

- Whether you're staying at the stylish Line Hotel in Adams Morgan or just stopping by, **The Cup We All**

Race 4 (1770 Euclid St. NW; ☏ **202/588-0525**) offers Counter Culture coffee drinks, herbal teas, and a selection of pastries and sandwiches. The classic cappuccino and maple latte with oat milk are excellent, although prices rival Starbucks' most expensive drinks.

- Just steps from Dupont Circle, **Emissary** (2032 P St. NW; ☏ **202/748-5655**) is a cozy independent coffeehouse, bar, and cafe. Go in the morning for almond butter toast topped with sliced strawberries and a house-brewed matcha latte. Then go again at night for the seasonal flatbread and craft beers. Happy hour is Monday to Friday from 4 to 7pm.

- Step inside the new Eaton Hotel to find **Kintsugi** (1201 K St. NW; ☏ **202/900-8417**), named after the revered Japanese art of repairing broken pottery with gold. Sit in the cozy, midcentury booths along the living plant wall and order from a menu that focuses on gluten-free and vegan pastries as well as ayurvedic beverages such as a Golden Turmeric Latte and Chaga Elixir.

hot fudge sundae, or six-layer carrot cake for dessert. The prix-fixe brunch menu (with a whopping five choices) is also meat-heavy: steak and eggs with "the perfect poached egg," egg frites and sausage, and French toast and sausage. Sit outside along Connecticut Avenue; yes, it can be noisy, but it's ideal for people-watching. Other locations are in **Capitol Hill/Barracks Row** (515 8th St. SE ☏ **202/601-7136**) and the suburbs of Bethesda, Maryland, and Arlington, Virginia.

3500 Connecticut Ave. NW (at Ordway St.). www.mediumrarerestaurant.com. ☏ **202/237-1432.** Reservations accepted. Dinner $23 per person; brunch $28 including bottomless juices, mimosas, and Bloody Marys. Mon–Thurs 5–10pm; Fri–Sat 5–11pm; Sat–Sun 10:30am–2:30pm.

EXPLORING WASHINGTON, D.C.

I f you've never been to Washington, D.C., your mission is clear: Get thee to the National Mall and Capitol Hill. Within this roughly 2½-by-⅓-mile rectangular plot lies the lion's share of the capital's iconic attractions (see "Iconic Washington, D.C.," in chapter 3), including presidential and war memorials, the U.S. Capitol, the U.S. Supreme Court, the Library of Congress, most of the Smithsonian museums, the National Gallery of Art, and the National Archives.

In fact, even if you have traveled here before, you're likely to find yourself returning to this part of town, to pick up where you left off on that long list of sites worth seeing, to visit new ones, like the **National Law Enforcement Museum** (p. 181), and to revisit favorites, which in the interim have often enhanced and updated their exhibits in the most captivating ways.

You'll want to know about the new **National Children's Museum**, just blocks from the National Mall and White House, and featuring a 33,000-square-foot play space. You'll want to tour the new **Hall of Fossils** at the **Smithsonian National Museum of Natural History,** which reopened its doors in 2019 following a complete renovation and representation of its more than 700 specimens, including near-complete skeletons of the T-Rex, triceratops, and a saber-toothed cat. And visit the **International Spy Museum** in its new space at L'Enfant Plaza, just south of the National Mall, offering a more wide-ranging version of its former Penn Quarter self.

Beyond the Mall and its attractions, iconic or otherwise, lie the city's charming neighborhoods, standalone museums, historic houses, and beautiful gardens; you don't want to miss those, either. Tour national landmarks and you'll gain a sense of what this country is about, both politically and culturally. Tour off-the-Mall attractions and neighborhoods and you'll get a taste of the vibrant, multicultural scene that is the real D.C. This chapter helps you do both.

CAPITOL HILL

The **U.S. Capitol** and flanking Senate and House office buildings dominate this residential neighborhood of tree-lined streets,

TOUR & TICKET WEBSITES VS. booking direct

Websites such as GetYourGuide.com, Viator.com, and ToursByLocals.com are undeniably convenient to use. In just a few minutes you can have advance reservations and/or tickets for tours, museums, historic sites, classes, guided walks, and more. These sites also include reviews from recent customers, and sometimes offer discounts on high-volume products like bus and boat tours.

But there are downsides to using these websites. Here in Washington, the biggest downside is directly related to its greatest upside: **Nearly all of the capital's famous attractions offer free admission and tours.** If you don't know better, you could be paying, sometimes significantly, for something that is yours for nothing. Here's an example: One tour and ticket website lists a $35-per-person, 3.5-hour "Capitol Building and Capitol Hill Walk" tour, which includes a walk from Union Station to the Supreme Court, a tour of the Library of Congress, and "reserved access and docent-led tour of the U.S. Capitol Building"—all of which cost nothing and are easy to do on your own. The outfitter's role seems more escort than professional tour leader, since the guide does not even conduct tours at each of the stops; in fact, Capitol and Supreme Court tours are docent-led only. As one reviewer noted, "Paid money for service that is free with no additional benefit."

Furthermore, many of these companies tout "priority," "VIP," or "reserved" access for a bit extra, allowing customers access to the "reserve line" rather than the regular one. The reality in Washington, D.C., is that all visitors must process through security screenings, whether equipped with a reserved pass or not, and the going can be slow. Just a small warning.

19th-century town houses, and pubs and casual eateries. Across the street from the Capitol lie the **U.S. Supreme Court** and the **Library of Congress;** close by are the smaller but still engrossing **Folger Shakespeare Library,** the **Belmont-Paul Women's Equality National Monument,** and **Eastern Market.** Only a half-mile or so away are **Union Station,** doing triple duty as historical attraction, shopping mall, and transportation hub; and an off-the-Mall Smithsonian, the **National Postal Museum.** But the neighborhood itself is a pleasure. Explore.

The Capitol ★★★ GOVERNMENT BUILDING   In Washington, D.C., one catches sight of the Capitol all around town. That's no accident: When planner Pierre L'Enfant laid out the capital in 1791, he purposely placed "Congress House" upon this bluff, overlooking the city. The importance of the Capitol and of Congress is meant to be unmistakable.

Incontrovertible, too, is the fact that a tour of this iconic American symbol is a necessary stop on any first-time tour of D.C. When you visit here, you understand, in a very visceral way, just what it means to govern a country democratically. The fights and compromises, the din of differing opinions, the necessity of creating "one from the many" (*e pluribus unum*) without trampling on the rights of that one. It's a powerful experience. And the ideals of the Congress are not just expressed in the debates on the floor of the House and Senate (though you should try to hear those if you can; see below), but in

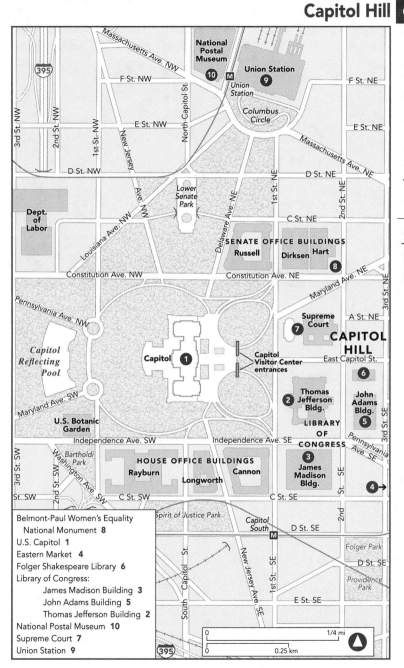

Belmont-Paul Women's Equality
    National Monument 8
U.S. Capitol 1
Eastern Market 4
Folger Shakespeare Library 6
Library of Congress:
        James Madison Building 3
        John Adams Building 5
        Thomas Jefferson Building 2
National Postal Museum 10
Supreme Court 7
Union Station 9

The Capitol Dome.

its masterful architecture, as well as within the many historical works of art and artifacts displayed within the massive building. For 135 years it sheltered not only both houses of Congress, but also the Supreme Court and, for 97 years, the Library of Congress.

Before entering the Capitol, stand back to admire the Capitol dome, from its base up to the pedestal of the "Statue of Freedom," the 19-foot, 6-inch bronze female figure at its crown. The Capitol dome weighs 9 million pounds, roughly the same as 20 Statues of Liberty. Its cast-iron exterior looks better than ever after the 2016 completion of a 2-year restoration, with 1,300 cracks sealed and scores of decorative ornaments recast.

The 45-minute guided tour (for procedures, see p. 122) starts in the Capitol Visitor Center, where you'll watch a 13-minute orientation film, then takes you to the Rotunda, National Statuary Hall, down to the Crypt, and back to the Visitor Center. Here's some of what you'll see:

The **Rotunda**—a huge 96-foot-wide circular hall capped by a 180-foot-high dome—is the hub of the Capitol. The dome was completed, at Lincoln's direction, while the Civil War was being fought: "If people see the Capitol going on, it is a sign we intend the Union shall go on," said Lincoln. Thirteen presidents have lain in state here, with former president George H. W. Bush, in 2018, the most recent; when John F. Kennedy's casket was displayed, the line of mourners stretched 40 blocks. It's an honor bestowed on only 31 people in 166 years, among them Senator John McCain, in 2018. On rare occasions, someone other than a president, military hero, or member of Congress receives posthumous recognition. In October 2005, Congress paid tribute to Rosa Parks by allowing her body to lie in honor here, different from lying in state. (Parks was the black woman who in 1955 refused to relinquish her seat to a white man on a bus in Montgomery, Alabama, thereby helping spark the civil rights movement. On February 27, 2013, Congress further honored Parks by adding a statue of her to **National Statuary Hall.**)

Embracing the Rotunda walls are eight immense oil paintings commemorating great moments in American history, such as the presentation of the Declaration of Independence and the surrender of Cornwallis at Yorktown. Inside the now-canopied inner dome of the Rotunda is an allegorical fresco masterpiece by Constantino Brumidi, *The Apotheosis of Washington,* a symbolic portrayal of George Washington surrounded by Roman gods and goddesses watching over the progress of the nation. Brumidi was known as the "Michelangelo of the Capitol" for the many works he created throughout the building. (Take another look at the fresco and find the woman directly below Washington; the triumphant *Armed Freedom* figure is said to be modeled after Lola Germon, a beautiful young actress with whom the 60-year-old Brumidi conceived a child.) Beneath those painted figures is a *trompe l'oeil* frieze depicting major developments in the life of America, from Columbus's landing in 1492 to the birth of the aviation age in 1903. Don't miss the sculptures in the Rotunda, including George Washington; a pensive Abraham Lincoln (sculpted from 1866 to 1870 by Vinnie Reams, the first woman artist to receive a government commission); a dignified Rev. Dr. Martin Luther King, Jr.; a ponderous trinity of suffragists, Elizabeth Cady Stanton, Susan B. Anthony, and Lucretia Mott; and a bronze statue of President Ronald Reagan, looking characteristically genial.

The **National Statuary Hall** was originally the chamber of the House of Representatives; in 1864 it became Statuary Hall, and the states were invited to send two statues each of native sons and daughters. There are 100 state-contributed statues in all throughout the Capitol. New Mexico completed the original collection with its contribution in 2005 of Po'Pay, a Pueblo Indian, who in 1680 led a revolt against the Spanish that helped to save Pueblo culture. States do have the prerogative to replace statues with new ones, which is

Heads-Up

Security precautions and procedures are a post-9/11 fact of life everywhere in America, but especially in the nation's capital, thanks to the preponderance of federal structures and attractions that are open to the public. What that means for you as a visitor is that you may have to stand in line to enter a national museum (like one of the Smithsonians) or a government building (like the U.S. Capitol). At many tourist sites, you can expect staff to search handbags, briefcases, and backpacks, either by hand or by X-ray machine. Some sites, including the National Air and Space Museum, require you to walk past metal detectors. During the busy spring and summer seasons, you may be queuing outside. Carry as little as possible, and certainly no sharp objects. Museums and public buildings rarely offer lockers for use by visitors.

what Florida did in 2018, authorizing the replacement of the state's 1922 choice of Confederate General Edmund Kirby Smith with that of civil rights activist and educator Mary McLeod Bethune. (Bethune was born and lived in Florida; she also worked for a while in Washington, D.C., where she founded the National Council of Negro Women and advised President Roosevelt; see p. 189.)

Because of space constraints, only 35 statues from the Statuary collection reside in the Hall, with the figures of seven presidents displayed in the Rotunda (the Rotunda holds three other presidents' statues, which are not part of the Statuary Hall Collection), 24 statues placed in the Visitor Center, and the remaining 34 standing in the Crypt (directly below the Rotunda), the Hall of Columns (directly beneath the Hall of the House of Representatives), and throughout the corridors of the Capitol. Statues include Ethan Allen, the Revolutionary War hero who founded the state of Vermont; and Missouri's Thomas Hart Benton—not the 20th-century artist famous for his rambunctious murals, but his namesake and uncle, one of the first two senators from Missouri and whose anti-slavery stance in 1850 cost him his Senate seat. Counting Mary McLeod Bethune (see above), 10 women are represented, including Alabama-born Helen Keller and Montana's Jeannette Rankin, the first woman to serve in Congress. The District of Columbia was finally allowed a statue in 2013: It added a full-sized bronze depiction of abolitionist Frederick Douglass, who stands in Emancipation Hall inside the Capitol Visitor Center. Congress has yet to recognize the District as its own state, but at least granted its constituents this representation!

In slow seasons, usually fall and winter, your public tour may include a visit to the **Old Supreme Court Chamber,** which has been restored to its mid-19th-century appearance. The Supreme Court met here from 1810 to 1860. Busts of the first four chief justices are on display—John Marshall, John Rutledge, John Jay, and Oliver Ellsworth—and so are some of their desks. The justices handed down a number of noteworthy decisions here, including in 1857 *Dred Scott v. Sandford,* which denied the citizenship of blacks, whether slaves or free, and in so doing precipitated the Civil War.

You will not see them on a tour, but the **south and north wings** of the Capitol hold the House and Senate chambers, respectively. You must obtain a pass from the office of your senator or representative to visit these galleries. (See below for info on watching Senate and House sessions.) The House of Representatives chamber is the setting for the president's annual State of the Union address.

A note on the area right outside the building: Immediately surrounding the Capitol itself are 58 acres of beautifully kept grounds, originally landscaped in 1874 by Frederick Law Olmsted, who also planned NYC's Central Park. The Capitol sometimes offers tours of the grounds in spring.

Procedures for Touring the Capitol: Tours of the Capitol are free and take place year-round, Monday through Saturday between 8:40am and 3:20pm. Capitol Guide Service guides lead the hour-long general-public tours, which

THE CAPITOL visitor center

The enormous, 4,000-person-capacity **Capitol Visitor Center** is underground, which means that as you approach the East Front of the Capitol, you won't actually see it. Look for signs and the sloping sets of steps on each side of the Capitol's central section, leading down to the center's entrances. Once inside you'll pass through security screening and then enter the two-level chamber.

Most visitors find it works best to explore the center after touring the Capitol. You can admire the 24 Statuary Hall statues scattered throughout and tour **Exhibition Hall,** a mini-museum of historic documents; check out interactive kiosks that take you on virtual tours of the Capitol, filling you in on history, art, and architecture; and view exhibits that explain the legislative process. **Emancipation Hall** is the large central chamber where you line up for tours; this is also where you'll find the 26 restrooms and 530-seat restaurant.

The visitor center is open Monday through Saturday year-round from 8:30am to 4:30pm, closed on Thanksgiving, Christmas, New Year's Day, and Inauguration Day.

can include as few as one or two people or as many as 40 or 50, depending on the season. Here I must sing the praises of these guides, who are often historians in their own right, repositories of American lore, traditions, anecdotes, and, of course, actual fact. Got a question? Ask away. These guides know their stuff.

You and everyone in your party must have a **timed pass,** which you can order online at **www.visitthecapitol.gov.** During peak spring and summer sessions, you should order tickets at least 2 weeks in advance. Same-day passes are also available daily from the "Visitors Without Reservations" walk-up line near the information desks on the lower level of the visitor center—even during peak times, the guides seem somehow to accommodate the crowds, so always try for a tour, even if the online system indicates that no passes are available. You can also contact your representative or senator in Congress and request constituent tours, which are usually limited to groups of 15 and conducted by congressional staff, who may take you to notable places in the Capitol beyond those seen on the public tour. Nevertheless, I would recommend you stick with the regular Capitol Guide tour, since the guides are more experienced and knowledgeable.

The Capitol has quite a list of items it prohibits; you can read the list online at www.visitthecapitol.gov (and also make sure that the Capitol will be open when you visit). Items ranging from large bags of any kind to food and drink are prohibited; leave everything you can back at the hotel.

The Capitol Guide Service also offers topical tours on a variety of subjects. Recent offerings included tours of the ornate Brumidi Corridors and tours that focused on civil-rights freedom fighters represented in the Capitol collections.

Procedures for Visiting the House Gallery or Senate Gallery: Both the Senate and House galleries are open to visitors whenever either body is **in**

session ★–★★★, so do try to sit in. (The experience receives a range of star ratings because a visit can prove fascinating or deadly boring, depending on whether a debate is underway and how lively it is.) Otherwise the Senate Gallery is open to visitors during scheduled recesses of 1 week or more, Monday to Friday 9am to 4:15pm. The House Gallery is open to visitors Monday to Friday 9am to 4pm. Children 5 and under are not allowed in the Senate gallery. You can obtain visitor passes at the offices of your representative and senators; District of Columbia and Puerto Rico residents can get passes from the office of their delegates to Congress. To find out your member's office location, go online at www.house.gov or www.senate.gov or call the main switchboard ℂ **202/225-3121.** You must have a separate pass for each gallery. Once obtained, the passes are good through the remainder of the Congress. *Note:* International visitors can obtain both House and Senate gallery passes by presenting a passport or a valid driver's license with photo ID to staff at the House and Senate appointments desks on the upper level of the visitor center.

The main, staffed offices of congressional representatives and delegates are in House buildings on the south (Independence Ave.) side of the Capitol; senators' main, staffed offices are located in Senate buildings on the north (Constitution Ave.) side. You should be able to pick up passes to both the Senate and House galleries in one place, at either your representative's office or one of your senators' offices. Visit the website of the Architect of the Capitol (**www.aoc.gov**) or the Visitor Center website (**www.visitthecapitol.gov**), or call the office of your senator or congressperson for more exact information about obtaining passes to the House and Senate galleries.

Call Ahead or Check Online

Here's a crucial piece of advice: **Call ahead or check the websites of the places you plan to tour each day before you set out.** Many of Washington's government buildings, museums, memorials, and monuments are open to the general public daily, year-round—except when they're not. Because buildings like the Capitol, the Supreme Court, and the White House are offices as well as tourist destinations, important business of the day may necessitate the closing of one of those sites, or at least sections, to sightseers. There's also the matter of maintenance. The steady stream of visitors to Washington's attractions necessitates ongoing caretaking, which may require closing an entire landmark, or part of it, or changing the hours of operation or procedures for visiting. Plus, Washington's famous museums, grand halls, and public gardens sometimes double as settings for press conferences, galas, special exhibits, festivals, and even movie sets. Dignitary visits also frequently shut down roads, restaurants, and attractions. And you might arrive at, say, the National Museum of American History and Culture on a Sunday afternoon, only to find some of its galleries off-limits because a movie or TV shoot is underway. (See the new *Wonder Woman 2* movie and you might catch several scenes of Georgetown.) To avoid frustration and disappointment, call ahead or check online for up-to-the-minute information.

Tip: You'll know that the House and/or the Senate is in session if you see flags flying over their respective wings of the Capitol (*Remember:* House, south side; Senate, north side), or visit their websites, **www.house.gov** and **www.senate.gov**, for schedules of bill debates in the House and Senate, committee markups, and links to your Senate or House representative's page.

Capitol and Capitol Visitor Center: E. Capitol St. (at First St. NW). www.visitthecapitol. gov, www.aoc.gov, www.house.gov, www.senate.gov. ✆ **202/225-6827** (recording), 202/593-1768 (Office of Visitor Services), or 202/225-3121 (Capitol operator). Free admission. Year-round Mon–Sat 8:30am–4:30pm (first tour at 8:50am, last at 3:20pm). Closed for tours Sun and Jan 1, Thanksgiving, Dec 25, and Inauguration Day. Parking at Union Station or on the streets. Metro: Union Station (Massachusetts Ave. exit) or Capitol South, then walk to the Capitol Visitor Center, located on the East Front of the Capitol.

Belmont-Paul Women's Equality National Monument ★

MUSEUM Welcome to a national park site dedicated to women's history, its status officially proclaimed by President Obama on April 12, 2016. The National Park Service roster of 417 national park units includes only a dozen or so focused on women's stories, so this is significant. Formerly known as the Sewall-Belmont House and Museum, this unassuming Federal-style, old brick house situated next to the Senate Hart Office Building has been the home of the National Woman's Party (NWP) since 1929. (In 1997, the NWP switched from being a political party to an organization focused on education and advocacy.) Suffragist and organizer extraordinaire Alice Paul founded the NWP in 1917 to fight for women's rights, including the right to vote, granted finally by Congress's passage of the 19th amendment on June 4, 1919, and eventual official adoption into the Constitution on August 26, 1920. The house is a repository of suffragist memorabilia, banners, political buttons, photos of events, and other artifacts, 2,600 in all, of which 250 are on view. You can walk through the first level on your own, but I'd recommend a staff-led tour— the guides tell the stories of individual heroines. Susan B. Anthony you will have heard of. But Alva Belmont, Inez Milholland Boissevain, and Febb Burn?

144 Constitution Ave. NE (at 2nd St.). www.nps.gov/bepa and www.nationalwomans party.org. ✆ **202/543-2240.** Free admission. Wed–Sun 9am–5pm for walk-ins, with guided tours typically available at 9:30am, 11, 2, and 3:30pm. Entrance is on 2nd St.— look for the signs. Closed Thanksgiving, Dec 25, and New Year's Day. Metro: Union Station or Capitol South.

Eastern Market ★

MARKET A mainstay of the historic Capitol Hill neighborhood and of the city itself, Eastern Market has been operating continuously since 1873, not even pausing after a fire in 2007 (indoor vendors moved to a parking lot across the street until the building reopened in 2009). Inside, 13 vendors in their separate stalls sell fresh produce, pasta, seafood, meats, cheeses, sweets, flowers, and pottery Tuesday through Sunday. Every Tuesday from 1 to 7pm, a farmers market operates outside the main hall. Things get really lively on weekends, when more than 100 arts and crafts merchants, plus an additional 20 or so farmers and open-air food vendors, sell their wares on the outdoor plazas surrounding the market. The street is closed to traffic in front of the market, and the block teems with families and singles doing their weekly grocery shopping, and even the occasional congressperson (many live in the neighborhood). For a real hometown experience, come for the blueberry buckwheat pancakes ("bluebucks") served for breakfast at Market Lunch inside the market, until 11am Tuesday through Friday, and until 1:30pm Saturday and Sunday.

225 7th St. SE (at North Carolina Ave.). www.easternmarket-dc.org. ✆ **202/698-5253.** Free admission. Indoor market: Tues–Fri 7am–7pm; indoor & outdoor markets: Sat 7am–6pm, Sun 9am–5pm. Closed Thanksgiving, Dec 25, and New Year's Day. Metro: Union Station or Capitol South.

Folger Shakespeare Library ★ LIBRARY   "Shakespeare taught us that the little world of the heart is vaster, deeper, and richer than the spaces of astronomy," wrote Ralph Waldo Emerson in 1864. More than a decade later, Amherst student Henry Clay Folger was profoundly affected by a lecture Emerson gave similarly extolling the Bard. Folger purchased an inexpensive set of Shakespeare's plays and went on to amass the world's largest collection of the Bard's works, today housed in the Folger Shakespeare Library. When the library opened in 1932 as a gift from the Folgers to the country, the collection comprised approximately 93,000 books, 50,000 prints and engravings, and thousands of manuscripts. Today, the collection has grown to include upwards of 260,000 printed books, more than 67,000 of which are rare (pre-1801), 60,000 manuscripts, 250,000 playbills, and a wealth of paintings, costumes, musical instruments, and other materials. Sadly, Henry Folger did not live to see the library's debut, having died suddenly in June 1930.

Most precious and best known of the Folger's possessions are its 82 copies of the **1623 First Folio of Shakespeare.** The first collected edition of Shakespeare's plays, it was published in 1623, 7 years after the playwright's death. It's the only source for 18 of Shakespeare's works, so had the First Folio not been printed, it's likely that the world would have been without *Macbeth, The Tempest*, and other of the Bard's masterpieces. On permanent display in the Folger's white-oak-paneled Tudor-ish **Great Hall** is one such First Folio, and next to it, a touchscreen that allows visitors to flip digitally from page to page.

Scholars and qualified researchers may apply to gain access to the collection and the library's Reading Rooms. The general public may visit the Reading Rooms by signing up online for the free, hour-long, docent-led tour held every Saturday at noon and Sunday at 1pm. Highlights include 16th- and 17th-century tapestries and a large stained-glass window portraying the Seven Ages of Man, as described by the character Jaques in *As You Like It*.

The **Great Hall** is always open to the public and, besides its First Folio display, mounts rotating exhibits of other items from the permanent collection—Renaissance musical instruments to centuries-old playbills. Just off the hall is the **Shakespeare Gallery,** which offers an orientation video and multimedia close-up look at some of the Folgers' treasures, as well as Shakespeare's life and works. Plan on spending at least 30 minutes here. Free docent-led tours take place daily; see information below.

At the end of the Great Hall is a theater designed to suggest the yard of an Elizabethan inn, where plays, concerts, readings, and Shakespeare-related events take place (see p. 226).

The Folger Shakespeare Library building itself has a marble facade decorated with nine bas-relief scenes from Shakespeare's plays; it is a striking example of Art Deco classicism. An **Elizabethan garden** on the east side of the building is planted with flowers and herbs of the period. Most remarkable here are eight sculptures by Greg Wyatt, each depicting figures from a particular scene in a Shakespeare play. The garden is also a nice, quiet place to have a picnic.

201 E. Capitol St. SE. www.folger.edu. ℂ **202/544-4600.** Free admission. Mon–Sat 10am–5pm; Sun noon–5pm. Free walk-in tours Mon–Sat 11am, 1, and 3pm; Sun noon and 3pm. Garden tours Sat 10am Apr–Oct. Reading Room tours Sat noon and Sun 1pm; reservations required. Check website for early closings. Closed federal holidays. Metro: Capitol South or Union Station.

Library of Congress ★★ LIBRARY You're inside the main public building of the Library of Congress—the magnificent, ornate, Italian Renaissance–style **Thomas Jefferson Building.** Maybe you've arrived via the tunnel that connects the Capitol and the Library of Congress, or maybe you've climbed the Grand Staircase facing First Street and entered through the main doors. In any case, you'll likely be startled—very startled—to find yourself suddenly inside a government structure that looks more like a palace. Before you line up for the tour, take time to stroll around the building and just gape. Admire the stained-glass skylights overhead; the Italian marble floors inlaid with brass and concentric medallions; the gorgeous murals, allegorical paintings, stenciling, sculptures, and intricately carved architectural elements. This building, more than any other in the city, is a visual treasure.

The Library of Congress.

Now for the history lesson: Established in 1800 by an act of Congress, "for the purchase of such books as may be necessary for the use of Congress," the library today also serves the nation, with holdings for the visually impaired (for whom books are recorded and/or translated into Braille), scholars and researchers in every field, college students, journalists, and teachers. Its first collection was destroyed in 1814 when the British burned the Capitol (where the library was then housed) during the War of 1812. Thomas Jefferson then sold the institution his personal library of 6,487 books as a replacement for roughly $23,000 in 1815, and this became the foundation of what is today the world's largest library.

The Jefferson Building was erected between 1888 and 1897 to hold the burgeoning collection and to establish America as a cultured nation with magnificent institutions equal to anything in Europe. Originally intended to hold the fruits of at least 150 years of collecting, the Jefferson Building was filled up in a mere 13 years. It is now supplemented by the **James Madison Memorial Building** and the **John Adams Building.**

Today the collection contains a mind-boggling 164 million items. Its buildings house more than 39 million catalogued books; 70 million manuscripts; millions and millions of prints and photographs, audio holdings (discs, tapes, talking books, and so on), movies, and videotapes; musical instruments from the 1700s; and the letters and papers of everyone from George Washington to Groucho Marx. Its archives also include the letters, oral histories, photographs, and other documents of war veterans from World War I to the present, all part of its **Veterans History Project;** go to www.loc.gov/vets to listen to or read some of these stories, especially if you plan on visiting the National World War II Memorial (p. 157).

In addition to its art and architecture, the Library exhibits objects from its permanent collections. "Shall Not Be Denied: Women Fight for the Vote," on view through September 2020, uses the personal papers and records of such figures as Susan B. Anthony, Elizabeth Cady Stanton, the National Woman's Party, and the National American Woman Suffrage Association, among others, to tell the long and determined push for women's suffrage and the legacy of this movement. An ongoing show is "Thomas Jefferson's Library." Always on view are two 1450s Bibles from Germany: the handwritten Giant Bible of Mainz, and the Gutenberg Bible, the first book printed with movable metal type in Europe.

The concerts that take place in the Jefferson Building's Whittall Pavilion and in the elegant **Coolidge Auditorium** are free but require tickets, which you can obtain through Eventbrite (www.eventbrite.com).

Across Independence Avenue from the Jefferson Building is the **Madison Building,** which houses venues for author readings and other events.

Using the library: Anyone 16 and over may use the library's collections, but first you must obtain a user card with your photo on it. You can get the process started by pre-registering online at wwws.loc.gov/readerreg/remote/. Whether preregistered or not, you must go to Reader Registration in Room LJ 139 (first floor of the Jefferson Building) and present your driver's license or passport. Staff will verify your identity, take a photo, and present you with your user card, which is good for 2 years. Then head to the Information Desk in either the Jefferson or the Madison building to find out about the research resources available to you and how to use them. Most likely, you will be directed to the Main Reading Room. All books must be used on-site.

Jefferson Bldg.: 10 First St. SE, btw. Independence Ave. and E. Capitol St. Madison Bldg.: 101 Independence Ave. SE (at First St. SE). www.loc.gov. *℃* **202/707-8000.** Free admission. Madison Bldg.: Mon–Fri 8:30am–9:30pm; Sat 8:30am–5pm. Jefferson Bldg.: Mon–Sat 8:30am–4:30pm. Stop at an information desk on the ground floor of the Jefferson Bldg. Docent-led tours of the Jefferson Bldg. are free, require no reservations or tickets, and take place Mon–Fri 10:30 and 11:30am, and 12:30, 1:30, 2:30, and 3:30pm; Sat 10:30 and 11:30am, and 1:30 and 2:30pm. Contact your congressional representatives to obtain tickets for congressional, or "VIP," tours (slightly more personalized tours). Metro: Capitol South.

National Postal Museum ★ MUSEUM   This Smithsonian museum is somewhat off the standard sightseeing route (most other Smithsonians are located on or near the National Mall), so it doesn't capture as many visitors as the other attractions. But if you're at all interested in the romance and adventure of the story of U.S. mail correspondence and its delivery (that's right, I said romance and adventure!), and in the international artistry and invention of that most miniature of art forms, the postage stamp, you really need to venture in.

You'll find yourself in the elegant lobby of a historic structure designed by Daniel Burnham in 1914. The building operated as a post office until 1986; it was reborn in 1993 as the Postal Museum.

I recommend that you head downstairs to tour the original part of the museum, where America's postal history from 1673 to the present is on display. Children usually make a beeline to the enormous blue freightliner truck front over in the corner, and climb up into the driver's seat. This is part of the central exhibit area called **Moving the Mail,** and you'll see planes, trains, and other postal vehicles that have been used at one time or another to transport the mail. Kids also delight in the sight of Owney the Dog, a replica of the scruffy pup that traveled with postal workers aboard Rail Mail Service trains in the late 19th century, becoming the unofficial mascot of the RMS.

In **Binding the Nation,** visitors can follow a path through a forest to trace the steps of mail carriers who traveled from New York to Boston in 1673, and climb into a stagecoach headed west. The exhibit introduces famous figures, like Buffalo Bill, of Pony Express renown; and founding father Benjamin Franklin in his role first as postmaster general for the British colonial post (until he was fired for his revolutionary activities) and then as postmaster general for the United Colonies.

Other exhibits cover mail's impact on city streets and rural routes (**Customers & Communities**), the journey a single letter takes through the postal system and how that process has changed over time (**Systems at Work**), and the history and current practice of getting mail delivered to and from military personnel (**Mail Call**). **Behind the Badge** reveals the work of the U.S. Postal

Inspection Service: Established in 1776, the federal agency is responsible for restoring mail service after disasters, spotting and preventing mail fraud, and keeping mail safe from the likes of Unabombers and lesser criminals.

Return upstairs to explore the **William H. Gross Stamp Gallery ★★★**, the world's largest stamp gallery. On view are displayed treasures from the museum's six-million-piece **National Stamp Collection,** including its rarest U.S. acquisition, the 1868 1-cent "Z-grill" stamp, one of only two known to be pressed into a grill pattern. Interactive kiosks, videos, and activities keep even the non-stamp-collector interested, enthralled even. The **World of Stamps** permanent exhibit features a hit list of famous stamps, starting with the very first postage stamp, the 1840 Penny Black, bearing the profile of a young Queen Victoria. **Stamps Around the Globe** displays international stamps from 24 countries, which make up more than half the Postal Museum's overall collection (everything from a colorful 1940 Egyptian stamp honoring the millennium of Cairo's first mosque to a rare "feather letter" from Sweden used in the mid-1700s to mid-1800s). Viewing these miniature artworks is a thrill.

Don't miss the last gallery, the **Postmasters Suite,** housed in a gorgeous, six-sided paneled room. It's reserved for special exhibits. Sports fans will love the exhibit **"Baseball: America's Home Run,"** coming on view in April 2020 and featuring hundreds of U.S. and international stamps commemorating great players and historic moments.

Tip: The Postal Museum's wall of windows features replicas of 54 historic U.S. stamps; come by at nighttime and you'll see the artwork illuminated.

2 Massachusetts Ave. NE (at First St.). www.postalmuseum.si.edu. © **202/633-5555.** Free admission. Daily 10am–5:30pm. Closed Dec 25. Metro: Union Station.

The Supreme Court of the United States ★★★ GOVERNMENT BUILDING   On many days, the Supreme Court is the most exciting place to be in town. Beginning on the first Monday in October, the nine justices hear cases, later to render opinions that can dramatically affect every American. Visitors may attend these proceedings, in which lawyers representing opposing sides attempt to make a convincing case for their clients, even as the justices interrupt repeatedly and question them sharply to clarify the constitutional principles at stake. It's a grand show, fast-paced, sometimes heated, and always full of weighty import (the justices hear only about 80 of the most vital of the 7,000 to 8,000 or so petitions filed with the Court every year). The Court's rulings are final, reversible only by an Act of Congress. And you, the visitor, get a close-up seat…if you're lucky (see below for info on getting in).

But even when the court isn't in session, touring the building is a worthwhile experience. During those periods, docents offer 30-minute lectures inside the Supreme Court chamber to introduce visitors of all ages to the Court's judicial functions, the building's history, and the architecture of the courtroom. Lectures take place every hour on the half-hour, beginning at 9:30am on days when the Court is not sitting and at a later time on Court days. You can also tour the building on your own. Architect Cass Gilbert, best known for his skyscrapers (such as New York's Woolworth building), designed the stately Corinthian marble palace that houses the Court. On the ground floor are exhibits and a film on the workings of the Court (an excellent preliminary to the docent lecture, so time your visit accordingly).

Getting in to see a case being argued: Starting the first Monday in October and continuing through late April, the Court "sits" for 2 weeks out of every month to hear two 1-hour arguments each day Monday through Wednesday, from 10am to noon, with occasional afternoon sessions scheduled as necessary from 1 to 2 or 3pm. You can find out the specific dates, names of arguments, and case descriptions on the Court's website and over the phone (see below).

Plan on arriving at the Supreme Court at least 90 minutes in advance of a scheduled argument during the fall and winter, and as early as 3 hours ahead in March and April, when students from schools on spring break lengthen the line. (Dress warmly; the stone plaza is exposed and can be witheringly cold.) Controversial cases also attract crowds; if you're not sure whether a particular case has created a stir, call the Court info line to reach someone who can tell you. The Court allots only about **150 first-come, first-served seats** to the public, but that number fluctuates, depending on the number of seats that have been reserved by the lawyers arguing the case, law clerks, special guests, and the press. The Court police officers direct you into one line initially; when the doors finally open, you form a second line if you want to attend only 3 to 5 minutes of the argument. Seating begins at 9:30am for those attending the full argument and at 10am for those who want to catch just a few minutes.

The justices release completed opinions in the courtroom throughout the argument term, October through April, and into May and June. If you attend an oral argument, you may find yourself present as well for the release of a Supreme Court opinion, since the justices precede the hearing of new oral arguments with the announcement of their opinions on previously heard arguments, if any opinions are ready. If you're visiting the Court in May or June, you won't be able to attend an argument, but you might still see the justices in action, delivering an opinion, during a 10am 15-minute session in the courtroom. To attend one of these sessions, you must wait in line on the plaza, following the same procedure outlined above.

Leave cameras, recording devices, and notebooks at your hotel—they're not allowed in the courtroom. Small children and infants are allowed but not recommended. *Note: Do* bring quarters. Security procedures require you to leave all your belongings—outerwear, purses, books, sunglasses, and so on—in a cloak room where coin-operated lockers accept only quarters.

1 First St. NE (btw. E. Capitol St. and Maryland Ave. NE). www.supremecourt.gov. ℂ **202/479-3000** or 202/479-3030 (recording). Free admission. Mon–Fri 9am–4:30pm. Closed all federal holidays. Metro: Capitol South or Union Station.

Union Station ★ ARCHITECTURAL ICON/MARKET   When it opened in 1907, this was the largest train station in the world. It was designed by noted architect Daniel H. Burnham, who modeled it after the Baths of

Diocletian and the Arch of Constantine in Rome, so its facade has Ionic colonnades fashioned from white granite and 100 sculptured eagles. Graceful 50-foot Constantine arches mark the entryways, above which are poised six carved figures representing Fire, Electricity, Freedom, Imagination, Agriculture, and Mechanics. Inside is the **Main Hall,** a massive rectangular room with a 96-foot barrel-vaulted ceiling, an expanse of white-marble flooring, and a balcony adorned with 36 Augustus Saint-Gaudens sculptures of Roman legion-

Union Station.

naires. Off the Main Hall is the **East Hall,** shimmering with scagliola marble walls and columns, a gorgeous hand-stenciled skylight ceiling, and stunning murals of classical scenes inspired by ancient Pompeiian art. (Today, this is the station's quietest shopping venue, with a handful of stores and stall vendors selling pretty jewelry and other accessories.)

In its time, this "temple of transport" has witnessed many important events. President Wilson welcomed General Pershing here in 1918 on his return from France. South Pole explorer Rear Admiral Richard Byrd was also feted at Union Station on his homecoming. And Franklin D. Roosevelt's funeral train, bearing his casket, was met here in 1945 by thousands of mourners.

But after the 1960s, with the decline of rail travel, the station fell on hard times. Rain caused parts of the roof to cave in, and the entire building—with floors buckling, rats running about, and mushrooms sprouting in damp rooms—was sealed in 1981. That same year, Congress enacted legislation to preserve and restore this national treasure, to the tune of $160 million. A remarkable 6-year restoration involving hundreds of European and American artisans returned the station to its original design.

Union Station never closes, never pauses. At least 40 million people come through its doors yearly, more than 100,000 a day. About 100 retail and food shops on three levels offer a wide array of merchandise and dining options. Several tour-bus companies use the station as a point of arrival and departure and operate ticket booths inside the front hall of the main concourse. (See p. 298 for info about tours.) Amtrak, the commuter MARC trains, Metrorail trains and Metrobuses, DC Circulator buses, taxis, rental cars, local drivers and pedestrians, and the DC Streetcar all converge on Union Station; see chapter 11 for details about Union Station as a transportation hub.

50 Massachusetts Ave. NE. www.unionstationdc.com. ✆ **202/289-1908.** Free admission. Station daily 24 hr. Shops Mon–Sat 10am–9pm; Sun noon–6pm. Machines located inside the station near the exit/entrance to the parking garage will validate your ticket, allowing you these reduced rates: $5 for the first hr., $7 for 2 hr., $20 for 2–10 hr., and $24 for up to 24 hr. Metro: Union Station.

THE NATIONAL MALL & MEMORIAL PARKS

This one's the biggie, folks. More than one-third of the capital's major attractions lie within this complex of parkland that the National Park Service calls the **National Mall and Memorial Parks.** The centerpiece of this larger plot, the National Mall (p. 149) extends from the Capitol to the Potomac River, and from Constitution Avenue to down and around the cherry-tree-ringed Tidal Basin. Presidential and war memorials, the Washington Monument, the Martin Luther King, Jr. Memorial, 11 Smithsonian museums, the National Gallery of Art, the National Archives, and the U.S. Botanic Garden are here waiting for you.

The National Mall itself, and the memorials, are open 24/7 for visiting, with Rangers on duty from 9:30am to 10pm daily, but not necessarily stationed at a specific memorial; rather, Rangers and volunteer guides rotate and rove from memorial to memorial throughout the day to answer questions. If you don't see a ranger at, say, the FDR Memorial, you might at your next likely stop, the nearby MLK Memorial. In addition to being available to respond to queries, rangers lead history-based or themed bike tours, talks, and walks throughout National Mall and Memorial Parks, almost daily and sometimes more than once a day. Check the National Mall and Memorial Parks calendar online (**www.nps.gov/nama/planyourvisit/calendar.htm**) to see what's on tap while you're here. All set? Let's get started.

Arts and Industries Building ★ ARCHITECTURE   Completed in 1881 just in time to host President James Garfield's inaugural ball, this red-brick and sandstone structure was the first Smithsonian museum on the Mall, and

Loop the National Mall Aboard the DC Circulator

Getting to the top attractions of the Mall is easy, thanks to the DC Circulator's National Mall route. This bus runs on a permanent, year-round, continuously looping National Mall circuit that begins and ends at Union Station, stopping at 15 points along the way. In winter, the Loop (my name for it, and I'm sticking with it) travels 7am to 7pm Monday to Friday, and 9am to 7pm Saturday to Sunday; in summer, the Loop operates 7am to 8pm Monday to Friday, and 9am to 8pm Saturday to Sunday. As with all the other Circulators, buses come by every 10 minutes and you may board them at any of its stops. The National Mall route from Union Station takes you down Louisiana Avenue and around the Mall via the inside roads of Madison, Jefferson, West Basin, East Basin, and Ohio drives, as well as Constitution Avenue. Stops include the National Gallery of Art, the National Museum of American History, the Washington Monument, the Lincoln Memorial, and more—every place you'd want to go, in other words. The fare is $1 and if you pay with a SmarTrip Card, you'll be able to reboard for free within a 2-hour window. I've noted when an attraction is served by the Circulator in the listings in this section.

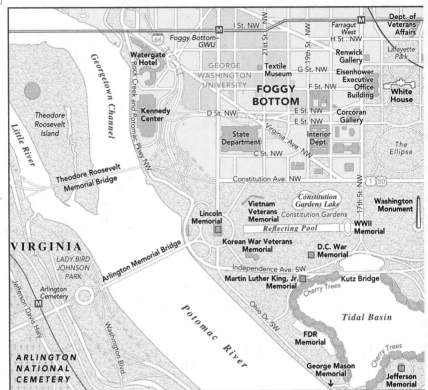

the first U.S. National Museum. But despite a 12-year-renovation completed in 2015, the building remains mostly closed to the public except for special events and exhibitions. You can always admire the building's exterior. Weather permitting, a 19th-century **carousel** operates across the street on the Mall.

900 Jefferson Dr. SW (on the south side of the Mall). www.aib.si.edu. Metro: Smithsonian (Mall exit). DC Circulator stop.

D.C. War Memorial ★ MONUMENT/MEMORIAL

This often-overlooked memorial commemorates the lives of the 499 citizens of Washington, D.C., who died in World War I. It's worth a stop on your way to grander, more famous edifices. President Herbert Hoover dedicated the memorial in 1931; John Phillip Sousa conducted the Marine band at the event. The structure is a graceful design of 12 Doric columns supporting a classical circular dome. The names of the 499 dead are inscribed in the stone base.

North side of Independence Ave. SW (btw. the National World War II and Lincoln memorials). www.nps.gov/nama/planyourvisit/dc-war-memorial.htm. Metro: Smithsonian (12th St./Independence Ave. exit), with a 25-min. walk. Near DC Circulator stop at MLK Memorial.

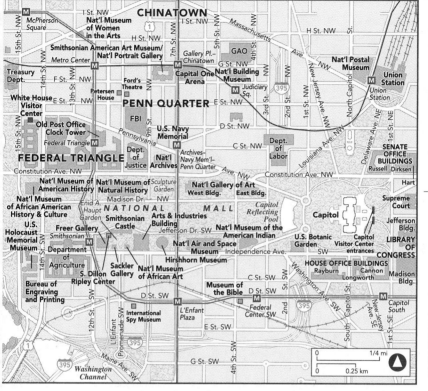

Enid A. Haupt Garden ★ GARDEN   Named for its donor, a noted sup-
porter of horticultural projects, this pretty 4¼-acre garden presents elaborate
flower beds and borders, plant-filled turn-of-the-20th-century urns, 1870s
cast-iron furnishings, and lush baskets hung from reproduction 19th-century
lampposts. The garden is planted on the rooftops of the subterranean Ripley
Center and Sackler and African Art museums.

Most captivating is the **parterre** of symmetrically arranged plots whose
vividly colorful and varied plantings change season by season. The ornamental garden patterns complement the Victorian architecture of the nearby
Smithsonian Castle. The tranquil **Moongate Garden** near the Sackler Gallery
employs water and granite in a landscape design inspired by a 15th-century
Chinese temple. Two 9-foot-tall pink-granite moon gates frame a pool paved
with half-rounds of granite. Benches backed by English boxwoods sit under a
canopy of weeping cherry trees.

The **Fountain Garden** outside the African Art Museum replicates an
Islamic garden, complete with elements of geometrical symmetry, low walls,
a central fountain, and water cascading down the face of a stone wall. Five

majestic linden trees shade a seating area around the **Downing Urn,** a memorial to American landscapist Andrew Jackson Downing, who designed the National Mall. Elaborate cast-iron carriage gates made according to a 19th-century design by James Renwick salute the Independence Avenue entrance.

10th St. and Independence Ave. SW. www.gardens.si.edu. © **202/633-2220.** Free admission. Daily dawn–dusk. Free tours May–Sept Wed 9:30 and 11:30am. Metro: Smithsonian (12th St./Independence Ave. exit). DC Circulator stop.

Franklin Delano Roosevelt Memorial ★★ MONUMENT/MEMORIAL

Since it opened in 1997, the FDR Memorial has proven to be one of the most popular of the presidential memorials. Its popularity has to do as much with its design as the man it honors. This 7½-acre outdoor memorial stretches out, mazelike, rather than rising up, across the stone-paved floor. Granite walls define the four "galleries," each representing a different term in FDR's presidency, from 1933 to 1945. Architect Lawrence Halprin's design includes waterfalls, sculptures (by Leonard Baskin, John Benson, Neil Estern, Robert Graham, Thomas Hardy, and George Segal), and Roosevelt's own words carved into the stone.

Great Depression sculpture at the FDR Memorial.

The many displays of cascading water can sound thunderous, as the fountains recycle an astonishing 100,000 gallons of water every minute. Their presence isn't a random choice: they reflect FDR's appreciation for the importance of H$_2$O. As someone afflicted with polio, he understood the rehabilitative powers of water exercises and established the Warm Springs Institute in Georgia to help others with polio. As president, FDR supported several water projects, including the creation of the Tennessee Valley Authority. A favorite time to visit the memorial is at night, when dramatic lighting reveals the waterfalls and statues against the dark parkland. (*Note:* Fountains are shut off in cold weather.)

Conceived in 1946, the FDR Memorial had been in the works for 50 years. Part of the delay in its construction can be attributed to the president himself: FDR had told his friend, Supreme Court Justice Felix Frankfurter, "If they are to put up any memorial to me, I should like it to be placed in the center of that green plot in front of the Archives Building. I should like it to consist of a block about the size [of this desk]." In fact, such a plaque sits in front of the National Archives (Pennsylvania Avenue entrance). Friends and relatives struggled to honor Roosevelt's request to leave it at that, but Congress and national sentiment overrode them.

As with other presidential memorials, this one opened to some controversy. Advocates for people with disabilities were incensed that the memorial sculptures did not show the president in a wheelchair, which he used after he contracted polio. President Clinton asked Congress to allocate funding for the additional statue of a wheelchair-bound FDR; it's at the very front of the memorial, to the right as you approach the first gallery. In the gift shop is a replica of Roosevelt's wheelchair, as well as a rare photograph of the president sitting in a wheelchair. The memorial is probably the most accessible tourist attraction in D.C.; as at most National Park Service locations, wheelchairs are available for free use on-site. Thirty minutes is sufficient for a visit.

On West Basin Dr., alongside the Tidal Basin in West Potomac Park (across Independence Ave. SW from the Mall). www.nps.gov/frde. (2) **202/426-6841.** Free admission. Open 24 hr. daily. Limited parking. Metro: Smithsonian (12th St./Independence Ave. exit), with a 20-min. walk. DC Circulator stop.

Freer Gallery of Art ★★ MUSEUM   Thanks to a wealthy donor of varied passions, a single museum houses one of the world's finest permanent collections of Asian art as well as the most comprehensive assemblage of the works of American artist James McNeill Whistler. This somewhat schizophrenic entity, which opened in 1923, was the first Smithsonian museum devoted to the fine arts.

The museum's namesake, Charles Lang Freer, was a self-taught connoisseur, who started out in the 1880s collecting American art, specifically living American artists, including his friend, the British-based Whistler. It was Whistler's affinity for Japanese and Chinese art that got Freer interested in collecting Asian art. (Galleries near the Peacock Room display other works by Whistler that clearly show the influence of Asian art and techniques on his own style.) Soon Freer's Asian art collection outgrew his American art collection; today, of the gallery's 25,000 objects spanning 6,000 years (from China, Japan, Korea, Syria, Iraq, Iran, India, Pakistan, Turkey, Central Asia, and Egypt), only a small number—1,708, to be exact—consists of American works.

This Italian Renaissance–style building, unlike many of its Smithsonian sisters, is usually blessedly uncrowded, making it a wonderful place to escape D.C.'s throngs. Furthermore, a nearly 2-year renovation of the Freer unveiled in late 2017 resulted in refurbished galleries, updated infrastructure, and an improved visitor experience. The main galleries lie on one level and encircle a lovely, landscaped central courtyard. It's possible to stroll unhurried through the skylit rooms, which hold an astonishingly wide array of wonders. Such as: fine jewelry from the Chinese Liangzhu culture (which flourished during the late Neolithic and Bronze ages—we're talking 6,000 years ago); a 1760 Japanese handscroll depicting "One Hundred Old Men Gathering for a Drink Party"; 12th-century illuminated manuscripts of sacred texts created by Jain artists of western India; a monumental hammered-brass Iranian candlestick from the late 12th century; exquisite Japanese screens; a beautiful, turquoise-glazed jar from late-12th-century Syria; giant and forbidding-looking

14th-century Japanese wooden figures that stood guard outside the entrance to a temple near Osaka; and the Freer's single permanent installation, Whistler's famous (and drop-dead gorgeous) *Harmony in Blue and Gold: the Peacock Room,* conceived as a dining room for the London mansion of wealthy client F. R. Leyland.

Jefferson Dr. SW at 12th St. SW (on the south side of the Mall). www.asia.si.edu. *©* **202/633-1000.** Free admission. Daily 10am–5:30pm except Christmas Day. Metro: Smithsonian (Mall/Jefferson Dr. exit). DC Circulator stop.

George Mason Memorial ★ MONUMENT/MEMORIAL   George Mason's name is not famous today, but it should be: He was the Virginia politician who authored the Virginia Declaration of Rights, upon which the first part of the U.S. Declaration of Independence is based, as well as the first 10 amendments to the U.S. Constitution, known as the Bill of Rights. Dedicated on April 9, 2002, the memorial consists of a bronze statue of Mason, dressed in 18th-century garb, from buckled shoes to tricorn hat, set back in a landscaped grove of trees and flower beds (lots and lots of pansies). Two stone slabs are inscribed with some of Mason's words, like these, referring to Mason's rejection of slavery: THAT SLOW POISON, WHICH IS DAILY CONTAMINATING THE MINDS & MORALS OF OUR PEOPLE. An interesting stand for a slave-owner to take, wouldn't you say? *Note:* The memorial is easy to miss, because it does not lie on the Tidal Basin path. As you approach the Jefferson Memorial from the direction of the FDR Memorial, or as you approach the FDR Memorial from the direction of the Jefferson, you'll come to the bridge that arches over the inlet leading from the Tidal Basin to the Potomac River; look straight across from the bridge, and there you'll see it.

E. Basin and Ohio drs. SW (btw. the Jefferson and FDR memorials). www.nps.gov/gemm. *©* **202/426-6841.** Free admission. Open 24 hr. daily. Limited parking. Metro: Smithsonian (12th St./Independence Ave. exit), with a 25-min. walk. DC Circulator stop.

Hirshhorn Museum and Sculpture Garden ★★ ART MUSEUM This cylindrically shaped, concrete-and-granite building holds provocative art at its best, from de Kooning to Jeff Koons. Look for Thomas Hart Benton's dizzying sprawl of figures in his 1920 painting *People of Chilmark,* Ellsworth Kelly's vivid minimalist paintings, Dan Steinhilber's sculpture made out of paper-clad wire hangers, Henri Matisse's bronze casts, and Damien Hirst's *The Asthmatic Escaped II, 1992,* in which one of two conjoined glass cases holds a camera on a tripod, and the other holds the clothing, inhaler, and other personal effects of "the escaped." The museum rotates works from its 12,000-piece collection, 600 at any one time, so if these exact artworks are not on view, others in the avant-garde family will be.

Don't overlook the special exhibits. The museum's current curators are unusually talented at picking of-the-moment, outside-the-box works, like the renowned *Waterfall* series of paintings from acclaimed abstract painter Pat Steir, on view until May 2020. The 28 large-scale, colorful paintings comprise Steir's first solo exhibition in Washington in nearly 50 years.

The Hirshhorn Art Museum.

The museum's 4.3-acre outdoor sculpture garden is undergoing its first renovation in almost 40 years, and at press time, an end date had not been released. The redesign, the work of Japanese artist and architect Hiroshi Sugimoto, calls for a complete redo of the formerly sunken garden. Adjacent to the National Mall, the below-ground garden was barely visible to both Mall and museum visitors. In 1974, acclaimed architect Gordon Bunshaft originally envisioned a much larger garden that traversed the entire National Mall's width and featured a substantial reflecting pool, but his ideas were never fully realized. As part of the renovation, the entrance will be enhanced, so that it's no longer below ground level. Initial concept designs also include reopening the underground passage connecting the garden to the museum plaza, which has been closed for 30 years. During construction, visitors will find many of the sculptures throughout the museum, while others will unfortunately not be on display. *Note:* The Hirshhorn's Sculpture Garden and the **National Gallery of Art's Sculpture Garden** (p. 147), located directly across the Mall from each other, **are not the same!** They offer two very different experiences.

The Hirshhorn exists thanks to a man named Joseph H. Hirshhorn, who was born in Latvia in 1899 but immigrated to the United States as a boy. In 1966, Hirshhorn donated his collection of more than 6,000 works of modern and contemporary art to the United States in gratitude for the country's welcome to him and other immigrants, and bequeathed an additional 5,500 upon his death in 1981. The museum opened in 1974.

Independence Ave. at 7th St. SW (on the south side of the Mall). www.hirshhorn.si.edu. © **202/633-4674.** Free admission. Museum daily 10am–5:30pm. Sculpture Garden daily 7:30am–dusk. Closed Dec 25. Metro: L'Enfant Plaza (Smithsonian Museums/Maryland Ave. or Smithsonian exit). DC Circulator stop.

Jefferson Memorial ★★ MONUMENT/MEMORIAL   President John F. Kennedy, at a 1962 dinner honoring 29 Nobel Prize winners, told his guests that they were "the most extraordinary collection of talent, of human knowledge, that has ever been gathered together at the White House, with the possible exception of when Thomas Jefferson dined alone." Jefferson penned the Declaration of Independence and served as George Washington's secretary of state, John Adams's vice president, and America's third president. He spoke out against slavery—although, like many of his countrymen, he kept slaves himself. He also established the University of Virginia and pursued wide-ranging interests, including architecture, astronomy, anthropology, music, and farming.

Franklin Delano Roosevelt, a great admirer of Jefferson, spearheaded the effort to build him a memorial, although the site choice was problematic. The Capitol, the White House, and the Mall were already located in accordance with architect Pierre L'Enfant's master plan for the city, and there was no spot for such a project that would maintain L'Enfant's symmetry. So the memorial was built on land reclaimed from the Potomac River, perched upon the lip of the manmade reservoir now known as the Tidal Basin. Roosevelt laid the memorial cornerstone in 1939 and had all the trees between the Jefferson Memorial and the White House cut down so that he could see the memorial every morning.

The memorial is a columned rotunda in the style of the Pantheon in Rome, whose classical architecture Jefferson himself introduced to this country (he designed his home, Monticello, and the earliest University of Virginia buildings in Charlottesville). On the Tidal Basin side, the sculptural group above the entrance depicts Jefferson with Benjamin Franklin, John Adams, Roger Sherman, and Robert Livingston, all of whom worked on drafting the Declaration of Independence. The domed interior of the memorial contains the 19-foot bronze statue of Jefferson standing on a 6-foot pedestal of black Minnesota granite. The sculpture is the work of Rudolph Evans, chosen from among more than 100 artists in a nationwide competition. Jefferson is depicted wearing a fur-collared coat given to him by his close friend, the Polish General Tadeusz Kościuszko. If you follow Jefferson's gaze, you see that the Jefferson Memorial and the White House have an unimpeded view of each other.

Ohio Dr. SW, at the south shore of the Tidal Basin (in West Potomac Park). www.nps. gov/thje. © **202/426-6841.** Free admission. Open 24 hr. daily. Limited parking. Metro: Smithsonian (12th St./Independence Ave. exit), with a 20- to 30-min. walk. DC Circulator stop.

Korean War Veterans Memorial ★ MONUMENT/MEMORIAL   This privately funded memorial, founded in 1995, honors those who served in the Korean War, a 3-year conflict (1950–53) that produced almost as many casualties as Vietnam. It consists of a circular "Pool of Remembrance" in a grove of trees and a triangular "Field of Service," highlighted by lifelike statues of 19 infantrymen who appear to be trudging across fields. A 164-foot-long black granite wall depicts the array of combat and support troops that served in Korea (nurses, chaplains, airmen, mechanics, cooks, and others); engraved markers along a walkway list the 22 nations that contributed to the UN's effort; and a commemorative area honors KIAs, MIAs, and POWs. Allot 15 minutes.

Southeast of the Lincoln Memorial, on the Independence Ave. SW side of the Mall. www.nps.gov/kowa. ✆ **202/426-6841.** Free admission. Open 24 hr. daily. Limited parking. Metro: Foggy Bottom, with 30-min. walk. DC Circulator stop.

Lincoln Memorial ★★★ MONUMENT/MEMORIAL When famed architect Charles Follen McKim was asked to work on the 1902 McMillan Commission to reshape the overall design for the Mall, he made his views clear on what he felt would be an important addition. "As the Arc de Triomphe crowns Place de l'Étoile in Paris, so should stand a memorial erected of the memory of that one man in our history as a nation who is worthy to be joined with George Washington—Abraham Lincoln."

Location was key, but where the monument should be was not entirely obvious: Until the late 1800s, a wider Potomac River had bumped up against the western edge of the National Mall. It was only after the Army Corps of Engineers had first reclaimed land from the river and created a mile-wide westward expanse of new terrain, and then landscaped and engineered the muddy morass, that the choice was clear. The memorial for honoring the president who had saved the Union would preside at one end of the Mall on a direct axis to the Washington Monument honoring the nation's founding president, both sites linked on the same axis further still to the symbol of the country itself, the U.S. Capitol, at the eastern end of the Mall.

Construction began in 1914, and what a job it was, shoring up the unstable wetlands and creating a foundation strong enough to support the majestic memorial that architect Henry Bacon had designed. The foundation rests on concrete piles that extend from 44 to 65 feet from original grade to bedrock. The retaining wall, keeping the river at bay, measures 257 feet wide by 187 feet deep by 14 feet high. The Lincoln Memorial itself weighs 38,000 tons. The monument finally opened in 1922 after 8 years of construction.

The neoclassical temple-like structure, similar in architectural design to the Parthenon in Greece, has 36 fluted Doric columns representing the states of the Union at the time of Lincoln's death, plus two at the entrance. On the attic parapet are 48 festoons symbolizing the number of states in 1922. (Hawaii and Alaska are noted in an inscription on the terrace.) Due east is the Reflecting Pool, lined with American elms and stretching 2,000 feet toward the Washington Monument and the Capitol beyond.

The memorial chamber has limestone walls inscribed with the Gettysburg Address and Lincoln's second inaugural address. Two 60-foot-high murals by Jules Guerin on the north and south walls depict, allegorically, Lincoln's principles and achievements. On the south wall, an Angel of Truth freeing a slave is flanked by groups of figures representing Justice and Immortality. The north-wall mural portrays the unity of North and South, and is flanked by groups of figures symbolizing Fraternity and Charity.

Most powerful, however, is Daniel Chester French's seated statue of Lincoln. Lincoln sits, gazing down on the visitors at his feet, the burdens of guiding the Union through the Civil War etched deeply in his face. Though 19 feet tall, the figure is eerily lifelike and exudes a fatherly compassion. Some say that his hands create the sign-language shapes for A (Abraham) and L (Lincoln), as a tribute to the fact that Lincoln signed legislation giving Gallaudet University, a school for the deaf, the right to confer college degrees. The National Park Service denies the symbolism, but it should be noted that French's own son was deaf, so the sculptor *did* know sign language.

Lincoln's legacy has made his memorial the site of numerous demonstrations by those seeking justice. Most notable was a peaceful demonstration of 250,000 people on August 28, 1963, at which Martin Luther King, Jr. proclaimed, "I have a dream." Look for the words I HAVE A DREAM. MARTIN LUTHER KING, JR., THE MARCH ON WASHINGTON FOR JOBS AND FREEDOM, AUGUST 28, 1963, inscribed and centered on the 18th step down from the chamber. The inscription, which the National Park Service added in July 2003, marks the precise spot where King stood to deliver his famous speech.

Thirty minutes is sufficient time for viewing this memorial. *Note:* Repair and restoration work is underway into 2020, but the plan is to keep the memorial open throughout. Plans are also in the works to open a visitor's center in the Lincoln Memorial undercroft, a soaring 15,000-square-foot space beneath the memorial.

On the western end of the Mall, at 23rd St. NW (btw. Constitution and Independence aves.). www.nps.gov/linc. ☏ **202/426-6841.** Free admission. Open 24 hr. daily. Limited parking. Metro: Foggy Bottom, with a 30-min. walk. DC Circulator stop.

Martin Luther King, Jr. National Memorial ★★ MONUMENT/MEMORIAL

I must confess my disappointment in the Martin Luther King, Jr. Memorial, which provides little context for King's life and work as, arguably, the United States' most important civil rights activist. I would have preferred a memorial more like the one for FDR, whose panels illustrate scenes from FDR's presidency; or like Lincoln's or Jefferson's, whose remarkable words are rendered more fully in the stone walls. Still, the very fact of its existence, here on the Mall among memorials to presidents and to those who fought in U.S. wars, affirms King's critical role in American history.

Authorized by Congress in 1996, the memorial debuted on October 16, 2011. Hurricane Irene prevented it from opening on its originally planned date, August 28, exactly 48 years after the Rev. Dr. Martin Luther King, Jr. delivered his momentous "I Have a Dream" speech on the steps of the Lincoln Memorial. On that original date, some 250,000 people gathered on the Mall during the March on Washington for Jobs and Freedom to pressure Congress to pass the Civil Rights Act. King was assassinated on April 4, 1968, at the age of 39.

The memorial's site along the northwest lip of the Tidal Basin is significant for the "visual line of leadership" it creates between the Lincoln Memorial, representing the principles of equality and civil rights as embodied in the personage of Abraham Lincoln and carried forward in King, and the Jefferson Memorial, which symbolizes the democratic ideals of the founding fathers. Set on a crescent-shaped, 4-acre parcel of land surrounded by the capital's famous cherry trees, the mammoth sculpture (created in China, a controversial decision) rests on 300 concrete piles driven into the muddy basin terrain. A 28-foot, 6-inch statue of Dr. King in a business suit, arms folded, stands front and center, representing the "Stone of Hope"; he is flanked by two enormous background pieces, representing the "Mountain of Despair." A curving boundary wall enclosing the grounds perhaps commemorates the slain civil rights leader best, with inscriptions of excerpts from his remarkable sermons and speeches. One of those excerpts, a paraphrased quote inscribed on the Stone of Hope saying "I was a drum major for justice, peace and righteousness," immediately faced controversy when poet Maya Angelou said it made King "look like an arrogant twit." In 2013, sculptor Lei Yixin returned to modify the memorial and remove the quote.

The memorial includes a bookstore and restrooms.

Adjacent to the FDR Memorial, along the northwest side of the Tidal Basin, at Independence Ave. SW, in West Potomac Park. www.nps.gov/mlkm. ℗ **202/426-6841.** Free admission. Open 24 hr. daily. Limited parking. Metro: Smithsonian (12th St./Independence Ave. exit), with a 25-min. walk. DC Circulator stop.

National Air and Space Museum ★★ MUSEUM   Big news: The Air and Space Museum has embarked on an enormous, multi-year, $1-billion makeover, which will most certainly affect your experience if you visit in

The Boeing Milestones of Flight Hall at the National Air and Space Museum.

2020. All 23 galleries will be transformed, and portions of the museum will be closed on a rolling basis, including the theaters, museum shop, and cafe. Should you still come? Well, of course! There's still lots to see. For example, the *Spirit of St. Louis,* the 1903 Wright Flyer, Bell X-1, the Apollo Lunar Module, and Skylab will *always* be on display despite the construction, which is expected to be fully completed by 2025.

Based on visitation numbers (7 million annually, prior to the renovation), this is America's favorite museum. And even in its current state, it's not hard to understand why. The National Air and Space Museum manages to tap into that most primordial of human impulses: the urge to fly. And it does so in a multi-layered fashion, mixing extraordinary artifacts with IMAX movies, videos, and hands-on exploration of displayed equipment.

The seeds of this museum were planted when the Smithsonian Institution acquired its first aeronautical objects in 1876: 20 kites from the Chinese Imperial Commission. By the time the National Air and Space Museum opened on the National Mall 100 years later, the collection had grown to tens of thousands of objects. Today, the inventory of historic aircraft and spacecraft artifacts numbers more than 66,000, the world's largest such collection.

The place is huge, as is much of its collection. Enormous aircraft and spacecraft dangle from the ceiling or are placed in floor exhibits throughout both levels. Visitors of all ages, but mostly families, take pictures of each other against the backdrops of the towering Pershing II (34.8 ft.) and SS20 Pioneer (54.1 ft.) missiles, or the Hubble Space Telescope (42 ft.), or just about anything in the museum, as most of the artifacts dwarf humans. Tours and demonstrations are in constant rotation.

And, unfortunately, there are often lines—many, many lines. The first is just to enter the building, and you can expect longer waits since the museum closed its entrance facing the National Mall for renovations. Then there are lines to get tickets for **IMAX films ★**, or a show at the **Einstein Planetarium ★.**

First-floor galleries cover the **Space Race** and the development of huge telescopes (**Explore the Universe**); the space-themed galleries upstairs highlight **Exploring the Moon** and **Time and Navigation** in space.

The central area on both floors takes a look at historic milestones and individuals in aviation and space research and development: Space and aviation artifacts in the first-floor **Boeing Milestones of Flight Hall** illustrate ways that aviation and flight transformed the world. This is where you'll see the first American jet aircraft, the *Spirit of St. Louis* ★★, flown solo by Charles Lindbergh across the Atlantic Ocean.

If you're short on time or simply overwhelmed, there are two things you shouldn't miss. The **Sky Lab Orbital Workshop ★★★**, in the Space Race gallery on the first floor (you enter the spaceship on the second floor), allows you to walk through the country's first space station. You're actually *inside* the astronauts' living quarters; if you look up, you'll see that most of the rocket's construction lies overhead. And be sure to visit the second-floor **Wright Brothers** exhibit, where the Wright brothers' **1903 Flyer ★★★**, the world's first successful airplane, is on display.

Amateur astronomers should head outside to the museum's east terrace to peer through the telescopes in the **Phoebe Waterman Haas Public Observatory.** The observatory is free and open to the public Wednesday to Sunday noon to 3pm for daytime sightings of moon craters and sun spots, and once or twice a month for nighttime observations (more info on the website).

Or take a load off your feet for a bit and watch an IMAX film, like the ever-popular *To Fly,* or *Planet Power 3-D,* or see a show at the **Albert Einstein Planetarium ★**, which offers a free show daily at 10:30am, but you must obtain a ticket from the box office. Otherwise, tickets for IMAX and planetarium films cost anywhere from $7.50 to $15 per person (plus $3.50 per-ticket processing fees), depending on the film, age of filmgoer, and whether the person is a Smithsonian Institution member.

Wonder where the museum has put all of the aircraft and equipment that used to occupy the west wing? Much of it now resides temporarily in the National Air and Space Museum's companion location, the **Steven F. Udvar-Hazy Center,** adjacent to Washington Dulles International Airport. If you're hungry to see more aviation artifacts and spacecraft, or if you've got a flight leaving from Dulles Airport and have time to kill, drive the 25 miles out to the satellite museum. Here you can explore one huge hangar filled with aviation objects and another with space objects, each arranged by subject (Commercial Aviation, Korea and Vietnam Aviation, Sport Aviation, and so on). Perhaps the center's most notable artifact is the **space shuttle** *Discovery.* The observation tower gives a bird's-eye view of planes landing and departing at Dulles Airport. IMAX movies and simulator rides also are options. *Note:* Admission is free at Udvar-Hazy, but there is a $15 fee for parking before 4pm, except December 15.

Mall museum: Independence Ave. SW, btw. 4th and 7th sts. (on south side of Mall, with two entrances, one on Jefferson Dr. and the other on Independence Ave.). Udvar-Hazy Center: 14390 Air and Space Museum Pkwy., Chantilly, VA. www.airandspace.si.edu. ☏ **202/633-2214** (Mall location), or **703/572-4118** (Virginia location). Free admission. Both locations daily 10am–5:30pm (Mall museum open until 7:30pm many days in summer). Free 1½-hr. highlight tours daily 10:30am and 1pm. Closed Dec 25. Metro: L'Enfant Plaza (Smithsonian Museums/Maryland Ave. exit) or Smithsonian (Mall/Jefferson Dr. exit). DC Circulator stop.

National Archives Museum ★★ MUSEUM The **Rotunda** of the National Archives displays the country's most important original documents: the Declaration of Independence, the Constitution of the United States, and the Bill of Rights (collectively known as the **Charters of Freedom**). Fourteen document cases trace the story of the creation of the Charters and the ongoing influence these fundamental documents have had on the nation and the world.

It proves to be an unexpectedly thrilling experience to stand among people from all over the world and peer in this dimly lit chamber at page after page of manuscript covered top to bottom in tiny, graceful script, whose forthright declarations founded our country and changed the world. It is gratifying, too, to see the documents given context within the exhibit. For example, one panel points to the role of "founding mothers" like Abigail Adams, who cautioned her husband in a letter, "If perticular [sic] care is not paid to the Ladies, we are determined to foment a Rebelion, [sic] and will not hold ourselves bound by any Laws in which we have no voice or Representation."

But the wonders don't end there: On display in the **David M. Rubenstein Gallery** is the original 1297 Magna Carta, one of only four known to exist in the world, and the only original version on public display in the United States. The Magna Carta anchors the permanent exhibit, **Records of Rights,** which presents hundreds of other landmark documents, as well as photographs, videos, and interactive items that help visitors trace the evolution of rights in the U.S. from its founding to the present day.

Beyond famous documents are the **Public Vaults,** an area that introduces visitors to the heart of the Archives: its 10 billion records, covering 2 centuries worth of documents, from patent searches to genealogical records to copies of George Washington's handwritten inaugural address, to census records, governmental records, and more.

Using the very latest in interactive museum design—listening booths, computer terminals, videos, you name it—the curators have mined the material for drama (and often presented it in a very kid-friendly fashion). In an area on patents, for example, the process is turned into a game: You read the patent application and then try to guess what well-known gadget it was for. A section on immigration presents the search for genealogical data as a cliffhanger mystery, detailing the steps and missteps of past Archives' users. President Nixon makes several eerie appearances: You read his resignation letter and listen to disturbing excerpts from the Watergate tapes. The **Lawrence F. O'Brien Gallery** rotates exhibitions of Archives documents. On view until 2021, "Rightfully Hers: American Women and the Vote" commemorates the 100th anniversary of the 19th Amendment through historical records, photos, letters, and other documents to reveal what it really took to win the vote for one-half of the populace. Its **Boeing Learning Center** offers hands-on activities for kids, encouraging them to grab a magnifying glass and white gloves to explore some of the Archives' collection themselves.

During the day, the **William C. McGowan Theater** continually runs dramatic films illustrating the relationship between records and democracy in the lives of real people. At night it serves as a premier documentary film venue for the city.

Beyond its exhibits, the Archives are a vital resource for researchers. Anyone 16 and over is welcome to use the National Archives center for genealogical research. Call for details.

Reading one of the many historical documents at the National Archives.

The National Archives building itself is worth an admiring glance. The neoclassical structure, designed by John Russell Pope (also architect of the National Gallery of Art and the Jefferson Memorial) in the 1930s, is an impressive example of the Beaux Arts style. Seventy-two columns create a Corinthian colonnade on each of the four facades. Great bronze doors mark the Constitution Avenue entrance, and four large sculptures representing the Future, the Past, Heritage, and Guardianship sit on pedestals near the entrances. Huge pediments crown both the Pennsylvania Avenue and Constitution Avenue entrances to the building.

In peak season, you may want to reserve a spot on a guided tour (Mon–Fri 9:45am) or simply a timed-visit entry, to avoid a long wait in line. Admission is always free, but you'll pay a $1 convenience fee when you place your order online at www.recreation.gov/ticket/facility/234645.

701 Constitution Ave NW (btw. 7th and 9th sts. NW). Tourists enter on Constitution Ave., researchers on Pennsylvania Ave. www.museum.archives.gov/. © **202/357-5000.** Free admission. Daily 10am–5:30pm. Call for research hours. Closed Dec 25. Metro: Archives–Navy Memorial. DC Circulator stop.

National Gallery of Art ★★★ ART MUSEUM   Best. Art museum. Ever. That's my opinion, but let me quickly say that world-renowned critics also consider the nearly 80-year-old National Gallery of Art to be among the best museums in the world. Its base collection of more than 130,000 paintings, drawings, prints, photographs, sculpture, decorative arts, and furniture trace the development of Western art from the Middle Ages to the present in a manner that's both informative and rapturously beautiful.

Now let me tell you why this is my favorite art museum, even one of my favorite places in Washington. I love the many ways the Gallery's design and programs make the artworks and the museum itself accessible to the ordinary visitor. Architect John Russell Pope (of Jefferson Memorial fame, see p. 139) modeled his design of the original West Building after the Pantheon in Rome, anchoring the main floor's interior with a domed rotunda, and then centered a colonnaded fountain beneath the dome. The overall feeling is of spaciousness and grace, especially when the huge fountain is encircled with flowers, as it often is. Extending east and west of this nexus are long and wide, light-filled, high-ceilinged halls, off which the individual **paintings galleries** lie, nearly 100 in all, leading eventually to lovely garden courts and more places to sit.

One hundred galleries? Yes, but the 1,000-some paintings are arranged in easy-to-understand order, in separate rooms by age and nationality: 13th-century Italian to 18th-century Italian, Spanish, and French artists on the west side; 18th- and 19th-century Spanish, French, British, and American masters on the east side. You may recognize some names: Leonardo da Vinci (whose ethereal portrait, *Ginevra de' Benci,* which hangs here, is the only da Vinci painting on public view in the Americas), Rubens, Raphael, Cassatt, El Greco, Brueghel, Poussin, Vermeer, van Dyck, Gilbert Stuart, Winslow Homer, Turner, and so on.

Down the sweep of marble stairway to the ground floor lie the West Building's remaining galleries. The light-filled, vaulted-ceilinged sculpture galleries include standouts by Bernini, Rodin, Degas, and Honoré Daumier, whose 36 small bronze busts of French government administrators are highly amusing caricatures. Other galleries display decorative arts, prints and drawings, photographs, even Chinese porcelain.

Across the street from the West Building is a Sculpture Garden that features 21 sculptures created by an international roster of artists in the last few decades, as well as a stunning Chagall mosaic.

The I. M. Pei–designed East Building showcases modern and contemporary art in galleries that lie off a dazzling atrium and includes three skylit towers and an outdoor sculpture terrace with a grand view of the city. In the East Building another world opens up, as graceful as the West Building, but here it's angular, airy, and capricious. An immense and colorful Calder mobile floats overhead, but where are the galleries? You're meant to wander, but you might miss something without a strategy. So here goes:

After arriving via the underground walkway from the West Building, find the elevator that will take you to the rooftop and its two towers. Tower 1's two-gallery space presents a study in contrasts, one gallery devoted to an array of mesmerizing colorblock Rothkos, the other displaying Barnett Newman's abstract, muted depictions of the Stations of the Cross. Tower 2 holds an entire roomful of Calders, many small and toylike, some swaying mobiles suspended from skylights, all colorful whimsies.

Take the elevator inside the Calder exhibit to the "Upper Level," one floor below, and head rightward out of the elevator, through the galleries on minimalist art and across the atrium to discover the softly lit room hung with 10 Matisse cutouts, decorative designs on paper that are mounted on canvas. Most attention-getting is "Large Decoration with Masks," a wall-covering paper mural of brightly colored rosettes. (This gallery's hours are limited, so make sure you visit before 2pm Mon–Sat, and before 3pm Sun.) The third tower is for temporary exhibitions; whether you go will depend on what's on.

Okay, now you're good to go explore on your own, back through the galleries of minimalist art, or on to pop art, photography, Picasso, American art from the first half of the 20th century, and French paintings from the last half of the 19th century and first half of the 20th.

If you make your way back to the West Building and exit onto 7th Street, you are directly across from the **Sculpture Garden.** Go! Positioned throughout its lushly landscaped 6 acres you'll find a stalking *Spider* by Louise Bourgeois, a tall, blue sculpture of five stacked chairs made of patinated bronze by Lucas Samaras, and 18 other modern sculptures. In the northwest corner is a delightful, large (10×17 ft.) glass and stone mosaic by Marc Chagall.

At the center of the Sculpture Garden is an expansive fountain, which turns into an ice rink in winter. The garden is famous for its summer Friday Jazz in the Garden series of concerts, which are free and draw a crowd.

The National Gallery also mounts killer special exhibits and offers a robust year-round schedule of films, tours, and talks, monthly after-hours events from October to April, and Sunday concert series (now in its 78th year)—all free, let me emphasize.

Not free, but recommendable, are five dining options, the best of which are the **Garden Café** (its menu sometimes is tied to the theme of a current exhibit) and the Sculpture Garden's **Pavilion Café.**

We have Andrew W. Mellon to thank for the museum. The financier/philanthropist, who served as ambassador to England from 1932 to 1933, was so inspired by London's National Gallery that he decided to give such a gift to his own country. The West Building opened in Washington, D.C., in 1941, the East Building in 1978, and the Sculpture Garden in 1999.

Constitution Ave. NW, btw. 3rd and 7th sts. NW (on the north side of the Mall). www.nga.gov. © **202/737-4215.** Free admission. Gallery: Mon–Sat 10am–5pm; Sun 11am–6pm. Sculpture Garden: Memorial Day to Labor Day Sat–Thurs 10am–7pm, Fri 10am–9pm, Sun 11am–7pm; Labor Day to Memorial Day Mon–Sat 10am–5pm, Sun 11am–6pm. Ice rink: Mid-Nov to mid-Mar Mon–Thurs 10am–9pm, Fri–Sat 10am–11pm, Sun 11am–9pm. Rink fees: $9 adults under 50 and children 13 and older, $8 adults 50 and over and children under 13, plus $4 skate rental, .50 locker rental ($5 deposit required). Closed Dec 25 and Jan 1. Metro: Archives–Navy Memorial, Judiciary Square (either exit), or Gallery Place/Chinatown (Arena/7th and F sts. exit). DC Circulator stop.

National Mall ★★★ ICON   As part of his vision for Washington, Pierre L'Enfant conceived of the National Mall as a bustling ceremonial avenue of distinguished buildings. Today's 2-mile, 700-acre stretch of land extending westward from the base of the Capitol to the Potomac River, just behind the Lincoln Memorial, fulfills that dream. Eleven Smithsonian buildings, plus the National Gallery of Art and its Sculpture Garden, and a stray government building (Department of Agriculture), stake out the Mall's northern border along Constitution Avenue and its southern border along Independence Avenue. More than 2,000 American elm trees shade the pebbled walkways paralleling Jefferson and Madison drives. In a single year, more than 35 million tourists and locals crisscross the Mall as they visit the Smithsonians, hustle to work, exercise, participate in whatever festival, event, or demonstration is taking place that day, or simply go for a stroll—just as L'Enfant envisioned, perhaps.

The National Park Service maintains the land with money from Congress and from the Trust for the National Mall (www.nationalmall.org), the Park Service's fundraising partner. A third organization of interested citizens, the National Coalition to Save Our Mall (www.savethemall.org), advocates for a public voice in Mall enhancement decisions, and for more support from Congress.

Improvement projects that may be underway in 2020 include the construction of a new amphitheater and wooded canopy for performances on the grounds of the Washington Monument, and a complete overhaul of the area known as Constitution Gardens (next to the Lincoln Memorial Reflecting Pool). *One noteworthy enhancement:* The Mall's oldest structure, the 1835 **Lockkeeper's House,** reopened in 2018 after a restoration to serve as the National Mall's own small visitor center. It is located on the southwest corner of the 17th Street and Constitution Avenue NW intersection, set within a wide plaza, across 17th Street from the Washington Monument grounds.

From the foot of the Capitol to the Lincoln Memorial. www.nps.gov/nama. ⓒ **202/426-6841.** Public space, open 365/24/7. Metro: Smithsonian. DC Circulator stop.

National Museum of African American History & Culture ★★★

MUSEUM   A profound and essential American experience awaits you at the Smithsonian's newest museum, which opened on September 24, 2016. Conceived as a place where visitors of all backgrounds might comprehend America's narrative through an African-American lens, the museum succeeds on every level. History exhibits, culture galleries, and the museum's architecture and design each express critical elements of the story.

Turns out, many, many people are interested in understanding that story, more people, in fact, than the museum can usually accommodate on any given day. So, a free **timed-pass system** has been instituted to control the crowds. You have two options for obtaining advance-entry passes: You can reserve them online 3 months in advance (recommended); these timed-entry passes are released the first Wednesday of every month for 3 months hence. Or you can rise at the crack of dawn to snag same-day time-entry passes online, which go up each morning at 6:30am (four passes per order) and last until they run out. For walk-up options, a limited number (300 or so) of same-day passes are offered weekdays starting at 1pm, at the museum's Madison Drive entrance. During certain months, a "Walk-Up Weekdays" policy is offered, in which no-pass entry is offered on a first come, first served basis; check the website to see if it's on when you visit. Frustrating as it all may be, the effort is worth it.

Located across from the Washington Monument, within view of the Lincoln Memorial and the White House, and next door to the National Museum of American History, the museum's very placement nudges the visitor toward a contextual appreciation. The building belongs within this panoply, but it speaks for itself, a remarkable standout in this cool landscape of white stone structures. A three-tiered shell of 3,523 bronze-colored panels, the "corona," sheaths the museum's glass-walled exterior, angling outward and upward, suggesting designs found in traditional West African sculpture and headware. The filigreed pattern of the corona mimics the ornate ironwork crafted by slaves in 19th-century New Orleans and Charleston. (As you move along inside, you will notice cutouts in the

The National Museum of African American History & Culture.

building's bronze scrim, which allow glimpses of surrounding landmarks, including the White House, Lincoln Memorial, and Arlington Cemetery, reinforcing the museum's emphasis on viewing the American experience through the eyes of an African American.)

When you enter the museum, you are stepping inside a 400,000-square-foot space, 60% of which lies below ground. And down is where visitors go first, to the History Galleries, or "crypts"—the heart of the experience.

The museum covers more than 500 years of history, starting in the 15th century with the transatlantic slave trade and continuing to slavery in the U.S., the Civil War, Reconstruction, segregation, the Civil Rights movement, and America since 1968. Ramps lead from one exhibit area and level to the next, creating different vantage points for viewing the artifacts and for connecting the gradual progression of events in time. This bottom-to-top touring offers a symbolic converse of that in place at the United States National Holocaust Memorial Museum (p. 167), where you begin at the top floor and descend (from the rise of Hitler and Nazism to the Final Solution). Exhibits at both museums reveal history through chronological storytelling that focuses on the lives of ordinary and heroic individuals. And both museums provide areas of contemplation and reflection, where visitors can sit and take everything in, from the tragic facts to celebrations of the indomitable human spirit.

Compelling, sometimes shocking, artifacts bring the history to life. These include shackles used by an enslaved child; an early 1800s weatherboard-clad slave cabin from Edisto Island, South Carolina; Harriet Tubman's shawl and hymn book; a vintage, open-cockpit biplane used at Tuskegee Institute to train African-American pilots during World War II; the Greensboro, North Carolina, Woolworth's lunch-counter stools occupied on a February day in 1960 by four black college students who refused to move after being denied service; and assorted documents and artifacts that capture more recent developments, from the presidency of Barack Obama to the Black Lives Matter movement.

On floors two and three above ground, "the Attic," are exhibits that highlight African-American struggles and achievements exploring stories of place, region, and migration; how African Americans carved a way for themselves in a world that denied them opportunities; and African Americans' contributions in sports and the military.

The fourth floor's Arts and Culture Galleries showcase African-American contributions in music, fashion, food, theater, and the visual arts. Artifacts displayed on these floors range from the outfit that Marian Anderson wore when she sang at the Lincoln Memorial in 1939 and Chuck Berry's red Cadillac convertible to artworks by Romare Bearden and Elizabeth Catlett.

The story of the museum itself is worth telling, too, and it is told here on the concourse level of the museum. "A Century in the Making" reveals that a group of black Civil War veterans are said to have proposed the idea for an African-American history museum in 1915. Congress took up the cause from time to time over the ensuing decades, finally enacting the NMAAHC Act in December 2003, establishing the museum within the Smithsonian Institution. A four-firm architectural unit won the design competition in 2009, groundbreaking took place on February 22, 2012, and construction began. Meanwhile, staff, starting from scratch, were traveling around the country amassing artifacts. Today, more than half of the museum's collection of 37,000 objects are donations.

Given the NMAAHC's multi-layered chronicling of African-American history from its very beginnings, it is moving that President Barack Obama, the country's first black president, was the person to cut the ribbon at its opening. But, say officials, that's not the end of the story for African-American progress, nor for the museum. This is a living museum, and it will continue to tell the ever-evolving story of African-American history and culture, which at this particular time in America is more necessary than ever.

If you have time, stop by **Sweet Home Café,** the museum's 400-capacity cafeteria serving African-American tastes rooted in regional cooking traditions: the agricultural south, Creole coast, north states, and the western range.

1400 Constitution Ave. NW, btw. 14th and 15th sts. NW, next to the Washington Monument, with entrances on Madison Dr. (main entrance) and Constitution Ave. www. nmaahc.si.edu. (C) **844/750-3012.** Free admission. Daily 10am–5:30pm. Closed Dec 25. Metro: Smithsonian or Federal Triangle. DC Circulator stop.

National Museum of African Art ★ MUSEUM

This inviting little museum does not get the foot traffic of its larger, better-known sister Smithsonians, but that only makes for a happier experience for those who do visit. Find it by strolling through the Enid A. Haupt Garden, under which the subterranean museum lies, and enter via the domed pavilions, stopping first to admire the tall artwork marking the entrance, the colorful fiberglass and goldleaf "Wind Sculpture VII," evocative of a ship's sail.

Traditional and contemporary African music plays lightly in the background as you tour the dimly lit suite of rooms on three sublevels. The galleries rotate works from the museum's 12,000-piece permanent inventory of ancient and modern art, spanning art forms and geographic areas. (The museum owns the largest public holdings of contemporary African art in the United States.) Sometimes the museum mounts special exhibits of works from private and public collections to emphasize a particular art genre, like the recent "Striking Iron: The Art of African Blacksmiths," which showcased 225 works including blades and currencies, wood sculptures studded with iron, musical instruments and elaborate body adornments, all incorporating iron, focusing on the region south of the Sahara. The museum also houses a collection of some 450,000 photographs.

A tour of the museum at any time turns up diverse discoveries: a circa 13th- to 15th-century ceramic equestrian figure from Mali; face masks from Congo and Gabon; or a 15th-century Ethiopian manuscript page.

The African Art Museum was founded in 1964, joined the Smithsonian in 1979, and moved to the Mall in 1987. If you descend to sublevel 3, you will reach the subterranean passage that takes you to the **Ripley Center** (p. 158).

950 Independence Ave. SW. www.africa.si.edu. (C) **202/633-4600.** Free admission. Daily 10am–5:30pm. Closed Dec 25. Metro: Smithsonian. DC Circulator stop.

does one museum possibly sum up the history of a nation that is 243 years old
and 3.8 million square miles in size and has a population of 326 million
people? And how does the museum sort through its collection of 1.8 million
artifacts, which include every imaginable American object, from George
Washington's uniform to an 1833 steam locomotive, from the Star-Spangled
Banner to a 1960s lunch box, and choose which to display? And finally, how
does the museum serve it up in such a way as to capture both the essence of
American history and culture, and the attention of a diverse and international
public?

As the National Museum of American History celebrates 56 years in 2020,
it is nearing the end of a massive reinvention of itself that is helping the
museum meet these daunting challenges. (*Note:* The full reinvention of the
West Wing will be completed in 2020 with the opening of new third-floor
exhibitions on entertainment, culture, and the arts.) I can tell you that a visit
to the National Museum of American History today is a more penetrating, fun,
and interesting experience than it ever was before.

In **Flag Hall** is the museum's star (or should I say "starred"?) attraction: the
original Star-Spangled Banner. This large 30×34-foot wool and cotton flag is
the very one that Francis Scott Key spied at dawn on September 14, 1814,
flying above Fort McHenry in Baltimore's harbor, signifying an American
victory over the British during the War of 1812. Key memorialized that
moment in a song that became the country's official National Anthem in 1931.
The threadbare 205-year-old treasure is on view behind a window in an environmentally controlled chamber; terrific, interactive displays bring to life the
significance and grandeur of this important artifact.

From Flag Hall, stay on the second floor to see more iconic Americana.
These include the original "Elmo" puppet from *Sesame Street*; a fragment of
Plymouth rock in **American Stories;** and objects such as Thomas Jefferson's
portable desk in the exhibit **American Democracy: A Great Leap of Faith,**
which explores the theme of what it takes to create a government of, by, and
for the people. **Many Voices, One Nation** pulls treasures from the museum's
vast collection to consider how cultural geography and identity contribute to
what it means to be American—two extremely timely exhibits. One of my
favorite exhibits is **Within These Walls,** which presents a partially reconstructed, two-and-a-half-level, 200+-year-old house transplanted from Ipswich, MA, and tells the stories of the five families who lived here over time,
from Colonial days to the early 1960s. Displays include authentic objects
from the pertinent time periods. You learn, for instance that Lucy Caldwell
occupied the house in the 1830s, played that square piano you see in the parlor, and formed the Ipswich Female Anti-Slavery Society with other women
in Ipswich, considering it her moral duty to "assume a public stand in favor of
our oppressed sisters."

American ingenuity is celebrated in first-floor exhibits; this is also the most
popular floor with young museumgoers. **Wegmans Wonderplace,** geared
toward kids under age 6, is a learning playroom where kids can "cook" in a

kitchen inspired by Julia Child's (on display on the first floor, see below) and find owls hidden in a miniature replica of the Smithsonian Castle. A revamped and much improved version of an old favorite attraction, the **Lemelson Center,** features **Places of Invention** and **Spark!Lab,** where interactive exhibits allow children ages 6 to 12 to learn about inventors and inventiveness hands-on.

Other first-floor exhibits focused on American ingenuity display patent models of inventions by Samuel Morse, Alexander Graham Bell, and Thomas Edison, as well as the **workshop of Ralph Baer,** the progenitor of video games. Stop by the museum's fresh exhibit on business history, **American Enterprise,** a kind of companion piece to the **Value of Money** exhibit here.

Assorted transportation vehicles command a lot of space and attention in **America on the Move,** but to my mind they're not nearly as interesting as the exhibit titled **FOOD: Transforming the American Table, 1950–2000.** Its *pièce de résistance* is **Julia Child's home kitchen,** kitchen sink to favorite skillet, which Child donated to the museum in late 2001.

If you're interested in American wars, politics, and fashion, head to the third floor, which holds the museum's most visited exhibit: **The First Ladies** features 26 first ladies' gowns and more than 1,000 objects, which round out our perceptions about the roles and personalities of these singular women. Covering their husband's stories is **The American Presidency: A Glorious Burden,** which attempts to shine a more personal light on those who have held the office. Continue to **The Price of Freedom: Americans at War,** which explores the idea of wars as defining episodes in American history.

Note: In the same area as the children's galleries is the **Wallace H. Coulter Performance Stage and Plaza,** where cooking demonstrations, jazz concerts, and other programs frequently take place. Around the corner from this area, just inside the Constitution Avenue entrance to the museum is the **Jazz Café,** where you can power up with ice cream cones, pastries, and sandwiches. Other attractions: racecar and flight simulator rides, a large cafeteria, and a theater showing 3D American adventure movies and Hollywood films.

Constitution Ave. NW, btw. 12th and 14th sts. NW (on the north side of the Mall, with entrances on Constitution Ave. and Madison Dr.). www.americanhistory.si.edu. ☏ **202/ 633-1000.** Free admission. Daily 10am–5:30pm. Closed Dec 25. Metro: Smithsonian or Federal Triangle. DC Circulator stop.

National Museum of the American Indian ★ MUSEUM This striking building, located at the Capitol end of the National Mall, stands out for the architectural contrast it makes with neighboring Smithsonian and government structures. It is the first national museum in the country dedicated exclusively to Native Americans, and Native Americans consulted on its design, both inside and out; the main architect was a Blackfoot Indian. The museum's rippled exterior is clad in golden sand–colored Kasota limestone; the building stands 5 stories high within a landscape of wetland grasses, water features, and 40 large uncarved rocks and boulders known as "grandfather rocks."

Although the interior design is breathtaking (you enter a 120-ft.-high domed "Potomac," or rotunda, whose central atrium shows off beautiful boats, each representing the handcrafted boatbuilding traditions of different native peoples), the experience of visiting here can be bewildering, thanks to the sheer number of artifacts (some 8,500) and the variety of tribes and tribal traditions portrayed. The best way to take it all in is by joining a Culture Connections highlights tour, usually scheduled daily at 1:30pm. But always check at the welcome desk to see if any other timed tours or events are available during your visit.

If you're exploring on your own, begin with the 13-minute *Who We Are* orientation film that plays throughout the day on the fourth level. It offers a good introduction to the diversity of traditions and contemporary Native American life that the museum explores. You'll add to that understanding of Native culture by visiting two other exhibits on the fourth floor: **Our Universes,** which focuses on Native cosmologies and the spiritual connection between man and nature, and **Nation to Nation,** which explores the history of treaty-making between the United States and American Indian nations, using 125 objects, such as wampum belts and peace medals, three videos, and four interactive touch-based media stations.

The second floor's **Return to a Native Place** tells the more local story of the Algonquian peoples of the Chesapeake Bay region (today's Washington, D.C., Maryland, Virginia, and Delaware). **Window on the Collections** (found on both the third and fourth levels) is for art lovers, showcasing 4,500 objects arranged in seven categories, including animal-themed figurines and objects, beadwork, dolls, and peace medals.

Two special exhibits are worth visiting: "The Great Inka Road: Engineering an Empire" (through June 1, 2020) presents the fascinating story behind the 20,000-mile road, a century in the making, traversing mountains, lowlands, rivers, and deserts to link places that are now part of Columbia, Bolivia, Peru, Argentina, Ecuador, and Chile. "Americans" (through 2022) highlights the ways in which American Indian images, names, and stories infuse American history and contemporary life, and it sets the record straight about historical figures, like Pocahontas, and historical events, such as the Battle of Little Big Horn.

Families should check out the children's **ImagiNations** activity center.

Opening in November 2020 on the grounds of the museum, the **National Native American Veterans Memorial** (https://americanindian.si.edu/nnavm/) will honor the contributions of American Indians, Alaska Natives, and Native Hawaiians who have served in the military. The large upright stainless-steel circle will sit atop a stone drum. Take a seat on any one of the benches and reflect while listening to the sounds of water, a symbol of sacred Native Indian ceremonies.

4th St. and Independence Ave. SW. www.americanindian.si.edu. ✆ **202/633-1000.** Free admission. Daily 10am–5:30pm. Closed Dec 25. Metro: Federal Center Southwest or L'Enfant Plaza (Smithsonian Museums/Maryland Ave. exit). DC Circulator stop.

National Museum of Natural History ★★ MUSEUM I'll be blunt: This museum can be just too much. And I mean that in, unfortunately, a negative way. Not only is it the second (after the Air and Space museum) most

The National Museum of Natural History rotunda.

popular museum in town (get ready to fight the crowds!), but there are so many exhibits, and so many items within the exhibits, that the average visitor experiences an uncomfortable sensory overload.

Let me give you some numbers: The museum's collection has more than 145 million artifacts and specimens (only a small percentage on display); the building measures 1.32 million square feet, of which 325,000 square feet is public space; and about 5 million people visit annually, making this the most visited natural history museum *in the world.*

Best advice: Know before you go. Use this guide and the museum's website to develop a strategy before you arrive. For instance, as the website suggests, try to visit on a Monday, Tuesday, or Wednesday, or on any weekday in September or February, when crowds are sparser. And if you still find yourself feeling overwhelmed on arrival, do as I did on a recent visit to the busy museum: Go up to one of the green- or tan-vested "Visitor Concierges" you'll see roaming the museum and ask them to name the two must-see things they would recommend in the particular exhibit. A concierge I approached in the Sant Ocean Hall responded immediately with the "live coral reef" and the "shark mouth," pointing me to these in the vast hall. Perfect suggestions. The variously colored coral reef tank holds fish of brilliant blue, purple, yellow, and pink hues. The enormous jaw of a *Carcharodon megalodon,* a shark that lived 5 million years ago, is enclosed in a glass case; the idea is for you to pose behind the glass case so that it appears as if you're inside the mouth—a great snapshot.

The museum has 22 different galleries, with exhibits that cover the story of natural history from the earliest beginnings of life to the present. The popular National Fossil Hall reopened in 2019 after a 5-year-long extreme makeover. The massive 31,000-square-foot exhibition space features some 700 specimens, including an Alaskan palm tree, early insects, reptiles and mammals, and dramatically posed giants like the meat-and-bone-eating tyrannosaurus that stomped the earth 66 million years ago. (The museum's display is one of the most complete T-Rex fossils in the world.) It's not just dinosaurs, either: A mastodon, woolly mammoth, and prehistoric shark are on display, too.

Meanwhile, on the second floor, the Hope Diamond is still holding court in its own gallery within the **Geology, Gems and Minerals** area. (The deep-blue, 45.52-carat diamond has a storied past, which you can read about on p. 277, in chapter 10.) The second floor is also where you'll find a small showpiece on 3,000-year-old mummies, notable for the beautifully decorated coffins on display; and a temporary exhibit (until 2021) on "Outbreaks: Epidemics in a Connected World," which tracks the rushed pursuit by scientists, medical personnel, and concerned citizens to identify and contain infectious disease outbreaks around the world.

And there's more: a live **butterfly pavilion;** a **Q?rius Jr. Discovery Room** of hands-on exhibits for young children; live tarantula feedings for thrill-seekers; and a newly renovated atrium featuring restaurants on two levels.

What to pick? That's up to you. Good luck.

Constitution Ave. NW, btw. 9th and 12th sts. (on the north side of the Mall, with entrances on Madison Dr. and Constitution Ave.). www.naturalhistory.si.edu. (C) **202/633-1000.** Free admission. Daily 10am–5:30pm (until 7:30pm in summer). Closed Dec 25. Metro: Smithsonian (Mall/Jefferson Dr. exit) or Federal Triangle. DC Circulator stop.

National World War II Memorial ★★ MONUMENT/MEMORIAL When this memorial was dedicated on May 29, 2004, 150,000 people attended, among them President George W. Bush; members of Congress; Marine Corps General (retired) P. X. Kelley, who chaired the group that spearheaded construction of the memorial; actor Tom Hanks and now-retired news anchor Tom Brokaw, both of whom had been active in soliciting support for the memorial; and last, but most important, thousands of World War II veterans and their families. These legions of veterans—some dressed in uniform, many wearing

a cap identifying the name of their division—turned out with pride, happy to receive the nation's gratitude, 60 years in the making, expressed profoundly in this memorial.

Designed by Friedrich St. Florian and funded mostly by private donations, the memorial fits nicely into the landscape between the Washington Monument grounds to the east and the Lincoln Memorial and its Reflecting Pool to the west. St. Florian purposely situated the 7½-acre memorial so as not to obstruct this long view down the Mall. Fifty-six 17-foot-high granite pillars representing each state and territory stand to either side of a central plaza and the **Rainbow Pool.**

The World War II Memorial.

Likewise, 24 bas-relief panels divide down the middle so that 12 line each side of the walkway leading from the entrance at 17th Street. The panels to the left, as you walk toward the center of the memorial, illustrate seminal scenes from the war years as they relate to the Pacific front: Pearl Harbor, amphibious landing, jungle warfare, a field burial, and so on. The panels to the right are sculptured scenes of war moments related to the Atlantic front: Rosie the Riveter, Normandy Beach landing, the Battle of the Bulge, the Russians meeting the Americans at the Elbe River. Architect and sculptor Raymond Kaskey sculpted these panels based on archival photographs.

Large, open pavilions stake out the north and south axes of the memorial, and semicircular fountains create waterfalls on either side. Inscriptions at the base of each pavilion fountain mark key battles. Beyond the center Rainbow Pool is a wall of 4,000 gold stars, one for every 100 American soldiers who died in World War II. People often leave photos and mementos around the memorial, which the National Park Service gathers up daily for an archive. For compelling, firsthand accounts of World War II experiences, combine your tour here with an online visit to the **Library of Congress's Veterans History Project,** at www.loc.gov/vets. See p. 128 for more info.

From the 17th Street entrance, walk south around the perimeter of the memorial to reach a ranger station, where there are brochures as well as registry kiosks for looking up names of veterans (also at **www.wwiimemorial.com**).

17th St., near Constitution Ave. NW. www.nps.gov/nwwm. ⓒ **800/639-4992** or 202/426-6841. Free admission. Limited parking. Metro: Farragut West, Federal Triangle, or Smithsonian, with a 20- to 25-min. walk. DC Circulator stop.

S. Dillon Ripley Center ★ CULTURAL INSTITUTION   Part of the Smithsonian complex but not officially counted as a museum, the S. Dillon Ripley Center is notable for hosting **Smithsonian Associates** arts, education, and entertainment programs (open both to members and to the general public; there's usually an admission fee) and **Discovery Theater** children's plays and entertainment. The center also mounts small rotating exhibits of works from various Smithsonian museums. Look for the copper-domed, hut-like structure next to the Smithsonian Castle. Its galleries and the Discovery Theater are subterranean and connect to the Freer, Sackler, and African Art museums.

1100 Jefferson Dr. SW. www.si.edu/museums/ripley-center. ⓒ **202/633-1000.** Free admission. Daily 10am–5:30pm. Closed Dec 25. Metro: Smithsonian (Mall exit). DC Circulator stop.

Sackler Gallery ★ MUSEUM   The Sackler is one-half of what is formally known as the **National Museum of Asian Art in the United States** (the Freer Gallery, p. 137, is the other half). Though the two museums are connected by purpose, research, staff—and subterranean passageway—they occupy separate buildings.

The Sackler Gallery exists because primary benefactor Arthur M. Sackler gave the Smithsonian Institution 1,000 works of Asian art and $4 million to put toward museum construction. When it opened in 1987, the gallery held mostly ancient works, including early Chinese bronzes and jades, centuries-old Near

East ceramics, and sculpture from South and Southeast Asia. Pieces from that stellar permanent collection continue to be on rotating view in several underground galleries, along with other precious works acquired over the years, like an assemblage of Persian book artistry and 20th-century Japanese ceramics. The collection now numbers 15,000 objects. Especially recommended is the "Encountering the Buddha: Art and Practice Across Asia" exhibition, whose displays include a Tibetan Buddhist shrine and a Sri Lankan *stupa* (domed Buddhist shrine), on view until November 2020.

On your way to viewing the Sackler's crown jewels in the subterranean galleries, you'll discover modern works. In the museum's street-level pavilion is a changing exhibit called **Perspectives,** always featuring captivating pieces by a contemporary Asian or Asian-diaspora artist. A recent exhibition, for example, was Indian artist Subodh Gupta's monumental installation *Terminal.* The artwork was a multi-spired tower created out of Indian household brass and stainless-steel vessels, a web of thread connecting the pieces together.

You'll encounter another work of contemporary art as you descend the stairs to tour the main galleries. The sculpture suspended from the skylit atrium and into the stairwell is called *Monkeys Grasp for the Moon* and was designed specifically for the gallery by Chinese artist Xu Bing. The work links 21 laminated wood pieces, each of which spells the word "monkey" in one of a dozen languages.

1050 Independence Ave. SW. www.asia.si.edu. ℂ **202/633-4880.** Free admission. Daily 10am–5:30pm. Closed Dec 25. Metro: Smithsonian (Mall/Jefferson Dr. exit). DC Circulator stop.

Smithsonian Information Center ("The Castle") ★ MUSEUM

This 1855 Medieval-style building, with its eight crenellated towers and rich red sandstone facade, lives up to its nickname, at least from the exterior. Its Great Hall interior is rather unattractive, but that doesn't matter, because you're just here for information, possibly restrooms, and perhaps a bite to eat.

There's not much else in this big building that's open to the public. The remains of Smithsonian benefactor James Smithson are buried in that big crypt in the Mall-side entrance area, which includes a small exhibit about the man. The pretty south-side entrance has been repainted to appear as it did in the early 1900s, when children's exhibits were displayed here. On the east side of the building is the **Castle Café,** which opens at 8:30am, earlier than any other building on the Mall. Coffee, pastries, sandwiches, and even beer and wine are sold. Situate yourself at a table inside, where there's free Wi-Fi, or outdoors in the lovely **Enid A. Haupt Garden,** and plot your day.

1000 Jefferson Dr. SW. www.si.edu. ℂ **202/633-1000.** Daily 8:30am–5:30pm (info desk 9am–4pm). Closed Dec 25. Metro: Smithsonian (Mall exit). DC Circulator stop.

United States Botanic Garden ★ GARDEN

For the feel of summer in the middle of winter and the sight of lush, breathtakingly beautiful greenery and flowers year-round, stop in at the Botanic Garden, located at the foot of the Capitol and next door to the National Museum of the American Indian. The grand conservatory devotes half of its space to exhibits that focus on the importance of plants to people, and half to exhibits that focus on ecology and the evolutionary biology of plants. But those finer points may escape you as you wander through the various chambers, outdoors and indoors, upstairs and down, gazing in stupefaction at so much flora. Throughout its 10 "garden rooms" and two courtyards, the conservatory holds about 1,300 living species, or about 3,000 plants. Individual areas include a high-walled enclosure, called "the Tropics," of palms, ferns, and vines; an **Orchid Room;** a garden of plants used for medicinal purposes; a primeval garden; and seasonal gardens created especially for children. Stairs and an elevator in the Tropics take you to a mezzanine level near the top of the greenhouse, where you can admire the jungle of greenery 24 feet below and, if condensation on the glass windows doesn't prevent it, a view of the Capitol Building. Just outside the conservatory is the **National Garden,** which includes the **First Ladies Water Garden,** a formal rose garden, a butterfly garden, an amphitheater, and a lawn terrace. Tables and benches make this a lovely spot for a picnic, though much of the garden is unshaded.

Ask at the front desk about guided tours, which don't follow a regular schedule. The USBG sometimes offers entertainment and special programs, such as the popular American Roots summer concert series.

The garden annex across the street holds **Bartholdi Park.** It's about the size of a city block and features a cast-iron classical fountain created by Frédéric Auguste Bartholdi, designer of the Statue of Liberty. Flower gardens bloom amid tall ornamental grasses, benches are sheltered by vine-covered bowers, and a touch and fragrance garden contains such herbs as pineapple-scented sage. Spring through fall, this is a pleasant place to enjoy a picnic at one of the many umbrella tables.

Note: When you visit Bartholdi Park, you may notice the **American Veterans Disabled for Life Memorial** (www.nps.gov/nama/planyourvisit/american-veterans-disabled-for-life.htm or www.avdlm.org; ✆ **877/426-6838**), located just across the street at 150 Washington Ave. SW. With its star-shaped fountain, continuously running reflecting pool, and panels of laminated glass etched with the images and quotations of injured soldiers, the memorial pays tribute to the more than 4 million soldiers injured while serving their country.

100 Maryland Ave. SW (btw. First and 3rd sts. SW, at the foot of the Capitol, bordering the National Mall). www.usbg.gov. ✆ **202/225-8333.** Free admission. Conservatory and National Garden daily 10am–5pm (National Garden open until 7pm in summer); Bartholdi Park dawn–dusk. Metro: Federal Center SW (Smithsonian Museums/Maryland Ave. exit). DC Circulator stop.

Vietnam Veterans Memorial ★★ MONUMENT/MEMORIAL The

Vietnam Veterans Memorial is possibly the most poignant sight in Washington: two long, black-granite walls in the shape of a V, each inscribed with the names of the men and women who gave their lives, or remain missing, in the longest war in American history. Even if no one close to you died in Vietnam, it's moving to watch visitors grimly studying the directories to find out where their loved ones are listed, or rubbing pencil on paper held against a name etched into the wall. The walls list close to 60,000 people, most of whom died very young.

The Vietnam Veterans Memorial.

Because of the raging conflict over U.S. involvement in the war, Vietnam veterans had received almost no recognition of their service before the memorial was conceived by Vietnam vet Jan Scruggs. The nonprofit Vietnam Veterans Memorial Fund raised $7 million and secured a 2-acre site in tranquil Constitution Gardens to erect a memorial that would make no political statement and would harmonize with neighboring memorials. By separating the issue of the wartime service of individuals from the issue of U.S. policy in Vietnam, the VVMF hoped to begin a process of national reconciliation.

The design by Yale senior Maya Lin was chosen in a national competition open to all citizens ages 18 and over. Erected in 1982, the memorial's two walls are angled at 125 degrees to point to the Washington Monument and the Lincoln Memorial. The walls' mirror-like surfaces reflect surrounding trees, lawns, and monuments. The names are inscribed in chronological order, documenting an epoch in American history as a series of individual sacrifices from the date of the first casualty in 1959. The National Park Service continues to add names as Vietnam veterans die eventually of injuries sustained during the war. Catalogs near the entrances to the memorial list names alphabetically and the panel and row number for each name that is inscribed in the wall. Elsewhere on the grounds of the Vietnam Veterans Memorial, though not part of Maya Lin's design, are two other sculptures honoring the efforts of particular servicemen and women: the **Three Servicemen Statue** and the **Vietnam Women's Memorial.**

Northeast of the Lincoln Memorial, east of Henry Bacon Dr. (btw. 21st and 22nd sts. NW, on the Constitution Ave. NW side of the Mall). www.nps.gov/vive. *C* **202/426-6841.** Free admission. Limited parking. Metro: Foggy Bottom, with 25-min. walk. DC Circulator stop.

Washington Monument ★★★ MONUMENT/MEMORIAL Step
inside the Washington Monument and onto the elevator that whisks visitors to

the 500-foot observation deck of this towering obelisk with views for miles in all directions. Or gaze up at the monument's exterior—it's hard not to; it stands out. And while you're gazing, keep this history in mind:

The idea of a tribute to George Washington was first broached 16 years before his death, by the Continental Congress of 1783. But the new nation had more pressing problems, and funds were not readily available. It wasn't until the early 1830s, with the 100th anniversary of Washington's birth approaching, that any action was taken.

First there were several fiascos. A mausoleum under the Capitol Rotunda was provided for Washington's remains, but a grandnephew, citing Washington's will, refused to allow the body to be moved from Mount Vernon. In 1830, Horatio Greenough was commissioned to create a memorial statue for the Rotunda. He came up with a bare-chested Washington, draped in classical Greek garb. A shocked public claimed he looked as if he were "entering or leaving a bath," and so the statue was relegated to the Smithsonian. Finally, in 1833, prominent citizens organized the Washington National Monument Society. The design of Treasury Building architect Robert Mills was accepted.

The cornerstone was laid on July 4, 1848, and construction continued for 6 years, until declining contributions and the Civil War brought work to a halt at an awkward 153 feet (you can still see a change in the color of the stone about one-third of the way up). It took until 1876 for sufficient funds to become available, thanks to President Grant's authorization for use of federal monies to complete the project, and another 4 years after that for work to resume on the unsightly stump. The monument's dedication ceremony took place in 1885, and it finally opened to the public in 1888.

In August 2011, a large earthquake struck the D.C. area and severely damaged the landmark's structure. The National Park Service launched a multi-year refurbishing effort to fix the landmark's elevator once and for all.

Visiting the Washington Monument: First off, even though admission is free, you'll need a ticket; see below for details. Travel light and definitely don't bring large backpacks, strollers, or open containers of food or drink, none of which are allowed inside the Monument. When you have your ticket, stand in line to pass through the new permanent security screening facility, and from there into the Monument's large elevator, which takes you upward for 70 seconds.

You won't arrive at the pinnacle of the 555-foot, 5⅛-inch-tall obelisk, but close to it: the 500-foot level of the world's tallest freestanding work of masonry. At this height, it's clear to see that the Washington Monument lies at the very heart of Washington, D.C., landmarks—and its 360-degree views are spectacular. Due east are the Capitol and Smithsonian buildings; due north is the White House; due west are the World War II and Lincoln memorials (with Arlington National Cemetery beyond); due south are the Martin Luther King, Jr. and Jefferson memorials, overlooking the Tidal Basin and the Potomac River. On a clear day, it's said you can see 20 miles in any direction.

Once you've gotten your fill of the views, head down the steps to the small museum (at level 490 ft.), where you can peer at bent lightning rods removed from the top of the Monument after it had been struck; discover that Pierre L'Enfant had hoped to honor George Washington with an equestrian statue; and read the prophetic quote by Sen. Robert Winthrop, at the 1885 dedication of the Washington Monument: THE LIGHTENING OF HEAVEN MAY SCAR AND BLACKEN IT. AN EARTHQUAKE MAY SHAKE ITS FOUNDATIONS...BUT THE CHARACTER WHICH IT COMMEMORATES AND ILLUSTRATES IS SECURE.

The Washington Monument, with the U.S. Capitol in the distance.

Ticket information: The National Park Service was still nailing down its new ticketing procedure when this book went to press. Admission to the Washington Monument is free, but you will need a ticket to get in. The ticket booth is located in the Monument Lodge, at the bottom of the hill from the monument, on 15th Street NW between Madison and Jefferson drives; it opens daily at 8:30am. Tickets are often gone by 9am, so plan to get here by 7:30 or 8am, especially in peak season. If you want advance tickets, call the **National Park Reservation Service** (𝄐 877/444-6777) or go to www.recreation.gov and type "Washington Monument DC" into the "Search for Places" field on the left-hand side of the page. You'll pay a minimal service fee per ticket if you order in advance, plus a little more for shipping and handling if you order 10 or more days in advance and want the tickets mailed to you; otherwise, you can pick up the tickets at the "Will Call" window at the ticket kiosk. To make sure that you get tickets for your desired date, reserve your tickets at least 2 weeks in advance. You can order up to six (6) tickets.

15th St. NW, directly south of the White House (btw. Madison Dr. and Constitution Ave. NW). www.nps.gov/wamo. 𝄐 **202/426-6841.** Limited parking. Metro: Smithsonian (Mall/Jefferson Dr. exit), with a 10-min. walk. DC Circulator stop.

SOUTHWEST OF THE MALL

Four top attractions are located across Independence Avenue from the National Mall. These sites are not National Park Service properties, so I separate them from other attractions located nearby in the southwest section of the National Mall and Memorial Parks category.

Bureau of Engraving and Printing ★ GOVERNMENT BUILDING
This is where they literally show you the money: A staff of about 1,172 works round-the-clock Monday through Friday churning it out at the rate of about

JAMES SMITHSON & the smithsonians

You must be wondering by now: How did the Smithsonian Institution come to be? It's rather an unlikely story, concerning the largesse of a wealthy English scientist named James Smithson (1765–1829), the illegitimate son of the Duke of Northumberland. Smithson willed his vast fortune to the United States, to found "at Washington, under the name of the Smithsonian Institution, an establishment for the increase and diffusion of knowledge." Smithson never explained why he left this handsome bequest to the United States, a country he had never visited. Speculation is that he felt the new nation, lacking established cultural institutions, most needed his funds.

Smithson died in Genoa, Italy, in 1829. Congress accepted his gift in 1836; 2 years later, half a million dollars' worth of gold sovereigns (a considerable sum in the 19th century) arrived at the U.S. Mint in Philadelphia. For the next 8 years, Congress debated the best possible use for these funds. Finally, in 1846, President James Polk signed an act into law establishing the Smithsonian Institution and authorizing a board to receive "all objects of art and of foreign and curious research, and all objects of natural history, plants, and geological and mineralogical specimens...for research and museum purposes." In 1855, the first Smithsonian building opened on the Mall, not as a museum, but as the home of the Smithsonian Institution. The red sandstone structure suffered a fire and underwent several reconstructions over the years, to serve today as the Smithsonian Information Center, known by all as "the Castle." Smithson's remains are interred in the crypt located inside the north vestibule (National Mall side).

Today, the Smithsonian Institution's 19 museums and galleries (D.C. has 17), 9 research centers, and the National Zoological Park comprise the world's largest museum complex. Millions of people visit the Smithsonians annually—nearly 30 million visitors toured the museums in 2018. The Smithsonian's collection of 156 million objects spans the entire world and all its history, its peoples and animals (past and present), and our attempts to probe into the future.

So vast is the collection that Smithsonian museums display only about 1% or 2% of the collection's holdings at any given time. Artifacts range from a 3.5-billion-year-old fossil to inaugural gowns worn by the First Ladies. Thousands of scientific expeditions sponsored by the Smithsonian have pushed into remote frontiers in the deserts, mountains, polar regions, and jungles of the world.

Individually, each museum is a powerhouse in its own field. The **National Museum of Natural History,** with 5 million annual visitors, is the most visited museum in the world. The **National Air and Space Museum** maintains the world's largest collection of historic aircraft and spacecraft. The **Freer** and **Sackler Galleries** house the largest Asian art research library in the United States. The **Smithsonian American Art Museum** is the nation's first-established collection of American art and one of the largest in the world. And so on.

To find out information about any of the Smithsonian museums, go to **www.si.edu**, which directs you to their individual home pages.

$300 million a day. Everyone's eyes pop as they walk past rooms overflowing with new greenbacks. But the money's not the whole story. The bureau prints security documents for other federal government agencies, including military IDs and passport pages.

A 40-minute guided tour begins with a short introductory film. Large windows allow you to see what goes into making paper money: designing, inking, engraving, stacking of bills, cutting, and examining for defects. The process combines traditional, old-world printing techniques with the latest technology to create counterfeit-proof currency. Additional exhibits display bills no longer in circulation and a $100,000 bill designed for official transactions. (Since 1969 the largest-denomination bill issued for the general public is $100.)

After you finish the tour, allow time to explore the **visitor center,** open from 8:30am to 7pm, with additional exhibits and a gift shop, where you can buy bags of shredded money, uncut sheets of currency in different denominations, and copies of historic documents, such as a hand-engraved replica ($200) of the Declaration of Independence.

Ticket tips: Many people line up each day to get a peek at all the moolah, so arrive early, especially during the peak tourist season. To avoid a line, consider securing VIP, also called "congressional," tour tickets from one of your senators or congresspersons; e-mail or call at least 3 months in advance. Tours take place April through August at 8:15 and 8:45am, and between 4 and 4:45pm.

Tickets for general-public tours are generally not required from September to February; simply find the visitors' entrance at 14th and C streets. March through August, however, every person taking the tour must have a ticket. To obtain one, go to the ticket booth on the Raoul Wallenberg (formerly 15th St.) side of the building. You'll receive a ticket specifying a tour time for that same day and be directed to the 14th Street entrance. You're allowed as many as four tickets per person. The ticket booth opens at 8am and closes when all tickets are dispersed for the day.

14th and C sts. SW. www.moneyfactory.gov. ℂ **866/874-2330.** Free admission. Mon–Fri 9am–2pm Sept to mid-March; 9am–6pm mid-March through Aug. Closed Sat–Sun, federal holidays, and Dec 25–Jan 1. Metro: Smithsonian (Independence Ave. exit). DC Circulator stop.

International Spy Museum ★★ MUSEUM   A visit to the International Spy Museum takes on a whole new meaning in the light of recent history. One can easily believe the claim made in the museum's 5-minute introductory film that Washington, D.C., has more spies than any other city in the world. Yikes. Well, if you can't flee them, join 'em. This museum gives you the chance to do just that, learning the tricks of the trade in interactive exhibits that allow you to take on a new identity and test your powers of observation. (Is that a lipstick tube in your purse or a gun?) Turns out, the most unlikely of people have acted as spies in their time. Would you believe Moses? George Washington? Julia Child?

The Spy Museum moved to its current location in 2019, doubling the floor space of the original museum and incorporating cool features in its design like the "glass veil suspended in front of an enclosed black box exhibition space," which allows the movement of people to be visible from both inside and outside. Its inventory of international-espionage artifacts numbers more than 7,000, in exhibits that cover history, as noted, as well as training, equipment, the "spies among us," legendary spooks, Civil War spies, and 21st-century cyber-spying. Explore Communist Berlin, including a Stasi office with all original artifacts, a border checkpoint, and original segments of the Berlin Wall. Or immerse yourself in the latest cyber-security threats and decipher possible future threats to the security of nations. It's a fascinating experience to hear about such a diverse cast, from the women whose analytical prowess facilitated the capture of Osama Bin Laden to James Lafayette, the African-American spy whose intelligence reports helped George Washington clinch victory in the American Revolution, and many others, famous, infamous, and unknown. 700 L'Enfant Plaza SW (at Independence Ave. SW). www.spymuseum.org. ⓒ **202/393-7798.** Admission $25 adults; $20 seniors/military/college students; $15 youths 7–12; children 5 and under free. Mon–Thurs 9am–7pm; Sun 10am–7pm; closed Fri and Sat. Metro: L'Enfant Plaza.

Museum of the Bible ★ MUSEUM   This eight-story, 430,000-square-foot museum is about the same mammoth size as the Smithsonian's National Museum of African American History & Culture. Like that museum, the Bible Museum's size indicates the epic nature of its subject—in this case, 3,500 years of history related to the Bible, and the Bible's impact on the world. There's a lot to see: Some 3,150 artifacts are on display, ranging from a fragment of an ancient Dead Sea Scroll to an illuminated manuscript from the 14th century to a copy of Elvis's personal Bible. And there's a lot to do: The center layers the traditional touring experience with immersive activities that have you walking through a re-creation of 1st-century Nazareth, complete with costumed villagers a la Williamsburg, or watching a film that flies you over the city of Washington, pointing out biblical inscriptions at capital landmarks as you go. Although the museum holds eight floors, the primary exhibits lie on floor 2 (**The Impact of the Bible on the World**), floor 3 (**The Stories of the Bible,** in entertainment

UPDATE ON NEW bills

You may have heard about the coming redesigns of the $20, $10, and $5 bills and may wonder whether you will see these new notes being printed during your tour. No, you will not. The task of redesigning the bills and incorporating the new designs into the Bureau's secure printing process takes time, and the Trump administration has delayed the process by at least 6 years. The original plan was for the Treasury Department to unveil the new $20, $10, and $5 notes in 2020, in conjunction with the 100th anniversary of the ratification of the 19th Amendment, giving women the right to vote. Latest reporting indicates that the official rollout date will take place in 2026 or later. Sometime in the future, then, we can look forward to seeing the $20 bill featuring abolitionist Harriet Tubman on the front and Andrew Jackson on the back; the $10 bill keeping Alexander Hamilton on the front but depicting suffragettes Lucretia Mott, Susan B. Anthony, Alice Paul, Elizabeth Cady Stanton, and Sojourner Truth on the reverse; and the $5 note keeping Abraham Lincoln on the face, but the flip side depicting historic events at the Lincoln Memorial involving First Lady Eleanor Roosevelt, singer Marian Anderson, and civil rights leader Dr. Martin Luther King, Jr.

form), and floor 4 (**The History of the Bible**). Visit levels B1, 1, and 5 to tour special exhibits and level 6 to enjoy good eats at **Manna** and take in an outstanding view of the capital. The museum is just a couple of blocks south of the National Museum of the American Indian and the National Mall.

I recommend my usual strategy for tackling a visit to an overwhelming museum: Start with a general guided tour, then ask your guide what exhibit or artifact is most meaningful to him or her. Or, if you have a particular interest, say, in what life was like in ancient Israel, head there first. In fact, a number of themed guided tours focus on one area or subject, such as "The Bible in American History," each lasting 45 minutes and costing an additional $9.99. I signed up for the highlights tour, whose designated top hits include Julia Ward Howe's original draft of the *Battle Hymn of the Republic,* written in 1861; and a fragment of a first edition of the Gutenberg Bible, circa 1455. My guide's personal recommendation was the "Impact of the Bible" section on criminal justice in America, specifically its collection of personal anecdotes, including that of a man in jail for life who nevertheless has found peace within himself through his newfound understanding of the Bible, and the tale of a jury that relied on Bible verses to find a man guilty of murder and deserving of the death sentence. Provocative.

The Bible Museum is Smithsonian in size and scope, but a different animal altogether. This is a privately funded facility, whose founders and primary funders are the evangelical billionaire Green family, owners of the chain of Hobby Lobby arts and crafts stores. Buy tickets online for discounted rates.

400 4th St. SW (at D St. SW). museumofthebible.org. © **866/430-6682.** Admission $20–$25 adults; $10–$15 children 7–17; free for children 6 and under. Daily 10am–5pm. Closed Thanksgiving, Dec 25, and Jan 1. Metro: Federal Center SW.

United States Holocaust Memorial Museum ★★ MUSEUM The

Holocaust Museum documents Nazi Germany's systematic persecution and annihilation of 6 million Jews and others between 1933 and 1945, presenting visitors with individual stories of both horror and courage in the persecuted people's struggle to survive. The museum calls itself a "living memorial to the Holocaust," the idea being for people to visit, confront the evil of which mankind is capable, and leave inspired to face down hatred and inhumanity when they come upon it in the world. A message repeated over and over is this one of Holocaust survivor and author Primo Levi: "It happened. Therefore it can happen again. And it can happen everywhere." Since the museum opened in 1993, more than 43 million visitors have taken home that message, and another: "What you do matters."

You begin your tour of the permanent exhibit on the first floor, where you pick the identity card of an actual Holocaust victim, whose fate you learn about in stages at different points in the exhibit. Then you ride the elevator to the fourth floor, where "Nazi Assault, 1933–1939" covers events in Germany, from Hitler's appointment as chancellor in 1933 to Germany's invasion of Poland and the official start of World War II in 1939. You learn that anti-Semitism was nothing new, and observe for yourself in newsreels how

Germans were bowled over by Hitler's powers of persuasion and propaganda. Exhibits tell stories of desperation, like the voyage of the *St. Louis* passenger liner in May 1939, which sailed from Germany to Havana with 900 Jews, but was turned away and returned to Europe.

The middle floor of the permanent exhibit covers the years 1940 to 1945, laying bare the horrors of the Nazi machine's "Final Solution" for the Jews, including deportations, the ghetto experience, and life and death in the concentration camps. Survivors tell their stories in taped recordings. Throughout the museum are artifacts like transport rail cars, reconstructed concentration camp barracks, and photographs of "killing squad" executions. One of the most moving exhibits is the "Tower of Faces," which contains photographs of the Jewish people who lived in the small Lithuanian town of Eishishok for some 900 years, before the Nazis killed nearly all, in 2 days in September 1941.

"The Last Chapter," on the second floor, documents the stories of heroes, like the king of Denmark, who was able to save the lives of 90% of Denmark's Jewish population. Exhibits also recount the Allies' liberation of the concentration camps and aftermath events, from Jewish emigration to America and Israel to the Nuremberg trials. At exhibit's end is the hour-long film, *Testimonies,* in which Holocaust survivors tell their stories. The tour finishes in the **Hall of Remembrance,** a place for meditation and reflection and where you may light a memorial candle.

Note: A group of Holocaust survivors volunteers at the museum, usually two each day. The volunteers stand near the information desk on the first floor and are there to answer questions.

Don't overlook the first-floor and lower-level exhibits. Always on view are **"Daniel's Story: Remember the Children,"** for children 8 and older, and the **"Wall of Remembrance"** (Children's Tile Wall), which commemorates the 1.5 million children killed in the Holocaust. The lower level is also the site for special exhibits. On view through 2021 is an exhibit that explores American responses to Nazism.

The museum also houses a Resource Center that includes a registry of Holocaust survivors and victims, a library, and archives, all of which are available to anyone who wants to research family history or the Holocaust.

Note: The museum's permanent exhibit is not recommended for children 11 and under; for older children, it's advisable to prepare them for what they'll see.

A cafeteria and museum shop are on the premises.

100 Raoul Wallenberg Place SW (formerly 15th St. SW; near Independence Ave., just off the Mall). www.ushmm.org. ℂ **202/488-0400.** Free admission. Daily 10am–5:30pm, open later in peak seasons. Closed Yom Kippur and Dec 25. Metro: Smithsonian (12th St./Independence Ave. exit). DC Circulator stop.

MIDTOWN

The **White House** is midtown's main attraction and offers reason enough to visit this part of town, even if you're only able to admire it from the outside. Midtown is where you'll find an off-the-Mall Smithsonian museum, the

Because the Holocaust Museum gets so many visitors (it has hosted as many as 10,000 people in a single day), passes specifying a visit time (in 15-min. intervals) are required in March through August, the busiest months. You can also obtain same-day passes by arriving early and standing in line on the 14th Street side of the museum's alley, where staff distribute passes starting at 9:45am. (If there's no line, head inside to the information desk.) The museum also offers a limited number of same-day passes online, starting at 6am on the day you hope to visit; or you can reserve as many as 55 tickets in advance at www.etix.com (search for "Holocaust"; you can also access the online etix system via the USHMM website), for $1 per pass (you print your own tickets). Passes are valid for entry within a 1-hour time frame from the time stamped on your pass. *Note:* Passes are for the museum's permanent exhibition on the first three floors. No passes are needed to see the lower-level exhibits.

Renwick Gallery, and smaller and more specialized art collections and several historic houses. Pick and choose from the offerings below, or follow the walking tour of the neighborhood outlined in chapter 10.

Art Museum of the Americas ★ ART MUSEUM

Contemporary Latin American and Caribbean artworks are on display inside this picturesque, red-tile-roofed, Spanish colonial–style structure. The museum rotates art from its permanent collection of 2,000 works, and sometimes collaborates with other organizations to mount special exhibits, often with the purpose of highlighting themes of democracy, development, and human rights. The Organization of American States opened the museum in 1976 as a gift to the U.S. in honor of its bicentennial.

201 18th St. NW (at Virginia Ave.). www.museum.oas.org. © **202/370-0147.** Free admission. Tues–Sun 10am–5pm. Closed federal holidays and Good Friday. Metro: Farragut West (18th St. exit) or Farragut North (K St. exit).

Daughters of the American Revolution (DAR) Museum ★ MUSEUM

The DAR Museum gives visitors a glimpse of pre-1840 American life through displays of folk art, rocking chairs, quilts and other furnishings, silverware, samplers, and everyday objects. Its 31 **Period Rooms** reflect trends in decorative arts and furnishings from 1690 to 1935. On display in the Americana Room are select items from the museum's archives of the paperwork of each period, from Colonial days through the Revolutionary War, up to the country's beginnings: diaries, letters, and household inventories. See p. 263 for more information.

1776 D St. NW (at 17th St.). www.dar.org/museum. © **202/628-1776.** Free admission. Museum and Period Rooms Mon–Fri 8:30am–4pm; Sat 9am–5pm. Americana Room Mon–Fri 8:30am–4pm. Closed federal holidays. Metro: Farragut West (17th St. exit) or Farragut North (K St. exit).

National Children's Museum ★★ MUSEUM

A 50-foot slide, an "immersive sandbox," interactive space exploration, and bubbles, so many bubbles. This sprawling 30,000-square-foot museum, which opened in late 2019, is designed to "spark curiosity and ignite creativity for kids and the young at heart." Highlights include a cloud-inspired climbing structure and slide spanning all four floors of the museum; a live green screen where kids get super powers to control the weather; life-sized bubbles; an immersive digital space focused on STEAM (science, technology, engineering, arts, and math) activities through play; and at opening, Disney's "Doc McStuffins, the Exhibit." The museum is also continuing its daily programming, including art classes, design/build experiments, and toddler activities.

Founded in 1974 as the Capital Children's Museum, the museum operated out of an old nunnery behind Union Station for nearly 30 years before becoming a "museum without walls" for several years. Its newest location will hopefully be a more permanent home for the community-focused museum.

The museum has a cafe with a fun, healthy menu and an espresso bar serving beer and wine for "former children."

1300 Pennsylvania Ave. NW (at 14th St. in the Ronald Reagan Bldg. and International Trade Ctr.). www.nationalchildrensmuseum.org. © **202/844-2486.** Admission $11 adults and kids 2–17. Check website for hours. Metro: Federal Triangle.

Octagon Museum ★ HISTORIC HOME   This is the country's oldest museum dedicated to architecture and design. Dr. William Thornton, first architect of the Capitol, designed the house, completed in 1801. As its name suggests, the structure is an architectural marvel. Eight sides, though? Nope, try six. Thornton made the house for Colonel John Tayloe III, a Virginia planter, breeder of racehorses, and friend of George Washington, who would come by to inspect the construction site from time to time. Upon its completion (which Washington did not live to see), the Octagon became a favorite social mecca, the Tayloes welcoming John Adams, Thomas Jefferson, James Madison, James Monroe, Daniel Webster, Henry Clay, and their ilk.

1799 New York Ave. NW (at 18th St.). www.architectsfoundation.org/octagon-museum. © **202/626-7439.** Free admission for walk-in, self-guided tours, or $5–$10 for guided tours of 5 or more (by appointment only). Thurs–Sat 1–4pm. Metro: Farragut West (17th St. exit).

Renwick Gallery of the Smithsonian American Art Museum ★★ ART MUSEUM   The Renwick Gallery is out to blow your mind. Long the city's go-to venue for lovers of American decorative arts, traditional and modern crafts, and architectural design, the museum in the past few years has morphed into a funhouse showcasing room-size installations of innovative, immersive artworks. Its 2018-2019 show *No Spectators: The Art of Burning Man,* which brought stampedes of visitors, is a good example. Showcasing the large-scale artworks made for the spirited desert gathering known as Burning Man, the second floor's 4,000-square-foot Grand Salon became a temple whose walls and ceiling were covered with small, decorative unstained wooden cutouts; visitors were invited to honor someone who'd died by writing the person's name or a message on one of these little curlicue blocks, leaving it behind. (The temple is on view until Jan 5, 2020.) There was also

The Renwick Gallery.

an 18-foot-high naked woman made of stainless steel, a 9-foot-high dragon crafted of recycled objects, and gigantic magic mushrooms that inflated and deflated when you stepped on a green-lit circle in front of each, not to mention virtual-reality activities and dressed-up mannequins.

The Renwick's galleries also showcase **Connections,** highlighting more than 80 objects "celebrating craft as a discipline and an approach to living differently in the modern world." The artworks span 90 years and numerous media.

On view in other rooms of the museum are objects from the permanent collection, such as Wendell Castle's *Ghost Clock.* An exhibit in the elegant Octagon Room uses photos, documents, and art objects to chronicle the building's history.

Designed by and named for James W. Renwick, Jr., architect of the Smithsonian Castle (p. 159), the Renwick was built in 1859, an example of French Second Empire–style architecture. A 2015 renovation restored the original 19th-century window configurations, and turned up some surprises, like long-concealed vaulted ceilings on the second floor. Located directly across the street from the White House, the Renwick originally was built to house the art collection of William Wilson Corcoran. The collection quickly outgrew the space, which led to the opening of the Corcoran Gallery of Art (currently closed to the public) just down the street, in 1874.

1661 Pennsylvania Ave. NW (at 17th St.). www.renwick.americanart.si.edu. ℂ **202/633-7970.** Free admission. Daily 10am–5:30pm. Closed Dec 25. Metro: Farragut West or Farragut North.

The White House ★★★ GOVERNMENT BUILDING It's amazing when you think about it: This house has served as residence, office, reception site, and world embassy for every U.S. president since John Adams. The White House is the only private residence of a head of state in the world that is open year-round to the public, free of charge, a practice that Thomas

Jefferson inaugurated. On a typical day, you'll be one of some 1,600 people touring the White House, knowing that meanwhile, somewhere in this very building, the president and staff are meeting with foreign dignitaries, congressional members, and business leaders, hashing out the most urgent national and global decisions. For tour info, see box, p. 175.

An Act of Congress in 1790 established the city now known as Washington, District of Columbia, as the seat of the federal government. George Washington and city planner Pierre L'Enfant chose the site for the president's house and staged a contest to find a builder. Although Washington picked the winner—Irishman James Hoban—he was the only president never to live in the White House. The structure took 8 years to build, starting in 1792, when its cornerstone was laid. Its facade is made of the same stone used to construct the Capitol. The mansion quickly became known as the "White House," thanks to the limestone whitewashing applied to the walls to protect them, later replaced by white lead paint in 1818. In 1814, during the War of 1812, the British set fire to the White House and gutted the interior; the exterior managed to endure only because a rainstorm extinguished the fire. What you see today is Hoban's basic creation: a building modeled after an Irish country house (in fact, Hoban had in mind the house of the Duke of Leinster in Dublin).

Insider tip: Tours of the White House exit from the North Portico. Before you descend the front steps, look to your left to see the window whose sandstone still remains unpainted as a reminder of the 1814 fire.

Additions over the years have included the South Portico in 1824, the North Portico in 1829, and electricity in 1891, during Benjamin Harrison's presidency. In 1902, repairs and refurnishing of the White House cost nearly $500,000. No other great change took place until Harry Truman's presidency, when the interior was completely renovated after the leg of Margaret Truman's piano cut through the dining room ceiling. The Trumans lived at Blair House across the street for nearly 4 years while the White House interior was shored up with steel girders and concrete.

In 1961, First Lady Jacqueline Kennedy spearheaded the founding of the White House Historical Association and formed a Fine Arts Committee to help restore the famous rooms to their original grandeur, ensuring treatment of the White House as a museum of American history and decorative arts. "It just seemed to me such a shame when we came here to find hardly anything of the past in the house, hardly anything before 1902," Mrs. Kennedy observed.

Every president and first family put their own stamp on the White House. President Trump has made subtle changes to the Oval Office, replacing maroon drapes with gold and swapping out camel-colored leather chairs for those covered in pale yellow fabric. The Obamas installed artworks on loan from the Hirshhorn Museum and the National Gallery of Art in their private residence, and chose works to hang in the public rooms of the White House. (Changing the art in the public rooms requires approval from the White House curator and the Committee for the Preservation of the White House.) Michelle Obama planted a vegetable garden on the White House grounds, and President Obama altered the outdoor tennis court so that it could be used for both basketball and tennis.

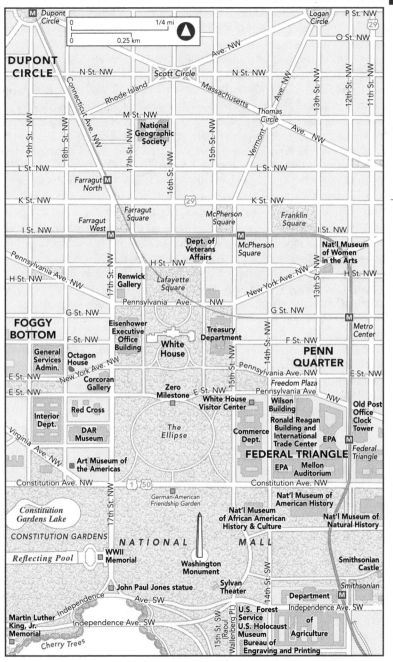

Highlights of the public tour include the gold and white **East Room,** the scene of presidential receptions, weddings, major presidential addresses, and other dazzling events. This is where the president entertains visiting heads of state and the place where seven of the eight presidents who died in office (all but James Garfield) lay in state. It's also where Nixon resigned. The room's early-18th-century style was adopted during the Theodore Roosevelt renovation of 1902; it has parquet Fontainebleau oak floors and white-painted wood walls with fluted pilasters and classical relief inserts. Note the famous Gilbert Stuart portrait of George Washington that Dolley Madison saved from the British torch during the War of 1812; the portrait is the only object to have remained continuously in the White House since 1800 (except during reconstructions).

You'll visit the **Green Room,** which was Thomas Jefferson's dining room but today is used as a sitting room. Mrs. Kennedy chose the green watered-silk wall covering. The oldest portrait in the White House hangs over the fireplace mantel, that of Benjamin Franklin, painted in 1767 by an artist named David Martin. If you glance out the windows you'll spot the Jefferson Memorial vividly standing out in the distance. In the **Oval Blue Room,** decorated in the French Empire style chosen by James Monroe in 1817, presidents and first ladies have officially received guests since the Jefferson administration. It was, however, Martin Van Buren's decor that began the "blue room" tradition. Grover Cleveland, the only president to wed in the White House, was married in the Blue Room. This room was also where the Reagans greeted the 52 Americans liberated after being held hostage in Iran for 444 days, and every year it's the setting for the White House Christmas tree.

The **Red Room,** with its red-satin-covered walls and Empire furnishings, is used as a reception room, primarily for afternoon teas. Several portraits of past presidents and a Gilbert Stuart portrait of Dolley Madison hang here. Dolley Madison used the Red Room for her famous Wednesday-night receptions.

From the Red Room, you'll enter the **State Dining Room.** Modeled after late-18th-century neoclassical English houses, this room is a superb setting for state dinners and luncheons. Below G. P. A. Healy's portrait of Lincoln is a quote taken from a letter written by John Adams on his second night in the White House (FDR had it carved into the mantel): I PRAY HEAVEN TO BESTOW THE BEST OF BLESSINGS ON THIS HOUSE AND ON ALL THAT SHALL HERE-AFTER INHABIT IT. MAY NONE BUT HONEST AND WISE MEN EVER RULE UNDER THIS ROOF.

1600 Pennsylvania Ave. NW (visitor entrance gate at E St. and E. Executive Ave.). www. whitehouse.gov. © **202/456-7041** or 202/208-1631. Free admission. All tours arranged only through congressional offices (see "How To's" box, below). Closed federal holidays. Metro: Federal Triangle.

The White House Visitor Center ★ MUSEUM Whether or not you're able to tour the White House, try to stop here for a behind-the-scenes understanding of the history and everyday life inside the executive mansion. Its wide range of intriguing offerings includes a 14-minute film, "White House: Reflections from Within," featuring the personal stories of the current and

THE "HOW TO'S" OF TOURING THE white house

You must have a reservation to tour the White House. No less than 21 days and as far as 3 months in advance of your trip, contact the office of one of your senators or representatives to request the tour, provide the number of people in your group, and ask for a specific tour date. Check your rep's website first (senate.gov or house.gov), since some members instruct you to call, while others require you to submit an online request; some members do not provide this constituent service at all. The tour coordinator consults with the White House on availability, and, if your requested date is available, submits your contact details and the size of your group to the White House. The White House then sends you confirmation of receipt of your request and asks you to register for the tour by submitting the names, birth dates, Social Security numbers (for those 18 and over), and other info for each person in your party. The White House reviews the information and contacts you 2 to 3 weeks before your requested date to let you know whether your request has been approved or denied. If approved, your confirmation letter/e-mail will include a confirmation number, the list of people in your group, and the date and time of your confirmed tour. (**Note:** International visitors should contact their embassy to submit a tour request.)

Hours: White House tours are available to the general public year-round from 7:30 to 11:30am Tuesday through Thursday and 7:30am to 1:30pm Friday and Saturday, and at other times depending on the president's schedule.

If the president is out of town, it's possible that more tours will be allowed past the usual cutoff time.

Format and timing: Tours are self-guided. Most people take no more than an hour to go through. Arrive about 15 minutes before your scheduled tour time.

Entry and ID: You'll enter at the side of East Executive Avenue, near the Southeast Gate of the White House. Bring valid, government-issued photo IDs whose information exactly matches that which you provided to your congressional member's office. Everyone in your party who is 18 or older must have an ID. **Important:** On the day of your tour, call ℭ **202/456-7041** to make sure the White House is open to the public that day and that your tour hasn't been cancelled.

Do not bring the following prohibited items: Backpacks, book bags, handbags, or purses; food and beverages; strollers; video recorders; tobacco products; personal grooming items, from cosmetics to hairbrushes; any pointed objects, whether a pen or a knitting needle; aerosol containers; guns; ammunition; fireworks; electric stun guns; maces; martial arts weapons/devices; or knives of any kind. Smartphones are okay, as are small cameras. The White House does not have a coat-check facility, so there is no place for you to leave your belongings while you take the tour. There are no public restrooms or telephones in the White House. **Best advice:** Leave everything but your wallet and camera back at the hotel.

former First Family occupants; interactive exhibits that allow you to explore inside and outside the White House with a touch of the screen; and exhibits of some 100 artifacts, like the mahogany desk that White House architect James Hoban fashioned out of the wood scraps left over from the construction of the building. National Park Service rangers staff the information desks and hand out White House touring pamphlets that you'll find helpful for your White House visit. The White House Historical Association mans the **gift shop** here (a great place to purchase mementos and presents, like the annually designed White House Christmas tree ornament). And here's a fact you might just want to know: The center has public restrooms.

1450 Pennsylvania Ave. NW (in the Department of Commerce Bldg., btw. 14th and 15th sts.). www.nps.gov/whho/planyourvisit/white-house-visitor-center.htm. *©* **202/208-1631.** Free admission. Daily 7:30am–4pm. Closed Jan 1, Thanksgiving, and Dec 25. Metro: Federal Triangle.

PENN QUARTER

Most of this bustling downtown neighborhood's attractions congregate near the Capital One Arena, on or just off 7th Street, the main artery. The ones that aren't there, like Ford's Theatre and the National Museum of Women in the Arts, are just a short walk away. If you enjoy layering your touring experience with stops for delicious meals or snacks, this is your neighborhood (see chapter 5 for Penn Quarter restaurants).

Ford's Theatre National Historic Site ★★ HISTORIC SITE   On April 14, 1865, President Abraham Lincoln was in the audience at Ford's Theatre, one of the most popular playhouses in Washington. Everyone was laughing at a funny line from Tom Taylor's celebrated comedy, *Our American Cousin,* when John Wilkes Booth crept into the President's Box, shot Lincoln, and leapt to the stage, shouting, *"Sic semper tyrannis!"* ("Thus ever to tyrants!") With his left leg broken from the jump, Booth mounted his horse in the alley and galloped off. Doctors carried Lincoln across the street to the house of William Petersen, where the president died the next morning.

The theater was closed after Lincoln's assassination and used as an office by the War Department. In 1893, 22 clerks were killed when three floors of the building collapsed. It remained in disuse until the 1960s, when the National Park Service remodeled and restored Ford's to its appearance on the night of the tragedy. Grand renovations and developments completed in phases between 2009 and 2012 have since brought about a wholly new experience for visitors.

Ford's Theatre today stands as the centerpiece of the **Ford's Theatre National Historic Site,** a campus of three buildings straddling a short section of 10th Street and including the **Ford's Theatre** and its **Ford's Theatre Museum; Petersen House,** where Lincoln died; and the **Aftermath Exhibits,** inside the **Center for Education and Leadership,** which debuted in 2012 and is dedicated to exploring Lincoln's legacy and promoting leadership.

I recommend visiting all four attractions if you have the time. Briefly, here's what you'll see at the Ford's Theatre National Historic Site:

The Ford's Theatre: The National Park Service presentations vividly re-create the events of that night, so try for a tour that includes one of these. The President's Box is still on view, but no, you are not allowed to enter it and sit where Lincoln sat. A portrait of George Washington hangs beneath the

President's Box, as it did the night Lincoln was shot. Ford's remains a working theater, so consider returning in the evening to attend a play. Ford's productions lean toward historical dramas and classic American plays and musicals; the 2019–20 season includes the drama *Silent Sky* and the 1950s musical comedy *Guys and Dolls*, until May 2020. The production schedule means that the theater, and sometimes the museum, may be closed to sightseers on some days; check the online schedule before you visit.

The **Ford's Theatre Museum,** on the lower level of the theater, displays artifacts that tell the story of Lincoln's presidency, his assassination, and what life was like in Washington and in the United States during that time. Unfortunately, when the museum is crowded, as it often is, it can be hard to get close enough to (and have enough time at) each of the exhibits to properly absorb the information. An exhibit about life in the White House shines a little light on Mary Todd Lincoln; a display of artifacts—including the actual gun (a little 45 derringer) that killed Lincoln—connects the dots between the assassin and those who aided him. Other affecting artifacts: Lincoln's size-14 boots, two Lincoln life masks, and a replica of the greatcoat he wore the night of the assassination—the real coat is here but too fragile for permanent display. (The bullet that killed Lincoln was actually removed by autopsy doctors and is now in the National Museum of Health and Medicine in Silver Spring, Maryland.)

Across 10th Street from the theater and museum is **Petersen House.** The doctor attending to Lincoln and other theatergoers carried Lincoln into the street, where boarder Henry Safford, standing in the open doorway of his rooming house, gestured for them to bring the president inside. So Lincoln died in the home of William Petersen, a German-born tailor. Now furnished with period pieces, the dark, narrow town house looks much as it did on that fateful April night. You'll see the front parlor where an anguished Mary Todd Lincoln spent the night with her son, Robert. In the back parlor, Secretary of War Edwin M. Stanton held a cabinet meeting and questioned witnesses. From this room, Stanton announced at 7:22am on April 15, 1865, "Now he belongs to the ages." Lincoln died, lying diagonally because he was so tall, on a bed the size of the one in the room. (The Chicago History Museum owns the actual bed and other items from the room.) The exit from Petersen House leads to an elevator that transports you to the fourth floor of the:

Aftermath Exhibits, in the Center for Education and Leadership, where your tour begins with the sights and sounds of the capital in the days following the assassination of Lincoln. You hear church bells tolling and horseshoes clopping and view exhibits of mourning ribbons, coffin handles, and newspaper broadsheets announcing the tragic news. Details convey the sense of piercing sorrow that prevailed: Twenty-five thousand people attended Lincoln's funeral on April 21, 1865, though not Mary Todd Lincoln, who was too overcome with grief. A staircase that winds around a sculptured tower of some 6,800 books all to do with Lincoln leads down to the center's third floor. Here, a short film, videos, and exhibits explore Lincoln's influence and legacy, including all sorts of commercial products with Lincoln's name, from the children's building blocks of Lincoln Logs to jewelry. Following the staircase

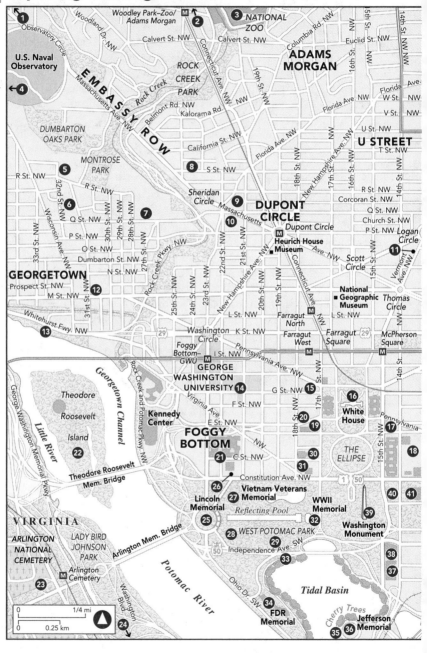

Albert Einstein Memorial 26
Anacostia Community
    Museum 75
African American Civil War
    Museum and Memorial 42
Anderson House 10
Arlington National Cemetery 23
Arts and Industries Building 62
Art Museum
    of the Americas 31
Belmont-Paul Woman's
    Equality National
    Monument 70
Bureau of Engraving
    and Printing 37
Corcoran Gallery 19
DAR Museum 30
DC War Memorial 29
Dumbarton House 7
Dumbarton Oaks 5
Eastern Market 74
Enid A. Haupt Garden 60
FDR Memorial 34
Folger Shakespeare Library 72
Ford's Theatre 46
Fred. Douglass Nat'l
    Historic Site 75

Freer Gallery of Art 56
George Mason Memorial 35
Georgetown Waterfront Park 13
Hillwood Museum 2
Hirshhorn Museum 64
International Spy Museum 63
Jefferson Memorial 36
Korean War Veterans
    Memorial 28
Kreeger Museum 4
Library of Congress 73
Lincoln Memorial 25
Madame Tussauds 45
Martin Luther King, Jr.
    Memorial 33
Mary McCleod Bethune
    Council House 11
Museum of the Bible 65
National Air and Space
    Museum 66
National Archives Museum 52
National Building Museum 47
National Children's Museum 18
National Gallery of Art 55
National Gallery of Art
    Sculpture Garden 54
National Law Enforcement
    Memorial and Museum 48
National Museum
    of African Art 61

National Museum of African American
    History & Culture 40
National Museum of American History 41
National Museum of the American Indian 67
National Museum of Natural History 53
National Museum of Women in the Arts 43
National Postal Museum 49
National Zoological Park 3
Octagon Museum 20
Old Post Office Clock Tower 51
Old Stone House 12
The Pentagon 24
Phillips Collection 9
Renwick Gallery 15
S. Dillon Ripley Center 58
Sackler Gallery 57
Smithsonian Information Center 59
Smithsonian American Art Museum
    and National Portrait Gallery 44
State Department Diplomatic Rooms 21
Supreme Court 71
Textile Museum 14
Theodore Roosevelt Island 22
Tudor Place 6
Union Station 50
U.S. Botanic Garden 68
U.S. Capitol 69
U.S. Holocaust Memorial Museum 38
Vietnam Veterans Memorial 27
Washington Monument 39
Washington National Cathedral 1
White House 16
White House Visitor Center 17
Woodrow Wilson House 8
World War II Memorial 32

another level down takes you to a gallery on real-life examples of brave individuals, such as Rosa Parks, to pose the question "What Would You Do?" in their circumstances.

The how-to: You'll need a timed ticket to tour any part of the campus. Tickets are free and tours take place daily. Visit the website, www.fords.org, for a list of offerings, which can range from a simple theater walk-through (15 min.) to a full tour encompassing the museum; the theater, including either a NPS ranger's interpretive program or a mini-play (these are great); the Petersen House; and the Aftermath Exhibits (a total of about 2 hr. and 15 min.).

A single ticket admits you to all parts of the campus, so don't lose it! Ford's really wants you to order tickets in advance online—only 20% of the daily allotment of tickets are available for same-day pickup. And even though Ford's says tours are free, online tickets incur processing fees, starting at $3 per ticket. You order the tickets online and print them yourself or pick them up at the theater's will-call booth. *Good to know:* When the Ford's Theatre website shows same-day tickets as unavailable, that just means they are unavailable to order online; go in person to the box office and you may score a same-day pass.

Spring through early fall, Ford's also sells tickets ($18 each, available online) to its popular "History on Foot" 2-hour **walking tours.** A costumed actor brings to life the events of April 14 and 15, 1865, leading tourists on a 1.6-mile traipse to about eight historically significant locations.

511 10th St. NW (btw. E and F sts.). www.fords.org. ℂ **202/347-4833.** Daily 9am– 4:30pm. Closed Thanksgiving, Christmas, and other days subject to the theatre's schedule. Timed tickets required for the free tours offered throughout the day. See above for details. Metro: Metro Center (11th and G sts. exit).

Madame Tussauds Washington, D.C. ★ MUSEUM   Calling all tweens! Justin Bieber's in the house! And OMG, is that Rihanna? On display throughout this museum are upwards of 100 lifelike wax figures, dressed and poised true to form, and grouped by theme: U.S. Presidents, First Ladies, Sports, Music, A-List Party, Cultural Icons, and Media and Entertainment. You can pretend to spar with Evander Holyfield, mingle with Jimmy Fallon, dance with Beyoncé, and shake hands with President Barack Obama. Said to be the most interactive of the 24 Madame Tussauds around the world, the D.C. Madame's best feature is its **3-D Presidential Gallery,** which arranges each of the 45 presidents with important historical figures of that day, at important moments in their presidencies. With the use of interactive devices and fun props, the gallery creates an entertaining learning experience targeted to children. Kids can try on period costumes and join George Washington in his boat crossing the Delaware River, or stand next to Woodrow Wilson and listen to the crowds cheer his arrival at the end of World War I.

1001 F St. NW (btw. 10th and 11th sts.). https://madametussauds.com/washington-dc/ en/. ℂ **866/823-9565** or 202/942-7300. Walk-up admission $22 plus tax ages 13 and over; $18 plus tax ages 3–12; free for children 2 and under. Purchase advance tickets online and receive a 20% or higher discount. Daily, but hours fluctuate; check the website for exact hours on the day you wish to visit. Metro: Metro Center (11th and G sts. exit).

On E Street NW between 4th and 5th streets, directly across the street from the National Building Museum and centered in the same plaza as the entrance/exit to the Judiciary Square Metro station, is the **National Law Enforcement Memorial** (www.nleomf.org; ✆ **202/737-3400**), dedicated to the federal, state, and local law enforcement officers who have died in the line of duty. The memorial is a landscaped park whose two tree-lined pathways embrace two curving, 304-foot-long blue-gray marble walls on which are inscribed the names of the more than 20,000 officers who have died protecting the nation and its people throughout U.S. history, starting in 1786. New names are added every May during National Police Week. Four sculptures of a lion protecting her cubs mark each pathway entrance; this is also where you find a catalog under Plexiglass, where you can locate the name of a particular officer in the memorial. Adjacent to the memorial to the south is the **National Law Enforcement Museum** ★ (444 E St. NW; www.LawEnforcement Museum.org; ✆ **202/737-3400**), which opened in fall 2018. Built mostly underground, the 57,000-square-foot museum tells its story through high-tech interactive exhibits, a comprehensive collection of artifacts, extensive resources for research, and diverse educational programming. It's open Sunday through Saturday 10am to 6pm (until 9pm Thurs), and admission is $22 adults, $20 seniors, military, law enforcement professionals, and college students, $15 youths 6–11, and free for children 5 and under.

National Building Museum ★ MUSEUM   The first thing you notice about the National Building Museum is the actual building, its pressed red-brick exterior and decorative terra-cotta frieze, and its *size,* 400 feet by 200 feet, big enough to hold a football field. Inside the impressive **Great Hall** is an Italian Renaissance courtyard, colossal Corinthian columns, 15-story-high ceiling, and central fountain. The structure, modeled after an Italian palazzo, was designed to house the Pension Bureau (its offices were located in those upper arcaded areas, overlooking the atrium) and to serve as a venue for grand galas. The building hosted its first event, President Grover Cleveland's inaugural ball, in 1885, even before construction was completed in 1887, and it's been the site of such balls and other events ever since.

In the 1980s, the building took on a new purpose as a museum dedicated to architecture, landscape architecture, engineering, urban planning, and historic preservation and opened to the public in 1985 as the National Building Museum. You can view the Great Hall and take a historic building tour for free, but the museum charges a fee to tour its exhibits, which are mounted in the galleries off the Great Hall on the first and second floors and change yearly. Two exhibits illustrate the museum's range of topics: **"Hoops"** (through Jan 2020) features a series of photographs of private and community basketball courts from around the nation and across the globe, and **"Animals, Collected"** (until spring 2020) highlights the museum's own collection of architectural objects depicting animals—both real and mythological—as ornaments on buildings, monuments, churches, and warehouses. The museum's year-round

Building Zone exhibit is a favorite for families with children ages 2 to 6, who can build a tower, drive a bulldozer, and explore a life-size playhouse.

If you're here in summer, you've got to stop by to experience the super-fun, interactive "Summer Block Party," which takes over the entire expanse of the Great Hall; one year it was a "beach" of nearly 1 million translucent plastic balls. Mid-May through mid-September, the museum partners with **Hill Country Barbecue** restaurant (p. 95) to serve barbecue, happy hours, and live music on its west lawn Wednesdays through Fridays. The museum gift shop is an especially good one (below), as is the on-site eatery **Firehook Bakery.**

401 F St. NW (btw. 4th and 5th sts.). www.nbm.org. ℭ **202/272-2448.** Admission $10 adults; $7 students (with ID), children 3–17, and seniors 60 and over. Building Zone only: $3. Summer Block Party: $16 adults; $13 students, children, and seniors. Mon–Sat 10am–5pm; Sun 11am–5pm. Closed Thanksgiving and Dec 25. Metro: Gallery Place (7th and F sts. exit) or Judiciary Square (F St. exit).

National Museum of Women in the Arts ★ ART MUSEUM   If you've never heard of Clara Peeters, a 16th-century Flemish painter of superbly rendered still-lifes; or Renaissance painter Lavinia Fontana; or Russian artist Sonia Delaunay, whose mastery of murals, theater sets, and ceramics led the Louvre in 1964 to choose her as its first living female artist to hold a retrospective there…it's a shame, but not surprising, given the historical short shrift accorded women's contributions to art. Here in D.C., we have an answer for that: the National Museum of Women in the Arts, where more than 4,500 works by women, 16th century to the present, are on display. Open since 1987, the museum remains the world's only major museum solely dedicated to recognizing women's creative accomplishments.

Inside the white marble Renaissance Revival museum building, built as a Masonic temple in 1908, is a space so elegant it's frequently in demand as a

Coffee Mugs & Celtic Bookends: Museum Gift Shops

Washington's museum shops hold a treasure trove of unusual gifts. Right now I'm loving the set of coffee mugs I bought my husband for Christmas at the **Folger Shakespeare Library** (p. 126) gift shop. They're covered in Shakespeare quotes, both for when you're in a foul mood ("Bolting-hutch of beastliness," "Thou art a boil, a plague sore") and for when you're feelin' the love ("Love is a smoke raised with the fume of sighs"). I've always had a weakness for the shop at the **National Building Museum** (p. 181), which is jammed with surprising, useful, and cleverly designed housewares and interesting games, including bookends embossed with

Celtic designs, Bauhaus mobiles, and collapsible strainers. And I can never visit the **National Gallery of Art** (p. 147) without lingering a little while in the store to admire captivating catalog books, notecards, posters, children's games, and a slew of other things. The Smithsonian's **National Museum of African Art** (p. 152) has unusual items from all over Africa, but I especially liked the interesting designs of the colorful dish towels, handbags, and headbands from Ghana. And then there's the woman-centric **National Museum of Women in the Arts** (above) gift shop, which has fab Frida Kahlo candles and leaning lady bookends.

wedding reception venue. Some of the artwork is on display in the Grand Hall, but most exhibits are in upstairs galleries, accessed via the sweeping marble double stairways. Among the works from the permanent collection are those by Rosa Bonheur, Mary Cassatt, Helen Frankenthaler, Barbara Hepworth, Georgia O'Keeffe, Lilla Cabot Perry, and Elaine de Kooning. Most popular is Frida Kahlo's self-portrait, the only Frida Kahlo on view in Washington. The museum mounts several special exhibits annually, which from September 19, 2020, to January 20, 2020, includes "Judy Chicago—The End: A Meditation on Death and Extinction," showcasing nearly 40 works of painted porcelain and glass, as well as two large bronze sculptures, from the feminist icon.

Also recommended is the museum's gift shop, which sells clever little items like a Dorothy Parker martini glass. And if you're hungry, have lunch in view of artworks at the **Mezzanine Café** (Mon–Fri 11am–2pm).

1250 New York Ave. NW (at 13th St.). www.nmwa.org. ✆ **800/222-7270** or 202/783-5000. Admission $10 adults; $8 students (with ID) and seniors 65 and over; free for youths 18 and under (general admission rates; special exhibition prices may be higher). Admission is free for all on the first Sun of every month. Mon–Sat 10am–5pm; Sun noon–5pm. Closed Jan 1, Thanksgiving, and Dec 25. Metro: Metro Center (13th St. exit).

Old Post Office Clock Tower ★ HISTORIC SITE   The Clock Tower offers a commanding view of the capital that's second only to that of the nearby Washington Monument. Now part of the Trump International Hotel Washington, D.C., the Tower is open to the general public for tours. As the second-tallest structure in D.C. after the Washington Monument, it offers fabulous 360-degree views, 270 feet up, of Pennsylvania Avenue, from the Capitol to the White House, and beyond to the National Mall. The building itself was used as the city's primary post office until 1914. It was slated for demolition in 1928, but a lack of funds during the Great Depression saved the structure. It wasn't until 1977 that complete renovation on the structure began, and in 1983, it reopened as offices and retail. The bells in the tower are rung at the opening and closing of Congress and for national holidays. The National Park Service operates and maintains the building and provides interpretive programming.

To reach the clock tower, you must venture down 12th Street, behind the hotel, to enter through the door marked "Starbucks & Clock Tower." Stride through the second set of glass doors, ignoring the Starbucks to your left, and keep going down the corridor to reach a wall-mounted exhibit of old photographs, maps, and documents that give you a little history of the building and the city. Proceed through security screening, then hop the elevator, the first of two that take you to the top (change elevators on the 9th floor).

1100 Pennsylvania Ave. NW (at 12th St.). www.nps.gov/opot. Entrance behind the Trump Hotel, off 12th St. NW. Free admission. Daily 9am–5pm. Metro: Federal Triangle.

Smithsonian American Art Museum and National Portrait Gallery ★★★ ART MUSEUM   Walt Whitman called this historic Greek Revival structure "the noblest of Washington buildings," and if he were around today, he'd likely stick with that opinion. If you've been flitting around the Penn Quarter, you had to have noticed it, with its porticoes modeled after the Parthenon in Athens, and its monumental footprint (405×274 ft.).

But it's what's inside we're interested in. The magnificent landmark, which served as the nation's patent office in the mid–19th century, now houses two distinct Smithsonian museums: the American Art Museum and the National Portrait Gallery, each occupying three levels of galleries that enclose a stunning, light-filled inner courtyard, museum wings meeting seamlessly.

Walt Whitman's name crops up again. He is here, yes he is, in portrait form, painted by John White Alexander in 1889, appearing rather old and tired, with blindingly white hair, full beard, and fluffy eyebrows, sitting at an angle and staring into the distance. Whitman's portrait hangs in the National Portrait Gallery's first-floor section, **American Origins,** a chronological arrangement of paintings of notables that tells the country's story, from Pocahontas to Harriet Beecher Stowe to Thomas Edison, in compelling fashion. Other permanent exhibits feature **20th Century Americans,** where Michele Obama's commissioned portrait now hangs, and **America's Presidents,** home to President Obama's official portrait.

The American Art Museum's collection of American art is one of the largest in the world—and the most diverse, with folk art, modern, African-American, and Latino art well represented. Standouts include Georgia O'Keeffe's take on *Manhattan;* Albert Bierstadt's idealized vision of the American West, *Among the Sierra Nevada;* a Nam June Paik video installation, *Electronic Superhighway: Continental U.S., Alaska, Hawaii;* and intriguing folk art, like James Hampton's creation of artwork out of garbage, *The Throne of the Third Heaven of the Nations' Millennium General Assembly.* You'll either love it or hate it, but you won't be able to look away from it.

In all, about 2,000 works are on display throughout both museums. You'll want to tour the top floor's two-level **Luce Foundation Center for American Art,** too, where thousands more works are stored but still on view, from walking canes to sculptures to dollhouses. In the adjacent **Lunder Conservation Center,** visitors can watch conservators work to preserve art pieces. Finally, make time to visit the museum's courtyard cafe, the setting for concerts including the monthly free jazz series of performances, *Take Five!*

Note: These two museums are open later than most in D.C., so you can schedule a visit for the end of the day.

8th and F sts. NW. www.americanart.si.edu or www.npg.si.edu. ℰ **202/633-1000.** Free admission. Daily 11:30am–7pm. Highlights tours are offered; check online or call for exact schedule. Closed Dec 25. Metro: Gallery Place–Chinatown (7th and F sts. exit, or 9th and G sts. exit).

DUPONT CIRCLE

In a city of national this-and-that attractions, Dupont Circle provides a charmingly personal counterpoint. Within this lively residential neighborhood of old town houses, trendy boutiques, and bistros are mostly historic houses (such as the Christian Heurich House), embassy buildings, and beloved art galleries (such as the Phillips Collection). Follow the walking tour of Dupont Circle and Embassy Row (p. 273) for a fuller picture of the neighborhood.

Anderson House ★ HISTORIC HOME   A visit to Anderson House is about marveling over the palatial architecture and interior design (love the ballroom), and the display of artwork—from Flemish tapestries to Asian and European paintings and antiquities to Revolutionary War artifacts. A bit of background: This limestone-veneered Italianate mansion, fronted by twin arches and a Corinthian-columned portico, was built between 1902 and 1905. Its original owners were career diplomat Larz Anderson III, who served as ambassador to Japan in 1912 and 1913, and his wife, heiress and philanthropist Isabel Weld Perkins, who as a Red Cross volunteer cared for the dying and wounded in France and Belgium during World War I, and who authored at least 40 books. The couple traveled a lot and filled their home with beautiful purchases from those journeys. Larz and Isabel were popular hosts in the capital and counted presidents and foreign dignitaries among their guests. Upon Larz's death in 1937, Isabel donated the house to the Society of the Cincinnati, and it has served ever since as headquarters and museum for the Society, founded in 1783 for descendants of Revolutionary War army officers. Anderson's great-grandfather was a founder and George Washington the organization's first president-general. Anderson House hosts exhibits, concerts, and lectures throughout the year; all are free and open to the public.

2118 Massachusetts Ave. NW (at Q St.). www.societyofthecincinnati.org. © **202/785-2040.** Free admission. Tues–Sat 10am–4pm, Sun noon–4pm; highlights tours hourly at 15 min. past the hour. Closed most federal holidays. Metro: Dupont Circle (Q St. exit).

Heurich House Museum ★ HISTORIC HOME   Wealthy German businessman and brewer Christian Heurich built this turreted, four-story brownstone and brick Victorian castle in 1894, and lived here with his family until he died in 1945. Old Heurich was a character, as a tour of the 31-room mansion/museum reveals. Allegorical paintings cover the ceilings, silvered plaster medallions festoon the stucco walls, and a *bierstube* (tavern room) in the basement sports the brewer's favorite drinking mottos—written in German, but here's one translation: "There is room in the smallest chamber for the biggest hangover." The **Castle Garden** is a good place to pause for a picnic or page through your guidebook. Enter the garden through the east gate on Sunderland Place NW.

1307 New Hampshire Ave. NW (at 20th St.). www.heurichhouse.org. © **202/429-1894.** Garden free admission; house tours $10, reservations suggested. Children under 10 not allowed. Tours Thurs–Sat 11:30am, 1, and 2:30pm. Garden weekdays 9am–5pm. Metro: Dupont Circle (19th St. exit).

National Geographic Museum ★ MUSEUM   You don't have to be an adventurer yourself to enjoy the exhibits mounted at the National Geographic Society headquarters. It does help, though, if you're a curious soul and appreciate the wonders of the natural world and of human exploration. Consider the museum's permanent exhibit, "National Geographic: Exploration Starts Here," displaying excavations of shipwrecks from the bottom of the ocean and video from the top of Mount Everest. From time to time, National Geo mounts a show that nobody can resist, like the recent 2019 "Queens of Egypt" exhibit, showcasing jewelry, sculpture, and artifacts from Egyptian queens like Nefertiti and Cleopatra VII. In addition to its free permanent exhibition, National Geographic always has at least one free photography show in its M Street lobby location; otherwise, exhibits and most lectures, films, and performances charge admission.

1145 17th St. NW (at M St.). www.natgeodc.org. ℭ **202/857-7700.** Permanent and photography exhibit admission free. Special exhibit admission $15 adults; $12 students/seniors; $10 children 5–12. Daily 10am–6pm. Closed Thanksgiving and Dec 25. Metro: Farragut North (Connecticut Ave. and L St. exit).

Phillips Collection ★★ ART MUSEUM The Phillips is beloved in Washington, mostly because of its French Impressionist and post-Impressionist paintings by van Gogh, Bonnard, Cezanne, Picasso, Klee, and Renoir, whose *Luncheon of the Boating Party* is the most popular work on display. But as familiar and traditional as these paintings may seem now, the works and their artists were considered daring and avant-garde when Duncan Phillips opened his gallery in 1921. The Phillips Collection, indeed, was America's first official museum of modern art.

Founder Phillips's vision for "an intimate museum combined with an experiment station" is one that the museum continually renews, through programs like its *Intersections* series of contemporary art projects exploring links between old and new artistic traditions, and in exhibits of provocative art. The **Wolfgang Laib Wax Room** is a good example: It is the first beeswax chamber that artist Laib created for a specific museum. That's right: beeswax. You smell it before you see it, kind of a musty, faintly honey-ish, cloying scent. The artwork is the size of a powder room, with a single light bulb dangling to illuminate walls and ceiling slathered thickly with wax that has the yellow hue of the fruit of a peach, flecked with bits of orangey brown. I sooo wanted to touch it, but that's not allowed. And a staff sentry stands near the entrance to make sure you don't. What is the Wax Room but an experiment station?

Today the museum's 3,000-work collection includes European masterpieces; treasures by American masters Dove, Homer, Hopper, Lawrence, and O'Keeffe; and works by living artists, such as Susan Rothenberg and Sean Scully. The Phillips complex joins the original 1897 Georgian Revival mansion—initially both the Phillips family home and public art gallery—with a modern gallery annex that doubles the space. The elegant mansion's graceful appointments—leaded- and stained-glass windows, elliptical stairway, oak-paneled Music Room, and tiled fireplaces—provide a lovely backdrop to the art and add to the reasons that locals love the Phillips.

Also consider gallery talks, the popular "Phillips after 5" socials every first Thursday, Sunday concerts in the **Music Room** (Oct–May; admission $45), and other events. The museum also has a charming **cafe** and a small gift shop.

1600 21st St. NW (at Q St.). www.phillipscollection.org. ℭ **202/387-2151.** Admission: Permanent collection free (donation welcome) on weekdays; Sat–Sun when no special exhibits are on view $10 adults; $8 seniors 62 and older and students 18 and older; free ages 18 and under. Ticketed special exhibits $12 adults; $10 seniors 62 and older and students 18 and older; free ages 18 and under. Admission price allows entry to both permanent and special exhibits. Tues–Sat 10am–5pm (Thurs until 8:30pm); Sun noon–7pm. Closed Mon and federal holidays. Metro: Dupont Circle (Q St. exit).

Woodrow Wilson House Museum ★ HISTORIC HOME   America's 28th president was too ill to attend the inauguration of his successor. Instead he was driven to his new home in the prestigious Kalorama neighborhood (yes, the very same neighborhood where former president Barack Obama currently lives). His final residence is preserved as he left it. The story here focuses on Wilson's Washington years (1912–24), examining his public persona while allowing a peek behind the draperies into his personal life, much of it quite tragic. Furnishings, White House objects, personal memorabilia, and elaborate gifts of state help tell the story. A mosaic of St. Peter hangs in the drawing room, a gift from Pope Benedict XV when the Wilsons toured Europe at the conclusion of World War I. A portrait of his wife Edith hangs above the mantle.

2340 S St. NW (at Massachusetts Ave.). www.woodrowwilsonhouse.org. ⓒ **202/387-4062.** Admission $10 adults; $8 seniors; $5 students; free for ages 11 and under. Feb–Dec Wed–Sat 10am–4pm; Sun and Tues noon–4pm; closed Mon. Guided tours only. Closed Jan and federal holidays. Metro: Dupont Circle (Q St. exit).

FOGGY BOTTOM

Known primarily as the locale for the George Washington University campus, the State Department, the International Monetary Fund, and the World Bank, Foggy Bottom is home also to the George Washington Museum and the Textile Museum, the John F. Kennedy Center for the Performing Arts (p. 224), and the State Department's Diplomatic Reception Rooms.

The George Washington Museum and the Textile Museum ★ MUSEUM   This two-museums-in-one building lies in the heart of the George Washington University's urban campus. Originally located in a charming Embassy Row mansion, the nearly century-old **Textile Museum** tripled its space and was, in a sense, reborn in 2015, when it moved to this custom-designed, 46,000-square-foot gallery in Foggy Bottom. Curators pull from the

museum's collection of some 20,000 textiles spanning 5,000 years and five continents to mount exhibits that in one way or another ask: How do clothes, adornments, and fabric furnishings articulate self and status within cultural, political, social, religious, and ethnic frameworks?

Meanwhile, on the second floor of the building, stemming off the Textile Museum's large gallery, is the **George Washington Museum's Albert H. Small Washingtoniana Collection,** totally unrelated to textiles but

Performance at the Kennedy Center.

In a grove of holly and elm trees at the southwest corner of the National Academy of Sciences grounds (22nd St. & Constitution Ave. NW), you'll find this dear memorial displaying the slouching figure of brilliant scientist, great thinker, and peace activist Albert Einstein. He sits slightly bent and sideways upon a granite bench, leaning on one hand and holding in the other a bronze sheet of paper on which are written mathematical equations for which he is famous. At his feet is a celestial map. His gaze looks worn and warm. The statue measures 12 feet in height and weighs 4 tons, yet children cannot resist crawling up on it and leaning against this man.

fascinating in its own right for the display of maps, prints, old photos, and rare letters that fill you in on life in the capital from the 17th to the 20th centuries.

701 21st St. NW (at G St.). https://museum.gwu.edu. ☏ **202/994-5200.** $8 suggested donation. Mon and Fri 11am–5pm; Wed–Thurs 11am–7pm; Sat 10am–5pm; Sun 1–5pm. Metro: Foggy Bottom.

State Department Diplomatic Reception Rooms ★ GOVERNMENT BUILDING   This is a fine-arts tour of 42 rooms that serve as our country's stage for international diplomacy and official entertaining. The rooms house a collection of early American paintings, furniture, and decorative arts dating from 1750 to 1825. Tours are by reservation only, made online or by phone, and are not recommended for children 12 and under. You must bring a valid photo ID, such as a driver's license, to enter the building.

2201 C St. NW (entrance on 23rd St. NW). www.receptiontours.state.gov. ☏ **202/647-3241.** Free admission. Guided tours only: Mon–Fri 9:30am, 10:30, and 2:45pm. Reservations required. Metro: Foggy Bottom.

U & 14TH STREET CORRIDORS

In the old stomping grounds of Duke Ellington and his fellow Black Broadway jazz greats, the main attractions are of the nightlife and dining variety—jazz clubs, like **Twins Jazz,** that carry Duke's legacy forward, and many restaurants and bars that cater to a range of appetites and interests. The two museums located here reflect the neighborhood's identity as a stronghold of African-American history and heroes. *Note:* The two museums below are located about half a mile from each other.

African American Civil War Memorial and Museum ★ MUSEUM Not everyone knows that thousands of African Americans, mostly slaves, fought during the Civil War. This modestly sized museum displays old photographs, maps, letters, and inventories, along with ankle shackles worn by slaves and other artifacts accompanied by text to tell the stories of the United States Colored Troops and the African-American involvement in the American Civil War. Walk across the street to view the African American Civil War Memorial. A semicircular Wall of Honor curves behind the sculpture; etched into the stone are the names of the 209,145 United States Colored Troops who served in the Civil War.

1925 Vermont Ave. NW (at 10th St.; in the Grimke Bldg.). www.afroamcivilwar.org. ⓒ **202/ 667-2667.** Free admission. Mon–Fri 10am–6:30pm; Sat 10am–4pm; Sun noon–4pm. Metro: U St./Cardozo (10th St. exit).

Mary McLeod Bethune Council House National Historic Site ★

HISTORIC HOME   This town house is the last D.C. residence of African-American activist/educator Bethune, who was a leading champion of blacks' and women's rights during FDR's administration. Born in South Carolina in 1875, the 15th of 17 children of former slaves, Mary McLeod grew up in poverty but learned the value of education through her schooling by missionaries. It was a lesson she passed forward. By the time she died in 1955 at the age of 79, McLeod—now Bethune, from her marriage in 1898 to Albert Bethune—had founded a school for "Negro girls" in Daytona Beach, Florida, that would later become the Bethune-Cookman College, today Bethune-Cookman University; received 11 honorary degrees; served on numerous government advisory commissions, including the National Child Welfare Commission; and acted as Special Advisor on Minority Affairs to President Franklin Delano Roosevelt from 1935 to 1944. Bethune also established this headquarters of the National Council of Negro Women to advance the interests of African-American women and the black community. Maintained by the National Park Service, the Bethune House exhibits focus on the professional achievements of this remarkable woman.

1318 Vermont Ave. NW (at O St.). www.nps.gov/mamc. ⓒ **202/673-2402.** Free admission. Daily 9am–5pm. Metro: U St./Cardozo (13th St. exit).

UPPER NORTHWEST D.C.: GLOVER PARK, WOODLEY PARK & CLEVELAND PARK

A handful of attractions lie in these just-beyond-downtown enclaves.

Hillwood Museum and Gardens ★ HISTORIC HOME   The magnificent estate of Post cereal heiress, businesswoman, and socialite Marjorie Merriweather Post encompasses the beautiful mansion where she lived from 1955 until her death in 1973, and 25 acres of gardens. The Georgian-style manse is filled with Post's collections of art and artifacts from 18th-century France and 18th- and 19th-century Russia, from Fabergé eggs to tapestries. The spectacular gardens include a Japanese-style plot, a Russian dacha, a French *parterre,* and a pet cemetery. A rather nice conclusion to your visit here is lunch or, on Sundays, afternoon tea, at **Hillwood's Café,** especially spring through fall, when the cafe opens up its terrace overlooking the gardens.

4155 Linnean Ave. NW (at Connecticut Ave.). www.hillwoodmuseum.org. ⓒ **202/686-5807.** Admission $18 adults; $15 seniors; $10 college students; $5 students 18 and under. $3 discount Mon–Fri and $1 Sat–Sun when you order tickets online. Tues–Sun 10am–5pm. Metro: Van Ness/UDC (east side of Connecticut Ave. exit), with a 20-min. walk.

National Zoological Park ★★ ZOO   The National Zoo was created by an act of Congress in 1889 and became part of the Smithsonian Institution in 1890. A leader in the care, breeding, and exhibition of animals, the zoo occupies 163 lushly landscaped and wooded acres and is one of the country's most delightful zoos. In all, the park is home to about 300 species—some 1,500 animals, many of them rare and/or endangered. You'll see cheetahs, zebras, gorillas, elephants, monkeys, brown pelicans, orangutans, a bison, and, of course, lions, tigers, and bears. The zoo's biggest draw continues to be its **giant pandas,** Mei Xiang and Tian Tian, and their 5-year old cub, Bei Bei.

Enter the zoo at the Connecticut Avenue entrance; you'll be right by the Education Building, where you can pick up a map and find out about feeding times and any special activities. *Note:* From this main entrance, you're headed downhill; the return uphill walk can prove trying if you have young children and/or it's a hot day. Unfortunately, waiting for families at the *bottom* of the hill is the **Kids' Farm** with ducks, chickens, goats, cows, and miniature donkeys, plus a vegetable garden and pizza sculpture. Let's face it: You might not get that far. But just in case, keep in mind that the zoo rents strollers, and snack bars and ice-cream kiosks are scattered throughout the park. Easier still: Simply catch the shuttle that loops continuously from top to bottom and back.

The zoo animals live in large, open enclosures—simulations of their natural habitats—along easy-to-follow paths. The **Olmsted Walk** winds from the zoo's Connecticut Avenue entrance all the way to the zoo's end, at Rock Creek Park. Stemming off the central Olmsted Walk is the **Asia Trail,** which takes you past sloth bears, those frolicking giant pandas, fishing cats, clouded leopards, and small-clawed otters. You can't get lost, and it's hard to miss a thing.

Like the big old **elephants.** Just across from the giant panda yard is **Elephant Trails,** the zoo's high-tech, environmentally friendly habitat for its seven Asian elephants. The enclosure includes 4 acres of indoor and outdoor space, a wading pool, a walking path for exercise, a barn with soft flooring for sleeping and geothermal heating, and, for real, a community center that offers the elephants the chance to socialize!

Moving on from there takes you to the **American Trail.** Located dead center in the zoo, the American Trail is home to animals native to the United States and Canada that were once in danger of becoming extinct. Bald eagles, seals, sea lions, gray wolves, beavers, and river otters are among the creatures

---

Early Risers?

Zoo grounds open daily at 8am, which might be too early for a lot of tourists, but not for families whose young children like to rise at the crack of dawn. If you find yourselves restless in the hotel room, hop on the Red Line Metro, which opens at 5am weekdays, 7am Saturday, and 8am Sunday (or drive—the zoo parking lot opens at 8am, too), get off at the Woodley Park–Zoo station, and walk up the hill to the zoo. A Starbucks, which opens at 5am Monday to Saturday and 6am Sunday, is directly across from the zoo entrance on Connecticut Avenue. Good morning.

living here. An artificial tidal pool is now part of the display, and visitors are welcome to dip their toes in and touch model sea creatures.

I also recommend **Amazonia,** where you can hang out and observe enormous 7-foot-long arapaima fish and itty-bitty red-tailed catfish, and look for monkeys hiding in the 50-foot-tall trees.

Not far from the Amazonia exhibit, stationed in front of the **Great Cats** habitat, home to lions, tigers, lynxes, and the like, is the zoo's solar-powered carousel, whose canopy is carved with 58 species of animals. Rides are $3.50. (But zoo admission is free.)

The zoo offers many dining options, stroller rental stations, a handful of gift shops, a bookstore, and several paid-parking lots. The lots fill up quickly, especially on weekends, so arrive early or take the Metro.

3001 Connecticut Ave. NW (adjacent to Rock Creek Park). www.nationalzoo.si.edu. © **202/633-4888.** Free admission. Apr–Oct (weather permitting) grounds daily 8am–7pm (last admittance at 6pm), animal buildings daily 9am–6pm; Nov–Mar grounds daily 8am–5pm (last admittance at 4pm), animal buildings daily 9am–4pm. Closed Dec 25. Metro: Woodley Park–Zoo or Cleveland Park.

Washington National Cathedral ★★ CATHEDRAL   Pierre L'Enfant's 1791 plan for the capital city included "a great church for national purposes." Possibly because of early America's fear of mingling church and state, more than a century elapsed before the foundation for Washington National Cathedral was laid. Its actual name is the Cathedral Church of St. Peter and St. Paul. The Church is Episcopal, but welcomes all denominations, seeking to serve the entire nation as a house of prayer for all people. It has been the setting for every kind of religious observance, from Jewish to Serbian Orthodox.

A church of this magnitude—it's the sixth-largest cathedral in the world, and the second largest in the U.S.—took a long time to build. Its principal (but

not original) architect, Philip Hubert Frohman, worked on the project from 1921 until his death in 1972. The foundation stone was laid in 1907 using the mallet with which George Washington set the Capitol cornerstone. Construction was interrupted by both world wars and by periods of financial difficulty. The cathedral was finally completed with the placement of the last stone on the west front towers on September 29, 1990, 83 years (to the day) after it was begun.

English Gothic in style (with several distinctly 20th-century innovations, such as a stained-glass window commemorating the flight of *Apollo 11* and containing a piece of moon rock), the

Washington National Cathedral.

cathedral is built in the shape of a cross, complete with flying buttresses and 112 gargoyles. Along with the Capitol and the Washington Monument, it is one of the dominant structures on the Washington skyline. Frederick Law Olmsted, Jr., designed the cathedral's 59-acre landscaped grounds, which include two lovely gardens (the lawn is ideal for picnicking), three schools, and two gift shops.

Among the many historic services and events that have taken place at the cathedral are celebrations at the end of World Wars I and II; the burial of President Wilson; funerals for presidents Eisenhower, Reagan, Ford, and George H. W. Bush; the burials of Helen Keller and her companion, Anne Sullivan, inside the cathedral; the Rev. Dr. Martin Luther King, Jr.'s final sermon; a round-the-clock prayer vigil in the Holy Spirit Chapel when Iranians held American hostages captive, and a service attended by the hostages upon their release; and President Bush's National Prayer and Remembrance service on September 14, 2001, following the cataclysm of September 11.

The best way to explore the cathedral is to take a 30-minute **guided highlights tour** (included in your admission price); the tours leave continually from the west end of the nave. You can also walk through on your own, using a self-guiding brochure available in several languages. Allow additional time to tour the grounds and to visit the **Pilgrim Observation Gallery ★**, where 70 windows provide panoramic views of Washington and its surroundings. Among the most popular special-interest tours are the Tuesday and Wednesday afternoon **Tour and Tea** events, which start at 1:30pm with an in-depth look at the cathedral and conclude in the Observation Gallery with a lovely "high tea," in both the British and literal sense—you're sitting in the cradle of one of the highest points in Washington, gazing out, while noshing on scones and Devon cream. The cost is $36 per person, and reservations are required. Call ✆ **202/537-2228** or book online at https://tix.cathedral.org.

The cathedral hosts numerous events: organ recitals and other types of concerts; choir performances; an annual springtime **Flower Mart** (with flowers, food, and children's rides); and the playing of the 53-bell carillon. The Cathedral's coffeehouse/cafe, **Open City at the National Cathedral,** operated by the owners of **Tryst** (p. 231) in Adams Morgan, is open Monday through Friday 7am to 6pm, Saturday and Sunday 8am to 6pm. The eatery is located inside the restored Old Baptistry, near the Bishop's Garden.

Note: When you visit in 2020, there's a good chance you'll still see exterior scaffolding. The earthquake of August 23, 2011, damaged some of the pinnacles, flying buttresses, and gargoyles at the very top of the cathedral's exterior, as well as some minor areas of the interior ceiling. Interior repair work was completed in 2015, so you'll see a fully restored nave, looking better than ever, in truth, because the restoration included cleaning clerestory windows and stones, the first time ever. Much exterior repair work remains, but the cathedral is completely safe to visit, and its programs continue as usual.

3101 Wisconsin Ave. NW (at Massachusetts Ave.). www.cathedral.org. ✆ **202/537-6200.** Admission $12 adults; $8 children and seniors. Cathedral Mon–Fri 10am–5pm; Sat 10am–4pm; Sun 12:45–4pm. Gardens daily until dusk. Daily (30-min.) tours Mon–Sat 10:15 am, 11, 1, 2, and 3 pm; Sun as available 1–3 pm. No tours on Palm Sunday, Easter,

Thanksgiving, Dec 25, or during services. Check website for service times. Metro: Tenleytown, with a 20-min. walk. Bus: Any N bus up Massachusetts Ave. from Dupont Circle, or any 30-series bus along Wisconsin Ave. This is also a stop on the Old Town Trolley Tour. Parking garage $6 per hr./$22 maximum weekdays until 11pm; flat rate $7 if you arrive after 4pm; flat rate $9 on Sat; free on Sun.

GEORGETOWN

One of the oldest parts of the city has long been best known for its major shopping opportunities, but we think the better reason to come here is to experience its rich history. A walking tour in chapter 10 will lead you to centuries-old estates and dwellings, including **Tudor Place,** the **Old Stone House, Dumbarton House Museum and Gardens,** and **Dumbarton House.**

Dumbarton House ★ HISTORIC HOME Built between 1799 and 1805, Dumbarton House is the headquarters for the National Society of Colonial Dames of America. Stop here to admire gorgeous architecture and antique decorative arts, and to glean a bit of early American history. Self-guide your way or call in advance to arrange a docent-guided tour.

2715 Q St. NW (at 27th St.). www.dumbartonhouse.org. ✆ **202/337-2288.** Admission $10; free for students. Feb–Dec Tues–Sun 10am–3pm. Closed federal holidays. Metro: Dupont Circle (Q St. exit), with a 20-min. walk or take the DC Circulator bus, two of whose routes run close by the house. Closed Jan.

Dumbarton Oaks ★ GARDEN & MUSEUM One block off the main drag of Wisconsin Avenue in upper Georgetown delivers you far from the madding crowds to the peaceful refuge of Dumbarton Oaks. The estate includes a museum devoted to Byzantine and pre-Columbian art, a research center and library, and 10 acres of formal and informal gardens. Frankly, many people skip the museum altogether simply to wander along the garden's hedge-lined walkways, into the orangery, past the weeping cherry trees, and all around the garden plots, admiring what's in bloom as they go. If it's April, you may see bluebells. August? Dahlias. The gardens are romantic, offer several pretty places to perch, and are adorned here and there with garden ornaments and artwork. *Note:* The gardens can get crowded in spring and early summer, when they are at their loveliest.

Do try to make time for the museum, however, whose newly renovated galleries display 1,200 Byzantine artifacts, including jewelry, lamps, icons, and illuminated manuscripts from the 4th to the 15th centuries; and pre-Columbian objects such as Aztec stone carvings, Inca gold ornaments, and Olmec heads. Other highlights include the Flemish tapestries and an El Greco painting, *The Visitation,* on display in the Renaissance-style **Music Room.** Like the Phillips Collection (p. 186), the museum's mansion setting adds to its charm.

The country house and gardens, which are situated at the highest point of Georgetown, belonged to a couple named Mildred and Robert Woods Bliss, who initiated these collections and gardens in the first half of the 20th century.

1703 32nd St. NW (garden entrance at 31st and R sts.). www.doaks.org. ✆ **202/339-6400.** Gardens: Mar 15–Oct. 31, Tues–Sun 2–6pm, $10 admission; Nov 1–Mar 14, Tues–Sun 2–5pm, admission free. Museum: Tues–Sun 11:30am–5:30pm; admission

Georgetown waterfront dock.

free. Closed national holidays and Dec 24. Metrobus nos. 30N, 30S, 31, 33, D1, D2, D3, D6, and G2, plus the DC Circulator bus all have stops close to the site.

Kreeger Museum ★ ART MUSEUM   You have to make an effort to visit the Kreeger, because it's located in a residential neighborhood away from downtown, the heart of Georgetown, and public transportation. But if you don't mind driving, taking a taxi, or riding the D6 bus from Dupont Circle, then walking a half-mile up the hill to the museum, you'll be well rewarded. On view throughout this unique Philip Johnson–designed building, besides the stunning architecture itself, are paintings, sculptures, prints, and drawings by 19th- and 20th-century European artists, Picasso (early and late), Kandinsky, Monet, Renoir, Munch, Pissarro, and Rodin among them. American works are on view, too, including some by Washington, D.C., artists such as Sam Gilliam and Gene Davis. Downstairs lies a small collection of traditional African masks and figures and Asian pieces. Outdoors is a sculpture terrace, where large works by Maillol and Henry Moore, and the sight of the distant Washington Monument, are some of the pleasures at hand. On the museum's north lawn is the separate **Sculpture Garden,** where works by the likes of George Rickey rise up. Situated on a summit, this 5½-acre estate, once the residence of collectors Carmen and David Kreeger, opened to the public in 1994.

2401 Foxhall Rd. NW (off Reservoir Rd.). www.kreegermuseum.org. ✆ **202/337-3050.** Museum: Admission $10 adults; $8 seniors and students; free for children 12 and under; Tues–Sat 10am–4pm. Sculpture Garden: Free admission; Tues–Sat 10am–4pm. Closed federal holidays. About 2 mi. from Reservoir Rd. and Wisconsin Ave. in Georgetown (a pleasant walk on a nice day); otherwise drive, take a taxi, or ride the D6 bus from Dupont Circle.

Old Stone House ★ HISTORIC HOME   This 1765 structure is said to be the oldest in Washington. The National Park Service owns and operates the house, and NPS rangers provide information and sometimes demonstrations related to the site's pre-Revolutionary history. See p. 272. The upper floors of the house opened with new exhibits in 2019.

3051 M St. NW (at 30th St.). www.nps.gov/places/old-stone-house.htm. ✆ **202/426-6851.** Free admission. Daily 11am–6pm. Garden open during daylight hours. Closed Dec 25. Metro: Foggy Bottom with a 15-min. walk, or take the DC Circulator.

Tudor Place ★ HISTORIC HOME   Designed by Dr. William Thornton, architect of the Capitol, Tudor Place was constructed between 1796 and 1816 for Martha Parke Custis, George Washington's step-granddaughter. Family descendants lived here until 1983. Tour the garden on your own; house tours are docent-led only. See p. 269.

1644 31st St. NW (at R St.). www.tudorplace.org. © **202/965-0400.** Reservations recommended. Mar–Dec: House admission $10 adults; $8 seniors and college students; $3 children 5–17. Garden admission $3. Feb: $1 admission to house and to garden. House and Garden Feb–Dec, Tues–Sat 10am–4pm; Sun noon–4pm. Closed Dec 25 and Jan. Metro: Dupont Circle (Q St. exit), with a 20-min. walk.

NORTHERN VIRGINIA
Arlington

The land that today comprises Arlington County, Virginia, was included in the original parcel of land demarcated as the nation's capital. In 1847 the state of Virginia took its territory back, referring to it as "Alexandria County" until 1920, when Arlington at last became "Arlington," a name change made to avoid confusion with the city of Alexandria.

And where did the county pick up the name "Arlington"? From its famous estate, Arlington House, built by a descendant of Martha Washington: George

---

MUSEUMS IN anacostia

This historic, largely black residential neighborhood located east of the Capitol and away from the center of the city is not a typical tourist destination, but two attractions do draw visitors. The **Frederick Douglass National Historic Site** (1411 W St. SE, at 14th St. SE; www.nps.gov/frdo; © **202/426-5961**) is by far the more compelling. Born a slave in 1818, Frederick Bailey escaped his Maryland plantation, became an abolitionist and gifted orator, changed his name to Douglass to avoid capture, and fled to Britain, where he purchased his freedom. Back in the United States a free man, Douglass picked up where he had left off, fighting against slavery and for equal rights for all, including women. This house, known as Cedar Hill, was Douglass's home for the last 17 years of his life. A National Park Service ranger begins your tour on the veranda, where you can see that the house crowns one of the highest hills in Washington. Then your guide takes you upstairs and down, filling you in on the life of the brilliant, brave, and charismatic abolitionist here at this house, and elsewhere: his love of reading, his escape from slavery, his married life, and his embrace of emancipation for all oppressed people.

See website for hours and admission, which is free, but by guided tour only. Also see the African-American History itinerary, p. 42, in chapter 3.

The **Anacostia Community Museum** (1901 Fort Place SE, off Martin Luther King Jr. Ave.; www.anacostia.si.edu; © **202/633-4820**) is a Smithsonian museum that primarily serves the neighborhood and the local community with exhibits that resonate with area residents, focusing on social, cultural, and historical themes. Especially noteworthy is the show "A Right to the City" (through Apr 20, 2020), which explores the history of neighborhood change throughout the capital.

Washington Parke Custis, whose daughter married Robert E. Lee. (Before that, "Arlington" was the name of the Custis family estate in Tidewater Virginia.) The Lees lived in Arlington House on and off until the onset of the Civil War in 1861. The beginnings of Arlington National Cemetery date from May 1864, when four Union soldiers were buried here, in the area now known as section 27, the oldest part of the cemetery.

The **Arlington Memorial Bridge** leads directly from the Lincoln Memorial to the Robert E. Lee Memorial at Arlington House, symbolically joining these two figures into one Union after the Civil War.

Beyond Arlington the cemetery is Arlington, a residential community from which most residents commute into Washington. In recent years, however, the suburb has come into its own, booming with businesses, restaurants, and nightlife, giving tourists more incentive to visit. Below are its worthwhile sites.

Arlington National Cemetery ★★ CEMETERY   Arlington National Cemetery is, without hyperbole, the United States' most important burial ground. This shrine occupies approximately 624 acres on the high hills overlooking the capital from the west side of Memorial Bridge. More than 400,000 people are buried here, including veterans of all national wars, from the American Revolution to the Iraq and Afghanistan conflicts; Supreme Court justices; literary figures; slaves; presidents; astronauts; and assorted other national heroes. Many graves of the famous at Arlington bear nothing more than simple markers.

Upon arrival, head to the **Welcome Center,** where you can view exhibits, pick up a detailed map, and use the restrooms (there are no others until you get to Arlington House). The Welcome Center also offers kiosks where you can access the cemetery's app, **ANC Explorer,** to find locations of and directions to individual gravesites plus self-guided tours of the cemetery. (Or download the free app ahead of time at the iTunes store or from the Arlington National Cemetery website.)

If you're here to visit a particular grave, you'll be gratified to know that the cemetery operates a free shuttle to individual gravesites. And if you're here as a tourist, and you've got plenty of stamina and it's a nice day, consider touring all or part of the cemetery on foot. Plenty of people do. I'd say it's worth it to spring for the narrated tour: It's a hop-on, hop-off tour that makes six stops on weekdays, with an additional three stops included on weekend tours, for those who so desire. All tours include stops at the gravesites of **Pres. John F. Kennedy, Gen. John J. Pershing,** the **U.S. Coast Guard Memorial,** the **Memorial Amphitheater** and **Tomb of the Unknown Soldier, Arlington House,** and the **Marine Corps Memorial.** The weekend add-ons are Sections 55 and 60, the **Columbarium Courts** and **Niche Wall,** and the **Pentagon Group Burial Marker,** a five-sided granite tombstone engraved with the names of the 184 people killed in the 9/11 attack on the Pentagon. The tour lasts an hour or more, depending on how many times you hop on and off, and how long you stay at each site. Service is continuous, and the narrated commentary is lively and informative. You can buy tickets online in advance (www.arlingtontours. com) or at the ticket counter in the Welcome Center. Tickets are $15 adults,

$11 seniors, $7.25 children 3 to 11; military and active-duty personnel receive discounted prices, and disabled and active-duty military in uniform are free (with proper ID).

Remember: This is a memorial frequented not just by tourists, but also by those attending burial services or visiting the graves of beloved relatives and friends who are buried here.

Cemetery highlights include the **Tomb of the Unknown Soldier,** which contains the unidentified remains of a service member from World War I in a massive, white marble sarcophagus; just west of the sarcophagus are three white marble slabs flush with the plaza, marking the graves of unknown service members from World War II, the Korean War, and the Vietnam War. But the crypt for the Vietnam War service member contains no remains. In 1998 the entombed remains of the unknown soldier from Vietnam were disinterred and identified as those of Air Force 1st Lt. Michael Blassie, whose A-37 was shot down in South Vietnam in 1972. The Blassie family buried Michael in his hometown of St. Louis. A 24-hour honor guard watches over the marble Tomb of the Unknowns and its companion gravesites with the changing of the guard taking place every half-hour April to September, every hour on the hour October to March, and every hour at night year-round.

Within a 20-minute walk, all uphill, from the Welcome Center is **Arlington House,** the **Robert E. Lee Memorial** (www.nps.gov/arho; © **703/235-1530**), which was begun in 1802 by Martha Washington's grandson (through her first marriage), George Washington Parke Custis, who was raised at Mount Vernon as George and Martha's adopted son. Custis's daughter, Mary Anna Randolph, inherited the estate, and she and her husband, Robert E. Lee, lived here between 1831 and 1861. When Lee headed up Virginia's army, Mary fled, and federal troops confiscated the property. A multi-year renovation project completed in 2019 restored the house to its 1860 appearance, adding detailed room displays and objects that belonged to George Washington and the Lee family, and opened a new museum and bookstore on the property.

It's worth visiting the Arlington House estate for the spectacular view of the capital from its hilltop location. Just below the house, look for **Pierre Charles L'Enfant's grave** at a spot that is believed to offer the best view of Washington, the city he designed.

Below Arlington House is the **gravesite of President John Fitzgerald Kennedy,** a 3-acre lawn terrace paved with irregular-sized stones of Cape Cod granite, tufts of grass growing between the stones. At the head of the gravesite is a 5-foot, circular fieldstone, with the Eternal Flame burning in the center. Embracing the terrace is a low crescent wall inscribed with quotations from President Kennedy's presidency. Slate headstones mark the graves for President Kennedy, Jacqueline Kennedy Onassis, and their two infant children. President Kennedy's two brothers, senators Robert Kennedy and Edward Kennedy, are buried close by. The Kennedy graves attract streams of visitors. Arrive close to 8am to contemplate the site quietly; otherwise, it's often crowded.

The **Women in Military Service for America Memorial** (www.womens memorial.org; © **800/222-2294** or 703/892-2606) is another recommended spot. It honors the nearly 3 million women who have served in the armed forces from the American Revolution to the present. The impressive memorial lies just beyond the gated entrance to the cemetery, a 3-minute walk from the visitor center. As you approach, you see a large, circular reflecting pool, perfectly placed within the curve of the granite wall rising behind it. Arched passageways within the 226-foot-long wall lead to an upper terrace and dramatic views of Arlington National Cemetery and the monuments of Washington; an arc of large glass panels (which form the roof of the memorial hall) contains etched quotations from famous people about contributions made by servicewomen. Behind the wall and completely underground is the **Education Center,** housing a **Hall of Honor,** a gallery of exhibits tracing the history of women in the military; a theater; and a computer register of servicewomen, which visitors may access for the stories and information about 265,000 individual military women, past and present. Hours are 8am to 5pm. Stop at the reception desk for a brochure for a self-guided tour through the memorial. The memorial is open every day except Christmas.

Just across the Memorial Bridge from the base of the Lincoln Memorial. www.arlington cemetery.mil. © **877/907-8585.** Free admission. Apr–Sept daily 8am–7pm; Oct–Mar daily 8am–5pm. Metro: Arlington National Cemetery. Parking $2/hr. The cemetery is also accessible as a stop on several tour bus services, including Old Town Trolley.

The Pentagon ★ GOVERNMENT BUILDING   Completed in January 1943 after a mere 16 months of construction, the structure is the world's largest low-rise office building. The Capitol could fit inside any one of its five wedge-shaped sections. Twenty-three-thousand people work at the Pentagon, which holds 17½ miles of corridors, 19 escalators, 284 restrooms, and 691 water fountains. Tours of this headquarters for the American military establishment were suspended for a while following the September 11, 2001, attack in which terrorists hijacked American Airlines Flight 77 and crashed it into the northwest side of the Pentagon, killing 125 people working at the Pentagon and 59 people aboard the plane. In the years since, the Pentagon has been completely restored and its tour program reinstated, in accordance with certain procedures (see below). More than 106,000 visitors tour the Pentagon annually.

An active-duty staff person from the National Capital Region's ceremonial unit conducts the free, 60-minute tour that covers 1½ miles. Your tour guide is required to memorize 20 pages of informational material, outlining the mission of each military branch. It's a fascinating introduction, as is seeing the building itself, its corridors commemorating the history, people, and culture of the Air Force, Navy, Army, Marine Corps, and Coast Guard. You'll see historical photos, the Hall of Heroes for Medal of Honor recipients, an exhibit recognizing U.S. prisoners of war and those missing in action, and paintings depicting the country's founding fathers.

The tour does not include a visit to the 2-acre **Pentagon Memorial,** better known as the **9/11 Memorial,** which is located outside, on the northwest side of the building near where the plane crashed. On view are 184 granite-covered benches, each engraved with a victim's name, and arranged in order of birth date. The names are written in such a way on each bench that you must face the Pentagon to be able to read the names of those killed there and face away from the Pentagon, toward the western sky, to read the names of those who perished on the plane. *Note:* You do not need to sign up for a Pentagon tour to visit the 9/11 Memorial, which is open to the public 24 hours a day, every day. The best way to reach the memorial is to take the Metro to the Pentagon station and walk the half-mile, following the signs that lead from the station to the northwest side of the Pentagon.

Pentagon tours are available Monday to Thursday 10am to 4pm, Friday noon to 4pm, and you must book your tour no sooner than 14 days and no later than 90 days in advance. Request the tour online at **https://pentagontours. osd.mil**, providing the Social Security number, birth date, and other info for each member of your party. There's no public parking at the Pentagon, so it's best to arrive by Metro—the Pentagon has its own Metro stop. Once you exit the Pentagon Metro station, look for the Pentagon Visitors Center near the station entrance and go to the Pentagon Tour Window.

Department of Defense, 1400 Defense Pentagon. https://pentagontours.osd.mil and www.pentagonmemorial.org. (C) **703/697-1776.** Free admission, but reservations required; guided tours only. Pentagon Mon–Thurs 10am–4pm; Fri noon–4pm. Pentagon Memorial daily 24 hr. Metro: Pentagon.

PARKS

More than 27% of Washington, D.C.'s land space is national parkland. When you add in the parks and gardens maintained by the D.C. Department of Parks and Recreation, as well as private estates that are open to the public, you're talking thousands and thousands of green acres!

Potomac Park ★★★

The National Mall and Memorial Parks' individual spaces known as West and East Potomac parks are 720 riverside acres divided by the Tidal Basin. The parkland is most famous for its display of **cherry trees,** which bloom for a mere 2 weeks, tops, every spring, as they have since the city of Tokyo first gave the U.S. capital the gift of the original 3,000 trees in 1912. Today more than 3,750 cherry trees grow along the Tidal Basin in West Potomac Park, East Potomac Park, the Washington Monument grounds, and other pockets of the city.

The sight of the delicate cherry blossoms is so special that the whole city joins in cherry-blossom-related hoopla, throwing the **National Cherry Blossom Festival** (Mar 20–Apr 12, 2020). The National Park Service devotes a home page to the subject, **www.nps.gov/cherry,** and the National Cherry Blossom Festival officially has another: **www.nationalcherryblossomfestival.org**. The trees usually begin blooming sometime between March 20 and April 17; April 4 is the average date at which the blooms reach their peak, defined as the point at which 70% of the Tidal Basin–sited cherry trees have blossomed.

To get to the Tidal Basin by car (*not* recommended in cherry-blossom season— actually, let me be clear: *impossible* in cherry-blossom season), you want to get on Independence Avenue and follow the signs posted near the Lincoln Memorial that show you where to turn to find parking. If you're walking, cross Independence Avenue where it intersects with West Basin Drive and follow the path to the Tidal Basin. There is no convenient Metro stop near here. If you don't want to walk or ride a bike, your best bet is a taxi.

West Potomac Park encompasses Constitution Gardens; the Vietnam, Korean, Lincoln, Jefferson, World War II, and FDR memorials; the D.C. World War I Memorial; the Reflecting Pool; the Tidal Basin and its paddleboats; and countless flower beds, ball fields, and trees. More than 1,500 cherry trees border the Tidal Basin, some of them Akebonos with delicate pink blossoms, but most are Yoshinos with white, cloudlike flower clusters.

East Potomac Park has 1,701 cherry trees in 10 varieties. The park also has picnic grounds, tennis courts, three golf courses, a large swimming pool, and biking and hiking paths by the water. East Potomac Park's **Hains Point** is located on a peninsula extending into the Potomac River; locals love to ride their bikes out to the point; golfers love to tee up in view of the Washington Monument. See "Outdoor Activities," p. 205, for further information.

Part of National Mall and Memorial Parks, bordering the Potomac River along the west and southwest ends. www.nps.gov/nama. ℂ **202/426-6841.** Free admission. Daily 24 hr. Metro: Smithsonian (12th St./Independence Ave. exit).

Rock Creek Park ★★★

Created in 1890, **Rock Creek Park** was purchased by Congress for its "pleasant valleys and ravines, primeval forests and open fields, its running waters, its rocks clothed with rich ferns and mosses, its repose and tranquility, its light and shade, its ever-varying shrubbery, its beautiful and extensive views," according to a Corps of Engineers officer quoted in the National Park Service's administrative history. A 1,754-acre valley within the District of Columbia, extending 12 miles from the Potomac River to the Maryland border, it's one of the biggest and finest city parks in the nation. Parts of it are still wild; coyotes have been sighted here, joining the red and gray foxes, raccoons, and beavers already resident. Most tourists encounter its southern tip, the section from the Kennedy Center to the National Zoo, but the park widens and travels much farther from there. Among the park's attractions are playgrounds, an extensive system of hiking and biking trails, sports facilities, remains of Civil War fortifications, and acres and acres of wooded parklands.

For full information on the wide range of park programs and activities, visit the **Rock Creek Nature Center and Planetarium,** 5200 Glover Rd. NW (ℂ **202/895-6070**), Wednesday through Sunday from 9am to 5pm. To get to the center by public transportation, take the Metro to Friendship Heights and transfer to bus no. E4 to Military Road and Oregon Avenue/Glover Road, then walk up the hill about 100 yards.

The Nature Center and Planetarium is the scene of numerous activities, including weekend planetarium shows, nature films, crafts demonstrations, live animal demonstrations, guided nature walks, plus a mix of lectures, films, and other events. Self-guided nature trails begin here. All activities are free,

Cyclists cruise through Rock Creek Park.

but for planetarium shows you need to pick up tickets a half-hour in advance. The Nature Center is closed on federal holidays.

At Tilden Street and Beach Drive, you can see the refurbished water-powered 1820s gristmill, used until not so long ago to grind corn and wheat into flour. It's called **Peirce Mill** (a man named Isaac Peirce built it). The mill is open for tours (Nov–Feb Sat–Sun noon–4pm; Mar Sat–Sun 10am–4pm; Apr–Oct Fri–Sun 10am–4pm); the mill seldom operates, however. Check the website, www.nps.gov/pimi, or call ✆ **202/895-6070.**

You'll find convenient free **parking** throughout the park.

In addition to the circumscribed 1,754-acre park, Rock Creek Park's charter extends to include the maintenance of other parks, gardens, and buildings throughout the city.

In Georgetown, the park's offerings include D.C.'s oldest standing structure, the 1765 **Old Stone House** (p. 194), located on busy M St. NW; the 10-acre, Potomac River–focused **Georgetown Waterfront Park** (www.georgetownwaterfront park.org), a swath of greenways, plazas, and walkways, with benches, a labyrinth, and overlooks—you owe it to yourself to take a stroll here; and in upper Georgetown, the family-friendly **Montrose Park,** a favorite place for picnicking and playing tennis; and **Dumbarton Oaks Park,** a 27-acre preserve of naturalistic gardens. Both Montrose and Dumbarton Oaks parks adjoin one another and the Dumbarton Oaks estate and formal gardens (p. 193).

Along 16th Street NW, about 1 mile north of the White House, is **Meridian Hill Park** (www.nps.gov/mehi), 12 acres in size, and located between the Adams Morgan and Columbia Heights neighborhoods. Meridian Hill Park is worth a visit for several reasons: Its view serves up the White House, the Washington Monument, and the Jefferson Memorial in the distance; its cascading fountain is the longest in North America; and planted amid its landscaped gardens are a potpourri of statues of famous people: Joan of Arc, Dante, President Buchanan. Best of all is the mix of people you'll find here, mostly from the nearby diverse neighborhoods, and the assorted activities they get up to: yoga lessons, soccer matches, and Sunday afternoon through evening, spring through fall, an African drum circle.

From the Potomac River near the Kennedy Center northwest through the city into Maryland. www.nps.gov/rocr. ✆ **202/895-6070.** Free admission. Daily during daylight hours. Metro: Access points near the stations at Dupont Circle, Foggy Bottom, Woodley Park–Zoo, and Cleveland Park.

Theodore Roosevelt Island Park ★

A serene, 88½-acre wilderness preserve, Theodore Roosevelt Island is a memorial to the nation's 26th president in recognition of his contributions to conservation. During his administration, Roosevelt, an outdoor enthusiast and expert field naturalist, set aside a total of 234 million acres of public lands for forests, national parks, wildlife and bird refuges, and monuments.

Native American tribes were here first, inhabiting the island for centuries until the arrival of English explorers in the 1600s. Over the years, the island passed through many owners before becoming what it is today—an island preserve of swamp, marsh, and upland forest that's a haven for rabbits, chipmunks, great owls, foxes, muskrats, turtles, and groundhogs. It's a complex ecosystem in which cattails, arrow arum, and pickerelweed grow in the marshes, and willow, ash, and maple trees root on the mud flats. You can observe these flora and fauna in their natural environs on 2.5 miles of foot trails.

In the northern center of the island, overlooking a terrace encircled by a water-filled moat, stands a 17-foot bronze statue of Roosevelt. Four 21-foot granite tablets are inscribed with tenets of his conservation philosophy.

To drive to the island, take the George Washington Memorial Parkway exit north from the Theodore Roosevelt Bridge. The parking area is accessible only from the northbound lane; park there and cross the pedestrian bridge that connects the lot to the island. You can also rent a canoe at Thompson Boat Center or Key Bridge Boathouse (p. 206) and paddle over, making sure to land at the north or northeast corner of the island; there is no place to secure the boat, so you'll need to stay with it. Or take the Metro to the Rosslyn Metro station, walk toward Key Bridge, and follow the short connecting trail leading downhill from the downstream side of the river and across the parkway into the parking lot. Expect bugs in summer and muddy trails after a rain.

In the Potomac River, btw. Washington and Rosslyn, VA (see above for access information). www.nps.gov/this. ✆ **703/289-2500.** Free admission. Daily 6am–10pm. Metro: Rosslyn, then follow the trail to the island.

Chesapeake & Ohio Canal National Historical Park

Hidden behind the bustling streets of Georgetown is the picturesque **C&O Canal** and its unspoiled towpath, which extends 184.5 miles into Maryland. You leave urban cares and stresses behind while hiking, strolling, jogging, cycling, or boating in this lush natural setting of ancient oaks and red maples, giant sycamores, willows, and wildflowers. But the canal wasn't always just a leisure spot for city people. It was built in the 1800s, when water routes were vital to transportation. Even before it was completed, though, the canal was being rendered obsolete by the B&O Railroad, which was constructed at about the same time and along the same route. Today its role as an oasis from unrelenting urbanity is even more important.

You can enter the towpath in Georgetown below M Street via Thomas Jefferson Street. If you hike 14 miles, you'll reach **Great Falls,** a point where the

Potomac becomes a stunning waterfall plunging 76 feet. This is also where the National Park Service runs its **Great Falls Tavern Visitor Center,** 11710 MacArthur Blvd., Potomac, MD (© **301/767-3714**), open year-round Wednesday through Sunday 9am to 4:30pm. At this 1831 tavern, you can see museum exhibits and a film about the canal; it also has a bookstore. The park charges for entrance: $15 per car, $7 per walker or cyclist (valid for 7 days).

The park offers many opportunities for outdoor activities (see below), but if you or your family prefer a less strenuous form of relaxation, consider a **mule-drawn 19th-century canal-boat trip,** led by Park Service rangers in period dress. They regale passengers with canal legend and lore and sing period songs. Boats operate at Great Falls spring through fall, Saturday and Sunday at 11am, 1:30, and 3pm; in summer, the boats operate on Fridays as well, at the same times. Barge rides last about 1 hour and 10 minutes, and cost $8 per adult, $6 for seniors, $5 per child, and free for children 3 and under. *Note:* Parts of the C&O Canal and its locks are under ongoing construction from either storm damage or restoration. Depending on when you visit, sections of the trail may be closed altogether. Call to confirm!

Enter the towpath in Georgetown below M St. via Thomas Jefferson St. www.nps.gov/ choh. © **301/767-3714.** Free admission. Daily during daylight hours. Metro: Foggy Bottom, with a 20-min. walk to the towpath in Georgetown.

ESPECIALLY FOR KIDS

As far as I know, Pierre L'Enfant and his successors were not thinking of children when they incorporated the long, open stretch of the Mall into their design for the city. But they may as well have been. This 2-mile expanse of lawn running from the Lincoln Memorial to the Capitol is a playground, really, and a backyard to the Smithsonian museums and National Gallery of Art, which border it. You can visit any of these sites assured that if one of your little darlings starts to misbehave, you'll be able to head right out the door to the National Mall, where numerous distractions await. Vendors sell ice cream, soft pretzels, and sodas. Festivals of all sorts take place on a regular basis, whether it's the busy **Smithsonian Folklife Festival** for 10 days at the end of June into July (see "Washington, D.C., Calendar of Events," in chapter 2, p. 23), or the **Kite Festival** on the Washington Monument grounds in spring. Weather permitting, a **19th-century carousel** operates in front of the Arts and Industries Building, on the south side of the Mall. Right across the Mall from the carousel is the child-friendly **National Gallery Sculpture Garden,** whose shallow pool is good for splashing one's feet in summer and for ice-skating in winter.

The Smithsonian's comprehensive calendar of events page (www.si.edu/ events/calendar) has a daily list of family-friendly fun at all 18 locations, letting you screen for children's activities. It's a great timesaver.

The truth is that many of Washington's attractions hold various enchantments for children of all ages. It might be easier to point out which ones are *not* recommended for your youngest: The Supreme Court, the chambers of Congress, the U.S. Holocaust Memorial Museum, and the State Department

Check for special children's events at museum information desks when you enter. I especially recommend a visit to the **International Spy Museum** (p. 165) for tweens and teens (and adults), for the fun interactive spy adventures; and the **National Building Museum** (p. 181), for kids ages 3 to 11, for the assortment of hands-on building-related activities. Here's a rundown of overall kid-pleasers in town:

○ **Discovery Theater, inside the S. Dillon Ripley Center** (p. 158): Right next to the Smithsonian Castle, this underground children's theater puts on about 30 productions each season—puppet shows, storytelling, dances, and plays.

○ **Gravelly Point:** Zzzzooom! It's a thrill for young airplane lovers to watch jets take off and land at this park just steps from Ronald Reagan Airport's runway. It's also an ideal spot to picnic, play ball, and walk along the Potomac River.

○ **Madame Tussauds Washington, D.C.** (p. 180): There are two kinds of people in this world: those who think wax museums are hokey, and children. Yeah, watch your offspring pretend to sing with Beyoncé, box with Evander Holyfield, stand tall next to George Washington, and whoop it up with Whoopi. Maybe you'll find your inner child and start loving these wax figures, too.

○ **National Air and Space Museum** (p. 143): Spectacular IMAX films (don't miss), planetarium shows, missiles, rockets, and a walk-through orbital workshop.

○ **National Museum of American History** (p. 153): This museum's got all your kids covered: the fabulous Wegmans Wonderplace is a playground for infants to 6-year-olds; the Lemelson Center introduces

visitors of all ages to the stories of inventors and inventions (Places of Invention), and invites kids ages 6 to 12, especially, to experiment and test their curiosity with plenty of hands-on activities (Spark!Lab). The museum has also gotten into simulated rides, where kids can practice driving a racecar or ride a roller coaster.

○ **National Museum of the American Indian** (p. 154): Children, and their parents too, enjoy themselves in the museum's imagiNATIONS Activity Center, where visitors learn basket weaving, kayak balancing, and other Native American skills, and play games to discover more about American Indian culture.

○ **National Museum of Natural History** (p. 155): This is a no-brainer: A Q?rius Jr. Discovery Room for youngsters, a Butterfly Pavilion, an insect zoo, shrunken heads, tarantula feedings, dinosaurs…

○ **National Zoological Park** (p. 190): Pandas! Cheetahs! Kids love zoos, and this is an especially good one.

○ **Rock Creek Park Nature Center and Planetarium** (p. 200): Kids can explore live turtles, fish, snakes, and an active beehive here, or stare up at the stars in the Planetarium, which hosts regular monthly programs. Afterward, walk the short stroll to the Rock Creek Horse Center, where young equestrians will love the 15-minute pony ride. ($22, reservations required).

○ **U.S. Botanic Garden** (p. 159): Kids get their hands dirty at the seasonal digging area outside the Children's Garden. Or head inside for a warm, fragrant experience. Don't miss the model train display during the holidays.

Diplomatic Rooms. The International Spy Museum is now recommending that its museum is most suitable for children 10 and over. Generally speaking, the bigger and busier the museum, the better it is for kids (see box above).

For more ideas, consult the online or print version of the Friday "Weekend" section of the *Washington Post,* which lists numerous activities (mostly free) for kids: special museum events, children's theater, storytelling programs, puppet shows, video-game competitions, and so forth. View the websites for the Kennedy Center and the National Theatre to find out about children's shows; see chapter 8 for details. For outdoor fun, consider the southwest waterfront's Wharf complex, studded with oversize game boards, bocce courts, mini-golf, bike rentals, and waterpark activities. And see p. 36 for a family-themed tour of the capital.

OUTDOOR ACTIVITIES

For information about spectator-sports venues, see chapter 8. But if you prefer to work up your own honest sweat, Washington offers plenty of opportunities in lush surroundings. See "Parks," earlier in this chapter, for complete coverage of the city's loveliest green spaces. And look to the waterfronts: In addition to **Georgetown Waterfront Park** (p. 201), the Capitol Riverfront's **Yards Park** is a magnet for parents who let their little ones play in the fountain and canal basin, and a popular spot for outdoor festivals and concerts. Best of all is the **Wharf at the Southwest Waterfront** (www.wharfdc.com/things-to-do), which offers a smorgasbord of outdoor recreational opportunities, including boat and bike rentals, yoga on the pier, fitness classes, sailing lessons, strolling, ice skating, you name it. Furthermore, East Potomac Park lies directly across the Washington Channel and a free ferry ride away from the Wharf; there you can play golf and tennis, swim, and jog (see those categories, below).

Biking

Biking is big in D.C., not just as a leisure activity but as an environmentally friendly form of transportation. Much of the city is flat, and paths are everywhere, notably around the National Mall and Memorial Parks. Rock Creek Park has a **9-mile paved bike route** ★ from the Lincoln Memorial through the park into Maryland. Or you can follow the bike path from the Lincoln Memorial over Memorial Bridge to Old Town Alexandria and on to Mount Vernon (see chapter 9). For a less-crowded ride, check out the **Anacostia Riverwalk Trail;** its 12 miles (of a planned 20-mile stretch) go from the Tidal Basin to the Capitol Riverfront neighborhood, and along the Anacostia River into other waterfront communities. *Warning:* Bike-path signage can be confusing or even missing altogether in the waterfront area and you may have to bike on neighborhood streets to pick up the path linking the Southwest Waterfront to the southeast portion of the Anacostia Riverwalk Trail.

The **C&O Canal Historical Park's towpath** (p. 202) is a popular bike path. The **Capital Crescent Trail** goes from Georgetown to the suburb of Bethesda, Maryland, following a former railroad track that parallels the Potomac River for part of the way and passes by old trestle bridges and pleasant residential neighborhoods. You can pick up the trail at the **Thompson Boat Center** in Georgetown, and at **Fletcher's Cove** along the C&O Canal; visit **www.cctrail.org** for info.

Capital BikeShare stations are located conveniently near the Tidal Basin and the National Mall; If you're here for more than a few days, consider a Capital BikeShare membership (www.capitalbikeshare.com; p. 297).

Bike rental locations include:

- The **Boat House at Fletcher's Cove,** 4940 Canal Rd. NW (www.fletcherscove.com; ✆ **202/244-0461**).

- **Bike and Roll/Bike the Sites** (www.bikeandrolldc.com; ✆ **202/842-2453**), with two locations: near the National Mall, at 955 L'Enfant Plaza SW, North Building, directly behind the new International Spy Museum location, daily tours and rentals (Metro: L'Enfant Plaza); and Old Town Alexandria, One Wales Alley, at the waterfront, self-guided tours, full-day advance-reservations rentals, and same-day walkup rentals (Metro: King St.). See p. 301 for info about their guided tours. Rates vary depending on the bike you choose but always include helmet, bike, lock, and pump; there's a 2-hour minimum.

- **Thompson Boat Center,** 2900 Virginia Ave. NW, at Rock Creek Parkway (www.thompsonboatcenter.com; ✆ **202/333-9543;** Metro: Foggy Bottom, with a 10-min. walk). Both Fletcher's and Thompson rent bikes, weather permitting, from about mid-March to the end of October.

- **Big Wheel Bikes,** 1034 33rd St. NW, near the C&O Canal just below M Street (www.bigwheelbikes.com; ✆ **202/337-0254**). You can rent a bike here March through late December Tuesday through Sunday.

Boating & Fishing

An enterprise called **Boating in DC** (www.boatingindc.com; ✆ **202/337-9642**) operates all of the boat rental locations I list below. Before you access the Boating in DC website, however, it might be helpful to read my descriptions below, which provide information geared toward visitors as much as locals.

Two places mentioned above that rent bikes also rent boats: **Thompson Boat Center** and the **Boat House at Fletcher's Cove;** they follow the same schedule as their bike rental season, basically March to November. Thompson has canoes, kayaks, and rowing shells (recreational and racing), and is open for boat and bike rentals daily in season. Fletcher's is right on the C&O Canal, about 2 miles from Key Bridge in Georgetown. In addition to renting bikes, canoes, rowboats, and kayaks, Fletcher's sells fishing licenses, bait, and tackle. Fletcher's is accessible by car (west on M St. NW to Canal Rd. NW) and has plenty of free parking.

Key Bridge Boathouse, 3500 Water St. NW (www.boatingindc.com; 𝒞 202/337-9642), located along the Georgetown waterfront beneath Key Bridge, is open daily mid-April to November for canoe and kayak rentals. Foggy Bottom is the closest Metro station. Sister boathouses include **Ballpark Boathouse,** on the Anacostia River in the Capital Riverfront neighborhood, at Potomac Avenue SE and First Street SE; and the **Wharf Boathouse,** at 700 Water Street SW, in the Southwest Waterfront neighborhood.

Also part of the Boating in DC dynasty are **paddleboats** ★, with footpedals to propel the boat over the surface of the Tidal Basin. The Tidal Basin is located between Independence Ave. SW and the Jefferson Memorial. Available for rent from 10am to 5pm daily mid-March to October 14 are fourseaters at $30 an hour, two-seaters at $18 an hour, and motorized two-seater "swan boats" at $34 an hour, for those who need a little help in getting around on the water.

Golf

The District's best and most convenient public golf course is the historic **East Potomac Golf Course** on Hains Point, 972 Ohio Dr. SW, in East Potomac Park (www.golfdc.com; 𝒞 202/554-7660). Golfers use the Washington Monument to help them line up their shots. The club rents everything but shoes. In addition to its three courses, one 18-hole and two 9-hole greens, the park offers a miniature golf course. Open since 1930, it's the oldest continually operating miniature golf course in the country.

Hiking & Jogging

Washington has numerous **hiking paths.** The C&O Canal offers 184.5 miles stretching from D.C. to Cumberland, Maryland; hiking any section of the flat dirt towpath or its more rugged side paths is a pleasure (and it's free). **Hiker/ biker campsites** along the way provide a picnic table, grill, and chemical toilet. Theodore Roosevelt Island is 88½ acres of wilderness but allows hikes on only three short trails. Rock Creek Park boasts 20 miles of hiking trails (visit www.nps.gov/rocr/planyourvisit/maps.htm for maps).

Joggers can run on the National Mall, along the path in Rock Creek Park, and around the 3.5-mile roadway that loops the 327-acre **East Potomac Park** (part of National Mall and Memorial Parks, www.nps.gov/nama) and takes you to Hains Point, the East Potomac Golf Course (see above) and tennis courts (see below).

Ice Skating

Georgetown's waterfront complex, the **Washington Harbour,** at 3050 K St. NW (www.thewashingtonharbour.com/ice-skating; 𝒞 202/706-7666), operates an ice rink that, at 11,800 square feet, is the largest outdoor skating venue in the city. (The recessed positioning of the rink obstructs what would otherwise be an awesome view of the Potomac River.) The season runs November to March, and the rink is open Monday and Tuesday noon to 7pm, Wednesday and Thursday noon to 9pm, Friday noon to 10pm, Saturday 10am to 10pm, and Sunday 10am to 7pm.

For a truly memorable experience, head to the **National Gallery Sculpture Garden Ice Rink** ★, on the Mall at 7th Street and Constitution Avenue NW (www.nga.gov/content/ngaweb/visit/ice-rink.html; ✆ **202/289-3360**), where you can rent skates, twirl in view of the sculptures, and enjoy hot chocolate in the Pavilion Café next to the rink. It's also open daily, November into March.

The Capitol Riverfront neighborhood has its own figure-eight-shaped ice rink in **Canal Park** (www.capitolriverfront.org/canal-park/ice-rink), open daily in winter.

The Wharf's ice skating rink (www.wharfdc.com/wharf-ice-rink), located on the Transit Pier in the Southwest Waterfront neighborhood, offers a rather small rink and unprotected exposure to the wind-whipping cold, but the river views missing at Washington Harbour are waiting for you here.

Each of these ice rinks charges for skate rentals and skating.

Swimming & Tennis

If it's summer and your hotel doesn't have a **pool,** you might consider one of the city's neighborhood pools, including a large outdoor pool at 25th and N streets NW (✆ **202/727-3285**) and the Georgetown outdoor pool at 34th Street and Volta Place NW (✆ **202/645-5669**). They are likely to be crowded.

One of the best places open to the public for swimming in summer and for other outdoor sports year-round is **Hains Point,** in **East Potomac Park** (p. 200), which lies within walking distance of Independence Avenue and across from the Wharf (see intro to this section) and has a large outdoor swimming pool (✆ **202/727-6523**).

Many of the same recreation centers equipped with pools also have **tennis courts,** so you'll find four courts at the 25th and N streets NW location and two courts at the Volta Place location, both cited above. In the same Georgetown neighborhood is **Montrose Park,** right next to Dumbarton Oaks (p. 193), with four courts, but no pool.

By far the best public tennis court facility is **East Potomac Park Tennis Center** at Hains Point (www.eastpotomactennis.com; ✆ **202/554-5962**), with 24 tennis courts (10 clay, 9 outdoor hard courts, and 5 indoor hard courts), including three illuminated at night; the park rents rackets as well. Fees vary with court surface and time of play.

For a list of public indoor and outdoor pools, go to **www.dpr.dc.gov** and click the "Find a Pool" link in the "Parks and Facilities" tab; for a list of public tennis courts, go to **https://dpr.dc.gov/publication/dpr-tennis-court-locations**.

SHOPPING

Washington, D.C.'s shopping scene is thriving, thanks to the city's strong economy. With its high-income population and vigorous spending statistics for both visitors and residents, Washington continues to attract major retailers. Local entrepreneurs, meanwhile, are also doing quite nicely, thank you very much. Wherever you are in the city, shops present a variety of wares, prices, and styles. This chapter leads you to some of the best.

THE SHOPPING SCENE

Most Washington-area stores are open from 10am to 5 or 6pm Monday through Saturday. Sunday hours vary, with some stores opting not to open at all and others open from noon to 5 or 6pm. Many stores in Georgetown and at Union Station keep later hours and are also open on Sunday. Other exceptions include antiques stores and art galleries, which tend to keep their own hours.

Sales tax on merchandise is 6% in the District, Maryland, and Northern Virginia. Most gift, arts, and crafts stores, including those at the Smithsonian museums, will handle shipping; clothing stores generally do not.

GREAT SHOPPING AREAS

UNION STATION   It's a railroad station, a historic landmark, an architectural marvel, and a shopping mall. Yes, the beauteous Union Station offers some fine shopping opportunities; it's certainly the best on Capitol Hill, with about 50 clothes, specialty, and souvenir shops. **Metro:** Union Station.

PENN QUARTER   The area bounded east and west by 7th and 14th streets NW, and north and south by New York and Pennsylvania avenues NW, continues to develop as a hopping shopping area. At the northern end of the quarter, the residential/office/dining/retail complex **CityCenterDC** (www.citycenterdc.com), on H St. NW (btw. 9th and 11th sts.), beckons 1-percenters and the curious to its high-end shops, Dior to David Yurman; but local enterprises are also here, including a weekly farmers market and outdoor yoga classes. Plus, the design of the site is cool, so check it out. The Penn Quarter has plenty of national chains such as Urban Outfitters, H&M, and Anthropologie; international chains such as Zara; as well as one-of-a-kind stores like the museum shops at the National Building

An art stall in the holiday market in Penn Quarter.

Museum, the Smithsonian American Art Museum and Portrait Gallery, and the National Museum of Women in the Arts. **Macy's** (formerly "Hecht's") at 12th and G streets, continues as the sole department store downtown. **Metro:** Metro Center, Gallery Place–Chinatown, or Archives–Navy Memorial.

ADAMS MORGAN   Centered on 18th Street and Columbia Road NW, Adams Morgan is known for secondhand bookshops and eclectic collectibles stores. It's a fun area for walking and shopping. **Metro:** Woodley Park–Zoo/ Adams Morgan (then walk south on Connecticut Ave. NW until you reach Calvert St., cross Connecticut Ave., and follow Calvert St. across the Duke Ellington Memorial Bridge until you reach the junction of Columbia Rd. NW and 18th St. NW) or Dupont Circle (exit at Q St. NW and walk up Connecticut Ave. NW to Columbia Rd. NW). ***Best bet:*** The DC Circulator bus, which runs between the McPherson Square and the Woodley Park–Zoo/Adams Morgan Metro stations.

CONNECTICUT AVENUE/DUPONT CIRCLE   Running from K Street north to S Street, Connecticut Avenue NW is the place to find clothing, from traditional business attire at Brooks Brothers or Ann Taylor to casual duds at Gap. The area closer to Dupont Circle is known for its art galleries, funky boutiques, and gift, stationery, and book shops. **Metro:** Farragut North at one end, Dupont Circle at the other.

U & 14TH STREET CORRIDORS AND SHAW   The number of cool shops has hit critical mass, winning the area widespread notice. If you shun brand names and box stores, you'll love the vintage boutiques and affordable fashion shops along U and 14th streets. Look for provocative handles, like Miss Pixie's Furnishings and Whatnot. **Metro:** U Street/African American Civil War Memorial/Cardozo and Mount Vernon Square/7th Street/Convention Center.

GEORGETOWN   Home to more than 200 stores, this neighborhood is and always will be the city's main shopping area. Most stores sit on one of the two main, intersecting streets, Wisconsin Avenue and M Street NW. You'll find both chain and one-of-a-kind shops, chic as well as thrift. Sidewalks are almost always crowded, and parking can be tough. **Metro:** Foggy Bottom, then catch the DC Circulator bus from the stop at 22nd Street and Pennsylvania Avenue (see p. 296 for more information). Metro buses (the no. 30 series) travel through Georgetown from different parts of the city. Otherwise, consider taking a taxi.

UPPER WISCONSIN AVENUE NORTHWEST   In a residential section of town known as Friendship Heights on the D.C. side and Chevy Chase on the Maryland side (7 miles north of Georgetown, straight up Wisconsin Ave.) is a quarter-mile shopping district that extends from Saks Fifth Avenue at one end to Sur La Table at the other. In between are malls, department stores, and top designer boutiques. The street is too wide and traffic always too snarled to make this a pleasant place to stroll. Drive if you want and park in the garages beneath the Mazza Gallerie, Chevy Chase Pavilion, or Bloomingdale's. Or take the **Metro;** the strip is on the Red Line, with the Friendship Heights exits leading directly into each of the malls.

THE WHARF   This Southwest Waterfront complex doesn't have a ton of shops—about 20 at last count—but the number is growing, and the stores on offer are pretty wonderful: offshoots of local favorites, such as the Politics and Prose bookstore, and delectable newcomers, such as the tiny Harper Macaw chocolate boutique. **Metro:** Waterfront.

OLD TOWN ALEXANDRIA   Old Town, in Virginia, resembles Georgetown in its picturesque location on the Potomac, streets lined with historic homes and plentiful shops, as well as in its less desirable aspects: heavy traffic, crowded sidewalks, difficult parking. Old Town extends from the Potomac River in the east to the King Street Metro station in the west, and from about 1st Street in the north to Green Street in the south, but the best shopping is in the center, where King and Washington streets intersect. Weekdays are tamer than weekends. **Metro:** King Street, then take a free King Street Trolley to reach the heart of Old Town.

SHOPPING A TO Z

Antiques

Georgetown, Adams Morgan, and the U and 14th Street Corridors all have concentrations of visit-worthy antiques stores. We recommend:

Brass Knob Architectural Antiques ★   When old homes and office buildings are demolished in the name of progress, these savvy salvagers spirit away salable treasures, from lots of light fixtures and chandelier glass to wrought-iron fencing. 2311 18th St. NW. www.thebrassknob.com. (C) **202/332-3370.** Metro: Woodley Park or Dupont Circle, with a 20-min. walk, or take the DC Circulator bus.

Cherub Antiques Gallery ★★   Open since 1974 (since 1983 at this location), this gallery specializes in Art Nouveau, Art Deco, Arts & Crafts, and Vienna Secession design periods. Look here for rare cocktail shakers and barware, candelabra, and jewelry. 2918 M St. NW. www.cherubantiquesgallery.com. ℂ **202/337-2224.** Metro: Foggy Bottom, then take the DC Circulator bus.

Good Wood ★★ Half flea market, half antique store, this delightful shop was opened by husband and wife Dan and Anna Kahoe in the early '90s. Come for the retro furniture and vintage goods as well as clothing, candles, and housewares. 1428 U St. NW (at Waverly Place NW). www.goodwooddc.com. ℂ **202/986-3640.** Metro: U Street/Cardozo.

Marston Luce Antiques ★★ Eighteenth- and 19th-century painted furniture, folk art, pottery, and garden items, specifically from Sweden and France—the owner lives more than half the year in Dordogne, France, and his inventory often reflects that provenance. 1651 Wisconsin Ave. NW. www.marstonluce.com. ℂ **202/333-6800.** Metro: Foggy Bottom, then take the DC Circulator bus.

Art Galleries

Art galleries abound in the capital. The following are among the best.

Addison/Ripley Fine Art ★ Representing internationally, nationally, and regionally recognized artists, Addison/Ripley shows works traditional to abstract, in all media and sizes, including large-scale paintings, sculpture, and photography. 1670 Wisconsin Ave. NW (Reservoir Rd.). www.addisonripleyfineart.com. ℂ **202/338-5180.** Metro: Foggy Bottom, then take the DC Circulator bus.

Foundry Gallery ★ Established in 1971, Foundry is nonprofit and artist-owned and -operated. It features the pieces of local artists, who work in various media and styles, from abstract painting on silk to mixed-media collages. The Foundry frequently hosts talks, workshops, demonstrations, and receptions. 2118 8th St. NW (btw. U and V sts.). www.foundrygallery.org. ℂ **202/232-0203.** Metro: U St./Cardozo (10th St. exit).

IA&A at Hillyer ★ The **International Arts & Artists** center occupies a three-room gallery in a restored historic carriage house situated in an alley behind the Phillips Collection. Its shows of contemporary art fulfill its mission to "increase cross-cultural understanding and exposure to the arts internationally." 9 Hillyer Court NW (21st St.). www.athillyer.org. ℂ **202/338-0325.** Metro: Dupont Circle (Q St. exit).

Studio Gallery ★ The city's oldest and most successful cooperative gallery, in existence for 63 years. It represents American and international artists, whose works are in all media: paintings, sculpture, installations, video, and mixed media. Don't miss the sculpture garden. 2108 R St. NW (20th St.). www.studiogallerydc.com. ℂ **202/232-8734.** Metro: Dupont Circle (Q St. exit).

Susan Calloway Fine Arts ★ On display are antique European and American oil paintings; contemporary art by local, regional, and international artists; and a carefully chosen selection of 17th- to 19th-century prints. 1643 Wisconsin Ave. NW (Q St.). www.callowayart.com. ℂ **202/965-4601.** Metro: Foggy Bottom, then take the DC Circulator bus.

Beauty

The city's best hair salons, cosmetic stores, and spas are in Georgetown.

Blue Mercury ★ Half "apothecary," half spa, this chain's five D.C. locations offer a full selection of facial, massage, waxing, and makeup treatments, as well as a smorgasbord of high-end beauty products, from Acqua di Parma fragrances to Kiehl's skincare line. www.bluemercury.com. Georgetown: 3059 M St. NW; ✆ **202/965-1300;** Metro: Foggy Bottom, then take the DC Circulator bus. Dupont Circle: 1619 Connecticut Ave. NW (✆ **202/462-1300**) and 1145 Connecticut Ave. NW (✆ **202/628-5567**); Metro: Dupont Circle (Q St. exit). Union Station: ✆ **202/289-5008;** Metro: Union Station. U & 14th St. Corridors: 1427 P St. NW; ✆ **202/238-0001;** Metro: U St./Carodozo (13th St. exit).

George at the Four Seasons ★★ If you have a hair emergency or just need a cut or styling and don't want to take any chances, George is a safe bet. George Ozturk has a devoted following, as does his team of 11. In addition to hair services, the salon offers waxing, makeup, and nail treatments. 2828 Pennsylvania Ave. NW (in the Four Seasons Hotel). www.georgefourseasonssalon.com. ✆ **202-342-1942.** Metro: Foggy Bottom, then take the DC Circulator bus.

Salon ILO ★ Gary Walker and Terry Bell (and their team of master hair and color stylists) have been delivering sleek cuts and treatments for more than 30 years. They count local politicians and known names among their clientele, but that's all I'm saying. 1637 Wisconsin Ave. NW. www.salonilo.com. ✆ **202-342-0350.** Metro: Foggy Bottom, then take the DC Circulator bus.

Books

A funny thing is happening in the capital: Real live bookstores are on the rise! Here is a smattering, starting with one I never saw coming.

Amazon Books ★ Open daily, Amazon's first D.C. brick and mortar bookshop sells new releases and books that are bestsellers and/or rated 4 stars or higher on its website. E-readers, Alexa devices, toys, and games are also for sale. The two-level store includes a cafe and kids section. 3040 M St. NW (at Thomas Jefferson St.). www.amazon.com. ✆ **202/333-2315.** Metro: Foggy Bottom, then take the DC Circulator bus.

Busboys and Poets ★ It's a bookstore, restaurant, community gathering place, theater, and political activist center. Its book inventory reflects all those angles, showcasing works by local authors, writers from diverse backgrounds, and subjects dealing with social and political struggles. The 14th St. location opened in 2005; others have followed, including a Busboys and Poets at 450 K St. NW (✆ **202/789-2227**). 2021 14th St. NW (V St.). www.busboysand poets.com. ✆ **202/387-7368.** Metro: U St./African American Civil War Memorial/ Cardozo Station (13th St. exit).

Capitol Hill Books ★ This longtime local favorite used-book store has books crammed into every possible bit of space throughout the two-story shop located directly across the street from Eastern Market. Look for foreign-language books in the bathroom and cookbooks in the kitchen sink! 657 C St. SE. www.capitolhillbooks-dc.com. ℰ **202/544-1621.** Metro: Eastern Market.

Kramerbooks & Afterwords Cafe ★★★   Opened in 1976, Kramer's was the first bookstore/cafe in Washington, maybe in this country, and has launched countless romances. It's jammed and often noisy; stages author readings, live music, and other events; and is open until 3am on Fridays and Saturdays. Paperback fiction takes up most of its inventory, but the store carries a little of everything. 1517 Connecticut Ave. NW. www.kramers.com. ℰ **202/387-1400** or 202/387-3825 for the cafe. Metro: Dupont Circle (Q St. exit).

The Lantern ★★   Rare, used, and out-of-print books—all donated—are this store's specialty. Books on antiques and philosophy, dramatic novels, and children's books can be found, along with sheet music, vinyl, and CDs. All proceeds benefit Bryn Mawr College. 341 P St. NW. www.lanternbookshop.org. ℰ **202/333-3222.** Metro: Foggy Bottom then walk 20 min., or take the DC Circulator Bus to the P Street stop.

Politics and Prose Bookstore ★★★   This much-cherished shop has vast offerings in literary fiction and nonfiction alike and an excellent children's department. It has expanded again and again over the years to accommodate its clientele's love of books in every genre, as well as a growing selection of greeting cards, journals, and other gifts. The shop hosts author readings nearly every night of the year, sometimes two or three in a single day. A warm, knowledgeable staff assists customers. Downstairs is a pleasant coffeehouse. Politics and Prose has another location at 70 District Square SW (ℰ **202/488-3867**) at the Wharf, in the Southwest Waterfront neighborhood, and another near Union Market, at 1270 Fifth St. NE (ℰ **202/544-4452**). 5015 Connecticut Ave. NW. www.politics-prose.com. ℰ **202/364-1919.** Metro: Van Ness–UDC, and walk, or transfer to an "L" bus to take you the ¾ mile from there.

Enjoy author readings at Politics and Prose Bookstore in Cleveland Park.

Reiter's Bookstore ★   Open since 1936, Reiter's is D.C.'s oldest independent bookstore. Located in the middle of the George Washington University campus, it's the go-to place for scientific, technical, medical, and professional books. The store is also known for its intriguing, sometimes amusing, mathematical and scientific toys in the children's section. 1900 G St. NW (19th St.). www.reiters.com. ℰ **202/223-3327.** Metro: Foggy Bottom.

Second Story Books ★ If it's old, out of print, custom bound, or a small-press publication, you'll find it here. The store also trades in used CDs and vinyl and has an interesting collection of campaign posters. 2000 P St. NW. www.secondstorybooks.com. ℰ **202/659-8884.** Metro: Dupont Circle (South/19th St. exit).

Cameras & Computers

Apple Store ★ Head to Massachusetts Avenue and Ninth Street NW in Mount Vernon Square to tour the beautifully renovated 116-year-old Carnegie Library and the Historical Society of Washington's three galleries showcasing D.C. history exhibits, and, yes, to check out Apple's D.C. flagship store. Or you can always visit the one in Georgetown, to hang out and fool around on the floor samples, study the merchandise, and get your questions answered by techy geeks roaming the room. 801 K St. NW. Metro: Mount Vernon Sq./7th St. Convention Center. 1229 Wisconsin Ave. NW. www.apple.com/retail/georgetown. ℰ **202/572-1460.** Metro: Foggy Bottom, then take the DC Circulator bus.

Leica Camera ★ This store is one of only eight the German company has opened in the U.S. If you know your way around cameras and don't mind spending a bit of money, this shop will likely delight. *FYI:* The store also sells used equipment and occasionally sponsors photo walks around the city. 977 F St. NW. www.leicastoredc.com. ℰ **202/787-5900.** Metro: Gallery Place (9th and G sts. exit).

Clothing

CHILDREN'S CLOTHING

Also consider **Macy's** at 1201 G St. NW (ℰ **202/628-6661**), in the Penn Quarter; and **GapKids** at 1258 Wisconsin Ave. NW (ℰ **202/333-2657**) in Georgetown, and at 664 11th St. NW (ℰ **202/347-0258**) in the Penn Quarter.

Egg by Susan Lazar ★ Classic footies are here. Designer boutique dresses are too, sizes newborn to girls 12. 1661 Wisconsin Ave. NW. www.egg-baby.com. ℰ **202/338-9500.** Metro: Foggy Bottom, then take the DC Circulator bus.

Little Birdies Boutique ★ This precious little shop sells precious little clothes for precious little children, newborns to size 7/8. Bella Bliss, Little English, and Petite Plume are among the brands for sale. 1526 Wisconsin Ave. NW. www.shoplittlebirdies.com. ℰ **202/333-1059.** Metro: Foggy Bottom, then take the DC Circulator bus.

MEN'S & WOMEN'S CLOTHING

See the "Great Shopping Areas" (p. 209) section if you're interested in such chain stores as **Urban Outfitters, Gap, Brooks Brothers,** or **H&M.** Below are stores that speak more to the fashion zeitgeist of D.C.

Betsy Fisher ★★ A walk past the store is all it takes to know that this shop is a tad different. Its windows and racks show off whimsically feminine fashions, shoes, and accessories by new American, French, and Italian designers. Betsy Fisher often hosts evening cocktail hours to introduce new lines or inventory. 1224 Connecticut Ave. NW. www.betsyfisher.com. ℰ **202/785-1975.** Metro: Dupont Circle (South/19th St. exit).

Hugh & Crye ★   This online retailer of "better-fitting menswear" launched in 2009 in Georgetown and maintains a brick-and-mortar version of the shop, open weekdays. Its two founders, Pranav Vora and Philip Soriano, felt called to act against "unsustainable clothing and manufacturing practices with adverse environmental and social impact," as well as ill-fitting menswear. Come check out their blazers, shirts, T-shirts, ties, and accessories. 3212 O St. NW. www.hughandcrye.com. ℂ **202/250-3807.** Metro: Foggy Bottom, then take the DC Circulator bus.

Maketto ★★   It's a cafe, it's a bar, it's a store, it's an award-winning restaurant (p. 85)—it's all of that and more. Maketto the shop is primarily about menswear, its inventory of international footwear, clothing, and accessories laid out in glass display cases and on open shelving. Neighborhood, Raised by Wolves, Vans, and Born N Raised are among the brands. 1351 H St. NE. www.maketto1351.com. ℂ **202/838-9972.** Metro: Union Station, then catch the DC Streetcar to the Atlas District.

The Outrage ★   Feeling the need to rise up in passionate resistance these days? Here's a shop that allows your clothing to speak for you. Tops and tees, sweatshirts, and pants are emblazoned with messages, including RESIST and THERE IS NO PLANET B. The rear space of the store is a membership-only spot for the feminist, progressive crowd. 1722 14th St. NW. www.the-outrage.com. ℂ **202/885-9848.** Metro: U Street/Cardozo.

Proper Topper ★★   For the longest time, I thought this store was just a hat boutique. Wrong! It's a one-stop shop for stocking stuffers and bigger gifts: lovely designs by Velvet and Victoria Road, pretty jewelry, adorable clothes for children, stationery, all sorts of gifty things, and yes, hats. 1350 Connecticut Ave. NW. www.propertopper.com. ℂ **202/842-3055.** Metro: Dupont Circle (19th St. exit).

Relish ★   To be blunt, you will need money—heaps of it—to shop here. But for fans of designer duds, this is your place. Dries van Noten, Calvin Klein, Marc Jacobs, and Simone Rocha are always in stock. Full-time stylists are also on hand to help you find that perfect look. 3312 Cady's Alley NW. www.relishdc.com. ℂ **202/333-5343.** Metro: Foggy Bottom, then take the DC Circulator.

Upstairs on 7th ★★   Ricki Peltzman's shop is neither upstairs nor on 7th Street (that was its original location) and its Pennsylvania Avenue street address is also misleading—you enter an office building at 12th and E streets and walk through the lobby to your left to find the shop, further obscured behind frosted glass. But believe me, Washington women in the know find their way here. Judges, restaurateurs, politicians, and other heavyweights speak truth to power through clothing they've purchased at Upstairs on 7th. Forget business-suit-oriented, though. No, Ricki sells fashionably fun and interesting apparel and accessories: Ray Harris's colorful and crinkly scarves, long-flowing Natalie Martin dresses, silky pajama-like St. Roche ensembles, New Form Perspective's magically adjustable sweaters. The shop also functions as a salon, with

Ricki hosting talks on timely subjects by notable women. 1299 Pennsylvania Ave. NW, Ste. 132R (enter at 12th and E sts., through the lobby of the Warner Building). www.upstairson7th.com. ✆ **301/351-8308.** Metro: Metro Center (12th and F sts. exit).

Violet Boutique ★★ This shop is a favorite of fashionistas on a budget. Feminine and trendy, the offerings range from cocktail dresses to colorful T-shirts, everything priced under $100. 1984 8th St. NW, Ste. 115 (entrance on Florida Ave. NW). www.violetdc.com. ✆ **202/621-9225.** Metro: Shaw-Howard University (R St. exit, btw. 7th and 8th sts.).

VINTAGE SHOPS

Meeps ★★ For men and women attracted to local designer wear and vintage clothes, from 1930s gabardine suits to 1950s cocktail dresses to satiny lingerie. 2104 18th St. NW. www.meepsdc.com. ✆ **202/265-6546.** Metro: U St./Cardozo (13th St. exit) or Woodley Park–Zoo, with a bit of a walk from either station.

Secondi Inc. ★ From the second floor of a building right above Starbucks, this high-style consignment shop sells women's clothing and accessories, including designer suits, evening wear, and more casual items—everything from Kate Spade to Chanel. Open since 1986, Secondi is the longest-running designer consignment shop for women in D.C. 1702 Connecticut Ave. NW (btw. R St. and Florida Ave.). www.secondi.com. ✆ **202/667-1122.** Metro: Dupont Circle (Q St. exit).

Via Gypset ★★ D.C. local Isabella Polles opened this quirky store in 2012, and it's become a favorite for vintage and retro looks, with some new pieces, along with shoes and accessories. 2311 Calvert St. NW. www.viagypset.com. ✆ **202/803-2874.** Metro: Woodley Park–Zoo.

Crafts

A Mano ★★ Owner Adam Mahr frequently forages in Europe and returns with unique handmade French and Italian ceramics, linens, and other decorative accessories for home and garden. 1677 Wisconsin Ave. NW. www.amano.bz. ✆ **202/298-7200.** Metro: Foggy Bottom, then take the DC Circulator bus.

Indian Craft Shop ★★ The Indian Craft Shop has represented authentic Native-American artisans since 1938, selling handwoven rugs and handcrafted baskets, jewelry, figurines, pottery, and other items. The shop is situated inside a federal government building, so you must pass through security and show photo ID to enter. It's open Tuesday to Friday and the third Saturday of each month. Department of the Interior, 1849 C St. NW, Rm. 1023. www.indiancraftshop.com. ✆ **202/208-4056.** Metro: Farragut West (17th St. exit), with a bit of a walk from the station.

The Phoenix ★ Around since 1955, the Phoenix sells high-end Mexican folk and fine art; clothing in natural fibers from American and international designers (Eileen Fisher and Flax are two); jewelry; and decorative doodads in tin, brass, copper, and wood. 1514 Wisconsin Ave. NW. www.thephoenixdc.com. ✆ **202/338-4404.** Metro: Foggy Bottom, then take the DC Circulator bus.

Torpedo Factory Art Center ★★ Once a munitions factory, this three-story building built in 1918 now houses more than 82 working studios, 7 galleries, and the works of about 165 artists, who tend to their crafts before your very eyes, pausing to explain their techniques or to sell their pieces. Artworks include paintings, sculpture, ceramics, glasswork, and textiles. 105 N. Union St., Alexandria, VA. www.torpedofactory.org. ✆ **703/746-4570.** Metro: King St., then take the free King Street Trolley or the DASH bus (AT2, AT5) eastbound to the waterfront.

Farmers & Flea Markets

Dupont Circle FreshFarm Market ★ About 50 local farmers sell flowers, fruits, vegetables, meat, poultry, fish, and cheeses here. The market sometimes features kids' activities, live music, and guest appearances by the chefs of some of D.C.'s best restaurants. It's open Sundays rain or shine, year-round, from 8:30am to 1:30pm. The FreshFarm Market organization stages other farmers markets on other days around town; see website. On 20th St. NW (btw. Massachusetts Ave. and Hillyer Place). www.freshfarm.org/washington-dc.html. ✆ **202/362-8889.** Metro: Dupont Circle (Q St. exit).

Eastern Market ★★★ Historic Eastern Market has been in continuous operation since 1873. Today the market's restored South Hall is a bustling bazaar, where area farmers, greengrocers, bakers, butchers, and others sell their

wares Tuesday through Sunday, joined by a second line of farmers outside on Tuesdays 1 to 7pm; on the weekend, 100 or so local artisans hawk jewelry, paintings, pottery, woodwork, and other handmade items on the outdoor plazas and streets surrounding the market. Best of all is the Saturday morning ritual of breakfasting on blueberry pancakes at the Market Lunch counter. The indoor market is open Tuesday to Friday 7am to 7pm, Saturday 7am to 6pm, and Sunday 9am to 5pm. 225 7th St. SE (North Carolina Ave.). www.easternmarket-dc.org. ✆ **202/698-5253.** Metro: Eastern Market.

Eastern Market.

Old Town Alexandria Farmers Market ★ The oldest continuously operating farmers market in the country (since 1753), this market offers locally grown fruits and vegetables, along with baked goods, cut flowers, and more. It's open year-round, Saturday mornings from 7am to noon. 301 King St. (at Market Square in front of the city hall), in Alexandria, VA. www.alexandriava.gov/market. ✆ **703/258-9115.** Metro: King St., then take the free King St. Trolley or the DASH bus (AT2, AT5) eastbound to Market Square.

Union Market ★ Worth a detour from sightseeing, this year-round indoor market includes pop-up marketers hawking a particular specialty, such as small-batch pickles. At least 40 vendors set up in stalls or at counters selling fresh produce, flowers, cheeses, artworks—everything from olive oil to oysters. Stop by Salt & Sundry for lovely handcrafted gifts; visit Sundays at noon and join a yoga class. There's always something popping up. It's open Monday to Wednesday 8am to 8pm, Thursday to Saturday 8am to 9pm, Sunday 8am to 8pm. 1309 Fifth St. NE. www.unionmarketdc.com. ℂ **301/347-3998.** Metro: NoMA–Gallaudet–U St.

Gifts/Souvenirs

See also "Crafts," earlier in this chapter; the Eastern Market listing above (weekend artisans sell excellent take-home gifts, such as Mary Belcher's Washington watercolors); and Hill's Kitchen under "Home Furnishings & Kitchenware," below. **Museum gift shops** (see chapter 6) are another excellent source. Also check out the **White House History Shop** (www.whitehousehistory.org/our-retail-shops) at Decatur House (1610 H St. NW; ℂ **202/218-4337**) and at the White House Visitor Center (1450 Pennsylvania Ave. NW; ℂ **202/208-7031**); see p. 174. It sells fun memorabilia, such as the White House Christmas tree ornament (newly designed each year) and sundry items related to the White House and its history.

Chocolate Moose ★ Its website welcomes browsers with the words "Serving weirdly sophisticated Washingtonians since 1978, but now attempting to reach out to the rest of you!" I guess my family qualifies as weirdly sophisticated, because we're longtime fans. Some of my favorite gifts, both given and received, are from this quirky little store. Think a "When Pigs Fly" tote bag; pink flamingo candles; wacky cards; hair clips; eccentric clothing; and other funny presents like a Cow Popper and a wind-up dinosaur. 1743 L St. NW. www.chocolatemoosedc.com. ℂ **202/463-0992.** Metro: Farragut North (L St. exit).

Shop Made in DC ★ This is the kind of shop I'm always looking for when I travel to another city. Everything in the shop, from the music playing to the coffee you're drinking (it's a cafe *and* a boutique) to the jewelry you're eyeing, is made by D.C. artisans and is for sale. The shop/cafe is a joint venture between a local entrepreneur and a D.C. government program. On a recent shopping trip here, I walked out with an owl print by Oh Bessie!, Pratt Standard Cocktail Co.'s (no relation) true ginger syrup, coffee from Lost Sock Roasters, and architecture-inspired earrings by D.C.'s Alissa Werres of Off on a Tangent. The shop sells hundreds of items and is happy to box and mail gifts for you. A new location opened at the Wharf in 2019 but does not have a cafe. 1330 19th St. NW (at Dupont Circle) and 10 District Square SW, Wharf District. www.shopmade indc.com. Metro: Dupont Circle (Q St. exit) and L'Enfant Plaza, then walk south.

Home Furnishings & Kitchenware

Cady's Alley ★ Cady's Alley refers not to a single store, but to the southwest pocket of Georgetown, where about 20 stores reside in and around said alley, which lies south of M Street. Look for tony, big-name places such as Waterworks and Design within Reach; European outposts, such as the hip kitchen furnishings of Bulthaup; and high-concept design stores, such as Contemporaria. 3314 M St. NW (btw. 33rd and 34th sts.). www.cadysalley.com. Metro: Foggy Bottom, then take the DC Circulator bus.

Hill's Kitchen ★★   This gourmet kitchenwares store occupies an 1884 town house adjacent to the Eastern Market Metro station on Capitol Hill. Precious take-homes include cookie cutters shaped like the Washington Monument and the Capitol dome; top-flight cooking utensils; and colorful aprons and towels. 713 D St. SE. www.hillskitchen.com. ℰ **202/543-1997.** Metro: Eastern Market.

Home Rule ★   Unique housewares; bath, kitchen, and office supplies; and gifts cram this tiny store. You'll see everything from French milled soap to martini glasses. 1807 14th St. NW (at S St.). www.homerule.com. ℰ **202/797-5544.** Metro: U St./Cardozo (13th St. exit).

Ligne Roset ★★★   For fans of all-things modern, this showroom showcases the very best in contemporary decor, from pearly translucent green bar stools to an asymmetrical settee in deep purple. Beds, lights, outdoor furniture, and rugs are also featured here. 2201 Wisconsin Ave. NW. www.ligneroset-dc.com. ℰ **202/248-3112.** Metro: Foggy Bottom, then catch Bus 31.

Miss Pixie's Furnishings & Whatnot ★   The name says it all. Vintage home furnishings from armoires to old silver cram the space. The owner buys only from auctions and only things that are in good shape and ready to use. New inventory arrives every Wednesday. 1626 14th St. NW. www.misspixies.com. ℰ **202/232-8171.** Metro: U St./Cardozo (13th St. exit).

Jewelry

In addition to the two shops below, consider the jewelry at the Phoenix, the Proper Topper, Upstairs on 7th, and Shop Made in DC, all listed above.

Mia Gemma ★   This pretty boutique sells the original designs of American and European artists, including Judy Bettencourt, Sarah Richardson, and Randi Chervitz. All pieces are handcrafted, either a limited edition or one of a kind. Customized design available, too. 933 F St. NW. www.miagemma.com. ℰ **202/393-4367.** Metro: Gallery Place/Verizon Center (9th St. exit).

Tiny Jewel Box ★★   Opened and owned by the same family since 1930, this jewelry store is the first place Washingtonians go for estate and antique jewelry, engagement rings, and the finest brands of watches. Tiny Jewel Box also sells the pieces of many designers, from Links of London to Alex Sepkus, as well as crystal and other house gifts. In the month leading up to Mother's Day, the Tiny Jewel Box holds its top-to-bottom sale, where you can save anywhere from 10% to 70% on many items. 1155 Connecticut Ave. NW. www.tinyjewelbox.com. ℰ **202/393-2747.** Metro: Farragut North (L St. exit).

Shoes

Comfort One Shoes ★   This locally owned family business was founded in Old Town Alexandria in 1993. Its three D.C. stores sell a great selection of popular styles for both men and women, including Doc Martens, Birkenstocks, and Ecco. You can always find something that looks smart and actually feels comfortable. 1630 Connecticut Ave. NW. www.comfortoneshoes.com. ✆ **202/328-3141.** Metro: Dupont Circle. Also at 1329 Wisconsin Ave. NW (✆ **202/735-5332**), Union Station (✆ **202/898-2430**), and several other locations.

Hu's Shoes ★   Fashion models in every D.C. photo shoot wear Hu's shoes, it seems. The Georgetown shop sells designer ready-to-wear footwear, handbags, and accessories. Owner Marlene Hu Aldaba travels to New York, Paris, and Milan in search of elegant specimens to suit her discriminating eye. Across the street, at 2906 M St. NW, is **Hu's Wear,** a two-level store selling designer outfits to accompany the darling shoes. 3005 M St. NW. www.husonline.com. ✆ **202/342-0202.** Metro: Foggy Bottom, then walk or take the DC Circulator bus.

Wine & Spirits

Barmy Wines & Liquors ★   Located near the White House, this store sells it all, but with special emphasis on fine wines and rare cordials. 1912 L St. NW. www.barmywines.com. ✆ **202/833-8730.** Metro: Farragut North (L St. exit).

Central Liquors ★   Dating back to 1934, Central Liquors is like a clearinghouse for liquor: Its great volume allows the store to offer the best prices in town. The store specializes in small estate wines, single-malt scotches, and small-batch bourbons. 625 E St. NW. www.centralliquors.com. ✆ **202/737-2800.** Metro: Gallery Place (9th and F sts. exit).

Schneider's of Capitol Hill ★   Two blocks south of Union Station is this family-run liquor store, in business for nearly 70 years. With a knowledgeable and enthusiastic staff, a 12,000-bottle inventory of wine, and a fine selection of spirits and beer, this shop is a find on Capitol Hill. 300 Massachusetts Ave. NE. www.cellar.com. ✆ **202/543-9300.** Metro: Union Station.

ENTERTAINMENT & NIGHTLIFE

8

D.C. nightlife is rollicking and diverse. One-third of the city's population is between 20 and 35, and thanks to the capital's strong economy, most have jobs and are ready to party. But just about everyone in this hard-charging city, from government wonks to high-powered attorneys, find themselves seeking a timeout at the end of long work days, whether that means a night out in the clubs or at the theater.

The best neighborhoods for nightlife are **Adams Morgan;** the **U & 14th streets NW crossroads** (U St. btw. 16th and 10th sts., and 14th St. btw. P and V sts.); **Shaw** (7th to 10th sts. NW, btw. Massachusetts Ave. NW and U St. NW); north and south of **Dupont Circle** along Connecticut Avenue; all over the **Penn Quarter; Georgetown;** the **Atlas District; Barracks Row** on Capitol Hill; **Capitol Riverfront** in southeast DC; and **Columbia Heights,** east of Adams Morgan and north of the U Street district; and the **Southwest Waterfront,** where the new Wharf complex has fast become a night and day destination.

Most of D.C.'s clubs and bars stay open until 1 or 2am Monday through Thursday and until 3am Friday and Saturday; what time they open varies. *Note:* The city allows establishments serving alcohol to open early and stay open until 4am for certain holidays, such as the 4th of July, and special events such as the World Cup. For current concert and club offerings, check the *Washington Post*'s online "Going Out Guide" (www.washingtonpost.com/going outguide). Available for free at Metro stations and newspaper racks is the Post's weekday tabloid publication *Express* (www.washington post.com/express), which focuses on local news and fun; the Thursday edition highlights nightlife and entertainment. Another free and excellent resource is the *Washington City Paper,* available at restaurants, bookstores, and other places around town, and online at **www.washingtoncitypaper.com**. (The printed version is easier to read, so it's worth getting your hands on one.)

One last note: Be sure to look closely at the calendars for all those places you visited during the day. Fun after-hours events are taking place at all sorts of unlikely venues, from the Library of Congress to the National Gallery of Art, many of them free or inexpensive to attend.

THE PERFORMING ARTS

Washington's performing-arts scene has an international reputation. We have not just one, but two Shakespeare theaters. The **Kennedy Center** reigns over all, staging opera, dance, classical/jazz/contemporary music performances, musicals, comedy, and traditional theater. **Arena Stage** is renowned for its innovative productions of American masters and new voices. And don't assume that these theaters present only classic renditions from a performing-arts hit list; no, each is wildly creative in its choices and presentations. For the most avant-garde theater, seek out smaller stages like the **Woolly Mammoth** and **Studio** theaters.

Seasons for both the Kennedy Center and Arena Stage run year-round; the Shakespeare Theatre's season (and that of other smaller theaters) is nearly year-round, taking a 4- to 6-week break July into August. The Kennedy Center often has performances going on throughout the day, but all theaters hold their major productions at 7:30 or 8pm nightly, with Saturday and Sunday matinee performances at 2pm and occasional midweek matinee performances on the schedule, especially at Arena Stage.

The bad news is that **ticket prices** have gone through the roof in the past couple of years. A lot of locals subscribe to the big three (Kennedy Center, Shakespeare, Arena), which leaves fewer one-off tickets available. Expect to pay $75 to $100-plus for a ticket—unless you're able to obtain a discounted ticket; see the "Getting Tickets" box, p. 227.

Major Theaters & Companies

Arena Stage ★★★ Founded in 1950, Arena Stage has long been about "putting the American spirit in the spotlight," as the company tagline phrases it. What that means is that the theater produces the works of American artists, choosing plays that explore themes of American diversity, challenges, and passions. A typical season features an American classic or two, a musical or two, new plays by emerging playwrights, world premieres, and, because

Arena is in the nation's capital, a play of political topicality. Many Arena Stage productions go on to win Tony Awards on Broadway, as did *Dear Evan Hansen*, the 2017 Tony winner for best new musical.

The theater is D.C.'s second-largest after the Kennedy Center. Officially called "The Mead Center for American Theater," the venue's three staging areas are the theater-in-the-round **Fichandler,** the fan-shaped **Kreeger,** and the intimate (200-seat), oval-shaped **Kogod Cradle.** Locals love Arena's productions, which draw more than 300,000 of us annually.

The Arena Stage.

Arena's 2019–20 season highlights include a play based on Khalid Hosseini's novel *A Thousand Splendid Suns,* about two Afghan women in Kabul; a "power play," *Celia and Fidel,* about Fidel Castro's political partner Celia Sanchez; a musical drama depicting a blues singer and his social circle, *Seven Guitars;* and *Toni Stone*, Lydia Diamond's play on the first woman to play baseball in the Negro leagues.

1101 6th St. SW (at Maine Ave.). www.arenastage.org. © **202/488-3300** for tickets, or 202/554-9066 for general information. Tickets $40–$110; discounts available for students, those under 30, patrons with disabilities, families, veterans, groups, and others. Metro: Waterfront.

John F. Kennedy Center for the Performing Arts ★★★

The capital's most renowned theater covers the entire realm of performing arts: Presentations of ballet, opera, plays, musicals, modern dance, jazz, hip hop, comedy, classical and chamber music, and children's theater all take the stage at this magnificent complex overlooking the Potomac River. The setting is gorgeous, the productions superb. As a living memorial to President John F. Kennedy, the Center is committed to fulfilling the president's mission to make the performing arts available to everyone. The Center's 3,000+ annual productions draw more than 3 million people.

Within the arts center's original 17-acre facility are eight different theaters and stages: the **Opera House, the Concert Hall, the Terrace Theater, the Eisenhower Theater, the Theater Lab, the Terrace Gallery, the Family Theater,** and **Millennium Stage.** A 4-acre expansion completed in 2019 added three pavilions housing rehearsal, performance, and education spaces; a reflecting pool; a grove of trees; an outdoor performance area; and a pedestrian bridge arching over Rock Creek Parkway, connecting the Kennedy Center to the Potomac riverfront.

The 2019–20 season lineup included the Washington National Opera's presentation of the race- and class-themed *Porgy and Bess,* Mozart's *Don Giovanni,* and a play about identity and connection, *Blue;* the National Symphony Orchestra's classical series covering the masters including Beethoven's 250th birthday, with guest appearances by high-profile soloists; a program of international theatrical productions; the annual engagements of the Alvin Ailey American Dance Theatre, the American Ballet Theatre, and the Mariinsky

---

Longer Than the Washington Monument Is Tall

Most Kennedy Center performances take place in theaters that lie off the Grand Foyer. But even if the one you're attending is on the Roof Terrace level, one floor up, make sure you visit the foyer anyway. Measuring 630 feet long, 40 feet wide, and 60 feet high, the Grand Foyer is one of the largest rooms in the world. It's even longer than the Washington Monument is tall (555⅝ ft.). Millennium Stage hosts free performances here nightly at 6pm; free yoga classes fill the space Saturday mornings at 10:15am; the famous Robert Berks sculpture of President John F. Kennedy is here; and just beyond the foyer's glass doors is the expansive terrace, which runs its length and overlooks the Potomac.

Ballet as well as the National Ballet of Canada's *Sleeping Beauty;* the modern dance presentations of Merce Cunningham, Matthew Bourne's *Swan Lake,* and Kyle Abraham's *A.I.M.;* a robust schedule of jazz concerts; and abundant children's presentations.

Visit the KenCen to attend a performance, for sure, but also consider stopping by for one of the free guided tours that take place throughout the day. Finish the visit by attending a free "Millennium Stage" performance, mostly concerts, but also dance, theater, comedy, and other forms of entertainment, staged every single evening at 6pm in the Grand Foyer, each night featuring a different act, local artists sometimes, but nationally known and international performers, too, and often performers appearing on a main stage later that evening.

Otherwise, expect to pay ticket prices that range from $20 for a family concert to $300 for opera; most tickets cost between $45 and $150.

2700 F St. NW (at New Hampshire Ave. NW and Rock Creek Pkwy.). www.kennedy-center.org. ℂ **800/444-1324** or 202/467-4600. 50% discounts offered (for select performances) to students, seniors, travelers with permanent disabilities, enlisted military personnel, and persons with fixed low incomes (ℂ **202/416-8340** for details). Garage parking $23 (pay $20 online in advance). Metro: Foggy Bottom (there's a free shuttle btw. the station and the Kennedy Center, departing every 15 min. Mon–Thurs 9:45am–11:30pm; Fri–Sat 10am–midnight; and Sun noon–11pm.) Bus: 80 from Metro Center.

National Theatre ★   Open since 1835, the National is the capital's oldest continuously operating theater and the country's third oldest. In earlier days, the likes of Sarah Bernhardt, Helen Hayes, and John Barrymore took the stage, and presidents Lincoln and Fillmore and others were among those in the audience. These days, the National is almost entirely about Broadway musicals. Past performances have included *School of Rock, Finding Neverland, A Bronx Tale,* and *Stomp.* The 1,672-seat National continues its free public-service programs: Saturday-morning children's theater (puppets, clowns, magicians, dancers, and singers) and screenings of classic films on select Monday nights.

1321 Pennsylvania Ave. NW (at 13th and E sts.). www.thenationaldc.org. ℂ **202/628-6161** for general info, 202/783-3370 for info about free programs, 800/514-3849 or go to www.etix.com to buy tickets. Tickets $25–$153 (most in the $70–$90 range). Metro: Metro Center (13th and G sts. exit) or Federal Triangle.

Shakespeare Theatre Company at the Lansburgh Theatre and Sidney Harman Hall ★★★   This is one of the best Shakespeare theaters in the country, known for its accessible interpretations of plays by Shakespeare, his contemporaries, and modern masters, from Oscar Wilde to Thomas Stoppard. Attend a play here and you're in for a thought-provoking, of-the-moment experience, whether it's the tweaking of a classic to address the political climate in D.C., the casting of people of color for the majority of roles, or the display of a little nudity. In its 34 years, the theater has won national and international acclaim, including a Regional Theater Tony Award and recognition by Queen Elizabeth II, who named the theater's former and longtime artistic director, Michael Kahn, an Honorary Commander of the Most Excellent Order of the British Empire for distinguished service to the arts and sciences. Washingtonians know to expect the best when they see the names of the theater's resident artists, like Edward Gero and Nancy Robinette. But it also brings in renowned guest performers, like Patrick Stewart and Marsha Mason.

The Shakespeare Theatre Company has two downtown locations (literally within a stone's throw of each other), the 451-seat **Lansburgh Theatre,** at 450 7th St. NW, and the 774-seat **Sidney Harman Hall,** at 610 F St. NW (across the street from the Capital One Arena); both houses frequently sell out. The 2019–20 season is the first for the Theatre's new artistic director Simon Godwin and includes Bard favorites *Much Ado About Nothing* and *Timon of Athens*, as well as an adaptation of *Peter Pan* and newer plays such as *Romantics Anonymous*. In addition, the Shakespeare Theatre screens live performances of London's National Theatre productions.

The theater hosts all kinds of talks, dance performances, discussions, cocktail hours, workshops, and other events, many of which target 20- to 30-somethings. Best deal for the under-35s is the sale of $25 tickets, available online with the promo code provided on the website.

Lansburgh Theatre: 450 7th St. NW (btw. D and E sts.). Sidney Harman Hall: 610 F St. NW. www.shakespearetheatre.org. ✆ **202/547-1122.** Tickets $25–$123; discounts available for military, patrons 21–35, seniors, and groups; check the website for all options. Metro: Archives–Navy Memorial or Gallery Place/Chinatown (7th St./Arena exit).

Smaller Theaters

Studio Theatre ★★, 1501 14th St. NW, at P Street (www.studiotheatre.org; ✆ 202/332-3300), since its founding in 1978, has grown in leaps and bounds into a four-theater complex, helping to revitalize its U Street neighborhood in the process. Productions are provocative and the season jam-packed, with at least eight plays on tap for the 2019–20 calendar. The Studio has had particular success in showcasing contemporary plays and nurturing local acting talent.

Ford's Theatre ★★, 510 10th St. NW, between E and F sts. NW (www.fords.org; ✆ 202/347-4833), is both a living museum—the site of President Abraham Lincoln's assassination in 1865—and a working theater staging multiple performances each year.

The **Woolly Mammoth Theatre Company** ★★ (www.woollymammoth.net; ✆ 202/393-3939) offers as many as 10 productions every year, specializing in new, offbeat, and quirky plays, often world premieres. The Woolly resides in a 265-seat, state-of-the-art facility at 641 D St. NW (at 7th St. NW), in the heart of the Penn Quarter.

I also highly recommend productions staged in the Elizabethan-styled **Folger Theatre** at the **Folger Shakespeare Library** ★★, on Capitol Hill, 201 E. Capitol St. SE, at 2nd Street (www.folger.edu; ✆ 202/544-7077), now in its 88th year. The theater typically produces three to four plays each season, using the same fine directors (Aaron Posner is a favorite) and casting the same excellent actors (Holly Twyford is always a treat), that you'll see at the Shakespeare Theatre and other stages around town. The main differences at the Folger are its design—its three-tiered wooden balconies, oak-carved columns, and half-timbered facade resemble the courtyard of an English Renaissance

GETTING tickets

Most performing-arts and live-music venues mentioned in this chapter require tickets, which you can purchase online at the venue's website, in person at the venue's box office, or through one of the ticket vendors listed below.

The best deals in town might be those posted on the website **www.goldstar.com**. It costs nothing to subscribe, and you'll immediately start receiving e-mail notices of hefty discounts on admission prices to performances and venues, including museums, all over the city.

TodayTix sells discounted and full-price last-minute tickets for shows in D.C. and its suburbs. You can browse and purchase tickets online at **www.todaytix.com**, but certain features, such as the use of ticket lotteries, are only available on the free downloadable app. *FYI:* Despite its name, the service works for tickets purchased up to a month in advance.

Ticket sellers **Live Nation Entertainment** (www.livenation.com; © 800/745-3000) and **www.ticketfly.com** (© 877/987-6487) operate in the D.C. area, selling full-price tickets for all sorts of performances. Expect to pay taxes plus a service charge, an order-processing fee, and a facility fee (if a particular venue tacks on that charge).

inn—and its intimacy: The theater holds just 270 people. The theater is also the setting for musical performances, lectures, readings, and other events.

Three more specialized theater companies are of note: **GALA Hispanic Theatre,** at 3333 14th St. NW in Columbia Heights (www.galatheatre.org; © 202/234/7174), which presents classic and contemporary plays in Spanish and English, as well as dance, music, and other programs; **Theater J** (www.theaterj.org; © 202/777-3210), praised by the *Washington Post* as "the most influential Jewish theater company in the nation," stages provocative performances on the Jewish experience in its renovated theater; and the tiny (130-seat!) **Keegan Theatre,** at 1742 Church St. NW, also in Dupont Circle (www.keegantheatre.com; © 202/265-3767), which often stages plays that embrace Irish writers and themes.

Concert Venues

The Anthem ★★★, 901 Wharf St. SW (www.theanthemdc.com; © 202/888-0020; Metro: Waterfront; L'Enfant Plaza, with free shuttle from L'Enfant Plaza station to the Wharf), which opened in October 2017, is the much-heralded new sibling of the 9:30 Club (p. 233), located at the Wharf. Expect to see rock acts, international artists, and local favorites at this "acoustically advanced" concert hall with a 2,500–6,000-person capacity.

Meanwhile, headliners like Ariana Grande, Jennifer Lopez, and Carrie Underwood continue to sell out the 20,000-seat **Capital One Arena ★★★,** 601 F St. NW, at 7th Street (www.capitalonearena.com; © 202/628-3200). Situated in the center of downtown, the Capital One Arena is a hotspot for music but also Washington's premier indoor sports arena (p. 236).

DAR Constitution Hall ★★ on 18th St. NW, between C and D streets (www.dar.org; © 202/628-4780), is housed in a beautiful turn-of-the-20th-century

A concert at the Capital One Arena.

Beaux Arts building and seats 3,746. Its excellent acoustics have drawn an eclectic group of performers over the years, from Duke Ellington to U2.

Under management by the 9:30 Club (p. 233), the historic **Lincoln Theatre ★**, 1215 U St. NW, at 13th Street (www.thelincolndc.com; ℂ **202/888-0050**), showcases indie favorites such as Imogen Heap, jazz legends like Roy Ayers, and assorted others. Once a movie theater, vaudeville house, and nightclub featuring black stars such as Louis Armstrong and Cab Calloway, this "Jewel on U" closed down in the 1970s and then reopened in 1994 after a renovation restored it to its former elegance.

The **Warner Theatre ★**, 513 13th St. NW, between E and F streets (www. warnertheatredc.com; ℂ **202/783-4000**), opened in 1924 as a movie/vaudeville palace known as the Earle Theatre. It was restored to its original, neoclassical-style appearance in 1992. It's worth coming by just to ogle the ornately detailed interior. The 2,000-seat auditorium offers year-round entertainment, alternating dance performances, like the Washington Ballet's Christmas performance of the *Nutcracker,* with comedy acts such as Wanda Sykes and Chelsea Handler and seasoned rockers like REO Speedwagon and Little Feat.

THE BAR SCENE

Some of the best and most popular bars in town are in hotels, including **Off the Record** at the Hay-Adams (p. 67), **Crimson** at the Pod DC (p. 67), the **Top of the Gate** at the Watergate (p. 75), and the **rooftop bars** at any of the hotels at the Wharf (p. 63). Here's a smattering of other favorites, old and new.

Barrel ★   The upstairs is a rustic dining room, often packed with Capitol Hillers noshing on the Southern fare (five-star vote for the fried chicken) and drinking craft cocktails and whiskeys. Downstairs, Rum-DMV is a—you guessed it—rum bar grooving to club sounds. 613 Pennsylvania Ave. SE (at 6th St.). www.barreldc.com. ℂ **202/543-3622.** Metro: Eastern Market.

Bluejacket Brewery ★★   A Washington Nationals baseball game at Nationals Park is one reason to visit the Capitol Riverfront neighborhood. Bluejacket is another. Opened by Greg Engert and his band of master brewers,

Bluejacket Brewery.

the same team behind ChurchKey (see below), Bluejacket brews 20 unique ales and lagers daily at its three-story site, from dry-hopped ales to barley wine. You can hang out at the bar in Bluejacket's restaurant, the **Arsenal,** and sample a few homebrews, dine here, or take a tour. Bluejacket offers two options, both of which require a reservation: a $29-per-person taste-as-you-go tour on Saturday at 1pm and a $35-per-person 7pm Friday night "Beers and Bites" tour. No tours on Nationals home-game days. 300 Tingey St. SE (at 4th St.). www.blue jacketdc.com. ✆ **202/524-4862.** Metro: Navy Yard/Ballpark (New Jersey Ave. exit).

ChurchKey ★   This mellow hangout draws a diverse mix, from boomers to their 20-something children, all sprawled on loungey banquettes or perched on stools at the long bar. It's a haven for beer lovers, with 50 drafts, 500 bottles, and five cask ales on tap. ChurchKey's downstairs sibling, **Birch & Barley,** is a popular eatery. 1337 14th St. NW (at Rhode Island Ave.). www.church keydc.com. ✆ **202/567-2576.** Metro: McPherson Square (14th St. exit) or U St./Cardozo (U and 13th sts. exit).

Columbia Room ★★   Shaw's Blagden Alley is home to several dining hotspots (see "Shaw-Thing" box, p. 114) and this nationally recognized cocktail bar. Its magical concoctions and energy derive from owner Derek Brown, esteemed mixologist, spirits historian, and perennial James Beard Award nominee. Columbia Room offers three spaces, a punch garden, spirits library, and a three- or five- course tasting menu of cocktails and snacks. 124 Blagden Alley NW (behind Ninth St., btw. M and N sts.). www.columbiaroomdc.com. ✆ **202/316-9396.** Metro: Mt. Vernon Square/7th St./Convention Center.

H Street Country Club ★   The main draw of this Atlas District fave is its assortment of activities: Skee-Ball, shuffleboard, and the District's only indoor miniature golf course. Up top is a huge rooftop deck. H Street serves pretty good Mexican food, too. 1335 H St. NE (at Linden Ct NE). www.hstreetcountryclub. com. ✆ **202/399-4722.** Metro: Union Station, then take a cab or the DC Streetcar, or walk.

Hill Country Barbecue ★★   Everybody knows to go to this Penn Quarter restaurant for awesome barbecue, strong drinks, and, downstairs, live

CHEAP EATS: happy hours TO WRITE HOME ABOUT

Certain restaurants around town set out tasty bites during happy hour, either free or for astonishingly low prices. The following are particularly generous:

Cheery **Oyamel**, 407 7th St. NW (www.oyamel.com; ℭ **202/628-1005**), has happy-hour specials featuring $7 margaritas, $5 Dos Equis or Tecate beer, and $6 glasses of wine, and appetizers such as ceviche ($4 each) or one of Oyamel's superb tacos for $2 (Mon–Fri 4–6pm).

Cuba Libre, 801 9th St. NW, at H St. (www.cubalibrerestaurant.com/en/washington/; ℭ **202/408-1600**), serves up an irresistible array of *picada* (bar bites), such as empanadas, fritters, sliders, and a cubano sandwich ($6 each). Drinks are a real deal: $5 beer, wine, or Sangria, $6 Cuban cocktails, either a Cuba Libre or a Caipirinha (Sun–Fri 4–7pm at the bar only).

The Denson, 600 F St. NW (www.densondc.com; ℭ **202/499-5018**), has happy-hour specials featuring $9 craft cocktails, $6 beer and wine, and local oysters for $20, a definite steal in this town. Even better? Happy hour continues on the weekend (daily 4:30–7pm).

The Hamilton (p. 232) hosts a decent sushi happy hour daily 3 to 6pm and after 11pm, serving half-priced classic rolls, signature rolls, nigiri, and sashimi.

---

music nearly nightly. The music tends toward outlaw country and honky-tonk; most Wednesday nights, the HariKaraoke Band provides live backup as a singer takes the microphone and "rocks 'n twangs" her heart out. 410 7th St. NW (at D St.). www.hillcountrywdc.com. ℭ **202/556-2050.** Metro: Gallery Place/Chinatown (7th and F sts. exit) or Archives–Navy Memorial.

Jack Rose Saloon ★★   Considered to be one of the best whisky bars in the country (its inventory numbers 2,600), this saloon has much going for it, including an expansive open-air (but enclosable) rooftop terrace with a great view of the neighborhood; a subterranean, speakeasy-like cellar; and all-around nods of approval for its comfort cooking. 2007 18th St. NW (btw. U and California sts.). www.jackrosediningsaloon.com. ℭ **202/588-7388.** Metro: Dupont Circle (19th St. exit), then 20-min. walk.

Lucky Bar ★   Looking for a good old-fashioned bar with booths, couches, a pool table, a jukebox, cheap beer, and sticky floors? Lucky Bar is the place. It's also Soccer Central, with TV screens broadcasting soccer matches from around the globe. Monday through Wednesday and Friday, Lucky Bar's happy hour runs from 3 to 8pm. Look for nightly specials, like $1 tacos on Tuesday nights and half-price cheeseburgers on Wednesday. 1221 Connecticut Ave. NW (at N St.). www.luckybardc.com. ℭ **202/331-3733.** Metro: Dupont Circle (South/19th St. exit) or Farragut North (L St. exit).

Marvin ★   Downstairs is a soul-food bistro, upstairs is the bar, which includes a lounge, rooftop beer garden, and live music/DJ space. Washington millennials come here to dance; it's always crowded after 10pm. 2007 14th St. NW (at U St.). www.marvindc.com. ℭ **202/797-7171.** Metro: U St./Cardozo (13th St. exit).

Quill ★★★ A pianist plays Tuesday through Saturday starting at 9pm, the perfect accompaniment to that Swept Away cocktail you're sipping and plate of charcuterie you're nibbling, at this chicest of lounges inside the city's chicest hotel. In the Jefferson Hotel, 1200 16th St. NW (at M St.). www.jeffersondc. com/dining/quill. ✆ **202/448-2300.** Metro: Dupont Circle (19th St./South exit) or Farragut North (L St. exit).

Tryst ★ Tryst is a coffeehouse bar. Coffee to charge you up in the am, drinks to get you going later in the day. It's got a good vibe, too: loungey in the pre-hipster sense of a comfort zone. Morning, noon, and night, customers sprawl on comfy old furniture, juggling laptops and beverages. Tryst also runs the **cafes** at the Phillips Collection (p. 186) and the Washington National Cathedral (p. 191). 2459 18th St. NW (at Columbia Rd.). www.trystdc.com. ✆ **202/232-5500.** Metro: U St./Cardozo or Woodley Park/Zoo/Adams Morgan, then take the DC Circulator.

Tune Inn ★ In business since 1947, this Capitol Hill watering hole is a veritable institution. The divey Tune Inn is open from early morning 'til late at night serving police officers, Hill staffers and their bosses, and folks from the hood. Sometimes they eat here, too, from a menu that includes burgers, fries, and crab cakes. 331 Pennsylvania Ave. SE (at 4th St.). ✆ **202/543-2725.** Metro: Capitol South.

THE CLUB & MUSIC SCENE
Live Music

If you're looking for a tuneful night on the town, Washington offers everything from hip jazz clubs to DJ-driven dance halls—places where you sit back and listen and places where you get up and rock out.

And Now for Something Completely Different

You can become part of the show at **ARTECHOUSE** (www.artechouse.com), a three-level, 15,000-square-foot funhouse that marries the arts and digital technology with sound, light, space, and visuals to create an immersive multimedia experience. In one 2019 exhibit, for example, D.C.'s cherry blossoms became an immersive experience, where a visitor's own heartbeat and touch controlled whether a bright cherry blossom tree flourished or withered. You really have to experience it for yourself. ARTECHOUSE is open during the day, but I recommend going at night, when visitors must be 21 or older and thus able to enjoy the augmented-reality cocktails (at $8–$12 each, the cocktail is real but the computer-generated images floating above the rim of your glass are not!). ARTECHOUSE mounts about eight major installations a year, changing every 1 to 2 months. You'll find it just southwest of the National Mall, at 1238 Maryland Avenue SW (12th St.). It's open daily Sunday to Thursday 10am to 7pm; after-hours 7–10pm; and Friday and Saturday 10am to 5pm and 5:30 to 11:30pm. Tickets are required. General admission is $20 adults; $15 seniors, students, and military-ID holders; and $10 children 2–14 (discounted tickets online in advance $16 adults; $13 seniors, students, and military-ID holders; and $8 children 2–14; some shows require visitors to be older than 12).

JAZZ & BLUES

If you're a jazz fan and are planning a trip to D.C. in early to mid-June, check out the fabulous 10- to 18-day **DC Jazz Festival** (www.dcjazzfest.org), which showcases the talents of at least 100 musicians in various venues around town, including many free events. Check the website for this year's exact dates. Other times of the year, check out the following venues:

The Birchmere Music Hall and Bandstand ★★★   This place started out 50 years or so ago showcasing primarily bluegrass and country acts. Its calendar now offers more range, stretching from Big Bad Voodoo Daddy to Joan Baez. Located in Alexandria, 6 miles and a $20 cab fare from downtown D.C., the Birchmere is well worth the trip. The hall seats 500 and serves food. Purchase tickets at the box office or online from www.ticketmaster.com. 3701 Mt. Vernon Ave. (off S. Glebe Rd.), Alexandria, VA. www.birchmere.com. ℂ **703/549-7500.** Tickets $25–$60. Take a taxi or drive.

Blues Alley ★★★   An inconspicuous alley off busy Wisconsin Avenue in Georgetown delivers you to the door of Blues Alley and another world entirely. It's a showcase for jazz greats like Arturo Sandoval and Benny Golson and up-and-comers. The club usually offers two sets a night, at 8 and 10pm, with the occasional midnight show on weekends. Blues Alley is a tiny joint filled with small, candlelit tables, so reservations are a must for the first-come, first-served seating. The supper club has been around since 1965 and looks it, but that's part of its charm. Its Creole menu features dishes named after stars (try Dizzy Gillespie's Jambalaya). 1073 Wisconsin Ave. NW (in an alley below M St.). www.bluesalley.com. ℂ **202/337-4141.** Tickets $16–$75 (most $20–$40), plus a $12-per-person food or drink minimum, plus a $6-per-person ticket surcharge. Metro: Foggy Bottom, then walk or take the DC Circulator.

Gypsy Sally's ★   Gypsy Sally's features bluegrass and "Americana" acts. Ticketed performances take place in the Music Room, which holds 300 people, and follow a Wednesday-through-Saturday schedule. Most shows offer a mix of reserved seating and general-admission standing. The club includes the **Vinyl Lounge** bar, which hosts no-cover performances Tuesday through Saturday; it has a separate entrance on 34th St. NW. Gypsy Sally's serves food and has a full bar. The club is located in Georgetown, down by the waterfront, underneath the Whitehurst Freeway. 3401 K St. NW (at 34th St.). www.gypsysallys.com. ℂ **202/333-7700.** Most tickets $10–$15. Metro: Foggy Bottom, then walk or take the DC Circulator.

The Hamilton ★★   Located on the subterranean level of a large restaurant, this live-music venue stages blues, rock, jazz, R&B, and folk performances nightly. Seating is at communal tables. The menu of pizza and sandwiches isn't stellar but will suffice if you haven't eaten before the show. Located in the heart of the Penn Quarter, the Hamilton is always worth checking out, with great sightlines, an eclectic lineup (world music, jazz, blues, you name it), and an excellent sound system. The **Loft at The Hamilton** is the venue's cozy, late-night bar on the restaurant's second floor; a band plays for free from 10:30pm to 1:30am, and the late-night menu features sushi items at half price. 600 14th St. (at F St.). www.thehamiltondc.com. ℭ **202/787-1000.** Live music acts $15–$50. Metro: Metro Center (13th St. exit).

Pearl Street Warehouse ★★   You're never more than 25 feet from the stage at this intimate Wharf venue, which only holds 150 to 300 people and showcases famous Americana rock, country, and blues artists. Everyone from singer Lilly Hiatt (John Hiatt's daughter) to the Jacob Jolliff Band (of Yonder Mountain String Band) has performed here. Some shows are seated, others are standing only, while some are a combo, so be sure to check online before arriving. All-American diner fare, craft brews, and cocktails are all available. 33 Pearl St. SW (at Maine Ave.). www.pearlstreetwarehouse.com. ℭ **202/380-9620.** Tickets $12–$40 plus $1 service fee. Metro: Waterfront.

ROCK, HIP-HOP & DJS
Below are primarily live-music clubs, but also a sprinkling of nightclubs known for their DJs and dance floors.

9:30 Club ★★★   The 9:30 Club is now a mini-dynasty, with the Lincoln Theatre (p. 228) and the Anthem (p. 227) part of the family. But this venue still rules. It's a 1,200-person-capacity concert hall with excellent sightlines, state-of-the-art sound system, four bars, and most important, a nightly concert schedule that features every possible star, rising or arrived, in today's varied rock world, from Patty Griffin to Adele. It's frequently voted the best live-music venue, certainly in D.C., but also countrywide. Unless advertised as seated, all shows are standing room only, general admission. 815 V St. NW (at 9th St.). www.930.com. ℭ **202/265-0930.** Tickets $12–$40. Metro: U St./Cardozo (10th St. exit).

Black Cat ★★★   This club is D.C.'s flagship venue for alternative music. When it opened on 14th Street in 1993, the neighborhood was a red-light district and D.C. was not a major player in the live-music scene. So hats off to the Black Cat, which played a part in the changes that have happened since. Today, local, national, and international groups play here, everyone from Arcade Fire to local trio Flasher. 1811 14th St. NW (btw. S and T sts.). www.blackcatdc.com.

A performance at the Black Cat.

© **202/667-4490.** Purchase tickets ($5–$25) online for concerts or arrive with cash; the club does not accept credit cards. Metro: U St./Cardozo (13th and U sts. exit).

Eighteenth Street Lounge ★★   Ever the hotspot, ESL is the place to go for dressing sexy and dancing to live music and DJ-spun tunes, a range of acid jazz, hip-hop, reggae, Latin jazz, soul, and party sounds. The setting is somewhat surprising: a restored, century-old mansion, once the home of Teddy Roosevelt, with fireplaces, high ceilings, and an outside deck. It's open Tuesday through Friday from 5pm and Saturday and Sunday from 9pm. 1212 18th St. NW (at Jefferson Place and Connecticut Ave.). www.eighteenthstreetlounge. com. © **202/466-3922.** Covers vary, usually $5–$15 after 10pm. Metro: Dupont Circle (South/19th St. exit) or Farragut North (L St. exit).

Rock & Roll Hotel ★   Located in the Atlas District, this club features a second-floor pool hall, a 400-person concert hall, a separate comfy bar for hanging out, and year-round rooftop deck and bar. Nightly acts range from local garage bands to national groups on tour. *Note:* Don't expect to stay overnight; despite its name, the hotel is just a club. 1353 H St. NE (at 14th St.). www.rockandrollhoteldc.com. © **202/388-7625.** Cover $8–$20. Metro: Union Station, then take the D.C. Streetcar, a taxi, or walk.

Comedy Clubs

In addition to the **Kennedy Center's** growing presence on the comedy circuit, the **Warner Theatre** (p. 228) sometimes features big-name comedians or troupes.

The Capitol Steps ★   *Make America Grin Again* is the name of the latest album released by this musical political satire troupe, following fast on the

---

THE best OF D.C.'S INTERNATIONAL SCENE

Washington is home to more than 180 embassies and international culture centers, which greatly contribute to the city's cosmopolitan flavor. Few embassies are open to the public on a walk-in basis (see p. 25 for info about embassy open houses in May), but many offer programs highlighting the culture of their countries. It's often some of the hottest nightlife in town.

The helpful website **www.embassy. org** provides a list of all the embassies, with links to their websites. If you explore the individual websites, you'll find that many host events that are open to the public—sometimes for free, sometimes at minimal cost. In my opinion, the French Embassy's **La Maison Française**

(www.frenchculture.org) and the Swedish Embassy's **House of Sweden** (www. swedenabroad.com) offer the most interesting events.

You can also buy tickets for **Embassy Series** (www.embassyseries.org; © **202/ 625-2361**) program events. These world-class, mostly classical-music performances are hosted by individual embassies and held at the embassy or the ambassador's residence. It's an intimate experience and tickets can be expensive. For example, on March 29, 2019, the Embassy of Austria staged a "night of Vienna" performed by cellist Julian Schwarz and pianist Marika Bournaki, along with a reception of wine and other Austrian tastes, for $75 per ticket, but well worth it!

heels of *Orange Is the New Barack, What to Expect When You're Electing, Mock the Vote,* and *How to Succeed in Congress Without Really Lying*—just five of the 40 albums the troupe has produced since it debuted in 1981. But really, it's best to see them perform their songs and skits in person, which you can do nearly every weekend at the Ronald Reagan Building and International Trade Center. The performers are former congressional staffers, and therefore well-equipped to satirize politicians. In the Ronald Reagan Bldg., 1300 Pennsylvania Ave. NW (at 13th St.). www.capsteps.com. © **202/312-1555.** Tickets $40.50. Metro: Federal Triangle.

The DC Improv ★ The Improv features headliners on the national comedy-club circuit as well as comic plays and one-person shows. Shows are about 1½ hours long and generally include three comics (an emcee, a feature act, and a headliner). Showtimes are at 7, 7:30, or 8pm Tuesday through Sunday, with a second show at 9:45pm or later on Friday and Saturday. Sometimes the club adds a third show at 11pm on weekends. Acts also take place in the more intimate 60-person lounge. You must be 18 to enter. 1140 Connecticut Ave. NW (btw. L and M sts.). www.dcimprov.com. © **202/296-7008.** Tickets $15–$45, plus a 2-item minimum per person. Metro: Farragut North (L St. exit).

THE LGBTQ SCENE

According to the *Washington Blade*, the D.C. publication covering the LGBT community, the nation's capital has the highest self-identified LGBT population in the country, at 9.8%. Here are three of the most popular bars favored by those 9.8 percenters.

The Green Lantern ★ This premier gay bar is "attitude free" and the place where everyone gets along with one another, so says the Lantern's owners. Tell the bartender you're visiting and you'll be instantly welcomed into "D.C.'s Queer Cheers." Open for more than 10 years now, the Lantern has a daily happy hour, and every Thursday, shirtless men drink free. The club also hosts karaoke and other themed and popular events. 1335 Green Court NW (off 14th St. NW). www.greenlanterndc.com. © **202/347-4533.** Metro: McPherson Square (14th St. exit).

J.R.'s Bar and Grill ★ This friendly place is always packed, whether it's Thursday night between 5 and 8pm, when $15 gets you all you can drink, or on "Showtunes Monday" nights. The all-male Dupont Circle club draws an attractive crowd, here to play pool, sing along, or simply hang out. 1519 17th St. NW (btw. P and Q sts.). www.jrsbar-dc.com. © **202/328-0090.** Metro: Dupont Circle (Q St. exit).

Nellie's Sports Bar ★ *Washington City Paper*'s **2018 Best of D.C.** issue reported that readers voted Nellie's Sports Bar their favorite in two categories, best sports bar and best gay bar. Clearly, Nellie's has her fans, and they aren't necessarily all gay. But if the idea of drag brunch or drag bingo appeals, or if you happen to be a whiz at trivia, or if you enjoy an entertaining social scene while you watch your favorite team play on TV, or if you fancy a cocktail on Nellie's roof deck overlooking U Street, you're bound to be happy at Nellie's. 900 U St. NW (at 9th St.). www.nelliessportsbar.com. ✆ **202/332-6355.** Metro: U St./ Cardozo (10th St. exit).

SPECTATOR SPORTS

Washington, D.C., has professional football, basketball, baseball, ice hockey, and soccer teams, and of those five, it's the **2018 Stanley Cup champions,** the Washington Capitals ice-hockey team, whose fans are the most passionate. And visible: In season you'll see red-jersey'd devotees swarming downtown before and after matches at the Capital One Arena. Tickets to the Caps games are attainable but not cheap. It's the tickets to the Redskins football games that remain most elusive, thanks to a loyal subscription base.

Annual Sporting Events

Citi Open This U.S. Open series event (formerly known as the Legg Mason Tennis Classic) attracts more than 72,000 people to watch big-time tennis pros compete for big bucks. A portion of the profits benefits the Washington Tennis and Education Foundation. The 9-day tournament takes place starting in mid- to late July at the Rock Creek Park Tennis Center in Rock Creek Park. www.citiopentennis.com. ✆ **202/721-9500.**

Marine Corps Marathon Thirty thousand runners compete in this 26.2-mile race (the third-largest marathon in the United States), which winds past major memorials. The race takes place on a Sunday in late October; 2020 marks its 45th year. www.marinemarathon.com. ✆ **800/786-8762.**

General Spectator Sports

Baseball Washington, D.C.'s Major League Baseball team, the **Nationals,** play at the finely designed **Nationals Park** (www.nationals.com; 1500 S. Capitol St. SE; ✆ **202/675-6287**), located in southeast Washington's Capitol Riverfront neighborhood. The 41,000-seat stadium is now the centerpiece of this newly vibrant waterfront locale, whose plentiful restaurants, bars, and fun activities will keep you busy, if you want to arrive early for the game or amuse yourself afterward. Metro: Navy Yard.

Basketball The 20,600-seat **Capital One Arena,** 601 F St. NW, where it meets 7th Street (www.capitalonearena.com; ✆ **202/628-3200**), in the center of downtown, is Washington's premier indoor-sports arena, where the **Wizards** (NBA), the **Mystics** (WNBA), and the **Georgetown University Hoyas** basketball teams play. Metro: Gallery Place/Chinatown.

Football The **Redskins** National Football League team plays at the 85,000-seat **FedEx Field** stadium, outside Washington, in Landover, Maryland. Obtaining tickets is difficult thanks to season-ticket holders, but if you want to try, visit www.redskins.com/fedexfield or www.stubhub.com.

Ice Hockey D.C. ice hockey fans rejoiced in 2018 when their beloved **Washington Capitals** brought home the Stanley Cup, winning its first NHL championship in franchise history. The team rink is inside the 20,600-seat **Capital One Arena,** 601 F St. NW (www.capitalonearena.com; ✆ **202/628-3200**), in the center of downtown. Metro: Gallery Place/Chinatown.

Soccer The D.C. men's Major League Soccer Club team, **D.C. United** (www.dcunited.com), which has been around since 1994, finally has its own arena, the 20,000-seat capacity **Audi Field,** 100 Potomac Ave. SW (www.audifielddc.com; ✆ **202/587-5000**), in an area called Buzzard Point, in the Southwest Waterfront, abutting the Capitol Riverfront neighborhood. The city's National Women's Soccer League team, **Washington Spirit** (www.washingtonspirit.com), also plays matches here. Metro: Navy Yard.

Tennis The World Team Tennis franchise team, the **Washington Kastles** (www.washingtonkastles.com), plays at the **Kastles Stadium at the Smith Center,** 600 22nd St. NW, on the campus of George Washington University. WTT is a coed professional tennis league; the Kastles team includes Venus Williams, Marta Kostyuk, Yoshihito Nishioka, and Frances Tiafoe (✆ **202/483-6647**). Metro: Foggy Bottom.

DAY TRIPS FROM D.C.

You've come as far as Washington, D.C.—why not travel just a bit farther to visit Mount Vernon, the home of the man for whom the capital is named? "Washington slept here" is a claim bandied about by many a town. "Washington lived here for 45 years" is a claim only Mount Vernon can make. The estate was George Washington's home from 1754 until his death in 1799 (as much as the American Revolution and Washington's stints as the new republic's first president would allow). And where did Washington go to sell his produce, kick up his heels, or worship? In nearby Old Town Alexandria. Its cobblestone streets and historic churches and houses still stand, surrounded now by of-the-moment eateries and chic boutiques. Make time, if you can, for visits to both Old Town and Mount Vernon.

MOUNT VERNON

Only 16 miles south of the capital, George Washington's Southern plantation dates from a 1674 land grant to the president's great-grandfather.

Essentials

GETTING THERE If you're going by car, take any of the bridges over the Potomac River into Virginia and follow the signs pointing the way to National Airport/Mount Vernon/George Washington Memorial Parkway. Travel south on the George Washington Memorial Parkway, the river always to your left, and pass by National Airport, also on your left. Continue through Old Town Alexandria, where the parkway is renamed "Washington Street," and head 8 miles farther, until you reach the large circle that fronts Mount Vernon.

You might also take a narrated bus or boat tour to Mount Vernon; prices include the cost of admission to Mount Vernon. **Gray Line** (www.graylinedc.com; ℭ **202/779-9894**) offers a 9-hour tour Tuesday, Thursday, and Saturday year-round ($105 adults, $40 children) that includes a brief stop at historic **Christ Church** (p. 250) in Old Town Alexandria on the way to Mount Vernon. Buses depart and return to Union Station, allowing you to explore Mount Vernon on

9

	9

DAY TRIPS FROM D.C. | Mount Vernon

> ## Fun Fact: The Parkway Is a Park
>
> Few people realize that the **George Washington Memorial Parkway** is actually a national park. The first section was completed in 1932 to honor the bicentennial of George Washington's birth. The parkway follows the Potomac River, running from Mount Vernon past Old Town and the nation's capital and ending at Great Falls, Virginia. Today the parkway is a major commuter route leading into and out of the city. But even the most impatient driver will find it hard to resist glances at the gorgeous scenery and monuments you pass along the way—it's a beautiful drive.

your own. The bus company **OnBoard Sightseeing** (http://washingtondctours.onboardtours.com/mount-vernon-tour; ✆ **301/839-5261**) offers a year-round 6-hour tour ($80 adults, $70 children Mon–Thurs; $90 adults, $80 children Fri–Sun) of Mount Vernon and Arlington Cemetery, via a drive-through of Old Town Alexandria. On this tour, your OnBoard tour guide not only narrates your experience on the bus, but also narrates your tour of Mount Vernon and Arlington Cemetery. The tour starts and returns to the White House Gifts shop at 15th Street NW and New York Avenue NW.

The narrated tour offered by **Spirit Cruises'** *Spirit of Mount Vernon* (www.cruisetomountvernon.com; ✆ **866/302-2469**) is a seasonal operation, cruising to Mount Vernon March through October (check online for daily schedules, which can vary). The vessel leaves from Pier 4 (6th and Water sts. SW; three blocks from the Green Line Metro's Waterfront station) at 8:30am, returning by 3pm. The cost is $51 plus tax per person (free for children 2 and under) and includes the price of admission into Mount Vernon.

The **Potomac Riverboat Company** (www.potomacriverboatco.com; ✆ **877/511-2628**) operates a narrated cruise aboard *Miss Christin* Tuesday through Sunday April through August, and Saturday and Sunday September until late October. It departs at 10:30am for Mount Vernon from the pier adjacent to the Torpedo Factory, where Union and Cameron streets intersect, at Old Town Alexandria's waterfront. The rate one-way is $48 adults, $39 children 2 to 11; round-trip $50 adults, $37 children; and always free for children 2 and under. Arrive at the pier 30 minutes ahead of time to secure a place on the boat. The narrated trip takes 90 minutes each way, stopping twice at Gaylord's National Harbor to pick up and discharge passengers. The boat departs Mount Vernon at 4pm to return to Old Town by 5:30pm, via National Harbor.

And here's a clever way to travel to and from Mount Vernon: The Potomac Riverboat Company and Bike and Roll have teamed up to offer **Bike and Boat,** which includes bike rental from Bike and Roll's Old Town Alexandria location at the waterfront, admission to Mount Vernon, and a narrated return trip back to Old Town aboard the *Miss Christin.* You pedal your own merry way along the Mount Vernon Trail (see box, "Biking to Old Town Alexandria & Mount Vernon," p. 249) to reach the estate, lock up your bike at Mount Vernon (where Bike and Roll staff pick it up), tour Mount Vernon, then board *Miss Christin* at 4pm to return to Old Town. You must pick up your bike in Old Town no later than 11:30am. Book through www.bikeandrolldc.com;

Tourists line up for a tour of Mount Vernon, the historic estate of George Washington.

more on p. 301. The package costs $79 ages 13 and older, $45 ages 6 to 12, and $25 ages 2 to 5.

If you're up for it, you can rent a bike and pedal the 18-mile round-trip distance at your own pace any time of year.

Finally, it's possible to take **public transportation** to Mount Vernon by riding the Metro to the Yellow Line's Huntington station and proceeding to the lower level, where you catch the Fairfax Connector bus no. 101 to Mount Vernon. *Note:* It seems Metro is always undergoing track work year-round; for details, see p. 293.

Touring the Estate

Mount Vernon Estate and Gardens ★★★

You could easily spend a full day soaking in the life and times of our first president, George Washington, when he lived at Mount Vernon. The 500-acre estate includes the centerpiece mansion, George and Martha Washington's home, and so much else: gardens, outbuildings, a wharf, slave quarters and burial grounds, a greenhouse, a working farm, an orientation center, education center, museum and, about 3 miles down the road, a working distillery and gristmill.

The plantation was passed down from Washington's great-grandfather, who acquired the land in 1674, to George's half-brother, and eventually to George himself in 1754. Washington proceeded over the next 45 years to expand and fashion the home to his liking, though the American Revolution and his years as president kept Washington away from his beloved estate much of the time.

What you see today is a remarkable restoration of the mansion, the oldest part of which dates from the 1740s. Interiors appear as they would have in 1799, with walls painted in the colors chosen by George and Martha, and with original furnishings and objects used by the Washington family on display. Historical interpreters stationed through the house answer questions as you pass through.

If time allows, visit the **Ford Orientation Center** prior to touring the estate. The Center is located inside the main entrance building, so it's easy to make this your first stop. The Orientation Center's 25-minute film, "We Fight to Be Free," offers some insight into Washington's character and career. Then, if you have time after your tour of the estate, we highly recommend you visit the **Donald W. Reynolds Museum and Education Center,** which lies on the path leading to shops and the food court, making this a logical last stop at Mount Vernon. The museum's 23 galleries, theater presentations, and display of 700 original artifacts help round out the story of this heroic, larger-than-life man.

Note: Visitors with limited time have to choose between visiting those centers or the historic sites scattered throughout the estate. If you're at Mount Vernon April through October, when Mount Vernon's shuttle operates (see information box, below) and the weather is most pleasant, I recommend doing the historic sites. Conversely, during the months of November through March, and in inclement weather, visits to the museum and education and orientation centers might be a better idea, both logistically and in terms of your personal comfort.

If you can, start with the **Outbuildings:** the kitchen, slave quarters, storeroom, smokehouse, overseer's quarters, coach house, stables, and working blacksmith shop with daily demonstrations. Walk or take the shuttle to the 4-acre **Pioneer Farm,** which includes a replica of Washington's 16-sided treading barn (built from his own design) and crops that he grew (corn, wheat, oats, and so forth). Historical interpreters in period costumes demonstrate 18th-century farming methods. At its peak, Mount Vernon was an 8,000-acre working farm, and Washington considered himself first and foremost a farmer.

tips FOR TOURING MOUNT VERNON

o   If you plan to visit Old Town Alexandria historic sites as well as Mount Vernon, buy a **Key to the City Museum Pass** (www.visitalexandriava. com/things-to-do/historic-attractions-and-museums/key-to-the-city) online or in person from the Alexandria Visitor Center (221 King St.). You'll receive a coupon for a 40% discount off the admission price for Mount Vernon (see details in the Old Town Alexandria section, below). If you're not interested in the Key to the City Pass, you can still save money by buying your Mount Vernon admission tickets online, which reduces the price by $2 for adults and seniors, $1 for children.

o   Your admission ticket is also your **timed entry ticket** to tour the mansion, so choose a tour time that allows you to first visit the Ford Orientation Center, where a 25-minute movie provides some good background for your visit.

o   You will also be given the choice of buying a standard tour ticket or, for

$30 more, a **premium tour ticket.** Again, consider the timing, and if it works, opt for the premium ticket. The difference is worth it: Instead of self-guiding your way through two floors of the mansion, usually a 15- to 20-minute experience, you'll receive a guided, 90-minute tour that takes you beyond the usual tourable rooms, with all your questions answered by your guide as you go. One other important perk of the premium ticket is that you avoid the very long entry line into the mansion, something you will most definitely appreciate on a hot summer day.

o   During the online ticketing process, you will have the chance to **add on specialty tours** covering areas beyond the mansion—for example, a 1-hour "Enslaved People of Mount Vernon Tour" for an additional $10. If you can manage it, add on a specialty tour—these tours truly bring history to life.

Not too far from the Pioneer Farm
is the wharf, where you can learn
about Washington's boat building
and fisheries, and take a 45-minute
narrated excursion on the Potomac
(mid-March to fall; $11 adults, $7
children). In Washington's time,
the river waters teemed with fish—
when the shad were running in the
spring, the surface of the Potomac
was said to sparkle like silver.

Back on land, you have more
to cover: the slave burial ground,
the greenhouse, and the tombs of
George and Martha Washington. Down the road from the estate are Washington's fully functioning distillery and gristmill. George Washington had
become one of the largest whiskey producers in the U.S. by 1799. The shuttle
travels the 2.7 miles to the site, which is open April through October and operated by costumed staff. Admission to the distillery and gristmill, as well as the
shuttle to and from Mount Vernon, are included in your ticket. Samplings of
the whiskey produced here are not included in your admission price, alas, but
you can purchase Mount Vernon–made whiskey and stoneground products at
the Shops at Mount Vernon. If you're not visiting Mount Vernon, the admission here is $5 per person; kids 5 and under free.

Mount Vernon belongs to the Mount Vernon Ladies' Association, which
purchased the estate for $200,000 in 1858 from John Augustine Washington
III, great-grandnephew of the first president. Today, more than a million
people tour the property annually. The best time to visit is off-season; during
the heavy tourist months (especially in spring, when schoolchildren descend
in droves), it's best to arrive in the afternoon on weekdays, or anytime early
Saturday or Sunday, because student groups will have departed by then.

3200 Mount Vernon Memorial Hwy. www.mountvernon.org. ✆ **703/780-2000.** Admission $20 adults, $19 seniors, $12 children 6–11, free for children 5 and under. Purchase
tickets online for $2 off all adult prices, $1 off children's prices. Apr–Oct daily 9am–5pm;
Nov–Mar daily 9am–4pm.

Dining & Shopping

Mount Vernon's comprehensive **Shops at Mount Vernon Complex** offers a
range of books, children's toys, holiday items, Mount Vernon private-label
food and wine, whiskey produced at the distillery, stoneground flour made at
the gristmill, and Mount Vernon–licensed furnishings. The Orientation Center
and slave quarters/greenhouse hold much smaller gift shops. A **food court**
features a menu of deli sandwiches, grilled items, pizza, and cookies. You
can't **picnic** on the grounds, but just a mile north on the parkway, **Riverside
Park** has tables and a lawn overlooking the Potomac. I do, however,

recommend a meal at the **Mount Vernon Inn restaurant** (see below); lunch or dinner at the inn is an intrinsic part of the Mount Vernon experience.

Mount Vernon Inn ★ AMERICAN TRADITIONAL   This quaint and charming Colonial-style restaurant comes complete with period furnishings and three working fireplaces. Lunch entrees range from baked turkey pie (a sort of early-American stew served with garden vegetables in an open pie shell) to a club sandwich. There's a full bar, and premium wines are offered by the glass. At dinner, tablecloths and candlelight give an elegance to the setting. The menu is mostly modern, but you may still see Colonial references in starters like hoecake (cornbread), here topped with country ham, crabmeat, and a hollandaise sauce; and the homemade peanut and chestnut soup. By the way, Mount Vernon has joined the happy-hour trend and now serves discounted beer, wine, and spirits, along with very un-Colonial appetizers (fried calamari, crab cake sliders) Tuesday through Friday from 4 to 8pm.

Near the entrance to Mount Vernon Estate and Gardens. www.mountvernon.org/inn. ℰ **703/799-6800.** Reservations recommended for dinner. Main courses $14–$26 lunch and dinner, $12–$24 brunch. Sun–Mon 11am–5pm; Tues–Sat 11am–9pm.

The Mount Vernon Shuttle

Good news! Mount Vernon offers free shuttle service around its estate, as well as to the gristmill and distillery, 2.7 miles down the road. The shuttle operates in high season only, from April to October, running continuously between the Museum and Education Center and the Pioneer Farm, near the Wharf, with a separate shuttle running back and forth between Mount Vernon Estate and its gristmill and distillery.

OLD TOWN ALEXANDRIA

Old Town Alexandria is about 8 miles S of Washington.

The city of Washington may be named for our first president, but he never lived there. No, he called this other side of the Potomac home from the age of 11, when he joined his half-brother Lawrence, who owned Mount Vernon. Washington came to Alexandria often, helping to map out the 60-acre town's boundaries and roads when he was 17, training his militia in Market Square and selling produce there from his Mount Vernon farm, worshipping at Christ Church, and dining and dancing at Gadsby's Tavern.

The town of Alexandria is actually named after John Alexander, the Scot who purchased the land of the present-day town from an English ship captain for "six thousand pounds of Tobacco and Cask." Incorporated in 1749, the town soon grew into a major trading center and port, known for its handsome homes.

Today, thanks to a multimillion-dollar urban renewal effort, some 200 structures from Alexandria's early days survive in Old Town's historic district. (Four thousand structures, in all, are deemed historic.) Market Square is the site of the oldest continuously operating farmers market in the country. (Catch it on Sat between 7am and noon, and you'll be participating in a 266-year-old tradition.) Christ Church and Gadsby's Tavern are still open and operating.

Many Alexandria streets still bear their original Colonial names (King, Queen, Prince, Princess, Royal), while others, like Jefferson, Franklin, Lee, Patrick, and Henry, are obviously post-Revolutionary. Wander down to King Street's waterfront and watch archaeologists excavating the 18th-century merchant ships that were discovered when developers started carving out land on which to build condos and commercial establishments.

Twenty-first-century America thrives in Old Town's many shops, boutiques, art galleries, bars, and restaurants. But it's still easy to imagine yourself in Colonial times as you listen for the rumbling of horse-drawn vehicles over cobblestone (portions of Prince and Oronoco sts. are still paved with cobblestone), dine on Sally Lunn bread and other 18th-century grub in the centuries-old Gadsby's Tavern, and learn about the lives of the nation's forefathers during walking tours that take you in and out of their former homes.

Essentials

GETTING THERE For spectacular views, consider biking to Old Town Alexandria (p. 249). If you're driving from the District, take the Arlington Memorial Bridge (be prepared for ongoing construction on the bridge—a rehabilitation project won't be complete until 2021) or the 14th Street Bridge to the George Washington Memorial Parkway south, which becomes Washington Street in Old Town Alexandria. Washington Street intersects with King Street, Alexandria's main thoroughfare. Turn left from Washington Street onto one of the streets before or after King Street (southbound left turns are not permitted from Washington St. onto King St.), and you'll be heading toward the waterfront and the heart of Old Town. If you turn right from Washington Street onto King Street, you'll still be in Old Town, with King Street's long avenue of shops and restaurants awaiting. Parking is inexpensive at nearby garages and at street meters, but if you want to pay nothing, drive a couple of blocks to streets off King Street, north of Cameron Street or south of Duke Street, where you can park for 2 or 3 hours for free. The town is compact, making it easy to get around on foot.

The easiest way to make the trip is by Metro (www.wmata.com); Yellow and Blue Line trains travel to the King Street station. (Metro platform construction here is scheduled to be completed in fall 2019, but don't be surprised if it's still ongoing in early 2020.) From the station, catch the free King Street Trolley, which operates Sunday to Wednesday 11am to 10:30pm, Thursday to Saturday 10:30am to midnight, making frequent stops between the Metro station and the Potomac River. The eastbound AT2, AT7, or AT8 blue-and-gold DASH bus (www.dashbus.com; ✆ **703/746-3274**) marked OLD TOWN or BRADDOCK METRO will also take you up King Street. Ask to be dropped at the corner of Fairfax and King streets, across the street from the Alexandria Visitors Center at Ramsay House. The fare is $1.75 in cash, or free if you're transferring from Metrorail or a Metrobus and using a SmarTrip card (p. 292). Or you can walk the 1½ miles from the station into the center of Old Town.

Or consider taking a **water taxi.** The **Potomac Riverboat Company** (www.potomacriverboatco.com; ✆ **877/511-2628**) operates year-round water

Old Town Alexandria

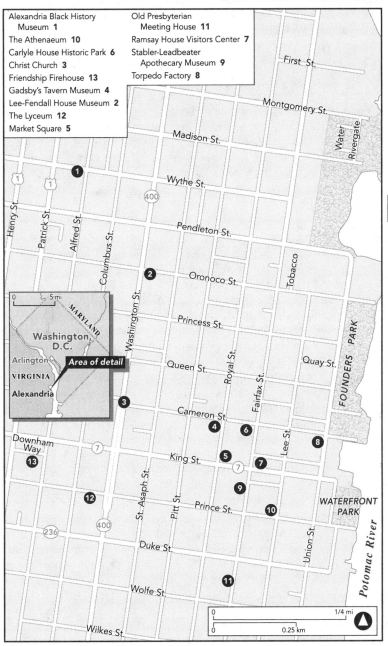

Alexandria Black History
    Museum **1**
The Athenaeum **10**
Carlyle House Historic Park **6**
Christ Church **3**
Friendship Firehouse **13**
Gadsby's Tavern Museum **4**
Lee-Fendall House Museum **2**
The Lyceum **12**
Market Square **5**

Old Presbyterian
    Meeting House **11**
Ramsay House Visitors Center **7**
Stabler-Leadbeater
    Apothecary Museum **9**
Torpedo Factory **8**

First St.

Montgomery St.

Water
Rivergate

Madison St.

Wythe St.

Pendleton St.

Henry St.

Patrick St.

Alfred St.

Columbus St.

Tobacco

Oronoco St.

Washington St.

Princess St.

FOUNDERS PARK

Quay St.

0   5 mi

MARYLAND

**Washington,
D.C.**

Arlington

VIRGINIA

Alexandria

Area of detail

Queen St.

Royal St.

Fairfax St.

Cameron St.

Lee St.

Downham
Way

King St.

St. Asaph St.

Pitt St.

Prince St.

WATERFRONT
PARK

Duke St.

Union St.

Potomac River

Wolfe St.

0   1/4 mi

0   0.25 km

Wilkes St.

taxi service between the Wharf and Georgetown, Old Town Alexandria, and National Harbor; and between Old Town Alexandria and National Harbor. The 30-minute ride is not cheap (starting at $28 adults, $14 children, round-trip), but is scenic for sure. Check the website for schedule and reservations.

VISITOR INFORMATION The **Visit Alexandria Visitor Center** at Ramsay House, 221 King St., at Fairfax Street (www.visitalexandriava.com; ✆ **800/388-9119** or 703/838-5005) is open April through September Sunday to Wednesday 10am to 6pm and Thursday to Saturday 10am to 8pm; October through March it's open daily 10am to 5pm (closed Thanksgiving, Dec 25, and Jan 1). Here you can pick up a map/self-guided walking tour and brochures about the area, and buy tickets to tours, shuttles, and nearby attractions (including Mount Vernon). Consider buying a $15-per-person **Key to the City Museum Pass** (here or in advance online), which includes admission to nine historic sites, a 40% off coupon for admission to Mount Vernon, and discounts at many attractions, shops, and restaurants. Valued at $44, the pass saves you $34 on admission prices alone, and more if you take advantage of the special offers.

ORGANIZED TOURS Though it's easy to see Alexandria on your own and with the help of Colonial-attired guides at individual attractions, you might consider taking a comprehensive walking tour. Architecture and history tours leave from the visitor center garden April through mid-November, at least once a day, weather permitting. Tours depart at 10:30am Monday through Saturday and at 2pm on Sunday, with additional tours during busy seasons. Call **Alexandria Tours** (✆ **703/329-1122**) for more information or to book a tour, which lasts 90 minutes and costs $15 per person (free for ages 6 and under). Or you can just show up at the appointed time and pay the guide when you arrive.

Many other organized tours are available, each focused on a particular subject. Ghost tours may be the most popular. The "Ghosts and Graveyard Tour" from **Alexandria Colonial Tours** (www.alexcolonialtours.com; ✆ **703/519-1749**) is offered March through December (weather permitting) at various times and days—call for the exact schedule. This 1-hour tour departs from Ramsay House and costs $15 for adults, $10 for children ages 7 to 17, and free for children 6 and under. Reservations are recommended, though not required, for these tours; or you can purchase tickets from the guide, who will be dressed in Colonial attire and standing in front of the visitor center.

CITY LAYOUT Old Town is very small and laid out in an easy grid. At the center is the intersection of Washington and King sts. Streets change from north to south when they cross King Street; for example, North Alfred Street is the part of Alfred north of King Street (closest to Washington, in other words). Guess where South Alfred Street is.

OVERNIGHTING It's not a bad idea to schedule an overnight in Old Town, especially if you're driving and plan a leisurely dinner here after a day of touring—and especially since the local lodging choices are so enticing. We recommend the comfy boutique charm of the **Morrison House, Autograph Collection** ★★, 116 S. Alfred St. (www.marriott.com/hotels/travel/wasmh-morrison-house-autograph-collection; ✆ **703/838-8000**), and the contemporary luxury of the **Kimpton Lorien Hotel & Spa ★★**, 1600 King St. (https://www.lorienhotelandspa.com; ✆ **877/956-7436**).

Alexandria Calendar of Events

Visit Alexandria posts its calendar of events online at www.visitalexandriava.com, or call ✆ **800/388-9119** or 703/746-3301 for further details about the following event highlights.

FEBRUARY

George Washington's Birthday is celebrated over the course of the entire month of February, including Presidents' Weekend, which precedes the federal holiday (the third Mon in Feb). Festivities typically include a Colonial-costume or black-tie banquet, followed by a ball at Gadsby's Tavern, special tours, "open houses" at some of Alexandria's most historic sites, a wreath-laying ceremony at the Tomb of the Unknown Soldier of the Revolution, a scavenger hunt around Alexandria, the nation's largest and oldest George Washington Birthday Parade, and a concert in Market Square. Most events, such as the parade and walking tours, are free. The **Birthnight Ball at Gadsby's Tavern** requires tickets for both the banquet and the ball. Go to www.washingtonbirthday.com.

MARCH

St. Patrick's Day Parade takes place on King Street on the first Saturday in March. Go to www.ballyshaners.org.

APRIL

Historic Garden Week in Virginia is celebrated with tours of privately owned local historic homes and gardens the third or fourth Saturday of the month. Check the website (www.vagardenweek.org) or call the Visitor Association (✆ **703/746-3301**) in early 2020 for details on tickets and admission prices for the tour. April 18–25, 2020.

JULY

Alexandria's birthday (its 271th in 2020) is celebrated with a free concert performance by the Alexandria Symphony Orchestra, fireworks, a patriotic birthday cake, and other festivities. Typically held the Saturday following the 4th of July.

SEPTEMBER

The King Street Art Festival (www.artfestival. com/festivals/alexandria-king-street-art-festival) features ceramics, sculpture, photography, and other works from more than 200 juried artists. The festival is free. Saturday and Sunday in mid- to late September.

OCTOBER

Ghost tours take place year-round but pick up around **Halloween.** A lantern-carrying guide in 18th-century costume describes Alexandria's ghosts, graveyards, legends, myths, and folklore as you tour the town and graveyards.

NOVEMBER

Christmas Tree Lighting is in Market Square. The ceremony, which includes a welcome by the Town Crier, musical performances, and an appearance by Santa, begins at 6pm. Stay after the tree lighting to stroll through Old Town and enjoy the thousands of tiny lights adorning the trees along King Street. Usually the Friday after Thanksgiving.

DECEMBER

The Annual Scottish Christmas Walk includes kilted bagpipers, Highland dancers, a parade of Scottish clans (with horses and dogs), caroling, fashion shows, storytelling, booths (selling crafts, antiques, food, hot mulled punch, heather, fresh wreaths, and holly), and children's games. 2020 is the 50th anniversary event, organized by and benefiting the nonprofit Campagna Center, whose programs assist local families, children, and the community. Go to www.campagnacenter. org/scottishwalkweekend or call ✆ **703/549-0111.** First weekend in December.

Holiday Boat Parade of Lights The water shines as dozens of lit boats cruise the Potomac River along Old Town Alexandria's historic waterfront, stretching for more than a mile. Pre-parade festivities include a beer garden, crafts, letters to Santa, and a hot chocolate bar. First weekend in December, after Scottish parade.

The Historic Alexandria Candlelight Tour visits seasonally decorated historic Alexandria homes and an 18th-century tavern. Travel through centuries of local history as

The Athenaeum in Old Town Alexandria.

you enjoy each historic site by candlelight, sip drinks, and taste food inspired by that time period. Admission is $25 adults, $20 seniors or active military, and $5 children 6 to 17. Go to www.alexandriava.gov/Candlelight Tours. Second Saturday in December.

What to See & Do

Colonial and post-Revolutionary buildings are Old Town Alexandria's main attractions. Our favorites are the **Stabler-Leadbeater Apothecary Museum, Carlyle House,** and **Gadsby's Tavern Museum,** but they're all worth a visit.

These sites are most easily accessible via the King Street Metro station, combined with a ride on the free King Street Trolley to the center of Old Town. The exceptions are the **Alexandria Black History Museum,** whose closest Metro stop is the Braddock Road station, and **Fort Ward Museum & Historic Site,** accessible via the AT5 DASH bus from the King Street Metro station, or by car or taxi.

Old Town is also known for its shopping opportunities. Brand-name stores, charming boutiques, antiques shops, art galleries, and gift shops sell everything you might desire. Notable local favorite shops include **Bellacara,** 1000 King St. (www.bellacara.com; ✆ **703/299-9652**), for fragrant soaps and more than 50 brands of luxe skin- and haircare products; **Society Fair,** 277 S. Washington St. (www.societyfair.net; ✆ **703/683-3247**), Cathal Armstrong's venture, part bakery/market/butchery/wine bar/demo kitchen; **An American in Paris,** 1225 King St., Ste. 1 (www.anamericaninparisoldtown.com; ✆ **703/ 519-8234**), where one must knock on the door to enter and sort through the beautiful, one-of-a-kind cocktail dresses and evening gowns; and **Red Barn Mercantile,** 1117 King St. (www.redbarnmercantile.com; ✆ **703/838-0355**), a great place to buy gifts, no matter the occasion or person, college graduate to toddler's birthday.

Note: Many Alexandria attractions are closed on Mondays.

Alexandria Black History Museum ★   In 1939, African Americans in Alexandria staged a sit-in to protest the segregation of blacks from Alexandria's main library. The black community built its own public library, and it is this 1940s building that now serves as the Black History Museum. The center exhibits photographs, documents, and memorabilia relating to the black citizens of Alexandria from the 18th century forward. In addition to the permanent collection, the museum presents rotating exhibits, genealogy workshops, book signings, and other activities. A half-hour is enough time to spend at the center.

The museum is actually on the outskirts of Old Town. Once you've explored the museum, walk into Old Town, rather than taking the Metro or even a taxi. Have a staff person point you in the direction of Washington Street, east of the center; if you choose, turn right (south) at Washington Street and walk two blocks to the **Lee-Fendall House** (p. 252) at Oronoco and Washington streets.

902 Wythe St. (at N. Alfred St.). www.alexblackhistory.org. ✆ **703/746-4356.** Admission $2. Tues–Sat 10am–4pm. Metro: Braddock Rd.; from the station, walk across the parking lot and bear right until you reach the corner of West and Wythe sts., where you'll proceed five blocks east along Wythe until you reach the center.

The Athenaeum ★   This grand building, with its Greek Revival architectural style, stands out among the narrow Old Town houses on the cobblestoned street. Built in 1851, the Athenaeum has been many things: the Bank of the Old Dominion, where Robert E. Lee kept his money prior to the Civil War; a commissary for the Union Army during the Civil War; a church; a triage center where wounded Union soldiers were treated; and a medicine warehouse. Now the hall serves as an art gallery and performance space. Pop by to admire the Athenaeum's imposing exterior, including the four soaring Doric columns

biking TO OLD TOWN ALEXANDRIA & MOUNT VERNON

One of the nicest ways to see the Washington skyline is from across the river while biking in Virginia. You'll have a breathtaking view of the Potomac and of Washington's grand landmarks. Rent a bike at one of **Bike and Roll**'s locations (http://bikeandrolldc.com/locations) or at the Thompson Boat Center, across from the Kennedy Center and right on the bike path (p. 206). Hop on the pathway that runs along the Potomac River and head toward the memorials and the Arlington Memorial Bridge. In Washington, this is the Rock Creek Park Trail; when you cross Memorial Bridge (near the Lincoln Memorial) into Virginia, the name changes to the **Mount Vernon**

Trail, which leads straight to Mount Vernon.

Of course, this mode of transportation is also a great way to see Old Town Alexandria and Mount Vernon. The trail carries you past Reagan National Airport via two pedestrian bridges that take you safely through the airport's roadway system. Continue to Old Town, where you should lock up your bike, walk around, tour some of the historic properties listed in this chapter, and take in some refreshment from one of the many excellent restaurants before proceeding on to Mount Vernon. The section from Memorial Bridge to Mount Vernon is about 19 miles in all.

and its interior hall: 24-foot-high ceilings, enormous windows, and whatever contemporary art is on display. Allot 20 minutes.

201 Prince St. (at S. Lee St.). www.nvfaa.org. ℂ **703/548-0035.** Free admission (donations accepted). Thurs–Sun noon–4pm. Closed major holidays.

Carlyle House Historic Park ★★   One of Virginia's most architecturally impressive 18th-century homes, Carlyle House also figured prominently in American history. A social and political center, the house was visited by the great men of the day, including George Washington. But its most important historic moment occurred in April 1755, when Major General Edward Braddock, commander-in-chief of His Majesty's forces in North America, met with five Colonial governors here and asked them to tax colonists to finance a campaign against the French and Indians. Colonial legislatures refused to comply, one of the first instances of serious friction between America and Britain.

When it was built, Carlyle House was a waterfront property with its own wharf. In 1753, Scottish merchant John Carlyle completed the mansion for his bride, Sarah Fairfax, a daughter of one of Virginia's most prominent families. It was designed in the style of a Scottish/English manor house and is lavishly furnished; Carlyle, a successful merchant, had the means to import the best furnishings and appointments available abroad for his new Alexandria home.

Tours are given on the hour and half-hour and take about 45 minutes; allow another 15 minutes if you plan to tour the tiered garden of brick walks and boxed parterres. Two of the original rooms, the large parlor and the dining room, have survived intact; the former, where Braddock met the governors, still retains its original fine woodwork, paneling, and pediments. The house is furnished in period pieces, but only a few of Carlyle's possessions remain. An architecture exhibit in an upstairs room depicts 18th-century building methods.

121 N. Fairfax St. (btw. Cameron and King sts.). www.novaparks.com/parks/carlyle-house-historic-park. ℂ **703/549-2997.** Admission $5 adults; $3 children 6–12; free for children 5 and under. Tues–Sat 10am–4pm; Sun noon–4pm.

Christ Church ★★   This sturdy redbrick Georgian-style church would be an important national landmark even if its two most distinguished members had not been Washington and Lee. It has been in continuous use since 1773; the town of Alexandria grew up around this building—it was once known as the "Church in the Woods." Over the years, the church has undergone many changes, adding the bell tower, church bell, galleries, and organ by the early 1800s, and the "wine-glass" pulpit in 1891. For the most part, the original structure remains, including the hand-blown glass in the windows.

Christ Church has had its historic moments. Washington and other early church members fomented revolution in the churchyard, and Robert E. Lee met here with Richmond representatives to discuss Lee's taking command of Virginia's military forces at the beginning of the Civil War. You can sit in the same pew where George and Martha sat with her two Custis grandchildren, or in the Lee family pew. You might also want to stroll through the churchyard, where some of the tombstones date from the mid- to late 1700s.

World dignitaries and U.S. presidents have visited the church over the years. One of the most memorable of these visits took place shortly after Pearl Harbor, when Franklin Delano Roosevelt attended services with Winston Churchill on the World Day of Prayer for Peace, January 1, 1942.

Of course, you're invited to attend a service (Sun at 8am, 10, and 5pm; Wed at 12:05pm). A guide gives brief lectures to visitors. A nearby **gift shop** (121 N. Columbus St., ☎ **703/836-5258**) is open Tuesday through Saturday 10am to 4pm and Sunday 9am to noon. Twenty minutes should do it here. Be sure to check out the website before you visit; it offers a wealth of information about the history of the church and town.

118 N. Washington St. (at Cameron St.). www.historicchristchurch.org. ☎ **703/549-1450.** Donations appreciated. Mon–Sat 9am–noon; Sun 2–4:30pm. Closed all federal holidays.

Fort Ward Museum & Historic Site ★

A short drive from Old Town is a 45-acre museum and park that transports you to Alexandria during the Civil War. The action here centers, as it did in the early 1860s, on an actual Union fort that Lincoln ordered erected, part of a system of Civil War forts called the "Defenses of Washington." About 90% of the fort's earthwork walls are preserved, and the Northwest Bastion has been restored with six mounted guns (originally there were 36). A model of 19th-century military engineering, the fort was never attacked by Confederate forces. Self-guided tours begin at the Fort Ward ceremonial gate.

Visitors can explore the fort and replicas of the ceremonial entrance gate and an officer's hut. A museum of Civil War artifacts on the premises features changing exhibits that focus on subjects such as Union arms and equipment, medical care of the wounded, and local war history.

There are picnic areas with barbecue grills in the park surrounding the fort. Living-history presentations take place throughout the year. This is a good stop if you have young children, in which case you could spend an hour or two here (especially if you bring a picnic).

4301 W. Braddock Rd. (btw. Rte. 7 and N. Van Dorn St.). www.fortward.org. ☎ **703/746-4848.** Free admission (donations welcome). Park daily 9am–sunset. Museum Tues–Sat 10am–5pm; Sun noon–5pm. Accessible via the AT5 DASH bus from the King Street Metro station, or by car or taxi: From Old Town, follow King St. west, go right on Kenwood Ave., then left on W. Braddock Rd.; continue for a mile to the entrance on the right.

Friendship Firehouse ★

Alexandria's first firefighting organization, the Friendship Fire Company, was established in 1774. In the early days, the company met in taverns and kept its firefighting equipment in a member's barn. Its present Italianate-style brick building dates from 1855; it was erected after an earlier building was, ironically, destroyed by fire. Local tradition holds that George Washington was involved with the firehouse as a founding member, active firefighter, and purchaser of its first fire engine, although research does not confirm these stories. The museum displays an 1851 fire engine, old hoses, buckets, and other firefighting apparatus. Allot 20 minutes to see this tiny place.

107 S. Alfred St. (btw. King and Prince sts.). www.friendshipfireco.com. ☎ **703/746-3891.** Admission $2. Sat–Sun 1–4pm.

Gadsby's Tavern Museum ★★ Alexandria commanded center stage in 18th-century America, and Gadsby's Tavern the spotlight. The tavern consisted of two buildings—one Georgian, one Federal, dating from around 1785 and 1792, respectively. Innkeeper John Gadsby combined them to create "a gentleman's tavern," which he operated from 1796 to 1808; it was considered one of the finest in the country. George Washington was a frequent dinner guest; he and Martha danced in the second-floor ballroom, and it was here that Washington celebrated his last birthday. The tavern also welcomed Thomas Jefferson, James Madison, and the Marquis de Lafayette (the French soldier and statesman who served in the American army under Washington during the Revolutionary War and remained close to Washington). It was the setting of lavish parties, theatrical performances, small circuses, government meetings, and concerts. Itinerant merchants used the tavern to display their wares, and traveling doctors treated a hapless clientele (these were rudimentary professions in the 18th century) on the premises.

The rooms have been restored to their 18th-century appearance. On the 30-minute tour, you'll get a good look at the **Tap Room,** a small dining room; the **Assembly Room,** the ballroom; typical bedrooms; and the underground icehouse, which was filled each winter from the icy river. Tours depart 15 minutes before and after the hour. Cap off the experience with a meal right next door, at the restored Colonial-style restaurant, **Gadsby's Tavern,** 138 N. Royal St., at Cameron Street (www.gadsbystavernrestaurant.com; ✆ **703/548-1288**).

134 N. Royal St. (at Cameron St.). www.gadsbystavern.org. ✆ **703/746-4242.** Admission $5 adults; $3 children 5–12; free for children 4 and under. Tours Apr–Oct Tues–Sat 10am–5pm, Sun–Mon 1–5pm; Nov–Mar Wed–Sat 11am–4pm, Sun 1–4pm. Closed most federal holidays.

Lee-Fendall House Museum ★★ Thirty-seven Lees occupied this handsome Greek Revival–style house over a period of 118 years (1785–1903), and it is a veritable Lee family museum of furniture, heirlooms, and documents. The politician and Revolutionary War officer "Light-Horse Harry" Lee never actually lived here, but he was a frequent visitor, as was his good friend George Washington. He did own the original lot but sold it to Philip Richard Fendall (himself a Lee on his mother's side), who built the house in 1785.

It was in this house that Harry wrote Alexandria's farewell address to George Washington, delivered when the general passed through town on his way to assume the presidency. (Harry also wrote and delivered the famous funeral oration to Washington that contained the words, "First in war, first in peace, and first in the hearts of his countrymen.") During the Civil War, the house was seized and used as a Union hospital.

Guided tours (45-min.) interpret the 1850s era of the home and provide insight into Victorian family life. Much of the interior woodwork and glass is original. The Colonial garden, with its magnolia and chestnut trees, roses, and boxwood-lined paths, can be visited as part of the tour or without a ticket.

614 Oronoco St. (at Washington St.). www.leefendallhouse.org. ✆ **703/548-1789.** Admission $5 adults; $3 children 5–17; free for children 4 and under. Wed–Sat 10am–4pm; Sun 1–4pm. Call ahead to make sure the museum is not closed for a special event. Tours on the hour 10am–3pm. Closed Jan and Thanksgiving.

The Lyceum ★   This Greek Revival building houses a museum depicting Alexandria's history from the 17th to the 20th centuries. It features changing exhibits and an ongoing series of lectures, concerts, and educational programs. The knowledgeable staff is happy to answer any questions.

The striking brick-and-stucco Lyceum also merits a visit. Built in 1839, it was designed in the Doric temple style to serve as a lecture, meeting, and concert hall. It was an important center of Alexandria's cultural life until the Civil War, when Union forces appropriated it for use as a hospital. After the war it became a private residence, and still later was subdivided for office space. In 1969, however, the city council's use of eminent domain prevented the Lyceum from being demolished in favor of a parking lot. Allow about 20 minutes here.

201 S. Washington St. (off Prince St.). www.alexandriava.gov/Lyceum. ✆ **703/746-4994.** Admission $2. Mon–Sat 10am–5pm; Sun 1–5pm. Closed Jan 1, Thanksgiving, and Dec 25.

Old Presbyterian Meeting House ★   Presbyterian congregations have worshiped in Virginia since the Reverend Alexander Whittaker converted Pocahontas in Jamestown in 1614. The original version of this Presbyterian Meeting House was built in 1774. Although it wasn't George Washington's church, the Meeting House bell tolled continuously for 4 days after his death in December 1799, and memorial services were preached from the pulpit here by Presbyterian, Episcopal, and Methodist ministers. According to the Alexandria paper of the day, "The walking being bad to the Episcopal church, the funeral sermon of George Washington will be preached at the Presbyterian Meeting House." Two months later, on Washington's birthday, Alexandria citizens marched from Market Square to the church to pay their respects.

Many famous Alexandrians are buried in the church graveyard, including John and Sarah Carlyle; Dr. James Craik (the surgeon who treated—some say killed—Washington, dressed Lafayette's wounds at Brandywine, and ministered to the dying Braddock at Monongahela); and William Hunter, Jr., founder of the St. Andrew's Society of Scottish descendants, to whom bagpipers pay homage on the first Saturday of December. It's also the site of a Tomb of an Unknown Revolutionary War Soldier. Dr. James Muir, minister between 1789 and 1820, lies beneath the sanctuary in his gown and bands. The cemetery has a larger burial ground nearby that has been used since 1809.

When lightning struck and set afire most of the original Meeting House in 1835, parishioners rebuilt the church in 1837, incorporating as much as they could from the earlier structure. This is the church you see today. The present bell, said to be recast from the metal of the old one, was hung in a newly constructed belfry in 1843, and a new organ was installed in 1849. The Meeting House closed its doors in 1889 and for 60 years was used sporadically. But in 1949 it was reborn as a living Presbyterian U.S.A. church, and today the Old Meeting House looks much as it did following its first restoration. The original parsonage, or manse, is still intact. There's no guided tour. Allow 20 minutes.

323 S. Fairfax St. (btw. Duke and Wolfe sts.). www.opmh.org. ✆ **703/549-6670.** Free admission. Open to the public Mon–Fri 9am–4pm (go to the church office right next door to obtain the key). Sun services 8:30, 11am (only 10am in summer).

Stabler-Leadbeater Apothecary Museum ★★ When its doors closed in 1933, this landmark drugstore was the second oldest in continuous operation in America. Run for five generations by the same Quaker family (beginning in 1792), the store counted Robert E. Lee (who purchased the paint for Arlington House here), George Mason, Henry Clay, John C. Calhoun, and George Washington among its famous patrons. Gothic Revival decorative elements and Victorian-style doors were added in the 1840s. Today the apothecary

Original gold-leafed bottles in the Stabler-Leadbeater Apothecary Museum in Alexandria.

looks much as it did in Colonial times, its shelves lined with original hand-blown gold-leaf-labeled bottles (the most valuable collection of antique medicinal bottles in the country), old scales stamped with the royal crown, patent medicines, and equipment for bloodletting. The clock on the rear wall, the porcelain-handled mahogany drawers, and two mortars and pestles all date from about 1790. Among the shop's documentary records is this 1802 order from Mount Vernon: "Mrs. Washington desires Mr. Stabler to send by the bearer a quart bottle of his best Castor Oil and the bill for it." The museum is open for guided tours only, which take place 15 minutes before and after the hour, and last 30 minutes.

105–107 S. Fairfax St. (near King St.). www.apothecarymuseum.org. (℡) **703/746-3852.** Admission $5 adults; $3 children 5–12; free for children 4 and under. Apr–Oct Tues–Sat 10am–5pm, Sun–Mon 1–5pm; Nov–Mar Wed–Sat 11am–4pm, Sun 1–4pm. Closed major holidays.

Torpedo Factory Art Center ★ This block-long, three-story structure was built in 1918 as a torpedo shell-case factory but now accommodates some 82 artists' studios, where 160 professional artists and craftspeople create and sell their own works. Here you can see artists at work in their studios, from potters to painters, as well as those who create stained-glass windows and fiber art. A volunteer or staff member is on hand to answer questions. Art lovers may end up browsing for an hour or two.

On permanent display are exhibits on the city's history from **Alexandria Archaeology** (www.alexandriaarchaeology.org; (℡) **703/746-4399**), which is headquartered here and engages in extensive city research—including the recent excavation of three Colonial-era merchant ships uncovered at Robinson Landing. It's an ongoing dig now, one that City Archaeologist Eleanor Breen called "one of the most archaeologically significant sites in Virginia."

105 N. Union St. (btw. King and Cameron sts., on the waterfront). www.torpedofactory. org. (℡) **703/746-4570.** Free admission. Daily 10am–6pm (Thurs until 9pm). Archaeology exhibit area Tues–Fri 10am–3pm; Sat 10am–5pm; Sun 1–5pm. Closed Jan 1, Easter, July 4, Thanksgiving, and Dec 25.

Where to Eat & Play

Old Town Alexandria is in the midst of a big redevelopment centered on its waterfront. The plan calls for new restaurants, shops, bars, town houses, and a rebuilt pier. A new, expanded Waterfront Park opened in 2019 at the foot of King Street, where visitors can now enjoy broadened views of the Potomac River. In the meantime, consider these other recommended restaurants and bars.

WHERE TO EAT

The following options satisfy assorted budgets, tastes, and styles; all are easily accessible via the King Street Metro station, combined with a ride on the free King Street Trolley to the center of Old Town.

Expensive

Hummingbird ★★★ SEAFOOD/AMERICAN   Owners Cathal (the chef) and Meshelle Armstrong are the married power couple behind Hummingbird, which *Washington Post* restaurant critic Tom Sietsema has called "Old Town's most appealing place to eat." (Other restaurants in the Armstrong family are the Filipino/Thai/Korean restaurant **Kaliwa,** at the Wharf in Washington, D.C.; **Eamonn's A Dublin Chipper,** below; and the bistro/market **Society Fair,** p. 248, in Old Town.) Hummingbird debuted in summer 2017 inside the new Hotel Indigo, scoring an early success for the city's waterfront redevelopment strategy. Come here for the wonderful water views, both inside through the glass doors and outside on the patio, where you can dine even in winter, warmed by stoked fire pits and blankets. The theme is nautical, with a navy and white decor. The food is as delicious as the setting, including lemon lobster bucatini, crab and corn fritters, excellent versions of chopped salad, lobster rolls, grilled fish, and, naturally, Southern-style hummingbird cake.

220 S. Union St. (in the Hotel Indigo, at the waterfront). www.hummingbirdva.net. ✆ **703/566-1355.** Reservations recommended. Main courses $8–$21 breakfast, $13–$21 brunch, $10–$20 lunch, $18–$32 dinner. Bar-menu items (available daily between lunch & dinner) $10–$20. Spring/summer hours Mon–Fri 6:30–10:30am and 11:30am–2:30pm; Sat–Sun 7am–2:30pm; Mon–Thurs 5:30–10pm; Fri–Sat 5:30–11pm; Sun 5–9pm.

Moderate

Blackwall Hitch ★ AMERICAN   If Hummingbird is booked, head here. The huge (seats 500), glass-enclosed restaurant and its two patios sit right on the waterfront, overlooking the Potomac River and the Torpedo Factory (see above). Inside are two dining rooms, an oyster bar, a bar/lounge where live music plays Thursday to Saturday evenings and at Sunday brunch, and the upstairs **Crow's Nest** bar, a perfect niche for boat- and people-watching. The menu leans halfway seaward, with options like oyster po'boys, softshell crabs, and fish tacos, and halfway good ol' American, with offerings of burgers and steaks, pasta, chicken, and flatbreads. The kids' menu has standard fare like chicken tenders, burgers, and pasta for $9 each.

5 Cameron St. (on the waterfront). www.theblackwallhitch.com. ✆ **703/739-6090.** Reservations recommended. Main courses $14–$42; Sun brunch $35 adults, $15 children 13 and under. Mon–Thurs 11am–midnight; Fri–Sat 11am–2am; Sun 10am–10pm.

Inexpensive

Eamonn's A Dublin Chipper ★ FISH & CHIPS   Fish and chips and a few sides (onion rings, coleslaw)—that's what we're talking here. But it's charming. Upstairs is **PX,** an exclusive lounge, where mixologist Todd Thrasher may be on hand to shake the drinks he's created. This is another in the strand of restaurant experiences from Cathal and Meshelle Armstrong (see Hummingbird, above); the Chipper is named after their son, Eamonn. The Armstrongs have a following, so expect a crowd.

728 King St. www.eamonnsdublinchipper.com. ✆ **703/299-8384.** Reservations not accepted. Main courses $6–$10. Mon–Wed 11:30am–10pm; Thurs 11:30am–11pm; Fri 11:30am–midnight; Sat noon–midnight; Sun noon–9pm.

Urbano 116 ★ MEXICAN   The sights and sounds of Mexico City followed chef Alam Méndez Florián to this Alexandria Oaxacan restaurant in the heart of Old Town. Its interior has a beamed ceiling, brick walls, cozy booths, leather bar seats, neon signs throughout, and a large mural backdrop dedicated to Mexico's theatrical professional wrestling pastime, *lucha libre.* Luchador masks (traditional Mexican wrestling masks) are on display.

The menu is dedicated to traditional Oaxacan cuisine, like moles, ceviche, and fresh takes on tacos, with fish, carnitas, *lengua* (beef tongue), and vegetarian options; octopus tacos come in a homemade heirloom corn tortilla. Starters include the usual guacamole and chips and salsa, but also plantain molotes ceviche. Entrees include braised short ribs, whole grilled trout, and a sirloin cap steak with guacamole and black beans. Passers-by can get a glimpse inside through a new "churro window." Wine, cocktails, and local beer are served.

116 King St. (btw. Union and Lee sts.). www.urbano116.com. ✆ **571/970-5148.** Reservations accepted. Main courses lunch and dinner $9–$28. Mon–Wed 11am–midnight; Thurs–Sat 11am–2am; Sun 10am–midnight.

NIGHTLIFE

Old Town Alexandria's nightlife options center on the bar scene, which is nearly as varied as the one across the Potomac in the District. Named for the patron saint of beer, St. Augustine, **Augie's Mussel House,** at 1106 King St. (www.eataugies.com; ✆ **703/721-3970**), reopened in 2019 after renovations, and features a Belgian menu from Chef Eric Reid and some of the best beers from around the world served indoors and on the expansive outdoor patio. If you're in the mood for raucous karaoke, DJ and local band performances, shuffleboard, and Skee-Ball, make your way to the **Light Horse,** 715 King St. (www.thelighthorserestaurant.com; ✆ **703/549-0533**). Downstairs is the restaurant, but upstairs is where you want to be. And for cocktails, live jazz, and Potomac views, snag a seat in the lounge of **Blackwall Hitch** (see "Where to Eat," above) Thursday through Saturday evenings and Sunday jazz brunch.

SELF-GUIDED WALKING TOURS

O ne of the greatest pleasures to be had in the nation's capital is walking. You round a corner and spy the Capitol standing proudly at the end of the avenue. You stroll a downtown street and chance to look up, and *bam*, there it is: the tip of the Washington Monument. People brush past you on the sidewalk speaking a pastiche of languages. You decide to walk rather than take the Metro or a taxi back to your hotel and discover a gem of a museum. A limousine pulls up to the curb and discharges—who? A foreign ambassador? A former prez? A famous author or athlete or human-rights activist?

Beautiful sights, historic landmarks, unpredictable encounters, and multicultural experiences await you everywhere in Washington. Follow any of these three self-guided walking tours and see for yourself.

10

WALKING TOUR 1: STROLLING AROUND THE WHITE HOUSE

START:	**White House Visitor Center, 1450 Pennsylvania Ave. NW (Metro: Federal Triangle or Metro Center).**
FINISH:	**The Penn Quarter (Metro: Federal Triangle or Metro Center).**
TIME:	**1½ hours to 2 hours (not including stops). It's a 1.6-mile trek.**
BEST TIME:	**During the day. If you want to hit all the museums, stroll on a Thursday or Friday.**
WORST TIME:	**After dark, as some streets can be deserted.**

The White House is the centerpiece of President's Park, an 18-acre national park that includes not just the house itself but also its grounds, from the Ellipse to Pennsylvania Avenue to Lafayette Square; the U.S. Treasury Building on 15th Street; and the Eisenhower Executive Office Building on 17th Street. As you wend your way from landmark to landmark, you'll be mingling with White House administration staff, high-powered attorneys, diplomats, and ordinary office workers. All of you are treading the same ground as early American heroes—like Stephen Decatur, whose house you'll see—and every president since George Washington (though the White House was not finished in time for him to live there).

This tour circumnavigates the White House grounds, with stops at historic sites and several noteworthy museums. The **White House Visitor Center** (see p. 174) is a good place to begin and end (for one thing, it's got restrooms!).

Note: Tours of the White House require advance reservations, as do tours of the U.S. Treasury Building. For White House tour info, see p. 175. See https://home.treasury.gov/services/tours-and-library/tours-of-the-historic-treasury-building for details about registering for a Treasury Building tour.

Start: From the White House Visitor Center, stroll up 15th Street to your first stop, at 15th and F streets NW.

---

1 U.S. Treasury Building

Lin-Manuel Miranda's brilliant musical *Hamilton* has brought the man and his times to life on Broadway and beyond. On this tour, you must settle for Hamilton, the statue. It stands outside the south end of the U.S. Treasury Building, too close to the White House for security's comfort to allow stray tourists a better look, so you must resign yourself to gazing at him from a distance through the black iron fencing. Hamilton, who devised our modern financial system, was the first secretary of the Treasury, established by Congress in 1789. Once you've caught a glimpse of Hamilton's statue, turn your attention to the Treasury's headquarters, Washington's oldest office building, initially erected in 1798 and severely damaged by fire not once, not twice, but three times (in 1801, 1814, and 1833), until reconstruction proceeded in fits and starts to completion in 1869. Its most notable architectural feature is the colonnade you see running the length of the building: 30 columns, each 36 feet tall, carved out of a single piece of granite. In its lifetime, the building has served as a Civil War barracks, a temporary home for President Andrew Johnson following the assassination of President Lincoln in 1865, and the site of President Ulysses S. Grant's inaugural reception. Today it houses offices for the U.S. treasurer, the secretary of the Treasury, its general counsel, and their staffs.

Continue north on 15th Street and turn left onto the Pennsylvania Avenue promenade, where you'll notice the statue of Albert Gallatin, the fourth secretary of the Treasury, standing accessibly on the north side of the Treasury Building. Continue along:

2 Pennsylvania Avenue

Say hello to the president, who resides in that big white house beyond the black iron fencing. Security precautions keep this two-block section of Pennsylvania Avenue closed to traffic. But that's a good thing. You may have to dodge bicyclists, roller skaters, joggers, and random Frisbees and sidestep soapbox orators and live newscasts, but not cars. Ninety Princeton American elm trees line the 84-foot-wide promenade, which offers plenty of great photo ops as you stroll past the White House. There are benches here, too, in case you'd like to sit and people-watch. L'Enfant's

Strolling Around the White House

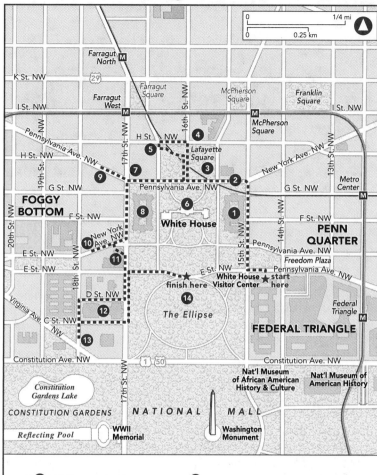

1 U.S. Treasury Building

2 Pennsylvania Avenue

3 Lafayette Square

4 St. John's Episcopal Church, Lafayette Square

5 Decatur House

6 White House

7 Renwick Gallery

8 Eisenhower Executive Office Building

9 GCDC Grilled Cheese Bar

10 Octagon House

11 Corcoran Gallery

12 DAR Museum and Period Rooms

13 Art Museum of the Americas

14 Ellipse

A bird's-eye view of Pennsylvania Avenue and the White House grounds.

original idea for Pennsylvania Avenue was that it would connect the legislative branch (Congress) at one end of the avenue with the executive branch (the president's house) at the other end.

Turn your back on the White House and walk across the plaza to enter:

3 Lafayette Square

This 7-acre public park is known as a gathering spot for protesters. In its early days, the grounds held temporary shelters for the slaves building the White House, then a race track, zoo, graveyard, and a military encampment. The park is named for the Marquis de Lafayette, a Frenchman who served under George Washington during the Revolutionary War. But it's General Andrew Jackson's statue that centers the park. Erected in 1853, this was America's first equestrian statue. It's said that sculptor Clark Mills trained a horse to maintain a reared-up pose so that Mills could study how the horse balanced its weight. Other park statues are dedicated to foreign soldiers who fought in the War for Independence, including Lafayette; Poland's Tadeusz Kosciuszko; Prussian Baron von Steuben; and Frenchman Comte de Rochambeau.

Walk through the park and cross H Street to reach 1525 H Street NW, the site of:

4 St. John's Episcopal Church on Lafayette Square

St. John's is known as "the Church of the Presidents" because every president since James Madison has attended at least one service here. If you tour the church, look for pew 54, eight rows from the front, which is the one traditionally reserved for the current president and first family. Other things to notice in this 1816 church, designed by Benjamin Henry Latrobe, are the steeple bell, which was cast by Paul Revere's son and has been in continuous use since its installation in 1822, and the beautiful stained-glass windows. The Lincoln Pew, at the very back of the church, is where Lincoln would sit alone for evening services during the Civil War, slipping in after other congregants had arrived and out before they left.

Directly across the street from St. John's is the Hay-Adams Hotel, which turns 92 this year (p. 67). Re-cross H Street to stand in front of 748 Jackson Place NW, the:

5 Decatur House

In addition to St. John's, Latrobe designed this Federal-style brick town house in 1818 for Commodore Stephen Decatur, a renowned naval hero in the War of 1812. Decatur and his wife, Susan, established themselves as gracious hosts in the 14 short months they lived here. In March 1820, 2 days after hosting a ball for President James Monroe's daughter, Marie, Decatur was killed in a gentleman's duel by his former mentor, James Barron. Barron blamed Decatur for his 5-year suspension from the Navy, following a court-martial in which Decatur had played an active role. Other distinguished occupants have included Henry Clay and Martin Van Buren, when each was serving as Secretary of State (Clay under Pres. John Quincy Adams, Van Buren under Pres. Andrew Jackson). Decatur House, which includes slave quarters, is open for free tours on a limited basis (www.whitehousehistory.org/events/tour-the-historic-decatur-house). The White House Historical Association gift shop is at the entry, at 1610 H St.

Walk back through Lafayette Square to return to the Pennsylvania Avenue plaza, where you'll have another chance to admire the:

6 White House

As grand as the White House is, it is at least one-fourth the size that Pierre L'Enfant had in mind when he planned a palace to house the President. George Washington and his commission went a different way and dismissed L'Enfant, though they kept L'Enfant's site proposal. An Irishman named James Hoban designed the building, having entered his architectural draft in a contest held by George Washington, beating out 52 other entries. Although Washington picked the winner, he was the only president never to live in the White House, or "President's Palace," as it was called before whitewashing brought the name "White House" into use. Construction of the White House took 8 years, beginning in 1792, when its cornerstone was laid. Its facade is made of the same stone used to construct the Capitol. See p. 171 for in-depth info about the White House and tours.

Turn around and head toward the northwest corner of the plaza, at 17th Street, to reach the:

7 Renwick Gallery

Its esteemed neighbors are the White House and, right next door, the Blair-Lee House (built in 1824), where the White House sends overnighting foreign dignitaries. The Renwick (p. 170), nevertheless, holds its own. This distinguished redbrick-and-brownstone structure was the original location for the Corcoran Gallery of Art. James Renwick designed the building (if it reminds you of the Smithsonian Castle on the Mall, it's because Renwick designed that one, too), which opened in 1874. When the collection outgrew its quarters, the Corcoran moved to its current location in 1897 (see below). Although the Renwick's mission has long focused on decorative arts and crafts from early America to the present, the gallery lately is gaining popularity for its special exhibits of ultra-inventive art by push-the-envelope contemporary artists, like the "Ginny Ruffner: Reforestation of the Imagination" show on view through January 5, 2020. Since 1972 the Renwick has operated as an annex of the

The U.S. Treasury Building.

Smithsonian American Art Museum, eight blocks away in the Penn Quarter. By all means, head inside.

Turn left on 17th Street, where you'll notice on your left the:

8 Eisenhower Executive Office Building

Old-timers still refer to this ornate building as the "OEOB," for "Old Executive Office Building"; the Eisenhower Executive Office Building houses the offices of people who work in or with the Executive Office of the President. When construction was completed in 1888, it was the largest office building in the world. During the Iran-Contra scandal of the Reagan presidency, the OEOB became famous as the site of document shredding by Colonel Oliver North and his secretary, Fawn Hall. Open to the public? Nope.

Cross 17th Street, then follow G Street west. See all the sandwich and coffee places? You can choose Subway if you'd like, but I'd rather you try a favorite, at 1776 G Street NW:

9 GCDC Grilled Cheese Bar ☕

The standard sandwich gets a gourmet makeover here, where you'll find grilled cheeses filled with everything from Gruyère and caramelized onions on challah bread ("The French Onion") to cheddar, kimchi, GCDC spicy sauce, and roast beef ("The Kim-Cheese Steak"). Pair it with GCDC's homemade tomato soup "with a kick" or summer gazpacho (www.grilledcheesedc.com; ✆ **202/393-4232**).

After you've satisfied your hunger, walk westward to 18th Street NW, turn left, and stroll three blocks to New York Avenue, where you'll spy the unmistakable:

10 Octagon House

Before you enter, admire the unique shape. Count its sides and you'll discover that the Octagon is, in fact, a hexagon. Designed by Dr. William Thornton, first architect of the U.S. Capitol, this 1801 building apparently earned its name from interior features, though experts disagree about that. Enter the Octagon to view the round rooms; the central, oval-shaped staircase that curves gracefully to the third level; the hidden doors; and the triangular chambers. Built originally for the wealthy Tayloe family, the Octagon served as a temporary president's home for James and Dolley Madison after the British torched the White House in

1814. On February 17, 1815, President Madison sat at the circular table in the upstairs circular room and signed the Treaty of Ghent, establishing peace with Great Britain. See p. 298 for more info about tours.

Cross New York Avenue and return to 17th Street, where you should turn right and walk to the Corcoran Gallery. It's unlikely that the gallery will be open for most of 2019, but if it is, you should definitely try to visit.

11 Corcoran Gallery of Art

This gallery, the first art museum in Washington and one of the first in the country, has always had a penchant for playing the wild card. In 1851, gallery founder William Corcoran caused a stir when he displayed artist Hiram Powers' *The Greek Slave,* which was the first publicly exhibited, life-size American sculpture depicting a fully nude female figure. (*The Greek Slave* is currently on view at the National Gallery of Art, p. 147.) Today the Corcoran Gallery of Art exists, but no longer as an independent entity. The George Washington University owns the building and the resident art school; the National Gallery owns 40% of the art, with the remaining 60% distributed to the American University Museum at the Katzen Arts Center (here in D.C.) and to Smithsonian museums and other institutions, including the Hirshhorn Museum and Sculpture Garden.

Walk to 17th Street and turn right, away from the White House. Follow it down to D Street and turn right, following the signs that lead to the entrance of the:

12 DAR Museum & Period Rooms

The National Headquarters of the Daughters of the American Revolution comprises three joined buildings that take up an entire block. The elegant middle building, Memorial Continental Hall, is the one you'll enter. The building cornerstone was laid in 1902 with the same trowel that George Washington used to lay the cornerstone for the Capitol. At the time, the front of the building faced the White House pasture, where presidential cattle grazed. What you're here for is the **DAR Museum,** which rotates exhibits of items from its 33,000-object collection, and the 31 period rooms, representing interior styles from the past, as interpreted by different states. The museum's collections veer from folk art to decorative arts and include old rocking chairs, ceramics, needlework samplers, and lots of silver. Quilters from far and wide come to admire the large collection of quilts, many of which are kept in glass sleeves that you can pull out from a case for better viewing. Highlights of the period rooms include the New Jersey Room, which replicates an English Council chamber of the 17th century, with woodwork and furnishings created from the salvaged oak timbers of the British frigate *Augusta,* which sank during the Revolutionary War; an opulent Victorian Missouri parlor; and New Hampshire's "Children's Attic," filled with 19th-century toys, dolls, and children's furnishings. You can tour the museum and period rooms on your own, but the free docent-led tour is more informative.

Exit the DAR, turning left and continuing along D Street to 18th Street, where you'll turn left again and follow to 201 18th Street NW, the Spanish colonial–style building that houses:

13 Art Museum of the Americas

The AMA showcases the works of contemporary Latin American and Caribbean artists. You'll be on your own; a visit takes 30 minutes, tops. *Not to miss:* a stunning loggia whose tall beamed ceiling and wall of deep-blue tiles set in patterns modeled after Aztec and Mayan art is a work of art on its own. A series of French (and usually locked) doors leads to a terrace and the museum garden, which separates the museum from the **Organization of American States (OAS) headquarters,** which owns it. When you leave the museum, you may notice the nearby sculptures of José Artigus, "Father of the Independence of Uruguay," and a large representation of liberator Simón Bolívar on horseback.

From 18th Street, head back in the direction of the White House, turning right on C Street and then left on 17th Street and follow it to E Street. Cross 17th Street and pick up the section of E Street that takes you between the South Lawn of the White House and the:

14 Ellipse

It's possible to bring a blanket and some food and picnic on the Ellipse, except when a White House event requires increased security and the Secret Service tell you to skedaddle. Otherwise, feel free to stroll the grounds. The Ellipse continues to be the site for the National Christmas Tree Lighting Ceremony every December, and a spot near the Zero Milestone monument remains a favored place for shooting photos against the backdrop of the White House. If you're ready to call it a day, keep walking a few more steps to return to 15th Street NW in the Penn Quarter, and its many options for an end-of-stroll repast.

WALKING TOUR 2: GEORGETOWN

START:	**Kafe Leopold's (DC Circulator bus; nearest Metro stop: Foggy Bottom).**
FINISH:	**Mount Zion United Methodist Church (DC Circulator bus; nearest Metro stop: Foggy Bottom).**
TIME:	**2½ to 3 hours (not including stops). The distance is about 3½ miles.**
BEST TIME:	**Weekday mornings are best to start out. If you want to attend a service at Mount Zion United Methodist Church, as well as do the house and museum tours, Sunday is your best day, and you should simply reverse the order of your stops, beginning at Mount Zion.**
WORST TIME:	**Saturday, when Georgetown's crazy social scene sometimes spills over into the back streets.**

The Georgetown famous for its shops, restaurants, and bars is not the Georgetown you'll see on this walking tour. Instead, the circuit takes you along quiet streets lined with charming houses and stately trees that remind you of the town's age and history. The original George Town, comprising 60 acres and named for the king of England, was officially established in 1751. It assumed

Georgetown.

new importance in 1790 when President George Washington, with help from his Secretary of State, Thomas Jefferson, determined that America's new capital city would be located on a site nearby, along the Potomac River. Georgetown was incorporated into the District of Columbia in 1871.

Get your stroll off to a good start by stopping first for pastries or something more substantial at 3315 Cady's Alley NW, the charming:

1 District Doughnut and Coffee ☕

Through a passageway and down a flight of stairs from busy M Street NW lies a cluster of chi-chi shops and District Doughnut and Coffee (www.district doughnut.com; ☏ **202/333-2594**), a modern doughnut shop that serves up the classic pastry handcrafted in a variety of creative flavors, like nutella cream, crème brûlée (torched to order), and baklava. Also look for local Compass Coffee here. Opens weekdays at 8am and at 9am weekends.

Return now to M Street, turn left, and continue to 3350 M Street NW, where you'll find the:

2 Forrest-Marbury House

No one notices this nondescript building on the edge of Georgetown near Key Bridge. But the plaque on its pink-painted brick facade hints at reasons for giving the 1788 building a once-over. Most significant is the fact that on March 29, 1791, Revolutionary War hero Uriah Forrest hosted a dinner here for his old friend George Washington and landowners who were being asked to sell their land for the purpose of creating the federal city of Washington, District of Columbia. The meeting was a success, and America's capital was born. Forrest and his wife lived here until Federalist William Marbury bought the building in 1800. Marbury is the man whose landmark case, *Marbury v. Madison,* resulted in the recognition of the Supreme Court's power to rule on the constitutionality of laws passed by Congress and in the institutionalization of the fundamental right of judicial review. The building has served as the Ukrainian Embassy since December 31, 1992, and the interior is not open to the public.

Walk to the corner of M and 34th streets, cross M Street, and walk up 34th Street one block to Prospect Street, where you'll cross to the other side of 34th Street to view 3400 Prospect Street NW:

3 Halcyon House

Benjamin Stoddert, a Revolutionary War cavalry officer and the first secretary of the Navy, built the smaller, original version of this house in 1789 and named it for a mythical bird said to be an omen of tranquil seas. (Stoddert was also a shipping merchant.) The Georgian mansion, like its neighbor Prospect House, is situated on elevated land, the Potomac River viewable beyond. Stoddert's terraced garden—designed by Pierre Charles L'Enfant, no less—offered unobstructed views of the Potomac River nearly 230 years ago.

Sometime after 1900, an eccentric named Albert Clemons, a nephew of Mark Twain, bought the property and proceeded to transform it, creating the four-story Palladian facade and a maze of apartments and hallways between the facade and Stoddert's original structure. Clemons is said to have filled the house with religious paraphernalia, and there are numerous stories involving sightings of shadowy figures and sounds of screams and strange noises in the night. Owners of Halcyon House since Clemons' death in 1938 have included Georgetown University and noted sculptor John Dreyfuss. Today, the name "Halcyon" refers to both the house and its resident nonprofit organization "designed to seek and celebrate creativity in all forms and galvanize creative individuals aspiring to promote social good."

Continue along Prospect Street to no. 3508, the site of:

4 Prospect House

This privately owned house was built in 1788 by James Maccubbin Lingan, a Revolutionary War hero and wealthy tobacco merchant. He is thought to have designed the house himself. Lingan sold the house in the 1790s to a prosperous banker named John Templeman, whose guests included President John Adams and the Marquis de Lafayette. In the late 1940s, James Forrestal, the secretary of defense under President Harry Truman, bought the house and offered it to his boss as a place for entertaining visiting heads of state, because the Trumans were living in temporary digs at Blair House while the White House was being renovated. The restored Georgian-style mansion is named for its view of the Potomac River. Note the gabled roof with dormer window and the sunray fanlight over the front door; at the rear of the property (not visible from the street) is an octagonal watchtower used by 18th-century ship owners for sightings of ships returning to port.

Keep heading west on Prospect Street until you reach 37th Street. Turn right and follow 37th Street to its intersection with O Street, where you'll see:

5 Georgetown University

Founded in 1789, Georgetown is Washington's oldest university and the nation's first Catholic university and first Jesuit-run university. Founder John

Strolling Around Georgetown

1. District Doughnut ☕
2. Forrest-Marbury House
3. Halcyon House
4. Prospect House
5. Georgetown University
6. Cox's Row
7. 3307 N St.
8. St. John's Episcopal Church, Georgetown
9. Martin's Tavern ☕
10. Tudor Place
11. Dumbarton House
12. Evermay
13. Oak Hill Cemetery
14. Dumbarton Oaks and Garden
15. Old Stone House
16. Mount Zion United Methodist Church

Carroll, the first Catholic bishop in America and a cousin of a Maryland signer of the Declaration of Independence, opened the university to "students of every religious profession." His close friends included Benjamin Franklin and George Washington, who, along with the Marquis de Lafayette, addressed students from "Old North," the campus's oldest building. After the Civil War, students chose the school colors blue (the color of Union uniforms) and gray (the color of Confederate uniforms) to celebrate the end of the war and to honor slain students. The 104-acre campus is lovely, beginning with the stunning, spired, Romanesque-style stone building beyond the university's main entrance on 37th Street. That would be the Healy Building, named for Patrick Healy, university president from 1873 to 1882 and the first African American to head a major, predominantly white university. The irony here is that Georgetown University now is reckoning with its earlier history, when in 1838 the college president sold 272 slaves to fend off financial ruin. Descendants of those slaves are demanding reparations.

Turn right on O Street and walk one block to 36th Street, where you'll turn right again. Continue to N Street to view Holy Trinity's parish chapel (3513 N St.). Built in 1794, the chapel is the oldest church in continuous use in the city. Continue farther on N Street, strolling several blocks to nos. 3327 to 3339, collectively known as:

6 Cox's Row

Built around 1805 to 1820 and named for the owner and builder, John Cox, these five charming houses exemplify Federal-period architecture, with dormer windows, decorative facades, and handsome doorways. Besides being a master builder, Cox was also Georgetown's first elected mayor, serving 22 years. He occupied the corner house at no. 3339 and housed the Marquis de Lafayette next door at no. 3337 when he came to town in 1824.

Follow N Street to the end of the block, where you'll see:

7 3307 N St. NW

John and Jacqueline Kennedy lived in this brick town house while Kennedy served as the U.S. senator from Massachusetts. The Kennedys purchased the house shortly after the birth of their daughter Caroline. Across the street at no. 3302 is a plaque on the side wall of the brick town house inscribed by members of the press in gratitude for kindnesses received there in the days before Kennedy's presidential inauguration. Another plaque honors Stephen Bloomer Balch (1747–1833), a Revolutionary War officer who once lived here.

Turn left on 33rd Street and walk one block north to O Street. Turn right on O Street and proceed to no. 3240, the site of:

8 St. John's Episcopal Church, Georgetown

Partially designed by Dr. William Thornton—first architect of the Capitol, who also designed the Octagon (p. 262) and Tudor Place (see below)—the church was begun in 1796 and completed in 1804. Its foundation and walls, at least, are original. Its early congregants were the movers and shakers of their times: President Thomas Jefferson (who contributed $50 toward the building fund), Dolley Madison, Tudor Place's Thomas and Martha Peter, and Francis Scott Key. To tour the church, stop by the office, just around the corner on Potomac Street, weekdays between 9am and 4pm, or attend a service on Sunday at 9am or 11am (10am in summer). Visit www.stjohnsgeorgetown.org for more info.

Follow O Street to busy Wisconsin Avenue and turn right, walking south to reach this favorite Washington hangout. Too early for a break? Return here or to another choice restaurant later; you're never far from Wisconsin Avenue wherever you are in Georgetown.

9 Martin's Tavern ☕

This American tavern, at 1264 Wisconsin Ave. NW (www.martinstavern.com; ℂ 202/333-7370), has been run by a string of Billy Martins since 1933. The original Billy's great-grandson runs the show today. So it's a bar, but also very much a restaurant (bring the children—everyone does), with glass-topped white tablecloths, paneled walls, wooden booths, and an all-American menu of burgers, crab cakes, Cobb salad, and pot roast. Martin's is famous as the place where John F. Kennedy proposed to Jacqueline Bouvier in 1953—look for booth no. 3. See p. 113.

Back outside, cross Wisconsin Avenue, follow it north to O Street, and turn right. Walk to 31st Street and turn left; follow it until you reach the entrance to 1644 31st Street NW:

10 Tudor Place

Yet another of the architectural gems designed by the first architect of the Capitol, Dr. William Thornton, Tudor Place crowns a hill in Georgetown, set among beautiful gardens first plotted nearly 215 years ago. The 5½-acre estate belonged to Martha Washington's granddaughter, Martha Custis Peter, and her husband, Thomas Peter. Martha Custis bought it in 1805 with an $8,000 legacy left to her by her step-grandfather, George Washington. Custis-Peter descendants lived here until 1983.

Tours of the house ($10) are docent-led only and reveal rooms decorated to reflect various periods of the Peter family tenancy. Exceptional architectural features include a clever floor-to-ceiling windowed wall, whose glass panes appear to curve in the domed portico (an optical illusion: It's the woodwork frame that curves, not the glass itself). On display throughout the first-floor rooms are more than 100 of George Washington's furnishings and other family items from Tudor Place's 15,000-piece collection. Docents reveal the rich history of the estate. From a sitting-room window in this summit location, Martha Custis Peter and Anna Maria Thornton (the architect's wife) watched the Capitol burn in 1814, during the War of 1812. The Peters hosted a reception for the Marquis de Lafayette in the drawing room in 1824. Friend and family relative Robert E. Lee spent his last night in Washington in one of the upstairs bedrooms.

Tours of the gardens ($3) are self-guided, with or without the use of an audio guide; a bowling green and boxwood ellipse are among the plum features. Tudor Place (www.tudorplace.org; ℂ 202/965-0400) is open Tuesday to Saturday 10am to 4pm and Sunday noon to 4pm, with tours given every hour on the hour; it's closed for the entire month of January.

From 31st Street, retrace your steps as far back as Q Street, where you'll turn left and walk several blocks to reach 2715 Q Street NW:

11 Dumbarton House

This stately redbrick mansion (www.dumbartonhouse.org; ✆ **202/337-2288**), originally called Bellevue, was built between 1799 and 1805. In 1915, it was moved 100 yards to its current location to accommodate the placement of nearby Dumbarton Bridge over Rock Creek. The house exemplifies Federal-period architecture, which means that its rooms are almost exactly symmetrical on all floors and centered by a large hall. Federal-period furnishings, decorative arts, and artwork fill the house; admire the dining room's late-18th-century sideboard, silver and ceramic pieces, and paintings by Charles Willson Peale. One of the original owners of Dumbarton House was Joseph Nourse, first register of the U.S. Treasury, who lived here with his family from 1805 to 1813. Dumbarton House is most famous as the place where Dolley Madison stopped for a cup of tea on August 24, 1814, while escaping the British, who had just set fire to the White House. It is open February to December Tuesday to Sunday from 10am to 3pm. Admission is $10, and tours are self-guided or guided on weekends at 10:30 am and 1:30 pm.

Exit Dumbarton House and turn right, retrace your steps along Q Street, and turn right on 28th Street. Climb the hill to reach 1623 28th Street NW, the estate of:

12 Evermay

The headquarters for a nonprofit organization, the Evermay Estate is not open to the public, unless you purchase a ticket to attend one of its concerts (http://rueno.org/evermay-series.html), which we can recommend. Otherwise, you'll have to content yourself with peering beyond the brick ramparts and thick foliage to view the impressive estate. As the plaque on the estate wall tells you, Evermay was built from 1792 to 1794 by Scottish real-estate speculator and merchant Samuel Davidson with the proceeds Davidson made from the sale of lands he owned around the city, including part of the present-day White House and Lafayette Square properties. By all accounts, Davidson was something of an eccentric misanthrope, guarding his privacy by placing menacing advertisements in the daily papers with such headlines as EVERMAY PROCLAIMS, TAKE CARE, ENTER NOT HERE, FOR PUNISHMENT IS NEAR.

Visitors approaching the entrance to Dumbarton House.

Georgetown Waterfront Park Harbour.

Follow the brick sidewalk and iron fence that run alongside to:

13 Oak Hill Cemetery

Founded in 1850 by banker/philanthropist/art collector William Wilson Corcoran (see Corcoran Gallery of Art, p. 263), Oak Hill is the final resting place for many of the people you've been reading about, in this chapter and in other chapters of this book. Corcoran is buried here, in a Doric temple of a mausoleum, along with the Peters of Tudor Place (see above) and the son of William Marbury of the Forrest-Marbury House (p. 265). Corcoran purchased the property from George Corbin Washington, a great-nephew of President Washington. The cemetery consists of 25 beautifully landscaped acres adjacent to Rock Creek Park, with winding paths shaded by ancient oaks. Look for the Gothic-style stone Renwick Chapel, designed by James Renwick, architect of the Renwick Gallery (p. 170), the Smithsonian Castle (p. 159), and New York's St. Patrick's Cathedral. The Victorian landscaping, in the Romantic tradition of its era, strives for a natural look: Iron benches have a twig motif, and many of the graves are symbolically embellished with inverted torches, draped obelisks, angels, and broken columns. Even the gatehouse is worth noting; designed in 1850 by George de la Roche, it's a beautiful brick-and-sandstone Italianate structure. Download a cemetery map (www.oakhillcemeterydc.org), or stop by the gatehouse (© **202/337-2835**) to pick one up. The grounds and gatehouse are open weekdays from 9am to 4:30pm; the grounds are also open Saturday 11am to 4pm and Sunday from 1 to 4pm.

Exit Oak Hill through the main entrance, and continue on the brick pathway to your right, strolling along R Street past Montrose Park until you reach the garden entrance to Dumbarton Oaks, on 31st Street. Or, if you'd prefer to visit the historic house and museum, continue around the corner to enter at 1703 32nd Street NW.

14 Dumbarton Oaks & Garden

Beyond the walls of Dumbarton Oaks is a tiered park of multiple gardens that include masses of roses, a pebble garden bordered with Mexican tiles, a wisteria-covered arbor, cherry-tree groves, overlooks, and lots of romantic, winding paths. The oldest part of Dumbarton Oaks mansion dates from 1801; since then the house has undergone considerable change, notably at the hands of Robert and Mildred Bliss, who purchased the property in 1920. As Robert was in the Foreign Service, the Blisses lived a nomadic life, amassing collections of Byzantine and pre-Columbian art, books relating to these studies, and volumes on the history of landscape architecture. After purchasing Dumbarton Oaks, the Blisses inaugurated a grand re-landscaping of the grounds and remodeling of the mansion to accommodate their collections and library, which now occupy the entire building. In 1940, the Blisses left the house, gardens, and art collections to Harvard University, Robert's alma mater. In the summer of 1944, at the height of World War II, Dumbarton Oaks served as the location for a series of diplomatic meetings that would cement the principles later incorporated into the United Nations charter. The conferences took place in the Music Room, which you should visit to admire the immense 16th-century stone chimney piece, 18th-century parquet floor, and antique Spanish, French, and Italian furniture. (See p. 193 for more info about the museum and gardens.) **Dumbarton Oaks Museum** (www.doaks.org; ✆ **202/339-6400**) is open year-round except major holidays Tuesday to Sunday 11:30am to 5:30pm, with free admission. The garden is open Tuesday to Sunday 2 to 6pm from March 15 to October 31 (admission fee $10); and Tuesday to Sunday 2 to 5pm November 1 to March 14 (free admission).

From the intersection of R and 31st streets, follow 31st Street downhill all the way to M Street and turn left to find your next destination at 3051 M Street NW:

15 Old Stone House

Located on one of the busiest streets in Washington, the unobtrusive Old Stone House offers a quiet look at life in early America, starting in 1765, when the Layman family built this home. Originally, the structure was simply one room made of thick stone walls, oak ceiling beams, and packed dirt floors. In 1800, a man named John Suter bought the building and used it as his clock shop. The grandfather clock you see on the second floor is the only original piece remaining in the house. Acquired by the National Park Service in the 1950s, the Old Stone House today shows small rooms furnished as they would have been in the late 18th century, during the period when Georgetown was a significant tobacco and shipping port. Park rangers provide information and sometimes demonstrate cooking in an open hearth, spinning, and making pomander balls. Adjacent to and behind the house is a terraced lawn and 18th-century English garden, a spot long frequented by Georgetown shop and office workers seeking a respite. Old Stone House (www.nps.gov/places/old-stone-house.htm; ✆ **202/426-6851**) is open daily 11am to 7pm; the garden is open daily dawn to dusk.

Turn left on M Street and walk two blocks to 29th Street, where you should turn left and walk about three blocks to:

16 Mount Zion United Methodist Church

Attend the 11am Sunday worship service here and you'll be among the city's oldest black congregation, established 204 years ago. By 1816, African Americans, both freed slaves and the enslaved, had already been living in Georgetown for decades. But blacks were not allowed to have their own church, so they worshipped at white churches, sitting in the balcony, apart from the white worshippers. In 1816, a man named Shadrack Nugent led 125 fellow black congregants to split from the nearby Montgomery Street Church (now Dumbarton United Methodist Church) and form their own congregation. The dissidents built a church, known as the "Little Ark," at 27th and P streets, and worshipped there until a fire destroyed the meeting house in 1880. (The congregation was all black, but the times still required a white man to be their pastor!) Meanwhile, a new and larger church was already under construction, on land purchased from a freed slave and prominent businessman named Alfred Pope, whose property adjoined the churches on 29th Street. The Mount Zion United Methodist Church held its first service in 1880, in the partially completed lecture hall, and dedicated the finished redbrick edifice you see today in 1884. The church proper actually lies on the second floor, whose high tin ceiling, beautiful stained-glass windows (called "comfort" windows for the sense of tranquility their pastel tints are said to imbue), and hand-carved pews are original features. A number of families in this 200-person congregation are descendants of the church's first founders, although only one or two congregants actually live in the neighborhood now. Mount Zion United Methodist Church welcomes all who are interested to attend its Sunday services, but otherwise is not open to the general public (www.mtzionumcdc.org; © **202/234-0148**).

Now retrace your steps to M Street. You're in the middle of Georgetown, surrounded by restaurants, shops, and bars. Go crazy! See chapters 5, 7, and 8 for recommendations.

WALKING TOUR 3: DUPONT CIRCLE/ EMBASSY ROW

START:	**Dupont Circle (Metro to Dupont Circle).**
FINISH:	**Vice President's Residence/U.S. Naval Observatory (take the N2, N4, N6 buses back to either Dupont Circle or Farragut North).**
TIME:	**2 hours (not including stops). The distance is about 2 miles.**
BEST TIME:	**Any day is fine unless you want to tour the Brewmaster's Castle and/ or Anderson House, in which case you should see the descriptions for their public tour days and times, and plan accordingly.**
WORST TIME:	**Nighttime, since you won't be able to see the details on the houses.**

This is a rather lengthy walk. It's worthwhile, I think, especially because you'll see nearly the whole world—or at least its embassies—on this route.

(To see more, look for the national flags of other embassies located on side streets a few steps to the left or right.)

If you feel yourself tiring, you can catch the N2 Metrobus at a number of stops along this route and it will take you back to Dupont Circle. Some of the walk is uphill, which is why I'm suggesting this precaution. You can do the walk in reverse, taking the bus to your starting point as well, though the more interesting Gilded Age sites are closer to Dupont Circle, and I want you to see those while you're still fresh.

Embassies are not normally open to visitors. But if you're here in May, you'll want to know about the annual embassy open-house events (see p. 25). Some embassies do organize exhibitions and concerts featuring homeland artists, and you'll sometimes see notices about them in the *Washington Post* and *Washington City Paper*. For ways to tap into embassy events, see "The Best of D.C.'s International Scene" box, p. 234.

As for food, you won't find much of it as you wander along. Better to pick up a picnic at **Teaism** (p. 109) and stop in one of the garden areas along the way.

---

1 Dupont Circle

We'll start right in the center of the traffic circle so you can get a good look around. Dupont Circle is one of the most famous place names in D.C., at one and the same time a historic district, a traffic circle, and a progressive neighborhood that's been home, since the mid-1970s, to the city's LGBTQ community. In fact, every year on the Tuesday before Halloween, thousands of Washingtonians turn out to watch dozens of outrageously dressed drag queens sprint in high heels down 17th Street in the heart of the Dupont Circle neighborhood, participating in the High Heel Race, an event that's taken place since 1986.

Named for Civil War Naval hero Samuel Francis Du Pont, the circle is placed exactly where Washington's famed architect Pierre Charles L'Enfant envisioned it, though construction didn't begin until 1871, long after L'Enfant's death. For its center, Congress commissioned a small bronze statue of the Admiral, but the proud Du Pont family would have none of it. Without asking permission, they commissioned the two men behind the Lincoln Memorial—sculptor Daniel Chester French and architect Henry Bacon—to create the fountain you see in front of you. It replaced the bronze statue in 1921; on its shaft are allegorical figures representing the elements a sea captain needs to navigate and propel the boat forward. See if you can figure out which is "the stars," which is "the sea," and which is "the wind."

Cross Massachusetts Avenue to New Hampshire Avenue until you come to Sunderland Place, and stop at 1307 New Hampshire Avenue:

2 The Brewmaster's Castle (the Christian Heurich House Museum)

Known in less polite circles as "burp castle," this is the house beer built. Christian Heurich was a highly successful brewer who, in the first half of

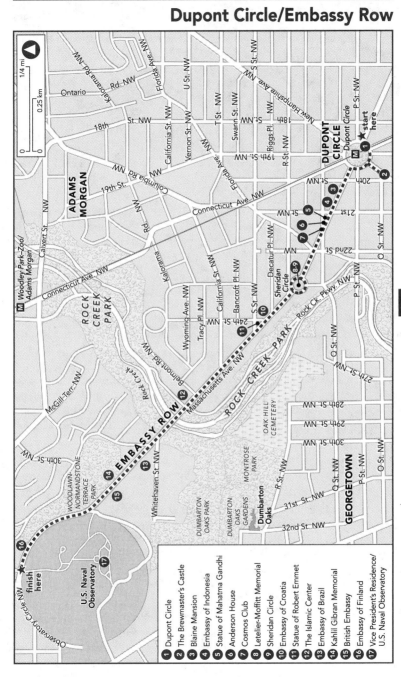

Dupont Circle/Embassy Row

1. Dupont Circle
2. The Brewmaster's Castle
3. Blaine Mansion
4. Embassy of Indonesia
5. Statue of Mahatma Gandhi
6. Anderson House
7. Cosmos Club
8. Letelier-Moffitt Memorial
9. Sheridan Circle
10. Embassy of Croatia
11. Statue of Robert Emmet
12. The Islamic Center
13. Embassy of Brazil
14. Kahlil Gibran Memorial
15. British Embassy
16. Embassy of Finland
17. Vice President's Residence/
    U.S. Naval Observatory

Daniel Chester French's marble fountain in the center of Dupont Circle.

the 20th century, was Washington, D.C.'s largest landowner and employer, after the federal government. He loved his work so much that he never retired, continuing to manage his brewery until his death at the age of 102 in 1945. That wasn't just a work ethic—the man had murals celebrating the joys of beer in his breakfast room and used as the slogan for his company, "Beer recommended for family use by Physicians in General." Yup, those were the days. You can see the interior on **tours** (Thurs–Sat 11:30am, 1, 2:30pm; $10 requested donation; no children under 10; www.heurich house.org; ✆ **202/429-1894**). If you can tour it, do so—the house is notable not just for the colorful history of its owner, but also for its importance architecturally. Built between 1892 and 1894, it is likely the first domestic structure framed with steel and poured concrete, an effort to make it fireproof. (The salamander symbol, at the top of the tower, was used as a superstitious shield against fire.) Many consider this Romanesque-style, 31-room structure to be one of the most intact late-Victorian structures in the country. But I really like spotting the gargoyles.

Walk toward 20th Street, turn right and continue north two blocks to Massachusetts Avenue. Turn left and on the corner you'll find 2000 Massachusetts Avenue, which is:

3 Blaine Mansion

The last standing mansion from the early days of Dupont Circle, this imposing brick and terra-cotta structure retains the name of its first owner: James G. Blaine. Had it not been for the Mugwumps—and don't you love it that we used to have political parties with such colorful names—he might well have become president instead of Grover Cleveland. As it was, charges of corruption involving illicit dealings with the railroads, ahem, derailed his campaign. This, despite the fact that Blaine had a longer and more distinguished career than most, having served as secretary of state twice, congressman and senator from Maine, and speaker of the House. The vertical sweep of the house surely impresses as much as the man, though to be honest, he barely lived here. Once the home was built, he decided it would be too costly to maintain and he leased it, first to Levi Leiter (an early co-owner of Marshall Field) and then to George Westinghouse. Yes, *that* Westinghouse. The latter bought it in 1901 and lived here until his death in 1914.

Continue in the same direction on Massachusetts Avenue to our first embassy at 2020 Massachusetts Avenue:

4 Embassy of Indonesia

The ornate structure occupied today by the Embassy of Indonesia is said to have cost $835,000 when it was built in 1903—the city's most expensive house at the time. Sadly, by the time the house was purchased by the Indonesians in 1951, the family fortune was so depleted that they let it go for a mere $350,000. A reminder that housing bubbles have been around for quite some time.

The man who commissioned its construction, Thomas Walsh, came to the United States from Ireland in 1869 at the age of 19. He headed west, and in 1876 struck it rich not once but twice, finding what is widely thought to be one of the richest veins of gold in the world. Suddenly a modern-day Midas, he moved to Washington, figuring a grand 60-room mansion was the way to make a splash in society. And remembering his roots, he's said to have embedded a nugget of gold ore in the porch. You'll notice that this neo-Baroque mansion is unusually curvaceous. That's because it's meant to evoke the look of an ocean liner. A grand staircase in the home itself is a direct copy of one on a White Star ocean liner.

The fortune depleter, daughter Evalyn Walsh McLean, was notable for the tragic turn her life took. Despite the jaunty title of her autobiography, *Father Struck It Rich!,* not much else went right in her life. Her son was killed at the age of 9 in a car crash and her daughter overdosed as a young woman. Husband Edward Beale McLean, an heir to the *Post* fortune, turned out to be an alcoholic, and together they burned through some $100 million. A large chunk of it went to the purchase of the famed Hope Diamond. Those who believe the diamond is cursed claim that McLean's misfortunes started with that purchase. She died nearly penniless at the age of 58. The diamond is now on display at the Smithsonian's Natural History Museum (see p. 155). The ornate and blindingly white statue poised outside the embassy depicts Saraswati, the Hindu goddess of learning and wisdom. Since Indonesia is home to the world's largest Muslim population, the display of a Hindu figure is intended to express Indonesia's respect for religious freedom.

Keep walking in the same direction to a small triangular park, where you'll find the:

5 Statue of Mahatma Gandhi

Striding purposefully, the man who led India to freedom from British rule in 1947 seems to be headed (aptly) for the **Embassy of India** (2107 Massachusetts Ave.), just across the adjacent side street. His walking stick, simple bowl, dress, and age in the sculpture suggest that this is a portrait of him on the famed protest march when he and a number of followers walked some 200 miles to the Arabian Sea to collect salt (and evade the British tax on that condiment). A turning point in the nonviolent fight for Indian freedom, it's an apt subject for this striking portrait.

6 Anderson House

Larz Anderson, an American diplomat, and his wife, Isabel Weld Perkins, author and Red Cross volunteer, took advantage of their immense Boston wealth and built not just a home but a palace. Their intent? To create a space large enough to serve as a headquarters for the Society of the Cincinnati, of which Larz was a member (and to which they bequeathed the home). Guided tours to this museum of the Gilded Age and clubhouse are available (see full write-up on p. 185). The membership of the society, founded in 1783, is composed of male descendants of officers in George Washington's Continental Army.

The building itself—sporting a cavernous two-story ballroom, a dining room seating 50, grand staircase, massive wall murals, acres of marble, and 23-karat gold trim—is palatial.

Head across the street to 2121 Massachusetts Avenue, the:

7 Cosmos Club

A prestigious private social club, Cosmos Club was founded in 1878 as a gathering place for scientists and public-policy intellectuals. The National Geographic Society spun off from the Cosmos 10 years later. The Cosmos Club's first meeting was held in the home of John Wesley Powell, the soldier and explorer who first navigated the Colorado River through the Grand Canyon in a dory. Since then, three presidents, two vice presidents, a dozen Supreme Court justices, 36 Nobel Prize winners, 61 Pulitzer Prize winners, and 55 recipients of the Presidential Medal of Freedom have numbered among its ranks. But none of them were women until 1988, when the Washington, D.C., Human Rights Office ruled that the club's men-only policy was discriminatory and illegal and the club admitted its first women members—a group of 18 that included the then-U.S. secretary of labor, a chief judge of the U.S. Court of Appeals, and several scientists and economists.

The club is the latest occupant of a French-inspired chateau built in 1901 with the railroad wealth of Richard and Mary Scott Townsend. His fortune came from the Erie Line; hers from the Pennsylvania Railroad (no joke). They hired the famed New York architectural firm of Carrère and Hastings, which created the New York Public Library, to build a chateau designed to resemble the Petit Trianon chateau—a royal hideaway at Versailles. Somewhat superstitious, the couple had the structure built around an older one. Apparently, a gypsy had once predicted that Mrs. Townsend would die "under a new roof." Despite these precautions, Mrs. Townsend did eventually pass away (darn!).

As you head toward Sheridan Square, look for the Romanian Chancery and the **Embassy of Ireland** (2234 Massachusetts Ave. NW). In front of these two is the:

8 Letelier/Moffitt Memorial

On September 21, 1976, Orlando Letelier, the former foreign minister of ousted Chilean President Salvador Allende, offered his colleague Ronni

Memorial bas-relief portraits of Orlando Letelier and Ronni K. Moffitt.

Karpen Moffitt and her husband, Michael, a ride home. A car bomb killed Letelier and Ronni Moffitt; Michael Moffitt survived. This small cylindrical monument honors the memory of Letelier and Moffitt. Thousands showed up later that week for a hastily organized protest funeral march. For years, rumors circulated that the American government was also in some way involved. But in 2016, the U.S. government released CIA documents that clearly laid the blame on Chilean dictator General Augusto Pinochet, the man who had ousted Allende in a military coup. Pinochet had sent Chilean secret police agents to the U.S. capital to carry out this terrorist act.

Turn away from the Memorial and look at:

9 Sheridan Circle

The Civil War officer mounted on his muscular horse is General Philip H. Sheridan, commander of the Union cavalry and the Army of the Shenandoah. His horse Rienzi, who carried him through 85 battles and skirmishes, became almost as famous during the war as "the steed that saved the day."

Sculpted by Gutzon Borglum, who carved the presidential faces on South Dakota's Mount Rushmore, the statue depicts Sheridan rallying his men at the Battle of Cedar Creek in northern Virginia on October 19, 1864. Sheridan was 15 miles north in the town of Winchester when a Confederate force under General Jubal A. Early surprised and drove back his army. Racing to the battle site on stout-hearted Rienzi, Sheridan led his men in a victorious counterattack.

Sheridan's wife is said to have chosen the site for the statue, which is flanked by two hidden pools. Sheridan's son, Second Lieutenant Philip H. Sheridan, Jr., served as a model for the statue. He was present at the unveiling in 1908, as was President Theodore Roosevelt. I suggest crossing (carefully) into the circle to get a close-up look.

10 General Philip Sheridan Memorial statue.

Carefully cross the Circle again, back to Massachusetts Avenue and continue going northwest to 2343 Massachusetts Avenue, the:

10 Embassy of Croatia

Outside the building the muscular figure of St. Jerome the Priest (A.D. 341–420) sits hunched over a book, his head in his hand. Jerome, the pedestal of the statue informs us, was "the greatest Doctor of the Church." This is a reference to his work in translating the Bible from Hebrew into Latin, a version called the Vulgate because it was in the language of the common people of the day. Historically, it is considered the most important vernacular edition of the Bible. At times in his younger years, Jerome's religious faith declined; he became involved in numerous theological disputes, and he spent several years in the desert leading an ascetical life while fighting temptations. I get the feeling this glum statue is commemorating those troubled times. The statue initially sat on the grounds of the Franciscan Abbey near Catholic University; it was moved here when the nation of Croatia was created at the breakup of Yugoslavia.

Continue walking to the 2400 block of Massachusetts Avenue where, in a triangular park, you'll see the:

11 Statue of Robert Emmet

Within a landscaped grove of Irish yew trees, the Irish revolutionary stands in a pose that he reportedly struck in Dublin in 1803 when a British court sentenced him to death by hanging. He appears to be gazing toward the Embassy of Ireland two blocks away. Born in 1778, Emmet led a failed uprising in Dublin on July 23, 1803. The statue was presented to the Smithsonian Institution in 1917 as a gift to the American public from a group of American citizens of Irish ancestry. It was moved to its present site in 1966, marking the 50th anniversary of Irish independence. In 2016, in honor of the centenary of the Easter Rising, the Irish ambassador re-dedicated the statue and the National Park Service refurbished the little park to make the bronze statue more visible.

Note the numerous embassies en route to the next stop, including the **Embassy of Japan** (2520 Massachusetts Ave.), set back behind a cobblestone courtyard. The 1932 Georgian Revival structure suggests the Far East with a subtle "rising sun" above the balcony over the door.

On the right is the **Embassy of Turkey** (2525 Massachusetts Ave.). The statue in front is of Mustafa Kemal Ataturk, the founder of modern Turkey.

Just before the bridge, head to 2551 Massachusetts Avenue:

12 The Islamic Center

The 160-foot-tall white limestone minaret, soaring above Embassy Row, makes the Islamic Center impossible to miss. From it, a loudspeaker intones the call to prayer five times daily. Built in 1949, the center does not line up directly with the street but faces Mecca. On Friday afternoons, throngs of the faithful pour into the mosque for prayer services, many of them embassy employees attired in their native dress. At times, prayer rugs are spread in the courtyard or even on the sidewalk outside the iron fence. This is when Embassy Row takes on its most dramatic multicultural look.

Visitors are welcome inside (daily 10am–5pm), but be sure to remove your shoes before entering the mosque itself; leave them in one of the slots provided on the entrance wall. Men should dress neatly; no shorts. Women are not allowed to wear sleeveless clothes or short dresses and must cover their hair. The interior, filled with colorful Arabic art, is well worth these preliminaries. Persian rugs blanket the floor, overlapping one another; 7,000 blue tiles cover the lower walls in mosaic patterns; eight ornate pillars soar overhead, ringing a huge copper chandelier. The carved pulpit is inlaid with ivory, and stained-glass windows add more color.

embassy row: **THE LOWDOWN**

Today, there are more than 170 foreign embassies, chanceries, or ambassadorial residences in Washington, D.C., and the majority of them are located on or near the 2-mile stretch of Massachusetts Avenue between Dupont Circle and Wisconsin Avenue NW. As a result, it's been dubbed Embassy Row.

A word on those distinctions: An *embassy* is the official office or residence

of the ambassador. Some ambassadors live and work in the embassy; others maintain separate residences, commuting to their job like the rest of us. A *chancery* is the embassy's office; this is where you might apply for a visitor's visa. It could be located within the embassy or not. Some countries also provide separate offices for special missions, such as the military attaché's office and for cultural centers.

Cross the bridge and look down: 75 feet below is Rock Creek Parkway as well as the 1,700-acre Rock Creek Park (p. 200). Walk on and take the time to look at the embassies you'll be passing until you get to 3006 Massachusetts Avenue, the:

13 Embassy of Brazil

This stately, palace-like building, next door to the black, boxlike circa-1971 Brazilian Chancery, is the ambassador's residence. Derived from an Italian Renaissance palazzo, the residence was designed in 1908 by John Russell Pope, a leader of the city's early-20th-century neoclassicist movement. The Jefferson Memorial, the West Building of the National Gallery of Art, and National Archives are among Pope's other local works.

Keep walking in the same direction and look to the right side to find the:

14 Kahlil Gibran Memorial

An elaborate 2-acre garden, eight-sided star fountain, circular walkway, shaded benches, and bronze bust celebrate the life and achievements of the Lebanese-American philosopher. Dedicated on May 24, 1991, it is a gift "to the people of the United States" from the Kahlil Gibran Centennial Foundation. Born in 1883 in a village near the Biblical Cedars of Lebanon, Gibran arrived in Boston as a child. Building a successful career as an artist and author, he published widely quoted books in English and Arabic. He died in New York City in 1931. Excerpts from his writings are etched into the memorial's circular wall, among them: WE LIVE ONLY TO DISCOVER BEAUTY. ALL ELSE IS A FORM OF WAITING. If you need to rest your feet, this lovely garden is the perfect place to do so.

Continue your stroll to 3100 Massachusetts Avenue, the:

15 British Embassy

Out in front and instantly recognizable in a familiar pose, **Sir Winston Churchill** stands in bronze. One foot rests on embassy property, thus British soil; the other is planted on American soil. Anglo-American unity is the symbolism, but the placement also reflects Churchill's heritage as the child of a British father and an American mother. His right hand is raised in the iconic familiar V for Victory sign he displayed in World War II. His other hand often sports a small bouquet of fresh flowers, left by admirers. The English-Speaking Union of the United States commissioned the statue, which was erected in 1965. The statue stands on a granite plinth; beneath it are blended soils from Blenheim Palace, his birthplace; the rose garden at Chartwell, his home; and his mother's home in Brooklyn, NY. Turn your back on Churchill for a moment and look directly across the street to see a smiling Nelson Mandela gazing back at you, his arm raised in a clenched fist. Churchill and Mandela appear to be communicating. Mandela stands in front of the South African Embassy, which erected this statue in 2013.

The U-shaped, redbrick structure rising behind the World War II prime minister is the main chancery, built in 1930. Sir Edwin Lutyens, one of Great Britain's leading architects of the day, designed both it and the ambassador's residence, located out of sight behind the chancery. The

An embassy in Washington, D.C., is different from embassies in most other capitals, where people visit them only if they have to; that is, to get a visa or to conduct official business. In Washington, D.C., embassies are expected to be much more. They need to be able to open windows on the life and culture of the countries they represent, not only for the select few, but for all Washingtonians and visitors to the capital who want to know. Many do, because Americans are curious by nature.

—Jukka Valtasaari, Finnish ambassador, 1988–1996 and 2001–2005

American Institute of Architects describes the pair as a "triumph," noting that Lutyens rejected the prevailing passion for neoclassical structures and instead created a colonial American design. Others suggest it looks like an 18th-century English country house. Whatever, it makes an impressive show. Too bad the concrete box on the right, an office building dedicated by Queen Elizabeth II in 1957, failed to match the architectural standard Lutyens set. The round glass structure, another unfortunately bland modern addition, is for conferences.

Cross Massachusetts Avenue at the stoplight and step from the crosswalk onto the grassy path straight ahead of you to find a steep, heavily wooded slope that drops into a slender canyon. It is Rock Creek Trail, and if you like, you can take a little nature detour. It's amazing how quickly, within 60 seconds really, you leave the hubbub of the city and find yourself in nature. Continue walking to 3301 Massachusetts Avenue, the dramatic:

16 Embassy of Finland

An abstract metal-and-glass front forms a green wall of climbing plants on a bronze, gridlike trellis. Within, huge windows in the rear look out onto a thickly forested slope, as if—to quote architectural historian William Morgan—"The Finns have brought a bit of the woods to Washington." Completed in 1994, the embassy was designed to display the life and culture of Finland. The embassy is open for tours one afternoon a month at 2pm, and you must register in advance. The embassy also welcomes the public on weekends and sometimes Wednesdays from 3 to 7pm when an exhibition is on view.

From the Finnish Embassy, look across the street to the green slope behind the tall iron fence. That white Victorian-style house partially visible atop the hill is the:

17 Vice President's Residence/U.S. Naval Observatory

Number One Observatory Circle is the official residence of the U.S. vice president. The wooded estate surrounding the residence is the site of the U.S. Naval Observatory; the large white dome holding its 12-inch refracting telescope is easily seen on the right. Built in 1893, the veep's house initially was assigned to the observatory's superintendent. But in 1923 the chief of naval operations took a liking to it, booted out the superintendent, and made the house his home. In 1974, Congress evicted the Navy and transformed it into the vice president's residence.

Up to that time, vice presidents occupied their own homes, as Supreme Court judges, Cabinet members, and congressional representatives and senators still do. But providing full security apparatus for the private homes of each new vice president became expensive. Nelson Rockefeller, veep in the Ford administration, was the first potential resident, but he used the house only for entertaining. So Vice President Walter Mondale became its first official occupant, leading the way for succeeding vice presidents. If you see a big tent on the front lawn, it usually means the vice president is hosting a gala reception.

The telescope at the U.S. Naval Observatory.

The observatory moved from Foggy Bottom to its present location in 1910. At the time, the hilltop site was rural countryside. One of the oldest scientific agencies in the country, the U.S. Naval Observatory was established in 1830. Its primary mission was to oversee the Navy's chronometers, charts, and other navigational equipment. Today it remains the preeminent authority on precise time. Scientists take observations of the sun, moon, planets, and selected stars, determine the precise time, and publish astronomical data needed for accurate navigation.

PLANNING YOUR TRIP

A s with any trip, a little preparation is essential. This chapter provides a variety of planning tools, including information on getting to D.C., tips on transportation within the city, and additional on-the-ground resources.

GETTING THERE
By Plane

Three airports serve the Washington, D.C., area. The following information should help you determine which airport is your best bet.

Ronald Reagan Washington National Airport (DCA) (www.flyreagan.com; ℰ **703/417-8000**). lies 4 miles south of D.C., across the Potomac River in Virginia, about a 10-minute trip by car in non-rush-hour traffic, and 15 to 20 minutes by Metro anytime. National's eight airlines fly nonstop to/from more than 95 destinations, nearly all domestic. Its proximity to the District and its direct access to the Metro rail system are reasons why you might want to fly into National. For Metro information, go online at **www.wmata.com**.

Washington Dulles International Airport (IAD) (www.flydulles.com; ℰ **703/572-2700**) is 26 miles outside the capital, in Chantilly, Virginia, a 35- to 45-minute ride to downtown in non-rush-hour traffic. Of the three airports, Dulles handles more daily nonstop international flights (56), with about 38 airlines flying nonstop to 138 destinations. The airport is not as convenient to the heart of Washington as National, but it's more convenient than BWI, thanks to an uncongested airport access road that travels half the distance toward Washington.

Last but not least, **Baltimore–Washington International Thurgood Marshall Airport (BWI)** (www.bwiairport.com; ℰ **410/859-7111**) is located about 45 minutes from downtown, a few miles outside of Baltimore. One factor especially has always recommended BWI to travelers: the major presence of **Southwest Airlines.** Its service comprises 70% of the airport's business, and it often offers real bargains. (Southwest also serves Dulles and National airports, but in a much smaller capacity.) BWI offers the greatest number of daily nonstop flights, 567, its 16 airlines flying to 79 domestic destinations and 13 international destinations.

GETTING INTO TOWN FROM THE AIRPORT

All three airports could really use better signage, especially since their ground transportation desks always seem to be quite a distance from the gate at which you arrive. Keep trudging, and follow baggage claim signs, because ground transportation operations are always situated near baggage carousels.

TAXI SERVICE For a trip to downtown D.C., you can expect a taxi to cost at least $15 for the 10- to 20-minute ride from National Airport, $68 for the 35- to 45-minute ride from Dulles Airport, and about $90 for the 45-minute ride from BWI. Expect taxis to add a $3 airport pickup charge to your fee.

SUPERSHUTTLE SuperShuttle (www.supershuttle.com; © **800/258-3826**) offers assorted car services, but its least expensive option is shared-ride travel in a van providing door-to-door service between the airport and your destination, whether in the District or in a suburban location. Make reservations by phone or online and proceed to the SuperShuttle desk or computerized kiosk in your airport to check in. The only drawback to this service is the roundabout route the driver must follow, as he or she drops off or picks up other passengers en route. If you arrive after the SuperShuttle desk has closed, you can summon a van by calling customer service at the above number or using the computerized kiosk on-site. The 24-hour service bases its fares on zip code, so to reach downtown, expect to pay about $15, plus $10 for each additional person, from National; $30, plus $10 per additional person, from Dulles; and $39, plus $10 per additional person, from BWI.

Public Transportation Options by Airport
FROM RONALD REAGAN WASHINGTON NATIONAL AIRPORT

If you are not too encumbered with luggage, you should take **Metrorail** into the city. Metro's Yellow and Blue Lines stop at the airport and connect via an enclosed walkway to level two, the concourse level of the main terminal, adjacent to terminals B and C. If yours is one of the airlines that still uses the "old" terminal A (Southwest, Air Canada, Frontier), you'll have a longer walk to reach the Metro. Signs pointing the way can be confusing, so ask an airport employee if you're headed in the right direction. **Metrobuses** also serve the area, should you be going somewhere off the Metro route. But Metrorail is fastest, a 15- to 20-minute non-rush-hour ride to downtown. If you haven't purchased a SmarTrip fare card online in advance (see box on SmarTrip cards, p. 292), you can do so at the Metro station. The base fare is $2, and goes up from there depending on when (fares increase during rush hours) and where you're going.

If you're renting a car from an on-site **car rental agency** (most are on-site in Terminal A), follow signs toward Terminal Parking Garage A, approximately 10 minutes from Terminals A & B and 15 minutes from Terminal C. You can also take the complimentary airport shuttle marked "Parking/Rental Car," which now stops at door 4 on the Ticketing Level/3rd Floor due to construction. Get off at the Terminal Garage A/Rental Car stop. If you've rented from an off-premises agency (such as Advantage), you'll want to take that same shuttle bus.

To get downtown by car, follow the signs out of the airport for the George Washington Parkway, headed north toward Washington. Stay on the parkway until you see signs for I-395 N. to Washington. Take the I-395 N. exit, which takes you across the 14th Street Bridge. Stay in the left lane crossing the bridge and follow the signs for Rte. 1, which will put you on 14th Street NW. (You'll see the Washington Monument off to your left.) Ask your hotel for directions from 14th Street and Constitution Avenue NW. Or take the more scenic route, always staying to the left on the GW Parkway as you follow the signs for Memorial Bridge. You'll be driving alongside the Potomac River, with the Capitol and memorials in view across the river; then, as you cross over Memorial Bridge, you're greeted by the Lincoln Memorial. Stay left coming over the bridge, swoop around to the left of the Memorial, take a left on 23rd Street NW, a right on Constitution Avenue, and then, if you want to be in the heart of downtown, left again on 15th Street NW.

Note: The Arlington Memorial Bridge is undergoing a multi-year rehabilitation project to repair structural issues and remove and repave sections of the bridge deck. Traffic may be significantly impacted if a lane or portion of the bridge is closed for work. Be prepared and check traffic before you go. For updates on the project, visit www.go.nps.gov/memorialbridge.

FROM WASHINGTON DULLES INTERNATIONAL AIRPORT Metrorail trains do not connect directly with Dulles Airport yet (latest word is that this will happen in late 2020 or possibly 2021), so you must first catch the **Washington Flyer Silver Line Express Bus** (www.flydulles.com/iad/silver-line-express-bus-metrorail-station; ✆ **888/927-4359**) to reach the closest Metro station, the Silver Line's Wiehle Ave./Reston East depot. Find the counter at Arrivals Door no. 4 in the main terminal or, if you're in the baggage claim area, go up the ramp at the sign for Door no. 4 to purchase the $5 ticket for the bus. Buses to the Wiehle Ave./Reston East Metro station run daily, every 15 to 20 minutes; the trip takes about 15 minutes. Once you arrive at the Metro station, you can purchase a Metro SmarTrip fare card to board a Silver Line train bound for Largo Town Center, which heads into D.C.

It may be more convenient to take the **Metrobus** (no. 5A) that runs between Dulles (buses depart from curb 2E, outside the ground transportation area) and the L'Enfant Plaza Metro station, located across from the National Mall and the Smithsonian museums. The bus departs every 30 to 40 minutes weekdays, hourly on weekends. It costs $7.50 (you must use a SmarTrip card—see box, p. 292—or have exact change) and takes 45 minutes to an hour.

If you're renting a car at Dulles, head down the ramp near the baggage-claim area and walk outside through door 2, 4, or 6 to curb 2C or 2F to wait for your rental car's shuttle bus. The buses come every 5 minutes or so en route to nearby rental lots. Almost all the major companies are represented.

To reach downtown Washington from Dulles by car, exit the airport and stay on the Dulles Access Road, keeping left as the road eventually leads right into I-66 E. Follow I-66 E., which takes you across the Theodore Roosevelt Memorial Bridge; be sure to stay in the center lane as you cross the bridge, and this will put you on Constitution Avenue (Rte. 29). Ask your hotel for directions from this point.

FROM BALTIMORE–WASHINGTON INTERNATIONAL AIRPORT
Washington's Metro service runs an Express Metro Bus ("B30") between its Metrorail Green Line Greenbelt station and BWI Airport. The airport has a bus stop on its lower level, in Concourse A/B. Look for PUBLIC TRANSIT signs to find the bus, which operates Monday through Friday only, departs every 60 minutes, takes about 30 minutes to reach the station, and costs $7.50. At the Greenbelt Metro station, you purchase a Metro farecard and board a Metro train bound for Branch Avenue, which will take you into the city. Depending on where you want to go, you can either stay on the Green Line or get off at the Fort Totten station to transfer to a Red Line train, whose stops include Union Station and various downtown locations.

You also have the choice of taking either an **Amtrak** (www.amtrak.com; *©* **800/872-7245**) or the Penn line of the **Maryland Rural Commuter (MARC)** train (http://mta.maryland.gov/marc-train; *©* **866/743-3682**) into the city. Both trains travel between the BWI Railway Station and Washington's Union Station, about a 30- to 45-minute ride. Both Amtrak (starting at $17 per person, one-way, depending on time and train type) and MARC ($7 per person, one-way) services run daily. A courtesy shuttle runs every 6 minutes or so (every 25 min. 1–5am) between the airport and the train station; stop at the desk near the baggage-claim area to check for the next departure time of both the shuttle bus and the train. Trains depart about once per hour.

BWI operates a large off-site **car rental facility.** From the ground transportation area, board a shuttle bus to the lot.

Here's how you reach Washington: Look for signs for I-195 and follow the highway west until you see signs for Washington and the Baltimore–Washington Parkway (I-295); head south on I-295. Get off when you see the signs for Rte. 50/New York Avenue, which leads into the District, via New York Avenue NE. Your hotel can provide specific directions from there.

National Airport Construction Alert!

Reagan National Airport is in the throes of a transformative improvement project, which does not affect flights into and out of the airport, but may well affect the roadway and Metro travel between the airport and the city. In 2020, construction at the airport means you can expect heavy traffic and delays, so allow extra time to get to and from National. For the latest details, visit National Airport's construction advisories webpage, **www.flyreagan.com/dca/construction-advisories**.

By Car

More than one-third of visitors to Washington arrive by plane, and if that's you, don't consider renting a car. The traffic in the city and throughout the region is abysmal, parking spaces are hard to find, garage and lot and metered street parking charges are exorbitant, and hotel overnight rates are even worse.

Furthermore, Washington is amazingly easy to traverse on foot, and our public transportation and taxi systems are accessible and comprehensive.

But if you are like most visitors, you're planning on driving here. No matter which road you take, there's a good chance you will have to navigate some portion of the **Capital Beltway** (I-495 and I-95) to gain entry to D.C. The Beltway girds the city, its approximately 64-mile route passing through Maryland and Virginia, with some 50 interchanges or exits leading off from it. The Beltway is nearly always congested, but especially during weekday morning and evening rush hours (roughly 5:30–9:30am and 3–7pm). Drivers can get a little crazy, weaving in and out of traffic.

The District is 240 miles from New York City, 40 miles from Baltimore, 700 miles from Chicago, 500 miles from Boston, and about 630 miles from Atlanta.

By Train

Amtrak (www.amtrak.com; ✆ **800/USA-RAIL** [872-7245]) offers daily service to Washington from New York, Boston, and Chicago. Amtrak also travels daily between Washington and points south, including Raleigh, Charlotte, Atlanta, cities in Florida, and New Orleans. Amtrak's **Acela Express** trains offer the quickest service along the "Northeast Corridor," linking Boston, New York, Philadelphia, and Washington, D.C. The trains travel as fast as 150 mph, making the trip between New York and Washington in times that range from less than 3 hours to 3 hours and 45 minutes, depending on the number of stops in the schedule. Likewise, Acela Express's Boston-Washington trip takes anywhere from 6½ hours to more than 8 hours, depending on station stops.

Amtrak runs fewer Acela trains on weekends and only honors passenger discounts (such as those for seniors or AAA members) on weekend Acela travel.

Amtrak offers a smorgasbord of rail passes and discounted fares; although not all are based on advance purchase, you often have more discount options by reserving early. Tickets for up to two children 2 to 12 cost half the price of the full adult fare when the children are accompanied by an adult. For more info, go to **www.amtrak.com**. *Note:* Most Amtrak travel requires a reservation, which means that every traveler is guaranteed, but not assigned, a seat.

Amtrak trains arrive at historic **Union Station** (see p. 131), 50 Massachusetts Ave. NE (www.unionstationdc.com; ✆ **202/371-9441**), a short walk from the Capitol, near several hotels, and a short cab or Metro ride from downtown. Union Station is D.C.'s transportation hub, with its own Metrorail station, Metrobus and DC Circulator bus stops, taxi stands, bikeshare and bike rental locations, rental car facilities, tour bus centers, intra-city bus travel operations, and connection to D.C. Streetcar service.

By Bus

Bus travel is now in vogue, thanks to the rise of fabulously priced, clean, comfortable, and fast bus services. Quite a number of buses travel between Washington, D.C., and New York City, and a growing number travel between D.C. and cities scattered up and down the East Coast.

BoltBus (www.boltbus.com; ✆ **877/265-8287**) travels multiple times a day between D.C. and NYC for $13 to $45 each way; and between D.C. and at least three other cities (Wilmington, Del., Philadelphia, and Newark) for similarly low fares. Ditto **Megabus** (www.megabus.com; ✆ **877/462-6342**), which travels between Union Station and NYC several times a day for as little as $1 and as much as $46, one-way (most fares run in the $13–$25 range); and offers cheap travel between D.C. and 28 other locations, including Boston, Toronto, and Charlotte. **Vamoose Bus** (www.vamoosebus.com; ✆ **212/695-6766**) travels between Rosslyn, Virginia's stop near the Rosslyn Metro station, and Bethesda, Maryland's stop near the Bethesda Metro station, and locations near NYC's Penn Station, for $20 to $60 each way, accruing one point for every dollar you've paid for your ticket. Collect 120 points and you ride one-way for free.

Greyhound (www.greyhound.com; ✆ **800/231-2222**), the company behind BoltBus, travels all over the country for rates as cheap as BoltBus and other operations; its bus depot is also at Union Station.

GETTING AROUND

Washington is one of the easiest U.S. cities to navigate, thanks to its manageable size and easy-to-understand layout. I wish I could boast as well about the city's comprehensive public transportation system. Ours is the second-busiest rail transit network and the sixth-largest bus network in the country. It used to be swell, but 40+ years of increased usage and inadequate maintenance put the system into crisis mode in 2009, which the Washington Metropolitan Transit Authority (WMATA) has been working hard to correct ever since. And the system *is* safer and more reliable. But the effort continues, as you will surely encounter firsthand if you visit in 2020.

Here's what I recommend as you plan your trip: **Choose lodging close to where you want to be,** whether the center of the city, near the offices where you're doing business, or in a favorite neighborhood, and then consider all the transportation options in this chapter. In addition, I recommend the website **www.godcgo.com**, which has info about traversing the city, from every angle, with links to *Washington Post* articles reporting on the latest traffic and transit news. You might just find yourself shunning transportation anyway, for the pleasure of walking or bike-riding your way around the compact capital.

City Layout

Washington's appearance today pays homage to the 1791 vision of French engineer Pierre Charles L'Enfant, who created the capital's grand design of sweeping avenues intersected by spacious circles, directed that the Capitol and the White House be placed on prominent hilltops at either end of a wide stretch of avenue, and superimposed this overall plan upon a traditional street grid. The city's quadrants, grand avenues named after states, alphabetically ordered streets crossed by numerically ordered streets, and parks integrated with urban features are all ideas that started with L'Enfant. President George Washington, who had hired L'Enfant, was forced to dismiss the temperamental genius after

L'Enfant apparently offended quite a number of people. But Washington recognized the brilliance of the city plan and hired surveyors Benjamin Banneker and Andrew Ellicott, who had worked with L'Enfant, to continue to implement L'Enfant's design. (For further background, see chapter 2.)

The U.S. Capitol marks the center of the city, which is divided into **northwest (NW), northeast (NE), southwest (SW),** and **southeast (SE) quadrants.** Most, but not all, areas of interest to tourists are in the northwest. The boundary demarcations are often seamless; for example, you are in the northwest quadrant at the National Museum of Natural History, but by crossing the National Mall to the other side to visit the Sackler Gallery, you put yourself in the southwest quadrant. Pay attention to the quadrant's geographic suffix; as you'll notice when you look on a map, some addresses appear in multiple quadrants (for example, the corner of G and 7th sts. appears in all four).

MAIN ARTERIES & STREETS From the Capitol, North Capitol Street and South Capitol Street run north and south, respectively. East Capitol Street divides the city north and south. The area west of the Capitol is not a street at all, but the National Mall, which is bounded on the north by Constitution Avenue and on the south by Independence Avenue.

The primary artery of Washington is **Pennsylvania Avenue,** which together with Constitution Avenue form the backdrop for parades, inaugurations, and other splashy events. Pennsylvania runs northwest in a direct line between the Capitol and the White House—if it weren't for the Treasury Building, the president would have a clear view of the Capitol—before continuing on a northwest angle to Georgetown, where it becomes M Street.

Constitution Avenue, paralleled to the south most of the way by Independence Avenue, runs east-west, flanking the Capitol and the Mall. Washington's longest avenue, **Massachusetts Avenue,** runs parallel to Pennsylvania (a few avenues north). Along the way, you'll find Union Station and then Dupont Circle, which is central to the area known as Embassy Row. Farther out are the Naval Observatory (the vice president's residence is here), the National Cathedral, American University, and, eventually, Maryland.

Connecticut Avenue, which runs more directly north (the other avenues run southeast to northwest), starts at Lafayette Square, intersects Dupont Circle, and eventually takes you to the National Zoo, on to the charming residential neighborhood known as Cleveland Park, and into Chevy Chase, Maryland, where you can pick up the Beltway to head out of town. Connecticut Avenue, with its chic-to-funky array of shops and clusters of top-dollar to good-value restaurants, is an interesting street to stroll.

Wisconsin Avenue originates in Georgetown; its intersection with M Street forms Georgetown's hub. Wisconsin Avenue basically parallels Connecticut Avenue; one of the few irritating things about the city's transportation system is that the Metro does not connect these two major arteries in the heart of the city. (Buses do, and, of course, you can always walk or take a taxi from one avenue to the other; read about the supplemental bus system, the DC Circulator, on p. 296.) Metrorail's first stop on Wisconsin Avenue is in Tenleytown, a residential area. Follow the avenue north and you land in the affluent Maryland cities of Chevy Chase and Bethesda.

FINDING AN ADDRESS   If you understand the city's layout, it's easy to find your way around. As you read this, have a map handy.

Each of the four corners of the District of Columbia is exactly the same distance from the Capitol dome. The White House and most government buildings and important monuments are west of the Capitol (in the northwest and southwest quadrants), as are major hotels and tourist facilities.

Numbered streets run north-south, beginning on either side of the Capitol with 1st Street. Lettered streets run east-west and are named alphabetically, beginning with A Street. (Don't look for J, X, Y, or Z streets, however—they don't exist.) After W Street, street names of two syllables continue in alphabetical order, followed by street names of three syllables; the more syllables in a name, the farther the street is from the Capitol.

Avenues, named for U.S. states, run at angles across the grid pattern and often intersect at traffic circles. For example, New Hampshire, Connecticut, and Massachusetts avenues intersect at Dupont Circle.

With this arrangement in mind, you can easily find an address. On lettered streets, the address tells you exactly where to go. For example, 1776 K Street NW is between 17th and 18th streets (the first two digits of 1776 tell you that) in the northwest quadrant (NW). *Note:* I Street is often written as "Eye" Street to prevent confusion with 1st Street.

To find an address on numbered streets, you'll probably have to use your fingers. For example, 623 8th Street SE is between F and G streets (the sixth and seventh letters of the alphabet; the first digit of 623 tells you that) in the southeast quadrant (SE). *One thing to remember:* You count B as the second

---

Be Smart: Buy a SmarTrip Card

If you are planning on using D.C.'s Metro system while you're here, do yourself a favor and order a **SmarTrip** card (www.wmata.com; (**888/762-7874**) online a couple of weeks in advance of your trip, so you'll have it with you when you arrive. SmarTrip is a permanent, rechargeable card that pays your way in the subway, on Metro and DC Circulator buses, and on other area transit systems, like the DASH buses in Old Town Alexandria, VA. It's easy to use: You just touch the card to the target on a fare-gate inside a Metro station, or farebox in a Metrobus. You can also purchase SmarTrip cards at vending machines in any Metro station; and at WMATA headquarters (Mon–Fri only), 600 5th St. NW;

its sales office at Metro Center (Mon–Fri only 8am–6pm), 12th and F streets NW; or at one of many retail outlets, such as CVS drugstores and Giant grocery stores. By purchasing the card in advance (but not too far ahead—the card expires if not used within 30 days of its purchase!), you'll avoid a hassle at the Metro station, where first-time use of the vending machines can be confusing. The cost of a SmarTrip card is $10: $2 for the card, plus $8 stored value to get you started. You can add value and special-value passes as needed online and at the SmarTrip Card Fare Vending/Passes machines in every Metro station, or even on a Metrobus, using the farebox. For more info, contact Metro.

To avoid risking the ire of fellow commuters, be sure to follow these guidelines: Stand to the right on the escalator so that people in a hurry can get past you on the left. And when you reach the train level, don't puddle at the bottom of the escalator, blocking the path of those coming behind you; move down the platform. Eating, drinking, and smoking are strictly prohibited on the Metro and in stations.

letter of the alphabet even though B Street North and B Street South are now Constitution and Independence avenues, respectively, but because there's no J Street, K becomes the 10th letter, L the 11th, and so on.

By Public Transportation
METRORAIL

The **Metrorail** system is in the midst of long-overdue repairs and reconstruction, which means you may encounter delays and possible cancellation of service on segments of different lines during your 2020 visit. Track and platform work is ongoing, and may even change day to day. Check Metro's website for the latest updates, or do as locals do: Sign up for Metro alerts (www. metroalerts.info) to receive timely announcements of Metrorail and Metrobus service delays, disruptions, schedule changes, advisories, and enhancements.

If you do ride Metrorail, try to avoid traveling during rush hour (Mon–Fri 5–9:30am and 3–7pm), since delays can be frequent, lines at fare machines long, trains overcrowded, and Washingtonians at their rudest. You can expect to get a seat during off-peak hours. All cars are air-conditioned.

Metrorail's base system of 91 stations and 118 miles of track includes locations at or near almost every sightseeing attraction; it also extends to suburban Maryland and northern Virginia. There are six lines in operation—**Red, Blue, Orange, Yellow, Green,** and the new **Silver** line. For now, the Silver Line has five stops that snake off the Orange line in Northern Virginia; future stops will lead to Washington Dulles Airport, by late 2020 if all goes as planned. The lines connect at several central points, making transfers relatively easy. All but Yellow, Green, and Silver Line trains stop at Metro Center; all except Red and Silver Line trains stop at L'Enfant Plaza; all but Blue, Orange, and Silver Line trains stop at Gallery Place–Chinatown. See the map inside the back cover of this book.

Metro stations are indicated by discreet brown columns bearing the station's name and topped by the letter M. Below the M is a colored stripe or stripes indicating the line or lines that stop there. To reach the train platform of a Metro station, you need a computerized **SmarTrip** card (see box above). **SmarTrip** card "Fare Vending" and "Add Value" machines are located inside the vestibule areas of the Metro stations. The blue SmarTrip Card Fare Vending machines sell SmarTrip cards for $10 ($2 for the card and $8 in trip value), add value up to $300, and add special-value passes to your SmarTrip Card; the

Metrorail doesn't go to Georgetown, and although Metro buses do (nos. 30, 31, 32, 33, 36, 38B, D1, D2, D5, D6, and G2), the public transportation I'd recommend is the **DC Circulator bus** (see box, p. 296), which travels two Georgetown routes: one that runs between the Rosslyn, VA, and Dupont Circle Metro stations, stopping at designated points in Georgetown along the way, and a second one that runs between Georgetown and Union Station. The buses come every 10 minutes from 6am to midnight Monday to Thursday; 6am to 3am Friday; 7am to 3am Saturday; and 7am to midnight Sunday. One-way fares cost $1.

machines accept debit and credit cards and bills up to $20, with change up to $10 returned in coins. The black Fare Vending machines are strictly for adding value to your current SmarTrip Card; the machines accept cash only, up to $20, with change up to $10 returned in coins.

Metrorail fares are calculated on distance traveled and time of day. Base fare during **non-peak hours** (Mon–Fri 9:30am–3pm; Mon–Thurs 7–11:30pm; Fri 7pm to 1am; Sat–Sun all day) ranges from a **minimum of $2** to a **maximum of $3.85.** During **peak hours** (Mon–Fri 5–9:30am and 3–7pm; Fri and Sat midnight–1am), the fare ranges from a **minimum of $2.25** to a **maximum of $6.**

For best value, consider buying a $14.75 **1-Day Rail/Bus** pass or a $38.50 **7-Day short trip** pass for travel on Metrorail. You can buy these online, adding the value to the SmarTrip card you're purchasing, or at the machines in the stations. See Metro's website for details.

Up to two children ages 4 and under can ride free with a paying passenger. Seniors (65 and older) and travelers with disabilities (with valid proof) ride Metrorail and Metrobus for a reduced fare.

To get to the train platforms, enter the station through the faregates, touching your SmarTrip card to the SmarTrip logo–marked target on top of the regular faregates or on the inside of the wide faregates. When you exit a station, you touch your card again to the SmarTrip logo–marked target on the faregate at your destination. If you arrive at a destination and the exit faregate tells you that you need to add value to your SmarTrip Card to exit, use the brown Exit-fare machines near the faregate to add the necessary amount—cash only.

Most Metro stations have more than one exit. To save yourself time and confusion, try to figure out ahead of time which exit gets you closer to where you're going. In this book, I **include the appropriate exit for every venue.**

Metrorail opens at 5am weekdays, 7am Saturday, and 8am Sunday, operating until 11:30pm Monday through Thursday, 1am Friday and Saturday, and 11pm Sunday. Visit www.wmata.com for the up-to-date info on routes and schedules.

METROBUS

The Transit Authority's bus system is a comprehensive operation that encompasses 1,500 buses traveling 325 routes, making about 11,500 stops, operating within a 1,500-square-mile area that includes major arteries in D.C. and the

Virginia and Maryland suburbs. The system is gradually phasing in new, sleekly designed red and silver buses that run on a combination of diesel and electric hybrid fuel.

The Transit Authority is also working to improve placement of bus stop signs. For now, look for red, white, and blue signs that tell you which buses stop at that location. Eventually, signage should tell you the routes and schedules. In the meantime, the Transit Authority has inaugurated electronic NEXT BUS signs at some bus stops that post real-time arrival information and alerts. You can also find out when the next bus is due to arrive at www.wmata.com (click on the NEXT BUS popup box on your screen and enter intersection, bus route no., or bus stop code).

Base fare in the District, using a SmarTrip card, is $2, or $4.25 for the faster express buses, which make fewer stops. There may be additional charges for travel into the Maryland and Virginia suburbs. Bus drivers are not equipped to make change, so if you have not purchased a SmarTrip card (see box, p. 292) or a pass, be sure to carry exact change.

If you'll be in Washington for a while and plan to use the buses a lot, buy a 1-week pass ($17.50), which loads onto a SmarTrip card.

Most buses operate daily around-the-clock. Service is quite frequent on weekdays, especially during peak hours, and less frequent on weekends and late at night. Up to two children 4 and under ride free with a paying passenger on Metrobus, and there are reduced fares for seniors and travelers with disabilities. If you leave something on a bus, on a train, or in a station, call **Lost and Found** Monday through Friday 9am to 5pm at ✆ **202/962-1195.**

By Car

If you must drive, be aware that traffic is always thick during the week, parking spaces hard to find, and parking lots ruinously expensive. Expect to pay overnight rates of $25 to $60 at hotels, hourly rates starting at $8 at downtown

---

Getting to the Atlas District

The long-awaited **DC Streetcar** is up and running, transporting people between Union Station and points along H Street NE in the hopping, nightlife-rich neighborhood known as the Atlas District. The distance between Union Station and the heart of the Atlas District is about 1 mile; the entire Union Station-to-Benning Road streetcar segment is 2.4 miles. All you have to do is ride the Metro to Union Station, and transfer to the streetcar from there. Here's the deal, though: When you arrive at the Union Station Metro stop, you must make your way up through the station to the bus deck level of the parking garage, then walk and walk and walk the marked pathway that leads to H Street, where you cross at the crosswalk to reach the streetcar stop. Dimly lit during the day, Union Station's garage is downright creepy at night. That's one drawback. Second, from Union Station, you're not that far, only a couple of blocks, from the start of the Atlas District; personally, I think it makes more sense most of the time to just walk the distance. For more information, go to www.dcstreetcar.com.

DC CIRCULATOR: fast, easy & cheap

Meet D.C.'s fantastic supplemental bus system. It's efficient, inexpensive, and convenient, traveling six routes in the city. These red-and-gray buses travel:

- The **Eastern Market to L'Enfant Plaza (EMLP) route** connecting the Eastern Market Metro Station, Barracks Row, the Navy Yard Metro station in Capitol Riverfront, the Southwest Waterfront and its Wharf, and L'Enfant Plaza near the National Mall, (Mon–Fri 6am–9pm, Sat–Sun 7am–9pm, with extended service on nights the Nationals have a game).

- The **Congress Heights-Union Station (CHUS) route** from Union Station to Barracks Row to Anacostia and back. (Mon–Fri 6am–9pm; Sat–Sun 7am–9pm).

- The **Union Station to upper Georgetown (GTUS) track** via the downtown (Mon–Thurs 6am–midnight; Fri 6am–3am; Sat 7am–3am; Sun 7am–midnight).

- The **Rosslyn to Dupont Circle route (RSDP)** that travels between the Rosslyn Metro station in Virginia and the Dupont Circle Metro station in the District, via Georgetown (Mon–Thurs 6am–midnight; Fri 6am–3am; Sat 7am–3am; Sun 7am–midnight).

- The **Woodley Park–Zoo to McPherson Square (WPAM) route** connecting those two Metro stations via Adams Morgan and the U & 14th Street Corridors (Mon–Thurs 6am–midnight; Fri 6am–3:30am; Sat 7am–3:30am; Sun 7am–midnight).

- The **National Mall (NM)** route, which loops the National Mall from Union Station and stops at 14 other sites en route (Winter: Mon–Fri 7am–7pm, Sat–Sun 9am–7pm; summer: Mon–Fri 7am–8pm, Sat–Sun 9am–8pm).

Buses stop at designated points on their routes (look for the distinctive red-and-gold sign, often topping a regular Metro bus stop sign) every 10 minutes. The fare is free (pending an ongoing initiative from Mayor Muriel Bowser). For easy and fast transportation in the busiest parts of town, you can't beat it. Go to www.dccirculator.com or call ☏ **202/671-2020.**

parking lots and garages, and flat rates starting at $20 in the most popular parts of town, such as Georgetown and Penn Quarter. If you're hoping to snag one of the 18,000 metered parking spaces on the street, you can expect to pay a minimum of $2.30 per hour by coin, credit or debit card, or smartphone. To use your smartphone, you must first sign up online at www.parkmobile.com, or download the app, to register your license plate number and credit card or debit card number. Once you arrive in D.C. and park on a street that requires payment for parking, you simply call the phone number marked on the meter or nearby kiosk (or use the app), and follow the prompts to enter the location ID marked on the meter and the amount of time you're paying for. If your parking space has neither a meter nor Parkmobile number to call, pay for parking at the nearby kiosk, print a receipt, and place it against the windshield.

D.C.'s traffic circles can be confusing to navigate. The law states that traffic already in the circle has the right of way, but you can't always depend on other drivers to obey that law. You also need to be aware of rush-hour rules: Sections of certain streets in Washington become **one-way** during rush hour: Rock

Creek Parkway, Canal Road, and 17th Street NW are three examples. Other streets change the direction of some of their traffic lanes during rush hour. Connecticut Avenue NW is the main one: In the morning, traffic in four of its six lanes travels south to downtown, and in late afternoon/early evening, downtown traffic in four of its six lanes heads north; between the hours of 9am and 3:30pm, traffic in both directions keeps to the normally correct side of the yellow line. Lit-up traffic signs alert you to what's going on, but pay attention. Unless a sign is posted prohibiting it, a right-on-red law is in effect.

FYI: If you don't drive to D.C. but need a car while you're here, you can rent one at the airport or at Union Station, as noted earlier in this chapter, or you can turn to a car-sharing service, such as **Zipcar** (www.zipcar.com), **Car2Go** (www.car2go.com), or **Enterprise CarShare** (www.enterprisecar share.com).

By Taxi, Uber, or Lyft

The D.C. taxicab system charges passengers according to time- and distance-based meters. Fares may increase, but at press time, fares began at $3.50, plus $2.16 per each additional mile and $1 per additional passenger. Other charges might apply (for example, if you telephone for a cab rather than hail one in the street, it'll cost you $2). Download the free DC Taxi app from the website www. dctaxionline.com, and order your transportation using your smartphone, à la Uber. *Note:* The big news about D.C. taxis is that they now accept credit cards.

Try **V.I.P. Cab Company** (✆ **202/269-9000**) or **Yellow Cab** (www.dcyellow cab.com; ✆ **202/544-1212**).

Or download the app for **Uber** (www.uber.com) or **Lyft** (www.lyft.com), both of which operate in the District.

By Boat

The many allures of the Southwest Waterfront Wharf include assorted transportation options for getting you there. In addition to public transportation, taxi, and bike-share programs already in place, the **Potomac Riverboat Company** (www.potomacriverboatco.com; ✆ **877/511-2628**) operates year-round water taxi service between the Wharf and Georgetown, Old Town Alexandria, and National Harbor; between Old Town Alexandria and the National Mall; and, in baseball season, between Old Town Alexandria and Nationals Park. A water jitney ferries passengers between the Wharf and East Potomac Park, April through November. Check **www.wharfdc.com** for details.

By Bike

Thanks to the city's robust bike-share program (**Capital BikeShare,** www. capitalbikeshare.com, ✆ **877/430-2453,** is the nation's largest, with more than 4,300 bikes and 500 bike stations), Washington, D.C., is increasingly a city where locals themselves get around by bike. The flat terrain of the National Mall and many neighborhoods make the city conducive to two wheels. Over 100 marked bike lanes traverse D.C. and bike paths through Rock Creek Park, the C&O Canal in Georgetown, along the waterfront via the Anacostia

Riverwalk Trail, and around the National Mall. Interested? Visit www.godcgo. com and click on the "Transportation Options" link under "Commuter" to download a map that shows bike lanes and Capital BikeShare stations, which are all over. The Capital BikeShare program might be a better option economically for members who use the bikes for short commutes, but be sure to consider that option, along with traditional bike-rental companies (see chapter 6, p. 206), which are also plentiful.

In addition to Capital Bikeshares, several dockless bike and electric scooter companies operate in D.C., including **Jump** (www.jump.com) and **Mobike** (www.mobike.com), so consider those if the thought of ditching your bike or scooter where you may appeals (rather than having to return it to a rack).

GUIDED TOURS

D.C. offers a slew of guided tours, from themed jaunts to sites where famous scandals occurred to Segway tours. Beyond those in this chapter are self-guided neighborhood walking trails on the **Cultural Tourism D.C.** website, **www.culturaltourismdc.org**. If you're here in September, be sure to check out Cultural Tourism D.C.'s Walkingtown D.C. offering of 50 free tours throughout the city over the course of 8 days.

On Foot

o **DC by Foot:** These tours are ostensibly free, but you are highly encouraged to tip at the end. Guides for **DC by Foot** (www.freetoursbyfoot.com/washington-dc-tours; © **202/370-1830**) like to spin humor with history as they shepherd participants around the sites. History is the emphasis on the popular National Mall tour, but other offerings cover such topics as spies and scandals or Lincoln's assassination; the outfit has expanded to include food, bike, bus, and photography tours. Unlike other guided tours, DC by Foot operates year-round.

o **Washington Walks:** Excellent guides and dynamite in-depth tours of neighborhoods off the National Mall make **Washington Walks** (www.washington walks.com; © **202/484-1565**) a long-time favorite. "Women Who Changed America" and "Abraham Lincoln's Washington" are among the most popular tours. Public walks ($20/person) take place April through November; private and group tours year-round.

o **DC Metro Food Tours: DC Metro** (www.dcmetrofoodtours.com; © **202/851-2268**) leads participants on 3½-hour-long gastronomic adventures in a particular neighborhood, serving side dishes of historical and cultural references. For example, a Georgetown tour might include a walk along the C&O Canal, a sampling of house-made pasta at a decades-old restaurant, tales of the neighborhood's famous residents (like President and Jacqueline Kennedy), and a sweet finish with dessert at one of the city's best bakeries. Ask about pub crawls. Rates vary from about $30 to $65 per person.

o **The Guild of Professional Tour Guides of Washington, D.C.:** Would you like your tour tailored to your interest in women's history or architecture?

The Guild (www.washingtondctourguides.com; ✆ **202/966-4935**), a membership organization for licensed, professional tour guides and companies, offers a slew of set tours, but also operates a guide-for-hire service on its website (click on "For Tourists," then "Book a Custom Tour"). Complete the online request form and then choose from among the responders. The price ranges from $40 to $60 per hour, for a minimum of 4 hours. These guides are the best of the best, with many members doubling as docents at places like the Capitol Visitor Center.

o **Segway Tours:** See the sights while riding self-propelling scooters that operate based on "dynamic stabilization" technology, which uses your body movements. **Segway Tours** (http://dc.citysegwaytours.com; ✆ **877/734-8687;** ages 16 and up) offers 2- and 3-hour tours year-round daily. The 2-hour tours cost $35 per person; the 3-hour tours cost $75 per person. (The cost includes training.) The operation also offers bike and walking tours and arranges tickets and passes for attractions.

By Bus

The three major companies that offer narrated bus tours of the city all operate out of Union Station: **Big Bus Tours** (www.bigbustours.com; ✆ **877/332-8689)**, **City Sights DC** (www.citysightsdc.com; ✆ **202/650-5444)**, and **Old Town Trolley Tours** (www.trolleytours.com/washington-dc/; ✆ **202/832-9800)**. Old Town Trolley Tours provides "entertainment narration" and is the only company authorized to operate the narrated tour throughout Arlington National Cemetery (p. 196). Big Bus Tours' Red Loop, National Mall route is the official sightseeing tour of National Mall and Memorial Parks. City Sights DC offers the most flexible array of add-on options, including a bike rental or boat tour. Big Bus and City Sights tour buses are double-deckers, which provide a fun point of view; and they also have air-conditioned interiors, which the trolleys do not (enclosed and heated in winter, the trolleys in summer open their windows). So each narrated tour has its individual appeals for you to mull over.

Old Town Trolley and Big Bus Tours allow you to buy tickets ahead of time online or at Union Station, which means you can begin your tour at any stop along the route, showing your ticket to board. City Sights DC allows you to purchase your tour online, but you must print out your voucher and redeem it at Union Station for the ticket that lets you board the bus. All three tour companies have booths at Union Station and include the station as a stop on their routes. At least one bus tour, Old Town Trolley Tours, provides scheduled free shuttle service between select hotels and a downtown stop on the tour, so be sure to inquire about that. All three of the bus tours provide hop-on, hop-off service and all three offer a night tour, which I recommend.

The basic narrated tour for each operation takes about 2 hours (if you don't get off and tour the sites, obviously), and trolleys/buses come by every 30 minutes or so. Rates start at $49/adult, $35/child for City Sights DC; $45/adult, $29/child for Old Town Trolley; and $49/adult, $35/child for Big Bus Tours. Check out each operation's website for full details.

By Boat

Potomac cruises offer sweeping vistas of the monuments and memorials, Georgetown, the Kennedy Center, and other Washington sights. Read the information below carefully, because not all boat cruises offer guided tours. Some of the following boats leave from Washington's waterfront, whether in Southwest or in Georgetown, and some from Old Town Alexandria. Parts of the Southwest Waterfront are still under development, so check boarding and parking information carefully online if you're booking a cruise that leaves from a D.C. dock. Consult the website, **www.wharfdc.com**, for the latest information about the Southwest Waterfront's newest cruise options.

o **Spirit of Washington Cruises,** Pier 4 at 6th and Water streets SW (www. spiritcruises.com/washington-dc; ℂ **866/302-2469;** Metro: Waterfront), offers trips daily year-round, including evening dinner, lunch, and brunch cruises, as well as a half-day excursion to Mount Vernon and back. Lunch and dinner cruises include DJ entertainment. The *Spirit of Washington* is a luxury, climate-controlled harbor cruise ship with four decks, including an outdoor observation deck, three bars, and windows designed for sightseeing.

o *Odyssey* (www.odysseycruises.com/washington-dc; ℂ **866/306-2469**) was designed specifically to glide under the bridges that cross the Potomac. The boat looks like a glass bullet, its wraparound, see-through walls and ceiling allowing for great views. You board the *Odyssey* at Pier 4, 580 Water Street NW (Metro: Waterfront). Year-round cruises available include lunch, Sunday brunch, and dinner excursions, with live entertainment provided during each cruise.

o The **Potomac Riverboat Company** ★ (www.potomacriverboatco.com; ℂ **877/511-2628** or 703/684-0580) offers several 90-minute round-trip, narrated tours aboard vessels that glide past Washington landmarks or along Old Town Alexandria's waterfront; certain cruises travel to Mount Vernon, where you hop off and reboard after you've toured the estate. You board the boats at the pier behind the Torpedo Factory in Old Town Alexandria at the foot of King Street, or, for the Washington monuments tour, at Georgetown's Washington Harbour or at the Wharf (at Transit Pier, on Wharf Street SW, between Blair Alley and 9th Street SW). A concession stand sells light refreshments onboard. April through October only.

o The **Capitol River Cruise**'s *Nightingales* (www.capitolrivercruises.com; ℂ **800/405-5511** or 301/460-7447) are historic 65-foot steel riverboats that can accommodate 90 people. The *Nightingales'* narrated jaunts depart Georgetown's Washington Harbour every hour on the hour, from 11am to 7pm, April through October (with an 8pm outing offered in summer months only). The 45-minute narrated tour travels past the monuments and memorials to National Airport and back. Bring a picnic or eat from the snack bar. To get here, take the Metro to Foggy Bottom and then walk into Georgetown, following Pennsylvania Avenue, which becomes M Street. Turn left on 31st Street NW and follow to the Washington Harbour complex on the water.

○ **DC Ducks** (www.dcducks.com; ℂ **202/966-3825**), operated by Old Town Trolley, feature land and water tours of Washington aboard the *DUKW,* an amphibious army vehicle (boat with wheels) from World War II. Ninety-minute guided tours aboard the open-air canopied craft include a land portion taking in major sights—the Capitol, Lincoln Memorial, Washington Monument, White House, and Smithsonian museums—and a 30-minute Potomac cruise. Passengers board just outside Union Station. Departures April through October are usually 10am to 4pm, every hour on the hour.

By Bike

Bike and Roll DC ★★ (www.bikeandrolldc.com; ℂ **202/842-2453**) offers a more active way to see Washington, from March to December. The company has designed several biking tours, including the popular Capital Sites Ride, which takes you past museums, memorials, the White House, the Capitol, and the Supreme Court. The ride takes 3 hours, covers 7 to 8 miles, and costs $44/hour adults, $34 children 12 and under. Bike the Sites provides a hybrid bicycle fitted to your size, a helmet, water bottle, light snack, and a professional guide. Tours depart from a location near the National Mall, at 955 L'Enfant Plaza SW, North Building Suite 905 (Metro: L'Enfant Plaza), and the guide imparts historical and anecdotal information as you go. Bike and Roll also offers this tour departing from the steps of the National Museum of American History, on the Mall. Bike and Roll rents bikes as well; see p. 153 in chapter 6.

[Fast FACTS] WASHINGTON, D.C.

Area Codes Within the District of Columbia, the area code is 202. In Northern Virginia it's 703, and in the Maryland suburbs, its 301. You must use the area code when dialing a phone number, whether it's a local 202, 703, or 301 phone number.

Business Hours Most museums are open daily 10am to 5:30pm; some, including several Smithsonians, stay open later in spring and summer. Most banks are open from 9am to 5pm weekdays, with some open Saturdays as well, for abbreviated hours. Stores typically open between 9 and 10am and close

between 8 and 9pm, Monday to Saturday.

Doctors Most hotels are prepared for medical emergencies and work with local doctors who are able to see ill or injured hotel guests. Also see "Hospitals," below.

Drinking Laws The legal age for purchase and consumption of alcoholic beverages is 21; proof of age is required and often requested at bars, nightclubs, and restaurants, so it's always a good idea to bring ID when you go out. Do not carry open containers of alcohol in your car or any public area that isn't zoned for alcohol consumption. The police can fine you on

the spot. Don't even think about driving while intoxicated.

Grocery stores, convenience stores, and other retailers can sell beer and wine 7 days a week. D.C. liquor stores are now open on Sunday. Bars and nightclubs serve liquor until 2am Sunday through Thursday and until 3am Friday and Saturday.

Electricity Like Canada, the United States uses 110–120 volts AC (60 cycles), compared to 220–240 volts AC (50 cycles) in most of Europe, Australia, and New Zealand. Downward converters that change 220–240 volts to 110–120 volts are difficult to find in the United States, so bring one with you.

Embassies & Consulates All embassies are located here in the nation's capital. Check for yours at www.embassy.org/embassies or call directory information at (202/555-1212.

Emergencies Call (911 for police, fire, and medical emergencies. This is a toll-free call.

If you encounter serious problems, contact the **Travelers Aid Society International** (www.travelersaid.org; (202/546-1127), a nationwide, nonprofit, social-service organization geared to helping travelers in difficult straits, from reuniting families separated while traveling to providing food and/or shelter to people stranded without cash. Travelers Aid operates help desks at Washington Dulles International Airport, Ronald Reagan Washington National Airport, and Union Station. At Baltimore–Washington International Thurgood Marshall Airport, a volunteer agency called **Pathfinders** ((410/859-7826) staffs the customer service desks throughout the airport.

Family Travel Field trips during the school year and family vacations during the summer keep Washington, D.C., crawling with kids all year long. More than any other city, Washington is crammed with historic sites, arts and science museums, parks, and recreational sites to interest young and old alike. Plus, the fact that so many attractions are free is a boon to the family budget.

Look for boxes on family-friendly hotels, restaurants, and attractions in their appropriate chapters.

Hospitals If you don't require immediate ambulance transportation but still need emergency-room treatment, call one of the following hospitals (and be sure to get directions): **Children's Hospital National Medical Center,** 111 Michigan Ave. NW ((202/476-5000); **George Washington University Hospital,** 900 23rd St. NW, at Washington Circle ((202/715-4000); **Medstar Georgetown University Hospital,** 3800 Reservoir Rd. NW ((202/444-2000); or **Howard University Hospital,** 2041 Georgia Ave. NW ((202/865-6100).

Internet & Wi-Fi Most hotels, resorts, cafes, and retailers now offer free Wi-Fi. Likewise, all three D.C. airports offer complimentary Wi-Fi. All D.C. hotels listed in chapter 4 offer Internet access, and most offer it for free.

Legal Aid While driving, if you are pulled over for a minor infraction (such as speeding), never attempt to pay the fine directly to a police officer; this could be construed as attempted bribery, a much more serious crime. Pay fines by mail or directly into the hands of the clerk of the court. If accused of a more serious offense, say and do nothing before consulting a lawyer. In the U.S., the burden is on the state to prove a person's guilt beyond a reasonable doubt, and everyone has the right to remain silent,

whether he or she is suspected of a crime or is actually arrested. Once arrested, a person can make one telephone call to a party of his or her choice. The international visitor should call his or her embassy or consulate.

LGBTQ Travelers The nation's capital is most welcoming to the gay and lesbian community. D.C.'s LGBTQ population is one of the largest in the country, with an estimated 7% to 10% of residents identifying themselves as such. The capital's annual, week-long Capital Pride celebration is held in June, complete with a street fair and a parade.

Dupont Circle, once the unofficial headquarters for gay life, continues to host the annual 17th Street High Heel Drag Race on the Tuesday preceding Halloween, and is home to long-established gay bars and dance clubs (see chapter 8), but the whole city is pretty much LGBTQ-friendly.

Mail At press time, domestic postage rates were 35¢ for a postcard and 55¢ for a letter. For international mail, a first-class letter of up to 1 ounce costs $1.15; a first-class postcard costs the same as a letter.

Mobile Phones AT&T, Verizon, Sprint, and T-Mobile are the primary cellphone networks operating in Washington, D.C., so there's a good chance you'll have full and excellent coverage anywhere in the city.

International visitors should check their **GSM (Global System for Mobile Communications) wireless**

	US$
Taxi from National Airport to downtown	18.00
Double room, moderate	250.00
Double room, inexpensive	180.00
Three-course dinner for one without wine, moderate	50.00
Glass of wine	12.00
Cup of coffee	2.75
1 gallon of regular unleaded gas	2.90
Admission to most museums	Free
1-day Metrorail pass	14.75

network to see where GSM phones and text messaging work in the U.S.

You can **rent** a phone before you leave home from **InTouch USA** (www.intouch usa.us; 🕾 **800/872-7626** in the U.S., or 703/222-7161 outside the U.S.).

You can purchase a pay-as-you-go phone from all sorts of places, from Amazon. com to any Verizon Wireless store. In D.C., Verizon has a store at Union Station (🕾 **202/682-9475**) and another at 1314 F St. NW (🕾 **202/624-0072**), to name just two convenient locations.

Money & Costs   If you are traveling to Washington, D.C., from outside the United States, you should consult a currency exchange website such as www.xe.com/curren-cyconverter to check up-to-the-minute exchange rates before your departure.

Anyone who travels to the nation's capital expecting bargains is in for a rude awakening, especially when it comes to lodging. Less expensive than New York and London, Washington, D.C.'s daily hotel rate nevertheless reflects the city's popularity

as a top destination among U.S. travelers, averaging $221 (according to most recent statistics). D.C.'s restaurant scene is rather more egalitarian: heavy on the fine, top-dollar establishments, where you can easily spend $100 per person, but with plenty of excellent bistros and small restaurants offering great eats at lower prices. When it comes to attractions, though, the nation's capital has the rest of the world beat, because most of its museums and tourist sites offer free admission.

In Washington, D.C., ATMs are ubiquitous, in locations ranging from the National Gallery of Art's gift shop to Union Station to grocery stores.

In addition to debit cards, credit cards are the most widely used form of payment in the United States. Beware of hidden credit card fees while traveling internationally. Check with your credit or debit card issuer to see what fees, if any, will be charged for overseas transactions. Fees can amount to 3% or more of the purchase price.

Newspapers & Magazines   The preeminent newspaper in Washington is the *Washington Post,* available online and sold in bookstores, train and subway stations, drugstores, and sidewalk kiosks all over town. These are also the places to buy other newspapers, such as the *New York Times,* and *Washingtonian* magazine, the city's popular monthly full of penetrating features, restaurant reviews, and nightlife calendars. The websites of these publications are www.washington-post.com, www.nytimes.com, and www.washingtonian.com. Also be sure to pick up a copy of *Washington City Paper,* a weekly publication available free all over the city, at CVS drugstores, movie theaters, you name it, but also online at www.wash-ingtoncitypaper.com.

Police   The number of different police agencies in Washington is quite staggering. They include the city's own Metropolitan Police Department, the National Park Service police, the U.S. Capitol police, the Secret Service, the FBI, and the

303

Metro Transit police. The only thing you need to know is: In an emergency, dial ℂ **911.**

Safety In the years following the September 11, 2001, terrorist attack on the Pentagon, the federal and D.C. governments, along with agencies such as the National Park Service, have continued to work together to increase security, not just at airports but also around the city, including at tourist attractions, and in the subway. The most noticeable and, honestly, most irksome aspect of increased security at tourist attractions can be summed up in three little words: **waiting in line.** Although visitors have always had to queue to enter the Capitol, the Supreme Court, and other federal buildings, now it can take more time to get through because of more scrutiny when you finally reach the door.

Besides lines, you will notice the intense amount of security in place around the White House and the Capitol, as well as a profusion of vehicle barriers.

Just because so many police are around, you shouldn't let your guard down. Washington, like any urban area, has a criminal element, so it's important to stay alert and take normal safety precautions. See "The Neighborhoods in Brief" in chapter 3 to get a better idea of where you might feel most comfortable.

Avoid deserted areas, especially at night, and don't go into public parks at night

unless there's a concert or a similar occasion attracting a crowd.

Avoid carrying valuables with you on the street, and don't display expensive cameras or electronic equipment. If you're using a map, consult it inconspicuously—or better yet, try to study it before you leave your room. In general, the more you look like a tourist, the more likely someone will try to take advantage of you. If you're walking, pay attention to who is near you as you walk. If you're attending a convention or event where you wear a name tag, remove it before venturing outside. Hold on to your purse, and place your wallet in an inside pocket. In theaters, restaurants, and other public places, keep your possessions in sight. Also remember that hotels are open to the public, and in a large hotel, security may not be able to screen everyone entering. Always lock your room door.

Senior Travel Members of **AARP** (www.aarp.org; ℂ **888/687-2277**) get discounts on hotels, airfares, and car rentals. Anyone over 50 can join.

With or without AARP membership, seniors often find that discounts are available to them at hotels, so be sure to inquire when you book your reservation. Venues in Washington that grant discounts to seniors include the Metro; certain theaters, such as the Shakespeare Theatre; and those few museums, such as the Phillips Collection, that charge

for entry. Each place has its own eligibility rules, including designated "senior" ages: The Shakespeare Theatre's is 60 and over, the Phillips Collection's is 62 and over, and the Metro discounts seniors 65 and over.

Smoking The District is smoke-free, meaning that the city bans smoking in restaurants, bars, and other public buildings. Smoking is permitted outdoors, unless otherwise noted.

Taxes The United States has no value-added tax (VAT) or other indirect tax at the national level. The sales tax on merchandise is 6% in the District, 6% in Maryland, and 6% in northern Virginia. Restaurant tax is 10% in the District, 6% in Maryland, and varied in Virginia, depending on the city and county. Hotel tax is 14.95% in the District, and averages 6% in Maryland and 4.3% in Virginia.

Telephones Most long-distance and international calls can be dialed directly from any phone. **To make calls within the United States and to Canada,** dial 1 followed by the area code and the seven-digit number. **For other international calls,** dial 011 followed by the country code, the city code, and the number you are calling.

Calls to area codes **800, 888, 877,** and **866** are toll free. However, calls to area codes **700** and **900** (chat lines, bulletin boards, "dating" services, and so on) can be expensive—charges of 95¢ to $3 or more per minute. Some numbers have minimum charges that can run $15 or more.

For **directory assistance** ("Information"), dial **411** for local numbers and national numbers in the U.S. and Canada. For dedicated long-distance information, dial 1, then the appropriate area code, plus 555-1212.

Time The continental United States is divided into **four time zones:** Eastern Standard Time (EST)—this is Washington, D.C.'s time zone—Central Standard Time (CST), Mountain Standard Time (MST), and Pacific Standard Time (PST). Alaska and Hawaii have their own zones. For example, when it's 9am in Los Angeles (PST), it's noon in Washington, D.C. (EST), 5pm in London (GMT), and 2am the next day in Sydney.

Daylight saving time is in effect from 2am on the second Sunday in March to 2am on the first Sunday in November. Daylight saving time moves the clock 1 hour ahead of standard time, so come that first Sunday in November, the clock is turned back 1 hour.

Tipping In hotels, tip **bellhops** at least $1 per bag ($2–$3 if you have a lot of luggage) and tip the **chamber staff** $1 to $2 per day (more if you've left a big mess). Tip the **doorman** or **concierge** only if he or she has provided you with some specific service (for example, getting you a cab or obtaining difficult-to-get theater tickets). Tip the **valet-parking attendant** $1 every time you get your car.

In restaurants, bars, and nightclubs, tip **service staff**

and **bartenders** 15% to 20% of the check, tip **checkroom attendants** $1 per garment, and tip **valet-parking attendants** $1 per vehicle.

As for other service personnel, tip **cab drivers** 15% of the fare; tip **skycaps** at airports at least $1 per bag ($2–$3 if you have a lot of luggage); and tip **hairdressers** and **barbers** 15% to 20%.

Toilets You won't find public toilets or "restrooms" on the streets of D.C. (other than in The Wharf), but they can be found in hotel lobbies, bars, restaurants, museums, service stations, and at many sightseeing attractions. Starbucks and fast-food restaurants abound in D.C., and these might be your most reliable option. Restaurants and bars in resorts or heavily visited areas may reserve their restrooms for patrons.

Travelers with Disabilities Although Washington, D.C., is one of the most accessible cities in the world, it is not perfect—especially when it comes to historic buildings, as well as some restaurants and shops. Theaters, museums, and government buildings are generally well-equipped. Still, for the least hassle, call ahead to places you hope to visit to find out specific accessibility features. In the case of restaurants and bars, I'm afraid you'll have to work to pin them down—no one wants to discourage a potential customer. Several sources might help. Destination: D.C.'s website offers some helpful, though hardly comprehensive, info,

http://washington.org/DC-information/washington-dc-disability-information, including links to the **Washington Metropolitan Transit Authority,** which publishes accessibility information on its website, www.wmata.com.

Visas The U.S. State Department has a Visa Waiver Program (VWP) allowing citizens of the following countries to enter the United States without a visa for stays of up to 90 days: Andorra, Australia, Austria, Belgium, Brunei, Chile, Czech Republic, Denmark, Estonia, Finland, France, Germany, Greece, Hungary, Iceland, Ireland, Italy, Japan, Latvia, Liechtenstein, Lithuania, Luxembourg, Malta, Monaco, the Netherlands, New Zealand, Norway, Portugal, San Marino, Singapore, Slovakia, Slovenia, South Korea, Spain, Sweden, Switzerland, Taiwan, and the United Kingdom. (**Note:** This list was accurate at press time; for the most up-to-date list of countries in the VWP, consult https://travel.state.gov/content/travel/en/us-visas/tourism-visit/visa-waiver-program.html.)

Even though a visa isn't necessary, in an effort to help U.S. officials check travelers against terror watch lists before they arrive at U.S. borders, visitors from VWP countries must register online through the Electronic System for Travel Authorization (ESTA) before boarding a plane or a boat to the U.S. Travelers must complete an electronic application providing basic personal and travel eligibility information.

Authorizations will be valid for up to 2 years or until the traveler's passport expires, whichever comes first. Currently, there is one $14 fee for the online application. Existing ESTA registrations remain valid through their expiration dates. *Note:* As of April 1, 2016, travelers from VWP countries must have an e-Passport to be eligible to enter the U.S. without a visa. E-Passports contain computer chips capable of storing biometric information, such as the required digital photograph of the holder.

Furthermore, the State Department states that "Under the Visa Waiver Program Improvement and Terrorist Travel Prevention Act of 2015, travelers in the following categories are no longer eligible to travel or be admitted to the United States under the Visa Waiver Program (VWP):

Nationals of VWP countries who have traveled to or been present in Iran, Iraq, Libya, Somalia, Sudan, Syria, or Yemen after March 1, 2011 (with limited exceptions for travel for diplomatic or military purposes in the service of a VWP country), and Nationals of VWP countries who are also nationals of Iran, Iraq, Sudan, or Syria.

These individuals will still be able to apply for a visa using the regular appointment process at a U.S. Embassy or Consulate."

Canadian citizens may enter the United States without visas, but will need to show passports and proof of residence.

Citizens of all other countries must have (1) a valid passport that expires at least 6 months later than the scheduled end of their visit to the U.S., and (2) a tourist visa.

For more information about U.S. visas, go to **www.travel.state.gov** and click "Visas."

Visitor Information

Destination D.C. is the official tourism and convention corporation for Washington, D.C., (www.washington.org; ☏ **202/789-7000**). Call staff "visitor services specialists" for answers to any specific questions about the city. Destination D.C.'s website is a good source for the latest travel information, including upcoming exhibits at the museums and anticipated closings of tourist attractions.

Once you've arrived, you're welcome to stop by Destination D.C.'s fourth-floor offices at 901 7th St. NW (Metro: Gallery Place–Chinatown, H St. exit) to pick up the visitors' guide and maps. Office hours are Monday to Friday 8:30am to 5pm.

National Park Service information kiosks are located inside or near the Jefferson, Lincoln, FDR,

Vietnam Veterans, Korean War, and World War II memorials, and at the Washington Monument (www.nps. gov/nama for National Mall and Memorial Parks sites; ☏ **202/426-6841** or 619-7222).

The **White House Visitor Center,** on the first floor of the Herbert Hoover Building, Department of Commerce, 1450 Pennsylvania Ave. NW (btw. 14th and 15th sts.; ☏ **202/208-1631,** or 202/456-7041 for recorded information), is open daily (except New Year's Day, Christmas Day, and Thanksgiving) from 7:30am to 4pm.

The **Smithsonian Information Center,** in the Castle, 1000 Jefferson Dr. SW (www.si.edu; ☏ **202/633-1000,** or TTY [text telephone] 633-5285), is open every day but Christmas from 8:30am to 5:30pm; knowledgeable staff answer questions and dispense maps and brochures.

Visit the D.C. government's website, **www. dc.gov,** and that of the nonprofit organization Cultural Tourism DC, **www.cultural tourismdc.org,** for more information about the city. The latter site in particular provides helpful and interesting background knowledge of D.C.'s historic and cultural landmarks, especially in neighborhoods or parts of neighborhoods not usually visited by tourists.

Index

See also Accommodations and Restaurant indexes, below.

General Index

A

Accommodations, 53–83. *See also* Accommodations Index
  Adams Morgan, 70–72
  alternative, 55–56
  best, 9
  best deals, 53–56
  Capitol Hill, 56–60
  Capitol Riverfront, 60–62
  Dupont Circle, 73–75
  extended stays, 70
  family-friendly, 66
  Foggy Bottom/West End, 75–78
  Georgetown, 78–80
  Midtown, 67–70
  National Mall, 62–63
  Old Town Alexandria, 246–247
  Penn Quarter, 64–67
  price categories, 57, 60
  prices (rates), 54–56
  Shaw, 80–81
  Southwest Waterfront, 63–64
  U & 14th Street Corridors, 81
  Woodley Park, 82–83
Adams, Abigail, 39
Adams Morgan, 47
  accommodations, 70–72
  restaurants, 106–107
  shopping, 210
Addison/Ripley Fine Art, 212
Addresses, finding, 292–293
African American Civil War Memorial and Museum, 46–47, 188–189
African Americans, 18
  African American Civil War Memorial and Museum, 46–47
  Black History Month, 23–24
  Emancipation Day, 25
  Frederick Douglass National Historic Site (Anacostia), 195
  history tour, 42–47
  National Museum of African American History & Culture, 41, 150–152
Air travel, 285–288
Albert Einstein Planetarium, 144–145
Alexandria. *See also* Old Town Alexandria
  layout, 246
Alexandria Archaeology, 254
Alexandria Black History Museum, 248, 249
Alexandria Colonial Tours, 246
Alexandria Visitor Center, 246

Allen, Ethan, 122
A Mano, 217
Amazon Books, 213
American Veterans Disabled for Life Memorial, 160
Amtrak, 288, 289
Anacostia, 47
Anacostia Community Museum, 195
Anacostia Riverwalk Trail, 47, 205
An American in Paris (Alexandria), 248
ANC Explorer (Arlington National Cemetery), 196
Anderson House, 185, 278
The Annual Scottish Christmas Walk, Alexandria, 247
The Anthem, 227
Anthony, Susan B., 121
Antiques, shopping for, 211–212
The Apotheosis of Washington (Brumidi), 121
Apple Store, 215
Architect of the Capitol, 124
Area codes, 301
Arena Stage, 223–224
Arlington, exploring, 195–199
Arlington House, 197
Arlington Memorial Bridge, 196
Arlington National Cemetery, 27, 196–197
Armed Freedom, 121
Armstrong, Louis, 52
Around the World Embassy Tour, 25
The Arsenal, 229
The Asthmatic Escaped II, 1992 (Hirst), 138
ARTECHOUSE, 231
Art galleries, 212
Art Museum of the Americas, 169, 264
Arts and Industries Building, 133–134
The Athenaeum (Alexandria), 249–250
Atlas District, restaurants, 84–85
Audi Field, 237
Augie's Mussel House (Alexandria), 256

B

Ballpark Boathouse, 207
Baltimore-Washington International Thurgood Marshall Airport (BWI), 285, 288
Banneker, Benjamin, 42–43
Barmy Wines & Liquors, 221
Barracks Row, 50
  restaurants, 85, 88–91
Barrel, 228
Barry, Marion, 13
Bars, 228–231
Barry Knob Architectural
Bartholdi Park, 160
Baseball, 236
"Baseball: America's Home Run" exhibit, 130

Basketball, 236
Beauty products and services, 213
Behind the Badge exhibit, 129–130
Bellacara (Alexandria), 248
Belmont-Paul Women's Equality National Monument, 24, 39, 125
Benton, Thomas Hart, 122, 138
Bethune, Mary McLeod, 122
  Mary McLeod Bethune Council House National Historic Site, 189
Betsy Fisher, 215
Bible Museum, 166–167
Big Wheel Bikes, 206
Bike and Boat, 239
Bike and Roll, 249
Bike and Roll/Bike the Sites, 206
Bike and Roll DC, 301
Biking, 205–206, 297–298
  to Old Town Alexandria & Mount Vernon, 249
  tours, 301
Binding the Nation, 129
Birch & Barley, 229
The Birchmere Music Hall and Bandstand, 232
Birthnight Ball at Gadsby's Tavern (Alexandria), 247
"Black Broadway," 18, 47
Black Cat, 233–234
Black History Month, 23–24
Blackwall Hitch (Alexandria), 256
Blaine Mansion, 276–277
Bluejacket Brewery, 228–229
Blue Mercury, 213
Blues Alley, 232
Boat House at Fletcher's Cove, 206
Boating in D.C., 206
Boat tours, 300
Boat travel, 297
Boeing Learning Center, 146
BoltBus, 290
Booking.com, 56
Books, 213–215
Booth, John Wilkes, 2
Bourgeois, Louise, 148
Bowser, Muriel, 20
Brass Knob Architectural Antiques, 211
Brazil, Embassy of, 282
The Brewmaster's Castle (Christian Heurich House Museum), 185, 274, 276
British Embassy, 282–283
Brown v. Board of Education of Topeka, 19
Brumidi, Constantino, 121
Bureau of Engraving and Printing, 163–165
Burnham, Daniel, 17, 129
Busboys and Poets, 213
Business hours, 301
Bus tours, 299
Bus travel, 289–290

C

Cady's Alley, 219–220
Calder, Alexander, 148
Caldwell, Lucy, 41
Calendar of events, 23–27
Calloway, Cab, 52
Cameras and computers, 215
Canal Park, 208
C&O Canal, 202, 203
C&O Canal Historical Park's
   towpath, 206
Capital Beltway, 289
Capital BikeShare, 206
Capital Crescent Trail, 206
Capital Fringe Festival, 26
Capital One Arena, 13, 20, 50,
   227, 236, 237
The Capitol, 117–118, 120–125
   procedures for touring,
   122–124
"The Castle" (Smithsonian
   Information Center), 159
"Capitol Building and Capitol Hill
   Walk" tour, 118
Capitol dome, 120
Capitol Guide Service, 122–123
Capitol Hill & Barracks Row, 7, 50
   accommodations, 56–60
   exploring, 117–132
   restaurants, 85, 88–91
Capitol Hill Books, 213–214
Capitol River Cruise, 300
Capitol Riverfront ("Navy
   Yard"), 50
   accommodations, 60–62
   restaurants, 91–92
The Capitol Steps, 234–235
Capitol Visitor Center, 123
Carlyle House Historic Park
   (Alexandria), 250
Carousel, 36, 134, 203
Car travel, 288, 295
Castle Garden, 185
Cedar Hill (Frederick Douglass
   National Historic Site), 43
Cellphones, 302–303
Central Liquors, 221
Charters of Freedom, 145
Cherry blossoms, 21
   National Cherry Blossom
      Festival, 24–25
Cherry trees, 199
Cherub Antiques Gallery, 211–212
Chesapeake & Ohio Canal
   National Historical Park,
   202–203
Child, Julia, 40, 154
Chinatown, 50
Chinese New Year Celebration, 24
Chocolate Moose, 219
Christ Church (Alexandria),
   250–251
Christmas Tree Lighting
   Alexandria, 247
   Washington, D.C., 27
Churchill, Sir Winston, 282
ChurchKey, 229
Citi Open, 26, 236
CityCenterDC, 50
Civil Rights era, 18

Civil War, 16–17
Cleveland Park, 50
   exploring, 189–193
   restaurants, 114–115
Clinton, Bill, 137
Clothing, 215–217
Club & music scene, 231–235
Coffee, 116
Columbia Heights, 50
Columbia Room, 229
Comedy clubs, 234–235
Comfort One Shoes, 221
Commission of Fine Arts, 17
Concert venues, 227–228
Congressional Cemetery, 10
Connecticut Avenue, 291
   shopping, 210
Connections (Renwick
   Gallery), 171
Constitution, U.S., 2–3
Constitution Avenue, 291
Constitution Gardens, 149
Coolidge Auditorium, 128
Corcoran, William Wilson, 271
Corcoran Gallery of Art, 263
Cosmos Club, 278
Cox's Row, 268
Crafts, 217–218
Crimson, 228
Croatia, Embassy of, 280
Crumbs and Whiskers, 10
Cuba Libre, 230

D

DAR Constitution Hall, 227–228
DAR Museum, 263
Daughters of the American
   Revolution (DAR) Museum, 169
David M. Rubenstein Gallery, 145
Day trips from D.C., 238–256
   Mount Vernon, 238–243
   Old Town Alexandria, 243-256
DC by Foot, 298
DC Circulator, 294, 296
   National Mall, 133
DC Ducks, 301
D.C. Fashion Week, 24
The DC Improv, 235
DC Jazz Festival, 26, 232
DC Metro Food Tours, 298
DC Streetcar, 295
D.C. United, 237
D.C. War Memorial, 134
Decatur House, 261
The Denson, 230
Destination DC, 55
Disabilities, travelers with, 305
Discounts, 54–56
Discovery Theater (S. Dillon
   Ripley Center), 158, 204
District Cutlery, 88
District of Columbia, 122
Doctors, 301
Dollar bills, 166
Donald W. Reynolds Museum and
   Education Center, 240
Douglass, Frederick, 18, 122
   Frederick Douglass National
      Historic Site (Cedar Hill), 43

Downing Urn, 136
Downtown, 50
Downtown & Penn Quarter,
   restaurants, 94–100
Dred Scott v. Sandford, 122
Drinking laws, 301
Dumbarton House, 193, 270
Dumbarton Oaks & Garden,
   193–194, 271–272
Dumbarton Oaks Museum, 272
Dumbarton Oaks Park, 201
Dupont Circle, 7, 35–36, 51
   accommodations, 73–75
   exploring, 184–187
   people-watching at, 6
   restaurants, 107–110
   shopping, 210
   walking tour, 273–284
Dupont Circle FreshFarm
   Market, 218

E

Eastern Market, 7, 125–126, 218
East Potomac Golf Course, 207
East Potomac Park, 200, 207, 208
East Potomac Park Tennis
   Center, 208
Egg by Susan Lazar, 215
Eighteenth Street Lounge, 234
Eisenhower Executive Office
   Building, 262
Electricity, 301–302
Elizabethan garden, 127
Ellington, Duke, 18, 47, 52
The Ellipse, 264
Ellsworth, Oliver, 122
Emancipation Day, 25
Emancipation Hall, 3, 122, 123
Embassies, 21
Embassies and consulates, 302
Embassy of Brazil, 282
Embassy of Croatia, 280
Embassy of Finland, 283
Embassy of India, 277
Embassy of Indonesia, 277
Embassy of Japan, 281
Embassy of Turkey, 281
Embassy Open Houses, 25
Embassy.org, 234, 234i
Embassy Row, 35–36, 51, 281
Embassy Series, 234
Emergencies, 302
Emerson, Ralph Waldo, 126
Emmet, Robert, Statue of, 280
Enid A. Haupt Garden, 135–136,
   152, 159
Entertainment and nightlife,
   222–237
   Alexandria, 256
   club & music scene, 231–235
   comedy clubs, 234–235
   current listings, 222
   hours, 222
   LGBTQ scene, 235–236
   performing arts, 223–228
   spectator sports, 236–237
   tickets, 227
EU Open House, 25
Evans, Rudolph, 140

Evermay, 270
Exhibition Hall, 123

F

Fall, 22
Families with kids, 302
    accommodations, 66
    best experiences for, 3–4
    best restaurants for, 4
    children's clothing, 215
    sights and attractions for,
      203–205
    suggested itinerary, 36–39
Federal Triangle, 18
FedEx Field, 236
Finland, Embassy of, 283
First Ladies Water Garden, 160
Fishing, 206
Fletcher's Cove, 206
FlipKey.com, 55
Flower Mart (Washington National
    Cathedral), 192
Foggy Bottom/West End, 51
    accommodations, 75–78
    exploring, 187–188
    restaurants, 110–111
Folger, Henry Clay, 126
Folger Shakespeare Library, 126–
    127, 182
Folger Theatre at the Folger
    Shakespeare Library, 226–227
Football, 236
Ford Orientation Center (Mount
    Vernon), 240
Ford's Theatre, 2, 17, 24, 226
Ford's Theatre Museum, 177
Ford's Theatre National Historic
    Site, 176–177, 180
Forrest-Marbury House, 265
Fort Ward Museum & Historic Site
    (Alexandria), 251
Fort Ward Museum & Historic Site
    (Old Town Alexandria), 248
Foundry Gallery, 212
Fountain Garden, 135–136
Franklin Delano Roosevelt
    Memorial, 136–137
Frederick Douglass House, 24
Frederick Douglass National
    Historic Site (Anacostia),
    43, 195
Freer, Charles Lang, 137
Freer Gallery of Art, 24, 137–138
Free things to do, best, 6–7
French, Daniel Chester, 141
Friday Jazz in the Garden, 148
Friendship Firehouse
    (Alexandria), 251

G

Gadsby's Tavern Museum
    (Alexandria), 252
GALA Hispanic Theatre, 227
George at the Four Seasons, 213
George Mason Memorial, 138
Georgetown, 51
    accommodations, 78–80
    exploring, 193–195

restaurants, 111–114
    shopping, 210–211
    walking tour, 264–273
Georgetown University, 266, 268
Georgetown Waterfront Park, 201
George Washington Memorial
    Parkway, 239
The George Washington Museum,
    Albert H. Small Washingtoniana
    Collection, 187–188
GetYourGuide.com, 118
Ghost tours, Alexandria, 247
Gifts and souvenirs, 219
Glover Park, 51
    exploring, 189–193
Goldstar.com, 227
Golf, 207
Good Wood, 212
Gravelly Point, 6, 204
Great Falls, 202–203
Great Falls Tavern Visitor
    Center, 203
Great Hall (Folger Shakespeare
    Library), 126
Guided tours, 298–301
The Guild of Professional Tour
    Guides of Washington, D.C.,
    298–299
Gypsy Sally's, 232

H

Hains Point, 200, 208
Halcyon House, 266
Hall of Columns, 122
Hamilton, Alexander, 258
The Hamilton, 230, 232–233
Harmony in Blue and Gold: the
    Peacock Room (Whistler), 138
Heurich House Museum, 185,
    274, 276
Hiking and jogging, 207
Hill Country Barbecue, 229–230
Hill's Kitchen, 220
Hillwood Museum and
    Gardens, 189
Hirshhorn Museum and Sculpture
    Garden, 138–139
Hirst, Damien, 138
The Historic Alexandria
    Candlelight Tour, 247–248
Historic Garden Week in Virginia
    (Old Town Alexandria), 247
History of Washington, D.C.,
    11–21
      birth of the capital, 15–16
      Civil Rights era, 18–20
      Civil War & Reconstruction,
        16–17
      early days, 14
      early 1800s, 16
      twenty-first century, 20–21
Holiday Boat Parade of Lights
    (Alexandria), 247
Holidays, 23
Holocaust Memorial Museum,
    United States, 167–169
HomeAway.com, 55
HomeExchange, 55

Home furnishings & kitchenware,
    219–220
HomeLink International, 55
Home Rule, 220
Hoover, Herbert, 134
Hospitals, 302
Hostelling International
    Washington, DC, 55
Hotels, 53–83. See also
    Accommodations Index
    Adams Morgan, 70–72
    alternative, 55–56
    best, 9
    best deals, 53–56
    Capitol Hill, 56–60
    Capitol Riverfront, 60–62
    Dupont Circle, 73–75
    extended stays, 70
    family-friendly, 66
    Foggy Bottom/West End,
      75–78
    Georgetown, 78–80
    Midtown, 67–70
    National Mall, 62–63
    Old Town Alexandria, 246–247
    Penn Quarter, 64–67
    price categories, 57, 60
    prices (rates), 54–56
    Shaw, 80–81
    Southwest Waterfront, 63–64
    U & 14th Street Corridors, 81
    Woodley Park, 82–83
Hotel search engines, 56
House Gallery, 123–124
House of Sweden, 234
House swapping, 55
Howard Theatre, 18
Howard University, 18
H Street Corridor (now known as
    the Atlas District), 19, 27, 47
H Street Country Club, 229
H Street Festival, 27
Hugh & Crye, 216
Hu's Shoes, 221
Hu's Wear, 221

I

IA&A (International Arts & Artists)
    at Hillyer, 212
Ice hockey, 237
Independence Day, 26
India, Embassy of, 277
Indian Craft Shop, 217
Indonesia, Embassy of, 277
Inside Airbnb, 55
International Spy Museum, 165–
    166, 204, 205
Internet and Wi-Fi, 302
The Islamic Center, 281
Itineraries, suggested, 28–52
    African-American history tour,
      42–47
    for families, 36–39
    iconic Washington, D.C.
      in 1 day, 28–33
      in 2 days, 33–34
      in 3 days, 35–36
    women's history tour, 39–42

J

Jack Rose Saloon, 230
Jackson, Andrew, 260
James Madison Memorial
  Building, 128
Japan, Embassy of, 281
Jay, John, 122
Jazz, 52, 74
  Sculpture Garden, National
    Gallery of Art, 6
Jazz and blues, 232–233
Jefferson, Thomas, 128
Jefferson Building, 127–128
Jefferson Memorial, 139–140
Jewelry, 220
Jogging, 8, 207
John Adams Building, 128

K

Kahlil Gibran Memorial, 282
Kastles Stadium at the Smith
  Center, 237
Keegan Theatre, 227
Keller, Helen, 122
Kennedy, Jacqueline, 172, 197,
  268, 298
Kennedy, John F., 19, 120,
  139–140, 268
  gravesite of, 197
Kennedy Center for the
  Performing Arts, 23, 36,
  223–225
  Millennium Stage performance
    at, 6, 224, 225
  vinyasa class in, 10
Key Bridge Boathouse, 207
Key to the City Museum Pass
  Mount Vernon, 241
  Old Town Alexandria, 246
King, Martin Luther, Jr., 19, 121
  Birthday of, 23
  Martin Luther King, Jr. National
    Memorial, 46, 142–143
King Street Art Festival (Old Town
  Alexandria), 247
Kite Festival, 203
Korean War Veterans Memorial,
  140–141
Kramerbooks & Afterwords
  Cafe, 214
Kreeger Museum, 194

L

Labor Day Concert, 26
La Cosecha, 88
Lafayette Square, 260
La Maison Française, 234
Lansburgh Theatre, 226
The Lantern, 214
Latrobe, Benjamin Henry,
  260, 261
Lawrence F. O'Brien Gallery, 146
Layout of Washington, D.C.,
  290–293
Le Bar à Vin, 112

Lee-Fendall House Museum
  (Alexandria), 252
Legal aid, 302
Leica Camera, 215
Lemelson Center, 154
L'Enfant, Pierre Charles, 140,
  149, 261
  grave, 197
Letelier/Moffitt Memorial,
  278–279
Leyland, F. R., 138
LGBTQ travelers, 302
LGBTQ scene, 235–236
Library of Congress, 34, 127–129
  National Book Festival, 26–27
  Veterans History Project, 158
Light Horse (Alexandria), 256
Ligne Roset, 220
Lin, Maya, 161
Lincoln, Abraham, 2, 17, 25, 120,
  121, 166
  Birthday, 24
  Lincoln Memorial, 46
Lincoln Memorial, 24, 32–33, 46,
  141–142, 166
Lincoln Theatre, 47, 228
Little Birdies Boutique, 215
Live music, 8
Live Nation Entertainment, 227
Lockkeeper's House, 149
Loft at The Hamilton, 232–233
Luce Foundation Center for
  American Art, 184
Lucky Bar, 230
Lunder Conservation Center, 184
The Lyceum (Alexandria), 253
Lyft, 297

M

McCain, John, 120
McKim, Charles Follen, 17, 141
McLeod Bethune, Mary, 18, 42
McMillan, James, 17
Madame Tussauds Washington,
  D.C., 180, 204
Mahatma Gandhi, Statue of, 277
Mail, 302
Maketto, 216
March on Washington for Jobs
  and Freedom (1963), 46
Marine Corps Marathon, 27, 236
Marshall, John, 122
Marshall, Thurgood, 18–19
Marston Luce Antiques, 212
Martin Luther King, Jr. National
  Memorial, 23, 46, 142–143
Marvin, 230
Maryland Rural Commuter
  (MARC), 288
Mary McLeod Bethune Council
  House National Historic Site,
  42, 189
Mason, George, Memorial, 138
Massachusetts Avenue, 291
Matisse, Henri, 148
Meeps, 217
Megabus, 290

Mellon, Andrew W., 149
Meridian Hill Park, 10, 50, 201
Metrobus, 286, 294–295
Metrorail, 286, 293
Mia Gemma, 220
Midtown, 50, 51
  accommodations, 67–70
  exploring, 168–176
  restaurants, 100–101
Miss Christin, 239
Miss Pixie's Furnishings &
  Whatnot, 220
Mobile phones, 302–303
Money and costs, 303
Montrose Park, 201, 208
Moongate Garden, 135
Moton, Robert Russa, 46
Mott, Lucretia, 121
Mount Vernon, 238–243
  biking to, 249
  shuttle service, 243
Mount Vernon Estate and
  Gardens, 240–242
Mount Vernon Ladies'
  Association, 242
Mount Vernon Trail, 249
Mount Vernon Triangle, 51
Mount Zion United Methodist
  Church, 42, 273
Moving the Mail exhibit area, 129
Mule-drawn 19th-century canal-
  boat trip, 203
Museum gift shops, 182
Museum of the Bible, 166–167
Museums, 6

N

National Air and Space Museum,
  4, 39, 143–145, 204
National Archives, 3, 32
National Archives Museum, 145
National Book Festival, 26–27
National Building Museum, 36,
  181–182, 204
National Cherry Blossom Festival,
  24–25, 199
National Children's Museum,
  169–170
National Christmas Tree
  Lighting, 27
National Coalition to Save Our
  Mall, 149
National Gallery of Art, 29,
  32, 182
  ice skating, 3
  Sculpture Garden, 139,
    147–149
National Gallery Sculpture
  Garden, 203
  Ice Rink, 208
National Garden, 160
National Geographic Museum,
  185–186
National Law Enforcement
  Memorial, 181
National Law Enforcement
  Museum, 181

The National Mall and Memorial Parks, 6–7, 29, 51–52, 133–163
accommodations, 62–63
Arts and Industries Building, 133–134
D.C. War Memorial, 134
exploring, 133–163
Franklin Delano Roosevelt Memorial, 136–137
Freer Gallery of Art, 137–138
George Mason Memorial, 138
Hirshhorn Museum and Sculpture Garden, 138–139
Jefferson Memorial, 139–140
jogging, 8
Korean War Veterans Memorial, 140–141
Martin Luther King, Jr. National Memorial, 142–143
National Air and Space Museum, 143–145
National Gallery of Art's Sculpture Garden, 139, 147–149
National Museum of African American History & Culture, 150–152
National Museum of African Art, 152
National Museum of American History, 153–154
National Museum of Natural History, 155–157
National Museum of the American Indian, 154–155
National World War II Memorial, 157–158
S. Dillon Ripley Center, 158
Sackler Gallery, 158–159
Smithsonian Information Center ("The Castle"), 159
southwest of, 163–168
United States Botanic Garden, 159–160
Vietnam Veterans Memorial, 160–161
Washington Monument, 161–163
National Memorial Day Parade, 25–26
National Museum of African American History & Culture, 23, 29, 41–42, 150–152
National Museum of African Art, 152, 182
National Museum of American History, 4, 36, 38, 40–41, 153–154, 204
National Museum of Asian Art in the United States (Sackler Gallery), 158–159
National Museum of Natural History, 155–157, 204
National Museum of the American Indian, 154–155, 204
National Museum of Women in the Arts, 42, 182–183
National Native American Veterans Memorial, 155

National Park Service, 149
National Portrait Gallery, 34
National Postal Museum, 129–130
Nationals Park, 236
National Stamp Collection, 130
National Statuary Hall, 121–122
National Theatre, 225
National Trust for Historic Preservation, 54
National Woman's Party (NWP), 125
National World War II Memorial, 157–158
National Zoological Park (National Zoo), 3, 38–39, 190–191, 204
Neighborhoods. See also specific neighborhoods
best for getting lost, 7
in brief, 47, 50–52
for nightlife, 222
Newspapers and magazines, 303
Nightlife and entertainment. See Entertainment and nightlife
9/11 Memorial (Pentagon Memorial), 198–199
9:30 Club, 233
NoMa, 52
Northern Virginia, 52, 195–199
Norton, Eleanor Holmes, 13, 20
N St. NW, 3307, 268

O
Oak Hill Cemetery, 10, 271
Obama, Barack, 20, 36, 172
Obama, Michelle, 36, 172
Octagon House, 262–263
Octagon Museum, 170–171
Offbeat experiences, best, 10
Off the Record, 228
Old Post Office Clock Tower, 183
Old Presbyterian Meeting House (Alexandria), 253
Old Stone House, 194, 201, 272
Old Supreme Court Chamber, 122
Old Town Alexandria, 7, 243–284
biking to, 249
calendar of events, 247–248
getting there, 244
organized tours, 246
overnighting, 246–247
shopping, 211
sights and attractions, 248–254
visitor information, 246
Old Town Alexandria Farmers Market, 218
Olmsted, Frederick Law, 17, 122, 192
OnBoard Sightseeing, 239
Outdoor activities, 205–208
Outdoor Yoga Mortis, 10
The Outrage, 216
Oyamel, 230

P
Paddleboats, 207
Parks, 199–203
Parks, Rosa, 121

Parks and gardens, 21
Paul, Alice, 125
Pearl Street Warehouse, 233
Peirce Mill, 201
Penn Quarter, 34, 50–52
accommodations, 64–67
exploring, 176–184
restaurants, 94–100
shopping, 209–210
Pennsylvania Avenue, 258, 260, 291
The Pentagon, 198–199
Pentagon Group Burial Marker (Arlington National Cemetery), 196
Pentagon Memorial (9/11 Memorial), 198–199
People of Chilmark (Benton), 138
Performing arts, 223–228
Period rooms (DAR Museum), 263
Petersen House, 177
Phillips Collection, 35, 186–187
Phoebe Waterman Haas Public Observatory, 144
The Phoenix, 217
Pilgrim Observation Gallery, 192
Pioneer Farm, 241
Planetarium, Albert Einstein 144–145
Rock Creek Nature Center and, 200, 204
Police, 303–304
Politics and Prose Bookstore, 214
Pollin, Abe and Irene, 13
Po'Pay, 121
Pope, John Russell, 147
Postal Museum, 129–130
Postmasters Suite gallery, 130
Potomac Park, 199–200
Potomac Riverboat Company, 239, 300
Presidents' Day, 24
President's Park, 257
Proper Topper, 216
Prospect House, 266
Public Vaults, National Archives Museum, 146

Q
Quill, 73, 231

R
Rainfall, average, 23
Rankin, Jeannette, 122
Reagan, Ronald, 121
Reagan National Airport, 288
Reams, Vinnie, 121
Records of Rights exhibit, 145
Red Barn Mercantile (Alexandria), 248
Reiter's Bookstore, 214
Relish, 216
Renwick Gallery of the Smithsonian American Art Museum, 169, 170–171, 261–262

Restaurants, 84–116. *See also*
    Restaurants Index
    Alexandria, 255–256
    Atlas District, 84–85
    best, 4–6
    Capitol Hill & Barracks Row, 85,
        88–91
    casual, 84
    Downtown & Penn Quarter,
        94–100
    Dupont Circle, 107–110
    family-friendly, 103
    Foggy Bottom/West End,
        110–111
    Midtown, 100–101
    price categories, 85
    Shaw, 114
    Southwest Waterfront, 92–94
    Union Market, 88
    U & 14th Street Corridors,
        102–106
    Woodley Park & Cleveland
        Park, 114–115
Restaurant Week, 23
Riverside Park (Mount
    Vernon), 242
Robert E. Lee Memorial, 197
Rock, hip-hop and DJs, 233–234
Rock Creek Nature Center and
    Planetarium, 200, 204
Rock Creek Park, 3, 200–201
Rock & Roll Hotel, 234
Ronald Reagan Washington
    National Airport (DCA), 285,
    286–287
Roosevelt, Franklin D., 18, 132
    Jefferson Memorial, 140
Rotunda
    the Capitol, 120–122
    National Archives, 145
Rutledge, John, 122

S
Sabah, 88
Sackler Gallery (National Museum
    of Asian Art in the United
    States), 158–159
Safety, 304
St. John's Church, 17
St. John's Episcopal Church,
    Georgetown, 268–269
St. John's Episcopal Church on
    Lafayette Square, 260
St. Patrick's Day Parade
    Old Town Alexandria, 247
    Washington, D.C., 24
Saint-Gaudens, Augustus, 17, 132
Salon ILO, 213
Salt cave, yoga in a, 10
Salt & Sundry, 88
Schneider's of Capitol Hill, 221
Sculpture Garden
    Kreeger Museum, 194
    National Gallery, 203
    National Gallery of Art, jazz
        in, 6
S. Dillon Ripley Center, 158
Seasons, 21–22

Secondi Inc., 217
Second Story Books, 215
Security precautions and
    procedures, 121
Segway Tours, 299
Senate Gallery, 123–124
Senior travel, 304
Sewall-Belmont House and
    Museum, 125
Shakespeare Gallery, 126
Shakespeare Theatre Company at
    the Lansburgh Theatre and
    Sidney Harman Hall, 225–226
Shakespeare Theatre Free for
    All, 26
Shaw, 52
    accommodations, 80–81
    restaurants, 114–115
    shopping, 210
Shepherd, Alexander "Boss," 17
Sheridan Circle, 279
Shoes, 221
Shop Made in DC, 219
Shopping, 209–221, 248
Shops at Mount Vernon
    Complex, 242
Sidney Harman Hall, 226
Sights and attractions, 117–208
    Arlington, 195–199
    Capitol Hill, 117–132
    Foggy Bottom, 187–188
    Georgetown, 193–195
    for kids, 203–205
    National Mall and Memorial
        Parks, 133–163
    Northern Virginia, 195–199
    parks, 199–203
    Upper Northwest D.C.: Glover
        Park, Woodley Park &
        Cleveland Park, 189–193
    U & 14th Street Corridors,
        188–189
1623 First Folio of
    Shakespeare, 126
SmarTrip card, 292, 293
Smithson, James, 164
The Smithsonian, 4
Smithsonian American Art
    Museum & National Portrait
    Gallery, 34, 183–184
Smithsonian Craft Show, 25
Smithsonian Folklife Festival,
    26, 203
Smithsonian Information Center
    ("The Castle"), 159
Smoking, 304
Soccer, 237
Society Fair (Alexandria), 248
Southwest Waterfront, 52
    accommodations, 63–64
    restaurants, 92–94
Spectator sports, 8, 236–237
Spider (Bourgeois), 148
Spirit Cruises' *Spirit of Mount
    Vernon*, 239
The Spirit of Freedom
    (sculpture), 46
Spirit of Washington Cruises, 300
Spring, 22

Stabler-Leadbeater Apothecary
    Museum (Alexandria), 254
Stamps Around the Globe
    exhibit, 130
Stanton, Elizabeth Cady, 121
State Department Diplomatic
    Reception Rooms, 188
Steir, Pat, 138
Steven F. Udvar-Hazy Center, 145
Street hockey, 10
Studio Gallery, 212
Studio Theatre, 226
Suffragist movement, 125
Summer, 22
SuperShuttle, 286
Supreme Court
    Old Supreme Court
        Chamber, 122
    tours, 118
Supreme Court of the United
    States, 2, 33, 130–131
Susan Calloway Fine Arts, 212
Swimming, 208

T
Taxes, 304
Taxis, 286, 297
Telephones, 304–305
Temperatures, average, 23
Tennis, 208, 237
    Citi Open, 26
Textile Museum, 187
Theater J, 227
Theodore Roosevelt Island
    Park, 202
Thomas Jefferson Building,
    127–128
Thompson Boat Center, 206
Ticketfly, 227
Tidal Basin, 140
Time zones, 305
Tiny Jewel Box, 220
Tipping, 305
Todaytix, 227
Toilets, 305
Tomb of the Unknowns, 27, 197
Tomb of the Unknown
    Soldier, 197
Top of the Gate, 228
Torpedo Factory Art Center, 218
Torpedo Factory Art Center
    (Alexandria), 254
Tour and Tea (Washington
    National Cathedral), 192
Tours, guided, 298–301
ToursByLocals.com, 118
Train travel, 289
Transportation, 290–298
    public, 293–295
Trump, Donald J., 166, 172
Tryst, 231
Tubman, Harriet, 166
Tudor Place, 195, 269
Tune Inn, 231
Turkey, Embassy of, 281
Twins Jazz, 188

U

U & 14th Street Corridors ("New U"), 18, 19–20, 52
  accommodations, 81
  exploring, 188–189
  restaurants, 102–106
  shopping, 210
Uber, 297
Union Market, 219
  restaurants, 88
Union Station, 131–132, 289
  shopping, 209
United Kingdom, Embassy of, 282
United States Botanic Garden, 159–160, 204
United States Holocaust Memorial Museum, 167–169
Upper Northwest D.C., exploring, 189–193
Upper Wisconsin Avenue Northwest, shopping, 211
Upstairs on 7th, 216–217
U.S. Capitol, 117–118, 120–125
  procedures for touring, 122–124
U.S. Capitol Building, 29
U.S. Postal Inspection Service, 129–130
U.S. Treasury Building, 258

V

Vamoose Bus, 290
Veterans Day, 27
Veterans History Project, 128
Via Gypset, 217
Viator.com, 118
Vice President's Residence/U.S. Naval Observatory, 283–284
Vietnam Veterans Memorial, 160–161
Vintage shops, 217
Violet Boutique, 217
Visas, 305–306
Visitor information, 306
VRBO, 55

W

Walking tours
  guided, 298–299
  self-guided, 257–284
    Dupont Circle/Embassy Row, 273–284
    Georgetown, 264–273
    around The White House, 257–264
Wallace H. Coulter Performance Stage and Plaza, 154
Warner Theatre, 228
Washington, District of Columbia, origin of name, 21
Washington, George, Birthday, D.C._24, Washington
  Old Town Alexandria, 247
Washington Capitals, 237
Washington Dulles International Airport (IAD), 285, 287–288

Washington Flyer Silver Line Express Bus, 287
Washington Harbour, 207–208
Washington Monument, 17, 24, 29, 32, 161–163
Washington National Cathedral, 51, 191–192
Washington National Cathedral Annual Flower Mart, 25
Washington Spirit, 237
Washington Walks, 298
Waterfall series (Steir), 138
Water taxis, Old Town Alexandria, 244–246
Weather, seasons, 22
Wegmans Wonderplace, 153–154
Welcome Center (Arlington National Cemetery), 196
West Potomac Park, 200
The Wharf, 52, 63
  ice skating rink, 208
  shopping, 211
Wharf at the Southwest Waterfront, 205
Wharf Boathouse, 207
Whistler, James McNeill, 137, 138
The White House, 29, 34, 168, 261
  exploring, 171–176
  touring, 175
White House Easter Egg Roll, 25
White House History Shop, 219
White House Visitor Center, 174–176, 258
William C. McGowan Theater, 146
William H. Gross Stamp Gallery, 130
Williams, Anthony, 13
Wilson, Woodrow, 35, 132
Wine and spirits, 221
Winter, 22
Wisconsin Avenue, 291–292
Women in Military Service for America Memorial, 197–198
Women's History Month, 24
Women's history tour, 39–42
Wonder Woman 2 (movie), 124
Woodley Park & Cleveland Park, 52
  accommodations, 82–83
  exploring, 189–193
  restaurants, 114–115
Woodrow Wilson House, 35–36
Woodrow Wilson House Museum, 187
Woolly Mammoth Theatre Company, 226
Works Progress Administration (WPA), 17
World of Stamps exhibit, 130

Y

Yards Park, 205
Yoga, 10
Yoga Factory, 10

Accommodations

Adam's Inn Bed & Breakfast, 72
AKA White House, 70
Avenue Suites, 76
Capitol Hill Hotel, 57
Conrad Washington DC, 64–65
Courtyard by Marriott Capitol Hill/Navy Yard, 61
Eaton Hotel DC, 53
The Fairfax at Embassy Row, 73–74
Fairfield Inn & Suites, 65–67
Georgetown Suites, 79–80
The Graham, 78–79
Hampton Inn & Suites Washington DC-Navy Yard, 61–62
The Hay-Adams, 67–68
Hilton Washington DC National Mall, 62
Hotel Hive, 77–78
Hotel Palomar, 74
Hotel Tabard Inn, 74–75
Hyatt House D.C., The Wharf, 66
Hyatt Regency Washington on Capitol Hill, 60
InterContinental Washington, D.C.-The Wharf, 63–64
The Jefferson, 73
Kalorama Guest House, 82–83
Kimpton George, 57
Kimpton Hotel Monaco Washington DC, 65
Kimpton Lorien Hotel & Spa (Old Town Alexandria), 247
Kimpton Mason & Rook, 81
The Line DC, 71
Morrison House, Autograph Collection (Old Town Alexandria), 246
The Normandy Hotel, 71–72
Omni Shoreham Hotel, 66, 82
One Washington Circle Hotel, 78
Pod DC Hotel, 67
Residence Inn Capitol, 63
The River Inn, 77
Rosewood Washington D.C., 79
The Watergate Hotel, 75–76
The W Hotel, 69–70
Willard InterContinental, 66, 68–69
Woodley Park Guest House, 83

Restaurants

Ali Pacha, 88
All Purpose Pizzeria, 114
Al Tiramisu, 108
Amparo Fondita, 88
Amsterdam Falafelshop, 107
Beefsteak, 5, 110–111
Belga Cafe, 89
Ben's Chili Bowl, 5, 20, 104–105
Blackwall Hitch (Alexandria), 255
In Blagden Alley, 115
Bombay Club, 5, 100–101
Brothers and Sisters, 106–107
Buttercream Bakery, 114

RESTAURANT INDEX

Café du Parc, 38, 100
Castle Café, 159
Central Michel Richard, 94
CherCher Ethiopian Restaurant, 102–103
Chez Billy Sud, 111–112
CHIKO, 90
Chloe, 91
Coconut Club, 88
Colada Shop, 105
Columbia Room, 115
Compass Coffee, 116
Convivial, 115
Cork Wine Bar & Market, 103–104
The Cup We All Race 4, 116
The Dabney, 115
Dabney Cellar, 115
Daikaya, 99
Del Mar, 92–93
District Doughnut and Coffee, 265
Duke's Counter, 39, 103
Eamonn's A Dublin Chipper (Alexandria), 256
El Cielo, 88
Emissary, 116
Espita Mezcaleria, 114
Estadio, 102
Fancy Radish, 84–85
Farmers Fishers Bakers, 110
Fiola, 95
Fiola Mare, 112–113
Five Guys Burgers and Fries, 99
Founding Farmers, 110

Gadsby's Tavern (Alexandria), 252
GCDC Grilled Cheese Bar, 262
Good Stuff Eatery, 4, 90–91
Hamilton, 5
Hank's Oyster Bar, 93
Hank's Pasta Bar, 94
Hill Country Barbecue, 4
Hill Country Barbecue Market, 95–96
Hummingbird (Alexandria), 255
Indique, 114–115
Iron Gate, 4, 108
Jaleo, 5, 96
Jazz Café, 154
Julia's Empanadas, 107
Kinship, 115
Kintsugi, 116
Kith and Kin, 93
Komi, 4, 108
Kramerbooks and Afterwords Cafe, 35
Le Diplomate, 102
Little Serow, 108–109
Maketto, 85
Martin's Tavern, 113, 269
Masseria, 88
Matchbox, 96
Maydan, 104
Medium Rare, 115
Metier, 115
Mount Vernon Inn, 243
Old Ebbitt Grill, 101, 103
Pavilion Café at the National Gallery Sculpture Garden, 32

Perry's Drag Brunch, 10
Philly Wing Fry, 93
Pineapple and Pearls, 88–89
Pinstripes, 4, 103
Pizzeria Paradiso, 4, 109
Plume, 4, 73
Qualia Coffee, 116
A Rake's Progress, 107
Rappahannock Oyster Bar, 5, 94
Rasika, 5, 97
Rose's Luxury, 89–90
The Salt Line, 91
Sei, 97–98
1789, 111
Shouk, 5
The Smith, 34, 98
Sweetgreen, 101
Tabard Inn, 109
Taco Bamba, 5, 99–100
Tail Up Goat, 106
Taqueria Nacional, 105–106
Teaism Dupont Circle, 109–110
Teaism Lafayette Square, 110
Teaism Penn Quarter, 110
Ted's Bulletin, 4, 90, 103
Tiger Fork, 5, 115
Unconventional Diner, 115
Urbana, 74, 107
Urbano 116 (Alexandria), 256
Via Umbria, 113
Whaley's, 92
Wingo's, 5
Yums II Carryout, 5
Zaytinya, 5, 98–99

Photo Credits

Cover, ©MDOGAN/Shutterstock.com; p. i: KazT; p. ii: Songquan Deng; p. iii: Tanarch; p. iv: Courtesy of Washington.org; p. v, top: Courtesy of washington.org; p. v, bottom left: Courtesy of washington.org; p. v, bottom right: Jon Bilous; p. vi, top: Courtesy of washington.org; p. vi, bottom: Orhan Cam/Shutterstock.com; p. vii, top: Courtesy of washington.org; p. vii, middle: Courtesy of washington.org; p. vii, bottom: angela n.; p. viii, top: Jorg Hackemann/Shutterstock.com; p. viii, bottom left: Courtesy of washington.org; p. viii, bottom right: Courtesy of the National Museum of American History/Hugh Talman; p. ix, top: Courtesy of washington.org; p. ix, bottom left: Courtesy of washington.org/Marquis Perkins; p. ix, bottom right: Robert Lyle Bolton; p. x, top left: Connor Mallon/Smithsonian's National Zoo; p. x, top right: Courtesy of washington.org; p. x, bottom: Courtesy of washington.org; p. xi, top: holbox; p. xi, middle: Courtesy of washington.org; p. xi, bottom: Courtesy of Rose's Luxury/Kate Warren; p. xii, top left: Jon Bilous; p. xii, top right: Andrea Izzotti; p. xii, bottom: Orhan Cam; p. xiii, top: Courtesy of washington.org; p. xiii, middle: Courtesy of washington.org; p. xiii, bottom: Andrea Izzotti; p. xiv, top left: Daniel X. O'Neil; p. xiv, top right: Carol M. Highsmith's America, Library of Congress, Prints and Photographs Division; Forms part of: Carol M. Highsmith's America Project in the Carol M. Highsmith Archive; p. xiv, bottom left: Courtesy of washington.org; p. xiv, bottom right: Courtesy of washington.org; p. xv, top: Courtesy of Visit Alexandria/R Kennedy for ACVA; p. xv, middle: Courtesy of Visit Alexandria/R Kennedy for ACVA; p. xv, bottom: Courtesy of George Washington's Mount Vernon; p. xvi, top: Albert Pego; p. xvi, bottom left: Anton_Ivanov/Shutterstock.com; p. xvi, bottom right: Courtesy of George Washington's Mount Vernon/Mount Vernon Ladies' Association; p. 2: Sergio TB; p. 3: bakdc/Shutterstock.com; p. 5: Courtesy of washington.org; p. 8: Gary Graves; p. 15: Hu Totya; p. 16: Library of Congress; p. 19, top: National Archives and Records Administration; p. 19, bottom: HST-AVC; p. 25: DVIDSHUB; p. 32: Anton_Ivanov/Shutterstock.com; p. 33: Paolo Vairo; p. 35: Orhan Cam; p. 38, top: Rain0975; p. 38, bottom: Courtesy NMAI; p. 43: Courtesy of washington.org; p. 46: TJ Brown/Shutterstock.com; p. 68: Courtesy of Hay-Adams; p. 69: David; p. 71: Courtesy of The Line DC/James Jackson; p. 76: Courtesy of the Watergate Hotel/Ron Blunt; p. 94: Wendy Harman; p. 97: Ted Eytan; p. 98: Jeff Martin; p. 112: Courtesy of Chez Billy Sud/Myki Wu; p. 120: Courtesy of Destination DC/Jake McGuire; p. 127: Sean Pavone/Shutterstock.com; p. 132: Heath Oldham/Shutterstock.com; p. 136: holbox; p. 139: 11photo/Shitterstock.com; p. 143: Eric Long, National Air and Space Museum, Smithsonian Institution; p. 146: Archives Foundation/Jeffrey Reed for the National Archives; p. 150: Courtesy of National Museum of African American History and Culture/Alan Karchmer; p. 156: Philip Cohen; p. 157: Courtesy of washington.org/Marquis Perkins, Destination DC; p. 161: mlbruno93; p. 163: Courtesy of Destination DC; p. 171: Courtesy of Smithsonian Renwick Museum/Joshua Yetman; p. 187: Anton_Ivanov/Shutterstock.com; p. 191: Steve Heap; p. 194: cdrin/Shutterstock.com; p. 201: TrailVoice; p. 210: Elvert Barnes; p. 214: Politics and Prose Bookstore; p. 218: apasciuto; p. 223: Courtesy of the Arena Stage; p. 228: Bossi; p. 229: Daniel Lobo; p. 233: Courtesy of The Black Cat/Shervin Lainez; p. 240: Frank Romeo/Shutterstock.com; p. 248: Josh; p. 246: Josh; p. 254: steph_ross; p. 260: Library of Congress/Carol M. Highsmith; p. 262: VICTOR TORRES; p. 265: Courtesy Georgetown BID/Sam Kittner; p. 270: Karsten Jung/Shutterstock.com; p. 271: Andriy Blokhin/Shutterstock.com; p. 276: Brian Holcomb; p. 279: Phil Pasquini/Shutterstock.com; p. 280: AgnosticPreachersKid; p. 284: Rory Finneren; Back cover: ©Dave Newman/Shutterstock.com

Map List

Iconic Washington, D.C.   30
Washington, D.C., for Families   37
A Women's History Tour of
    Washington, D.C.   40
An African-American History Tour of
    Washington, D.C.   44
Washington, D.C., at a Glance   48
Washington, D.C., Hotels   58
Washington, D.C., Restaurants   86

Capitol Hill   119
The National Mall   134
The White House Area   173
Exploring Washington, D.C.   178
Old Town Alexandria   245
Strolling Around the White House   259
Strolling Around Georgetown   267
Dupont Circle/Embassy Row   275

Frommer's EasyGuide to Washington D.C. 2020, 7th Edition

Published by
FROMMER MEDIA LLC

ISBN 978-1-62887-470-9 (paper), 978-1-62887-471-6 (e-book)

Editorial Director: Pauline Frommer
Developmental Editor: Alexis Lipsitz Flippin
Production Editor: Lynn Northrup
Cartographer: Roberta Stockwell
Photo Editor: Meghan Lamb
Assistant Photo Editor: Phil Vinke
Indexer: Maro Riofrancos

For information on our other products or services, see www.frommers.com.

Frommer Media LLC also publishes its books in a variety of electronic formats. Some content that
appears in print may not be available in electronic formats.

Manufactured in the United States of America

5 4 3 2 1

ABOUT THE AUTHOR

Meredith Pratt is an avid traveler, writer, art lover, and a Washingtonian for more than 15 years. Her work has profiled international travel locales, high-powered personalities, and top D.C. destinations. She has a Bachelor of Journalism from the University of Maryland, College Park. Meredith previously authored several Frommer's *Washington, D.C., Day by Day* guidebooks. Her writing has also appeared in *USA Today; Executive Travel; Baltimore Magazine; WebMD, the Magazine; Washington Flyer;* and many others. She and her husband share their home just outside of D.C. with two adventurous little girls.

ABOUT THE FROMMER'S TRAVEL GUIDES

For most of the past 50 years, Frommer's has been the leading series of travel guides in North America, accounting for as many as 24% of all guidebooks sold. I think I know why.

Though we hope our books are entertaining, we nevertheless deal with travel in a serious fashion. Our guidebooks have never looked on such journeys as a mere recreation, but as a far more important human function, a time of learning and introspection, an essential part of a civilized life. We stress the culture, lifestyle, history, and beliefs of the destinations we cover, and urge our readers to seek out people and new ideas as the chief rewards of travel.

We have never shied from controversy. We have, from the beginning, encouraged our authors to be intensely judgmental, critical—both pro and con—in their comments, and wholly independent. Our only clients are our readers, and we have triggered the ire of countless prominent sorts, from a tourist newspaper we called "practically worthless" (it unsuccessfully sued us) to the many rip-offs we've condemned.

And because we believe that travel should be available to everyone regardless of their incomes, we have always been cost-conscious at every level of expenditure. Though we have broadened our recommendations beyond the budget category, we insist that every lodging we include be sensibly priced. We use every form of media to assist our readers, and are particularly proud of our feisty daily website, the award-winning Frommers.com.

I have high hopes for the future of Frommer's. May these guidebooks, in all the years ahead, continue to reflect the joy of travel and the freedom that travel represents. May they always pursue a cost-conscious path, so that people of all incomes can enjoy the rewards of travel. And may they create, for both the traveler and the persons among whom we travel, a community of friends, where all human beings live in harmony and peace.

Arthur Frommer